RENEWALS 458-4574

DATE DUE

WITHDRAWN
UTSA LIBRARIES

Library
University of Texas
at San Antonio

Privilege and the Politics of Taxation in Eighteenth-Century France offers a lucid new interpretation of the Ancien Régime and the origins of the French Revolution. It examines what was arguably the most ambitious project of the eighteenth-century French monarchy: the attempt to impose direct taxes on formerly tax-exempt privileged elites. Connecting the social history of the state to the study of political culture, Michael Kwass describes how the crown refashioned its institutions and ideology to impose new forms of taxation on the privileged. Drawing on impressive primary research from national and provincial archives, Michael Kwass demonstrates that the levy of these taxes, which struck elites with some force, not only altered the relationship between monarchy and social hierarchy, but also transformed political language and attitudes in the decades before the French Revolution. *Privilege and the Politics of Taxation in Eighteenth-Century France* sheds new light on French history during this crucial period.

MICHAEL KWASS is Assistant Professor of History at the University of Georgia.

PRIVILEGE AND THE POLITICS OF TAXATION IN EIGHTEENTH-CENTURY FRANCE

PRIVILEGE AND THE POLITICS OF TAXATION IN EIGHTEENTH-CENTURY FRANCE

LIBERTÉ, ÉGALITÉ, FISCALITÉ

MICHAEL KWASS

University of Georgia

PUBLISHED BY THE PRESS SYNDICATE OF THE UNIVERSITY OF CAMBRIDGE
The Pitt Building, Trumpington Street, Cambridge, United Kingdom

CAMBRIDGE UNIVERSITY PRESS
The Edinburgh Building, Cambridge, CB2 2RU, UK
http://www.cup.cam.ac.uk
40 West 20th Street, New York, NY 10011-4211, USA
http://www.cup.org
10 Stamford Road, Oakleigh, Melbourne 3166, Australia

© Michael Kwass 2000

This book is in copyright. Subject to statutory exception and to the provisions of relevant
collective licensing agreements, no reproduction of any part may take place without the
written permission of Cambridge University Press.

First published 2000

Printed in the United Kingdom at the University Press, Cambridge

Typeset in Baskerville 11/12.5pt [CE]

A catalogue record for this book is available from the British Library

Library of Congress cataloguing in publication data
Kwass, Michael.
Privilege and the politics of taxation in eighteenth-century France:
liberté, égalité, fiscalité / Michael Kwass.
p.   cm.
Includes bibliographical references and index.
ISBN 0 521 77149 8 (hb)
1. Taxation – France – History – 18th century.   2. France – Politics and government –
18th century.   3. Privileges and immunities – France – History – 18th century.
4. Representative government and representation – France – History – 18th century.
5. Capital levy – France – History – 18th century.   6. Tax exemption – France – History –
18th century.   7. Elite (Social sciences) – France – 18th century.
8. Taxation – France – Caen – History – 18th century.   I. Title.
HJ2646.K85   2000
336.2′00944′09033 – dc21   99–29135   CIP

ISBN 0 521 77149 8 hardback

For my parents

Contents

List of illustrations	*page*	xi
List of figures		xii
List of tables		xiii
Acknowledgements		xiv
List of abbreviations		xvii

Introduction: why taxes?   1

PART ONE. REASSESSING PRIVILEGE   21

1   The economy of privilege and the challenge of universal
taxation   23
    Stories of fiscal privilege   24
    Fiscal–military rivalry and the establishment of universal taxes   33
    Persuading the public: the crown's own stories   38
    From courts and communities to administrators and individuals   47

2   A kingdom of taxpayers   62
    Universal taxation in the *pays d'élections*   71
    Universal taxation in the *pays d'états*   95
    Universal taxes on targeted privileged groups   103

PART TWO. THE POLITICS OF TAXATION AND THE LANGUAGE
OF DISPUTE   117

3   Petitioning for "justice": tax disputes in the administrative
sphere   119
    Petitions and the clamor for justice   120
    Administrative justice   139

4   Taking "liberty" to the public: tax disputes in the
institutional sphere   155

The calm before the storm   158
Jansenists and taxpayers, 1760–1764   161
Maupeou and beyond, 1771–1782   194

5   Taxation, Enlightenment, and the printed word: debate
    in the literary sphere   213
    The circulation of texts on the royal finances   214
    The ideas and rhetoric of literature on taxation   222

PART THREE. FROM RESISTANCE TO REVOLUTION   253

6   Turning taxpayers into citizens: reform, revolution, and
    the birth of modern political representation   255
    Provincial assemblies and the dawn of a "New Regime"   256
    The call for estates and constitutional revolution   273
    The empowerment of the Third Estate and social revolution   283
    Revolution and the "active" citizen   303

    Conclusion: liberté, égalité, fiscalité   311
    Tocqueville and Habermas reconsidered   319

Select bibliography   324
    Archival sources   324
    Published primary sources   327
    Secondary works   330
Index   342

Illustrations

(Reproduced by kind permission of the Bibliothèque Nationale)

5.1 *Virtue rewarded*   *page* 245
6.1 *Let's hope that I will soon be done with this*   286
6.2 *The past age*   287
6.3 *I knew our turn would come*   288
6.4 *The present time demands that each support the great Burden*   289
6.5 *He would like to knock down that which sustains them*   290

Figures

2.1 The *capitation* paid by privileged and commoner in the   *page*
generality of Caen   72
2.2 The *capitation* on the privileged in the generality of Caen   75
2.3 The *capitation* on the nobility in the generality of Caen   75
2.4 The *capitation* on officers of justice in the generality of Caen   78
2.5 The *capitation* on the bourgeoisie in the generality of Caen   82
2.6 The *capitation* and the *taille* on commoners in the
generality of Caen   83
2.7 The *dixième* and *vingtième* in the generality of Caen   85
2.8 Taxes on Brittany   98
2.9 Taxes on Languedoc   98
2.10 The rolls of the *vingtième* in Languedoc in 1783   102
2.11 The *capitation* paid by the city of Paris in 1701   108
5.1 The number of texts on finance, 1695–1789   219

Tables

3.1 The *capitation* and the nobility: reductions and failures
    to pay   143
3.2 The *capitation* and officers of justice: reductions and
    failures to pay   143
3.3 The *capitation* and the *privilégiés*: reductions and failures
    to pay   144
3.4 The *capitation* and the bourgeoisie: reductions and failures
    to pay   144

Acknowledgements

It is fitting that a book about new forms of taxation in eighteenth-century France should begin by recognizing the debts I incurred while producing it. My chief debt is to David Bien, who oversaw the dissertation on which the book is based. As my advisor at the University of Michigan, David generously shared his deep understanding of the Old Regime and offered just the right balance of encouragement and criticism at several points in my graduate education. As a teacher, he exhibited that rare combination of good humor and erudition that makes the study of history as enjoyable as it is meaningful. And, as an historian, he possesses a true sense of the craft, thinking through historical problems with care, imagination, and style. He, more than anyone, has shaped my understanding of what a scholar should be.

At Michigan I also had the good fortune to take seminars and discuss my work with William Sewell, Marvin Becker, Michael MacDonald, and Kenneth Lockridge. Michael MacDonald, Ken Lockridge, and Marvin Becker brought early modern culture to life and, in very different ways, forced me to think harder about the period's distinctive qualities. Each evoked a past that seemed distant and foreign and yet intriguingly accessible. Bill Sewell stimulated my interest in social and cultural theory and demonstrated the extent to which theory can enrich historical analysis; although it is not always obvious, much of the theory I began reading at Michigan underpins the structure of this book. I also thank Raymond Grew and Elizabeth Eisenstein and, beyond Michigan, Martin Wolfe, Hilton Root, and Michael McCahill, for teaching me enough about the writing of history to allow me to produce a book of my own.

I owe a debt of gratitude to my Ann Arbor friends who, by making graduate school fun, sustained me in this project. The music, meals, and conversation – did I mention the meals? – provided by fellow members of the Hutchins Institute, Steve Soper, Tom Schrand, Jon Mogul, and Dennis Sweeney, lifted my spirits after long days of toiling over tax rolls. It was reassuring to belong to a group of historians-in-the-making who could throw a party (or a whiffleball) after a day spent thinking about the past. Jay Smith, as a more senior Bien student, showed me the ropes and happily shared his increasingly sophisticated vision of Old Regime France.

My two years of research in France were funded generously by a grant from the Fulbright-Hayes Foundation and a Bourse Chateaubriand from the French government. In Paris, I benefited from a seminar on the social history of the state led by Robert Descimon and Alain Guéry at the École des Hautes Études en Sciences Sociales. As a young scholar, it was both exciting and challenging to have the opportunity to participate, however modestly, in the intellectual life of that renowned institution. I also learned a great deal from numerous conversations with Richard Bonney and Joël Félix. Richard Bonney helped to make my first several months in the archives far more productive; routinely eating lunch at the counter of *Le Petit Berri*, we recounted the morning's discoveries in the archives and discussed the gritty details of Old Regime finance and administration. I am grateful to Richard for sharing his expertise on the French state and its archives, and for providing guidance during a crucial stage in my research. Thanks as well to Joël Félix, who befriended me and initiated many thought-provoking discussions of eighteenth-century legal and financial institutions. My conversations with Richard and Joël allowed me to see the shape of my argument well before I started to write.

Thanks in part to a grant from the Rackham School of Graduate Studies of the University of Michigan and a Sarah Moss fellowship from the University of Georgia, I was able to take the time needed to digest the evidence I harvested in France. During that process, several colleagues read parts or all of my manuscript and offered much-needed advice. In Athens, David Schoenbrun and Joshua Cole were kind enough to suggest ways to improve my analysis of the tax data; I am grateful for their encouragement and their friendship. Beyond Athens, I owe special debts to three model colleagues – Gail Bossenga, Peter Jones, and Tom Kaiser – who graciously agreed to read the entire manuscript as I was revising it. I took their extensive comments to heart and have no doubt that their suggestions vastly improved this work. I hope they will recognize some of their contributions in the pages that follow. The anonymous readers for Cambridge University Press were equally helpful in steering me away from dangerous errors and emboldening me to clarify parts of my argument.

The publishers of *The Journal of Modern History* and of *Crises, revolutions and self-sustained growth: Essays in European fiscal history, 1130–1830* kindly allowed me to use material published previously in different form. The Bibliothèque Nationale granted me permission to publish the illustrations that appear in chapters 5 and 6.

Finally, I pause to thank Laura Mason. My debt to her is unusual in that it takes so many forms. In her various roles as provider of personal support, tireless reader, peerless editor, and French historian extraordinaire, she has endured the production of this book like no other. Make no mistake about it: the exchange was not a fair one. In reading my work she may have learned more about Old Regime taxes than she cared to know, but I have become a better historian. Thanks.

This book is dedicated to my mother and father, Phoebe and George Kwass. They did more than simply ensure that I receive a good education. They offered warm encouragement, confidence, and enthusiasm, trusting me to use that education as I wished. They have shaped this book more than they probably know.

Abbreviations

AD Calvados	Archives Départementales du Calvados
AD Seine-Maritime	Archives Départementales de la Seine-Maritime
AN	Archives Nationales
AN, AP	Archives Nationales, Archives Privées
Annales E.S.C.	*Annales: Economies, sociétés, civilisations*
AP	*Archives parlementaires*
BN	Bibliothèque Nationale
BN, JdF	Bibliothèque Nationale, Collection Joly de Fleury
BN, Ms. Fr.	Bibliothèque Nationale, Manuscrits français
BN, NAF	Bibliothèque Nationale, Nouvelles Acquisitions Françaises
FHS	*French Historical Studies*
JMH	*Journal of Modern History*
RHES	*Revue d'histoire économique et sociale*

Introduction: Why taxes?

Taxation has long been associated with the outbreak of the French Revolution. Ever since revolutionaries wrested the power to tax from the monarchy in 1789, no other single issue has come to symbolize so vividly the twin evils of the Old Regime: despotism and privilege. As the president of the Constituent Assembly's committee on taxation, the duc de la Rochefoucauld, explained to his fellow deputies in August of 1790, "the vicious system of taxation under which France has groaned for so long" was the product of both "despotism," by which royal ministers callously violated the rights of the nation, and "privileges," which unjustly exempted certain subjects from taxes.[1] The committee was so repulsed by the system of taxation it was charged to dismantle that it not only recommended the creation of an entirely new tax system but suggested, in addition, that the very word for tax, *impôt*, "disappear from our language."[2]

Following the proposals of the committee, legislators scrapped much of the old tax system and created new taxes called "*contributions publiques*," a phrase that evoked the nation's newly constituted social contract, according to which all citizens were to possess political rights, be equal before the law, and make contributions to the state. In the address that introduced the Revolution's new tax system to the public, the Assembly proclaimed to every citizen that nothing less than "your political existence stems from the fact that each citizen, by the share that he gives in proportion to his income, obtains a useful share of all public services – services paid for by the like contributions that fellow citizens have pooled with his."[3] These were not idle words. Between 1789 and 1791 the Assembly defined

[1] *AP*, XVIII, pp. 143–5, speech by Rochefoucauld, 18 August 1790.
[2] *AP*, XVIII, pp. 158–9, report of the comité de l'imposition, 18 August 1790.
[3] Camille Bloch, ed., *Les contributions directes; instructions, receuil de textes et notes* (Paris, 1915), pp. 263–4.

the rights of citizenship and built a system of political representation on the basis of taxation: the right to vote, eligibility for election, and the distribution of representatives to the nation's legislature were all determined in part by the payment of taxes.

The sheer noise level generated by the issue of taxation at the end of the Old Regime and the beginning of the Revolution has led generations of historians to believe that taxes were a primary cause of the Revolution. According to the most dramatic historical accounts, taxes became so oppressive under the Old Regime that the popular classes, unable to bear the burden, rose up to overthrow the old order and establish a new society based on freedom and equality. In stirring prose, the nineteenth-century republican Jules Michelet wrote that under the Old Regime "tax collection was nothing less than an organized war: it unleashed an army of 200,000 scavengers who weighed heavily on the soil. These locusts razed everything, sweeping the place clean. To squeeze revenue from a people thus devoured, it was necessary to impose cruel laws, a terrible penance, the galleys, the gallows, the wheel." To make matters worse, Michelet continued, the king "gave (or sold at great profit) exemptions from taxes ... Thus, the fisc worked against itself: as it increased the sum to be levied, it reduced the number of those who paid; the weight, bearing down on fewer shoulders, grew heavier and heavier." On the morning of the Revolution the wretched people of France, having received no relief from their supposed savior, the king, awoke like a hero to throw off the burdens of the past. Lest his readers misconstrue the true meaning of the Revolution, Michelet urged them to bear witness to the misery of the Old Regime: "Sensitive men who cry about the evils of the Revolution (with good reason undoubtedly), shed some tears also for the evils that incited it."[4] In the twentieth century the economic historian Ernest Labrousse added statistical substance to Michelet's romantic evocation of the causes of the Revolution by claiming that taxes and seigneurial dues became more burdensome prior to the Revolution as the agricultural sector of the economy languished.[5]

Was fiscal oppression one of the "evils" that incited the Revolution? The question is plain enough and yet today, when the connections between social oppression (or social change in general)

---

[4] Jules Michelet, *Histoire de la Révolution française* (repr., Paris, 1979), I, p. 86.
[5] Ernest Labrousse, *La crise de l'économie française à la fin de l'ancien régime et au début de la Révolution* (Paris, 1944).

and the origins of the Revolution are far from clear, it seems strangely out of place. In fact one could argue that the royal fisc was equally if not more brutal in the seventeenth century than it was in the eighteenth, as Michelet himself admitted, and that no such relation between a growing fiscal burden and the outbreak of revolution existed. But if this were the case, why was taxation a burning public issue in the decades before the Revolution? And if *non*-revolutionary tax revolts were as endemic to the Old Regime as royal bankruptcies, why had the issue of taxation come to be invested with special revolutionary meaning by 1789?

I pose these questions at a moment when the field of Old Regime and revolutionary France is undergoing dramatic change, change with which we need to be familiar if we are to understand why studying something as mundane as taxation might be of significance. In the past decade and a half, interpretations of the Old Regime, the Revolution, and the relationship between the two have converged on the concept of political culture. The term "political culture" arose from an effort to direct the historiography of eighteenth-century France away from what had become a stale debate between proponents of the classic social interpretation of the French Revolution, who contended that the Revolution was the product of long-term social and economic change, and Revisionists, who sought to discredit "the Marxist interpretation" by subjecting its assumptions to intense empirical scrutiny. This is not the place to rehash the story of the debate – it has been told well already[6] – but suffice it to say that by the late 1970s the Revisionists were claiming victory. They had shattered a once oversimplified conception of "bourgeois revolution" by demonstrating with great skill that the Revolution was not the work of a coherent capitalist bourgeoisie, that many clergymen, nobles, lawyers, royal office-holders, and other nonbourgeois elites participated in making the Revolution, and that these groups shared with the bourgeoisie similar kinds of property and attitudes towards wealth. The mounting evidence on the structure of eighteenth-century society and the background of the revolutionary players themselves made it clear that class conflict could no longer provide a viable framework for understanding the roots and course of the Revolution. In 1979, the ardent Revisionist George Taylor proclaimed that "the class-struggle thesis of the French Revolution has

---

[6] See William Doyle, *Origins of the French Revolution* (Oxford, 1980), part I.

expired and is interred in the graveyard of lost paradigms assassinated by critical research."[7]

Although dramatic at the time, Taylor's words seem somewhat hollow in retrospect. The assassins to whom he refers, the practitioners of empirical social and economic historical research, had indeed deployed the weapons of their trade to slay the classic social interpretation, but they were unable to breathe life into a new, equally compelling theory. If the origins of the Revolution could not be traced to class conflict or the rise of a specific social group, the bourgeoisie, then who or what did cause the Revolution? While social, political, and institutional historians continued to grapple with this question, the most spectacular attempts to reconceptualize the origins of the Revolution were made by more philosophically minded intellectual and cultural historians such as François Furet, Keith Baker, and Roger Chartier, who cleared a vast domain of research by asserting that the political culture of the Old Regime created the intellectual conditions of revolution. Consider the recent statements of Baker and Chartier. Baker writes,

The conceptual space in which the Revolution was invented, the structure of meanings in relationship to which the quite disparate actions of 1789 took on a symbolic coherence and political force, was the creation of the old regime. If the revolutionaries came to a profound sense of the character of their actions and utterances as constituting a radical departure, that claim too was historically constituted (and rhetorically deployed) within an existing linguistic and symbolic field. The problem for the historian is to show how the revolutionary script was invented, taking on its power and its contradictions, from within the political culture of the absolute monarchy.

Chartier adds that searching for the origins of the Revolution is no longer a matter of determining "causes" but one of locating the conditions that made the Revolution "possible because it was conceivable."[8]

Thus post-Revisionist historians replaced what was a relatively specific agent of change, the bourgeoisie, with a considerably more vague one: a new political imagination that manifested itself most vividly in the spread of subversive political discourse among various French subjects. Over the course of the eighteenth century, philo-

---

[7] Quoted in Jack R. Censer, "The Coming of a New Interpretation of the French Revolution?" *Journal of Social History* 21 (Winter, 1987), p. 296.
[8] Keith Baker, *Inventing the French Revolution: Essays on French Political Culture in the Eighteenth Century* (Cambridge, 1990), p. 4; Roger Chartier, *The Cultural Origins of the French Revolution*, trans. Lydia G. Cochrane (Durham, NC, 1991), p. 2.

sophes, journalists, pamphleteers, magistrates, lawyers, ministers of state, and royal officials – nearly anyone with a public voice – increasingly used language that implicitly or explicitly criticized existing social structures and political practices and, in the most extreme cases, evoked the possibility of a new order. Words such as "citizen," "liberty," "despotism," "nation," and "public opinion" flowed easily from the quills and tongues of the literate, shifting the symbolic locus of power outward from king to civil society. By 1789 many members of the middling and upper ranks of society, whom we might expect to have been defenders of the established order, were prepared to redefine the political structure of the kingdom.

The question now facing historians is why. Why did royal subjects, especially those in positions of power, reconceive their political existence? Why did revolutionary mentalities and discourse develop within the confines of absolutism? Although the intellectual and cultural historians who recast the field have achieved great success in tracking the emergence of a new political culture and in deconstructing its linguistic and ideological features, they have been far less successful in explaining why and how that culture arose when it did. Most, like Chartier, eschew the very word "cause" and feel uncomfortable discussing "underlying" reasons for the dramatic changes in political culture that they have depicted, in part because the notion of an underlying causal explanation smacks of the determinism associated with the classic social interpretation of the Revolution. To say, however, that the Revolution was possible because its ideas became conceivable or its discourse speakable is to flirt with a circular logic disconnected from social experience.

It is one of the great ironies of current historiography, therefore, that post-Revisionists, in their effort to liberate political rhetoric and ideology from overbearing social referents, have drawn from two formidable thinkers who advanced rigorous sociological explanations for the cultural and ideological changes France experienced before the Revolution. Alexis de Tocqueville and Jürgen Habermas have been enlisted in the service of constructing a new interpretation of the Old Regime and Revolution, but scholars have stripped away the causal mechanisms that drive their work.

Since the publication of Furet's tremendously influential book *Interpreting the French Revolution*, Tocqueville has become the figurehead for the history of prerevolutionary political culture. A nineteenth-century liberal notable, Tocqueville argued that the egalitarian ethos of the French Revolution did not spring anew from the revolutionaries – despite what the revolutionaries themselves believed – but was in fact the product of a long process of "administrative centralization" that occurred under the Old Regime. As the absolutist state swallowed up local institutions and crushed structures of decentralized aristocratic rule, it leveled and atomized society, making it seem as if all individuals were equal, if only in their subjugation to and dependence on a centralized royal administration. At the same time, Tocqueville explained, the monarchy created more and more social privileges to comfort nobles and others whom it had exiled from the world of political rule. The resentment engendered by the patently unjust spread of privilege, combined with the rise in the spirit of equality that came with a centralized state, was enough to undermine the stability of the Old Regime, but when men of letters with no political experience began filling their readers' minds with utopian visions of a perfect society, and when the monarchy itself initiated a string of major reforms, the Old Regime finally gave way to revolution. It is worth emphasizing that the single driving force in this story was state centralization: state centralization created an impotent but privileged nobility; it encouraged a sense of equality among subjects of different social status; it deprived the intelligentsia of the political experience it needed to temper its naive and reckless ideas; and it exposed the public to the notion of thorough-going reform. In this way, Tocqueville emphasized, the central state cleared the way for French democracy at the expense of political liberty. The Revolution was merely the dramatic culmination of this long-term historical process.[9]

The only figure who has matched Tocqueville in providing historians with a broad, cogent, and adaptable sociological model is Habermas, who received lavish attention after the translations of a seminal work, *The Structural Transformation of the Public Sphere*, into French in 1978 and English in 1989.[10] According to Habermas, a modern "public sphere" developed in Europe in the seventeenth and eighteenth centuries, creating an arena in which individuals rationally discussed matters of common interest and, for the first time in history, generated what people were beginning to call

[9] Alexis de Tocqueville, *The Old Régime and the French Revolution*, trans. Stuart Gilbert (New York, 1955).
[10] Jürgen Habermas, *The Structural Transformation of the Public Sphere: An Inquiry into a Category of Bourgeois Society*, trans. Thomas Burger (Cambridge, MA, 1989).

"public opinion." That opinion, in turn, was meant to guide the decision-making of rulers, including the supposedly absolute kings of France, who would now be held accountable for their actions before a critical and reasoning public. What produced this extraordinary public? Borrowing from Marx and Weber, Habermas argued that the two historical engines behind the formation of a politicized public sphere were the rise of commerce and the growth of a bureaucratic state, both of which became clearly discernible in the age of mercantilism. On the one hand, the ascendancy of trade gave rise to private family life while simultaneously fueling a "traffic in news" that would ultimately make news itself a commodity. Hence the specifically "bourgeois" origins of what would become a mature public sphere of urban salon-goers, newspaper readers, coffee-house conversationalists, and others making public use of their capacity to reason.

On the other hand, Habermas observed, "civil society came into existence as the corollary of a depersonalized state authority." Rather than emerging on its own, a critical, politicized public was hailed into existence by a bureaucratizing state whose printed decrees addressed it and whose economic interventions provoked it into an awareness of itself as the state's opponent. In the late seventeenth and eighteenth centuries, as European rulers made more and more "continuous administrative contact" with "capitalists" (literate merchants, bankers, entrepreneurs, and manufacturers who represented the public), "official interventions into the privatized household finally came to constitute the target of a developing critical sphere." Only after suffering the intrusions of state mercantilist policy did a public of producers and consumers seize hold of the printing press, an instrument formerly monopolized by the state, to generate an oppositional, independent public opinion that in France ultimately destabilized absolutist society.[11]

For Tocqueville, then, the rise of a centralized state generated the sensibilities and ideas that would lead to revolution; for Habermas the friction between a mercantilist state and a growing number of capitalists gave rise to a new political force, the public, which he believed achieved its full powers in France during the Revolution.

---

[11] Habermas, *Public Sphere*, pp. 19–24. Although Habermas believes that the French public sphere took a weaker literary form under the Old Regime and did not reach maturity until the Revolution, most historians agree that it had developed with some vigor by the middle of the eighteenth century and was therefore as much a cause of the Revolution as a result.

Given the compelling nature of their theses, it is not altogether surprising that many of the historians who are redefining the field of eighteenth-century France in the aftermath of the Revisionist victory have turned to Tocqueville and Habermas.

What is curious and of particular relevance to the design of this study, however, is the uneven way in which current historical literature has drawn from these two thinkers. If we think about their arguments in terms of mechanisms of change and the effects of those mechanisms, historians have tended to concentrate on the effects side of the equation. This is most clear in the case of Habermas. Although most historians of political culture prefer to leave the thorny problems of state mercantilism and capitalist development aside, they have produced path-breaking research on the evolution of public opinion. It is now evident that the idea of public opinion became increasingly important over the eighteenth century and began to rival the monarchy as the symbolic center of political authority. Writers, lawyers, magistrates, and royal officials, who deferred rhetorically to "public opinion" in an effort to legitimize their political claims, encouraged the belief that the nation had a voice that deserved a role in government.[12] Moreover, some historians have gone beyond intellectual history, beyond the study of public opinion as a rhetorical device, to attempt to describe the actual content of public opinion itself.[13] Listening to subjects detained by the Paris police for seditious speech, eavesdropping on conversations in salons, reading popular books and pamphlets, and reconstructing the legal profession's engagement with the public, historians have painted a portrait of a vibrant public opinion colored by touches of Jansenism and Rousseauism, political libel and philosophical reflection, deep mistrust of ministerial authority and in some cases outright hostility to the king himself. Whatever its content, most agree that public opinion, as both an idea and a body of consciously shared attitudes, weakened the authority of the crown and encouraged new ways of conceptualizing the political order.

---

[12] For the notion of public opinion, see Baker, *Inventing*, pp. 167–99; Mona Ozouf, "L'opinion publique," in *The Political Culture of the Old Regime*, ed. Keith Baker (Oxford, 1987), pp. 419–34; and Chartier, *Cultural Origins*, ch. 2. For the ways in which lawyers appealed to public opinion, see Sarah Maza, *Private Lives and Public Affairs: The Causes Célèbres of Prerevolutionary France* (Berkeley, CA, 1993); and David Bell, *Lawyers and Citizens: The Making of a Political Elite in Old Regime France* (Oxford, 1994).

[13] See, for example, Arlette Farge, *Subversive Words: Public Opinion in Eighteenth-Century France*, trans. Rosemary Morris (University Park, PA, 1995).

But we are already a long way from Habermas' emphasis on capitalism and the mercantilist state. What of Habermas' contention that the emergence of public opinion had discrete long-term causes? The question of economic growth, neglected by historians suspicious of the "bourgeois" origins of the public sphere, is now resurfacing in studies of consumer culture, but we are still unsure of how the central state's "official interventions into the privatized household" helped to shape public opinion. This book seeks to shed light on this important problem.

Attention to Tocqueville has also been somewhat distorted. Furet provided brilliant insights into the thought of Tocqueville but was not inclined to pursue archival research into processes of state formation and the sensibilities that resulted from them. Instead, Furet validated Tocqueville's thesis that state centralization "closed off the channels of communication between society and the State" and produced the dangerous "literary politics" of the Enlightenment in which utopian "abstract right" was substituted for more responsible "consideration of facts."[14] Furet also added the ideas of Augustin Cochin to those of Tocqueville, arguing that, in addition to the prominent role played by men of letters, philosophical societies contributed to the genesis of revolutionary consciousness by virtue of their "democratic sociability." Such societies, which took the form of Masonic lodges, cafés, salons, and literary societies, not only introduced a significant degree of equality among their members, thus contradicting the steep social hierarchy that existed everywhere outside their doors, but were also drawn to the Rousseauian notion of an indivisible general will that was "patterned on the 'absolute' power of the monarch."[15] All that was needed to ignite the explosive ideas emanating from philosophical societies and literary figures was the power vacuum of 1789. Once power was seen as vacant and accessible it was only a matter of time before the logic of Rousseauian discourse drove the Revolution to its radical and violent conclusions.

Furet's assertions have not gone unchallenged of course. It turns

[14] François Furet, *Interpreting the French Revolution*, trans. Elborg Forster (Cambridge, 1981), pp. 36–8.

[15] Furet, *Interpreting*, p. 38. Furet's ideas on philosophical societies and revolutionary sovereignty are developed, respectively, in Ran Halévi, *Les loges maçonniques dans la France d'Ancien Régime aux origines de la sociabilité démocratique* (Paris, 1984); and Marcel Gauchet, *La révolution des droits de l'homme* (Paris, 1989).

out that men of letters were not altogether isolated from politics; new forms of sociability were not necessarily wedded to a Rousseauian idea of indivisible sovereignty; and the Revolution was not driven by the logic of ideology alone.[16] But I raise Furet's argument to underscore the way in which he chose to direct his analysis toward the effects of absolutism without grounding that analysis in a reconsideration of the problem of state formation. Furet emphasized the indivisibility of royal sovereignty under the Old Regime to explain the successful reception of Rousseau's idea of an equally indivisible general will during the Revolution, but, unlike Tocqueville, he was interested neither in how the royal state worked in practice nor in how it left a particular mental imprint on the individuals who came into contact with it. It was at the level of daily life, Tocqueville insisted, that the state shaped the political mentalities of the French; the writings of men of letters (and, we may add, the attitudes of members of philosophical societies) only reinforced a state-induced predilection for reform and equality over liberty.

This is not to suggest that every *dix-huitièmiste* need systematically test the causal underpinnings of the arguments of Tocqueville and Habermas, nor do I mean to imply that all the answers are to be found in the work of these two thinkers. But in concentrating our attention on cultural, linguistic, or ideological phenomena without thoroughly investigating their social or political context, we risk making it appear as if those phenomena were self-generating. We also run the risk of losing much of the explanatory power that Marxist historians once wielded. Although the project of liberating politics and ideology from the straitjackets of class conflict and material interest – or rescuing them from the indifference of earlier generations of *Annalistes* – has undoubtedly enriched the field of prerevolutionary France, divorcing the history of political culture from social referents of all kinds makes it difficult to offer satisfying explanations for transformations in the meaning of political

---

[16] The first criticism, made of Tocqueville but equally applicable to Furet, is discussed in Baker, *Inventing*, pp. 20–3. The fact that voluntary societies possessed Lockean, rather than Rousseauian, characteristics is demonstrated in Margaret Jacob, *Living the Enlightenment: Freemasonry and Politics in Eighteenth-Century Europe* (Oxford, 1991). And the thesis that social differences (if not class, then wealth and status) as well as political circumstance played important roles in the formation of revolutionary consciousness has been revived by Timothy Tackett, *Becoming a Revolutionary: The Deputies of the French National Assembly and the Emergence of a Revolutionary Culture (1789–1790)* (Princeton, NJ, 1996).

discourse.[17] Is this the price we have to pay for moving beyond the Marxist–Revisionist debate onto the terrain of political culture? Not necessarily, as a number of scholars have shown.

Historians have avoided this conundrum by following one of three intersecting paths, each of which pays special attention to the environment in which political language evolved. The first path, which I have already mentioned, returns to the promising question of socio-economic change by looking at patterns of production and consumption and considering how changes in material culture affected perceptions of society and politics. It is entirely possible that the expansion of consumption among the popular classes may have undermined traditional social relations and broadened the dimensions of the public sphere, even if it did not create an easily identifiable revolutionary bourgeoisie.[18]

The second route, more relevant to this study, is that of institutional history. Not traditional institutional history, but a kind of history that delves inside a monarchy that was only theoretically absolute to look at how institutions functioned in practice, at the factions and patronage networks that were in operation, at the motivations, interests, and attitudes of members of corporate bodies, and at their engagement with a wider public. Forays of this kind into two institutional worlds, those of law and finance, have yielded particularly promising results.

In reconstructing judicial politics, historians of the world of law have shown how the magistrates of the kingdom's highest courts, the parlements, fashioned a potent language of opposition to the crown.[19] Responding initially to the persecution of Jansenists by the monarchy and upper clergy, magistrates publicized the threat of "despotism," stressed the need for the crown to adhere to the

[17] The problem of analyzing discourse without sufficient regard for the social or material world has been raised by William Sewell, *A Rhetoric of Bourgeois Revolution: The Abbé Sieyes and "What Is the Third Estate?"* (Durham, NC, 1994), pp. 22–40; Robert Darnton, *The Forbidden Best-Sellers of Pre-Revolutionary France* (New York, 1996), pp. 173–80; and Colin Jones, "Bourgeois Revolution Revivified: 1789 and Social Change," in *Rewriting the French Revolution*, ed. Colin Lucas (Oxford, 1991), pp. 69–118.

[18] Jones, "Bourgeois Revolution"; Daniel Roche, *France in the Enlightenment*, trans. Arthur Goldhammer (Cambridge, MA, 1998).

[19] Works on the parlements are too numerous to list here. For the crucial period of the third quarter of the eighteenth century, see Jean Egret, *Louis XV et l'opposition parlementaire, 1715–1774* (Paris, 1970); and Julian Swann, *Politics and the Parlement of Paris under Louis XV, 1754–1774* (Cambridge, 1995). For a sensible appraisal of parlementary politics in general, see William Doyle, "The Parlements," in Baker, ed., *Political Culture*, pp. 157–67.

"fundamental laws" of the kingdom, and, in their bolder moments, advanced theories of national sovereignty. And where magistrates exercised restraint, lawyers were known to exhibit unusual enthusiasm. The men of the bar made direct appeals to the transcendent authority of public opinion, all but substituting that authority for the sovereignty of the king, and published, in the last two decades of the Old Regime, unprecedented runs of legal briefs filled with dramatic tales of political abuses and aristocratic corruption.[20] Although the bridge between judicial appeals to the public and the actual content of public opinion remains under construction – the foundation laid thus far has been generally Jansenist and Parisian in nature – it is likely that the printed materials emanating from the courts influenced the views of the thousands of subjects who eagerly read them. We shall have occasion to construct another piece of this bridge in chapter 4.

Meanwhile, as the legal world comes into sharper focus, historians of state finance are exploiting Tocqueville's insight that even the most mundane fiscal and administrative practices helped to recast the mentality of royal subjects. At the heart of the royal finances lay a fundamental contradiction between a system of credit in which a cash-hungry monarchy borrowed from corporate bodies and other creditors in exchange for fiscal privileges, and a system of taxation that was limited by the very privileges the monarchy had distributed. Both sides of this contradiction, according to David Bien and Gail Bossenga, had profound political ramifications. Borrowing tested public confidence in the monarchy and may have paradoxically reinforced democratic habits of political participation internal to corporate groups; taxing led to resentment of privilege and triggered debates about the meaning of citizenship. Although we have a firmer grasp of the social and political consequences of eighteenth-century royal debt, there is still much to learn about the tax system and its implications.[21]

Finally, historians venturing down the third path, rather than approaching the Old Regime through the doorways of specific

---

[20] Bell, *Lawyers and Citizens*; and Maza, *Private Lives*.

[21] David Bien, "Old Regime Origins of Democratic Liberty," in *The French Idea of Freedom: The Old Regime and the Declaration of Rights of 1789*, ed. Dale Van Kley (Stanford, CA, 1994), pp. 23–71; Gail Bossenga, *The Politics of Privilege: Old Regime and Revolution in Lille* (Cambridge, 1991); and Gail Bossenga, "Taxes," in *A Critical Dictionary of the French Revolution*, ed. François Furet and Mona Ozouf, trans. Arthur Goldhammer (Cambridge, 1989), pp. 582–9.

institutions, have seized upon highly contentious public issues and unpacked the meaning of the controversy swirling around them. Notable travelers on this path include Dale Van Kley, who has looked at Jansenism and eighteenth-century political ideology, and Steven Kaplan, who has studied the politics of the eighteenth-century grain trade.[22] The advantage of both these studies is their breadth. By taking up a single issue, the two historians are able to draw connections between such diverse historical subjects as royal policy, literary debate, judicial conflict, and popular culture. Rather than examining these matters in isolation from each other, the issue-driven approach draws them together, allowing the historian to examine a compact cross-section of Old Regime political life.

This book straddles the second and third paths. It examines a single yet omnipresent issue of Old Regime politics – taxation – and considers how long-term changes in fiscal institutions altered the relationship between monarchy and social hierarchy and, in turn, helped to transform political culture. Instead of covering the entire system of taxation, I focus on what was arguably the most ambitious project of the eighteenth-century monarchy: the attempt to levy direct taxes on tax-exempt privileged elites.

Until recently it was understood that such an attempt was utterly doomed. During the Third Republic (1870–1914), as French writers debated the merits of a progressive income tax, Marcel Marion and other financial historians looked to the example of the past and found in the Old Regime a society saturated with privilege. "All-powerful in appearance," Marion stated, "the government was in reality continually held in check by privileged corps stronger than it, by a spirit of general resistance that it felt incapable of surmounting."[23] The privileged were so effective in protecting their interests, he argued, that they consistently confounded royal tax reforms, driving the crown to bankruptcy and the people to revolution. A similar theme was sounded by the twentieth century's Marxist historians who used the example of fiscal privilege to demonstrate that the Old Regime state was a construct of dominant social classes. According to Michel Vovelle, the monarchy was "taken over, or more accurately steadily infiltrated by privileged

---

[22] Among their many works, see Dale Van Kley, *The Damiens Affair and the Unraveling of the Ancien Régime, 1750–1770* (Princeton, NJ, 1984); and Steven Kaplan, *Bread, Politics and Political Economy in the Reign of Louis XV* (The Hague, 1976).

[23] Marcel Marion, *Histoire financière de la France depuis 1715: I, 1715–1789* (Paris, 1919), I, p. vi.

groups, who used it as an instrument to serve their class interests."[24] Perry Anderson recounted much the same story to the English-speaking world in his widely-read *Lineages of the Absolutist State.* "From the beginning to the end of the history of absolutism," he wrote, the nobility "was never dislodged from its command of political power" and the state was never anything more than the nobility's "political carapace." "The fiscal crisis which detonated the revolution of 1789 was provoked by [the state's] juridical inability to tax the class which it represented."[25]

The thesis that the monarchy was incapable of taxing the privileged was first challenged in 1963 by the founding mother of Revisionism, C. B. A. Behrens, who claimed that, contrary to the assumptions of both Tocqueville and Marxist historians, French nobles in the eighteenth century did in fact pay substantial amounts in taxation, rendering them comparable to their often virtuously depicted British counterparts.[26] Behrens further advanced that whatever fiscal privileges did exist, far from being the preserve of the first two orders, belonged to many members of the third estate as well. Both parts of this argument have been well integrated into Revisionist orthodoxy. Although the familiar refrain about the failure of the monarchy to impose taxes on elites can still be heard in the occasional textbook, few historians today would suggest that nobles paid no taxes at all or that privilege was restricted exclusively to the upper orders.

Beyond these now commonplace ideas, however, there is still a great deal of uncertainty regarding the value of fiscal privilege and the social incidence of the direct taxes that were aimed at elites. We still know little about the burden of taxation on the nobility and other privileged groups, the ways in which the privileged evaded the payment of the sums for which they were assessed, and the extent to which taxation consumed their income. Responding to Gerald Cavanaugh's criticisms of her work, Behrens herself was later forced to admit that "in the present state of knowledge the truth [about direct taxation and noble privilege] cannot be established."[27] Since that admission there has been a number of important works dealing

[24] Michelle Vovelle, *La chute de la Monarchie, 1787–1792* (Paris, 1972), pp. 48–9.
[25] Perry Anderson, *Lineages of the Absolutist State* (London, 1974), pp. 18 and 112.
[26] C. B. A. Behrens, "Nobles, Privileges, and Taxes in France at the End of the Ancien Régime," *Economic History Review* 2nd ser. 15 (April 1963), pp. 451–75.
[27] "A Revision Defended: Nobles, Privileges, and Taxes in France," *FHS* 9 (1976), p. 522.

with taxation and finance in eighteenth-century France, all of which underscore the significance of new forms of taxation and raise the possibility, as Behrens did, that the privileged paid much more in direct taxes than was once thought. These studies, which will receive due attention in the second chapter, contain much useful evidence on the tax assessments of the privileged, but few look at actual tax payments and sort out definitively the extent to which various social groups were taxed over the long term. For all we have learned about French finances in recent decades, the question of the incidence of taxation, so crucial to our understanding of prerevolutionary state and society – and political culture – remains elusive. To what extent did the eighteenth-century monarchy change the distribution of direct taxes and alter a centuries-old regime of fiscal privilege? Which individuals and social groups ended up paying taxes, and how much did they pay? By providing fresh archival evidence on taxation and by measuring expansions and contractions in fiscal privilege in the century before the French Revolution, this book seeks to answer these fundamental questions and put the issue to rest.

Determining the incidence of new forms of taxation is merely a preliminary step toward a broader examination of the politics of taxation. The distribution of taxes, after all, was the outcome of constant conflict and negotiation between kings and administrators, on the one side, and courts of law, regional political bodies, cities, guilds, families, and individuals, on the other. We must be sure to look at the human interaction behind the statistics. How did the monarchy approach different social groups when it levied, or tried to levy, taxes? What methods of persuasion or coercion did royal officials employ when confronted with recalcitrant elites? No doubt taxpayers went to great lengths to protect their wealth but we know little about the means by which they did so. How would a court of law, a municipality, or an individual noble, shopkeeper, or peasant go about exerting influence on or blocking the claims of royal officials? Who was successful and why? This study aims to capture the vitality of disputes over taxation and illuminate basic patterns of contestation between the crown and the individuals, groups, and institutions that composed the socio-legal hierarchy of the kingdom.

Once the structures and outcomes of disputes have been laid bare, it is essential to go on to consider the cultural space in which disputes unfolded. Although historical sociologists have skillfully "brought the state back in" to analyses of long-term social change and revolutions, they have tended to leave political culture and ideology out.[28] This study seeks to redress that problem by extending its analysis of taxation to treat the cultural field between state and society, and this is precisely where the book converges with current historical work on political discourse and public opinion. To see in disputes only clashes between competing interests is to miss what is most essential to the history of political culture: the ideas and language through which those interests were expressed and negotiated. Keith Baker's linguistic definition of political culture is quite useful in this respect:

> It sees politics as about making claims; as the activity through which individuals and groups in any society articulate, negotiate, implement, and enforce the competing claims they make upon one another and upon the whole. Political culture is, in this sense, the set of discourses or symbolic practices by which these claims are made ... It constitutes the meanings of the terms in which these claims are framed, the nature of the contexts to which they pertain, and the authority of the principles according to which they are made binding. It shapes the constitutions and powers of the agencies and procedures by which contestations are resolved, competing claims authoritatively adjudicated, and binding decisions enforced.[29]

If we apply Baker's abstract definition to the context of this book, political culture is about the claims and counterclaims articulated by crown and subjects as they wrestled over the problem of taxation in the century before the Revolution. It is possible to interpret the meaning of these claims by amplifying the sounds of contestation and listening to the voices residing in a variety of documents, including royal decrees, statements issued by judicial institutions, petitions submitted by ordinary taxpayers, treatises printed by men of letters, and ultimately the proclamations of revolutionaries. Rather than treating these texts as isolated or inert objects of intellectual content, this study places them in their proper historical

---

[28] The social history of the state has been newly examined in such works as Charles Tilly, *Coercion, Capital, and European States, AD 990–1992* (Cambridge, MA, 1992); Theda Skocpol, *States and Revolutions: A Comparative Analysis of France, Russia, and China* (Cambridge, 1979); and Peter Evans, Dietrich Rueschmeyer, and Theda Skocpol, eds., *Bringing the State Back In* (Cambridge, 1985). For a critique of Skocpol that raises the question of ideology, see William Sewell, "Ideologies and Social Revolutions: Reflections on the French Case," *JMH* 57 (March, 1985), pp. 57–85.

[29] Baker, *Inventing*, pp. 4–5.

context – as ideological "moves" in a game of power.[30] Though played by the kingdom's elite, this was no trivial parlor game; it was a struggle over the power to appropriate the economic surplus of France.

The clash of claims and counterclaims, in which implicit and explicit assertions about royal authority and social hierarchy were inscribed, produced a kind of ideological or linguistic fallout as questions of a potentially subversive nature were thrust into public debate. What makes royal authority legitimate? How can the actions of the state be made accountable to its citizens? How equal or unequal should members of the same society be? By the second half of the eighteenth century finance ministers, magistrates, men of letters, and ordinary taxpayers all advanced what they understood to be the best constitutional blueprint for resolving the problem of taxation. At stake was the very composition of state and society.

The issue of taxation, then, is worth studying because it provides a powerful lens through which we can observe the development of political discourse and public opinion without losing sight of the long-term transformations in state and society that helped to shape them. By connecting the social history of the state to newer concerns about language and culture, this study seeks to offer a fresh interpretation of the Old Regime and its relationship to the French Revolution.

The book is divided into three parts. Part One (chapters 1 and 2) describes the regime of fiscal privilege that pervaded early modern French society and examines the crown's attempt in the eighteenth century to extricate itself from that regime by shifting some of the burden of taxation onto the elite. As chapter 1 explains, it was international fiscal–military rivalry that first prompted the monarchy to establish two "universal" direct taxes, the *capitation* and the *dixième*, which were designed to strike all subjects regardless of where they stood in the social hierarchy of the kingdom.[31] To institute these taxes the monarchy refashioned its ideology and its bureaucracy, elaborating a new rhetoric of fiscal equality and transferring admin-

---

[30] For the ways in which texts represent ideological "moves," see J. G. A. Pocock, *Virtue, Commerce, and History: Essays on Political Thought and History Chiefly in the Eighteenth Century* (Cambridge, 1985), pp. 1–34.

[31] I use the term "universal" taxes after the spirit of the laws that established them. How close the taxes came to meeting the claims made in royal tax decrees is the subject of ch. 2.

istrative power from judicial officials to an increasingly modern branch of administration. Chapter 2 presents data on the incidence of universal taxes and measures the force with which they struck various privileged and nonprivileged groups in different parts of the kingdom.

Naturally, the levy of universal taxes and the ideological and bureaucratic changes in royal authority that supported it met with strong opposition. But unlike the popular tax revolts of the seventeenth century, which were communal and violent, resistance to universal taxation in the eighteenth century tended to manifest itself in nonviolent institutional conflict and learned public debate. Part Two (chapters 3–5) looks at the politics of universal taxation and the language it generated in three distinct spheres: administrative, institutional, and literary. Chapter 3 examines contestation in the administrative sphere, where legions of privileged taxpayers routinely petitioned royal administrators in search of "justice." The frequency with which taxpayers contested their assessments, the rhetorical strategies that petitioners employed for the purposes of persuasion, and the responses of administrators to such appeals reveal the ways in which ordinary subjects formulated claims and entered into negotiations with the crown on a day-to-day basis. Chapter 4 looks at disputes too, but at the institutional level, where conflict unfolded on a grand scale as the monarchy clashed with sovereign courts of law. Filled with privileged individuals now subject to taxation, and forced to yield critical areas of jurisdiction over taxation to the crown, these institutions publicly protested against tax increases in language that transcended the vocabulary of justice to speak of despotism, liberty, and citizenship. It is clear that the publicity of such language politicized the issue of taxation and encouraged taxpayers to reflect on their relationship to the monarchy and to demand political change. Finally, in the literary sphere, citizens of the republic of letters raised the issue of taxation by publishing books and pamphlets. Gauging the diffusion of these texts during the Enlightenment, chapter 5 examines how the century's most popular books on finance characterized the problem of taxation and exposed principles of natural law, social contract, citizenship, publicity, and political participation to ever-growing numbers of readers.

The public decrees issued by the crown, the petitions of taxpayers, the protests of institutions, and the treatises of men of letters constituted a kingdom-wide dialogue on taxation and, by extension, on justice, citizenship, equality, liberty, and national sovereignty. Part Three (chapter 6) delineates how the multiple dialogues on taxation contributed to the outbreak of two revolutions, one against absolutism and the other against privilege. On the one hand, all taxpayers, nobles as well as commoners, used language produced by tax disputes to demand representation in a permanent constitutional government that would protect the liberty and property of citizens from an overextended state. On the other hand, the third estate and its allies stretched this constitutional revolution by seizing upon the conceptual link between taxation and citizenship to assert its own claims to political equality. Hence, as we shall see, the issue of taxation constitutes a kind of passageway that leads from the contentious politics of the Old Regime to the dramatic constitutional revolution of 1789 to the edge of the social revolution that radicalized the new political order as it was taking shape.

PART ONE

Reassessing privilege

The economy of privilege and the challenge of universal taxation

"Revenue is the chief preoccupation of the state. Nay more it is the state."

— Edmund Burke[1]

From the fourteenth to the eighteenth century not everyone in the kingdom of France had to pay direct taxes. Despite the growing needs and appetites of the royal treasury, many subjects enjoyed the valuable privilege of tax exemption. Between 1695 and 1789, however, the monarchy sought to expand its revenues by attempting to tax all those whom it had formerly deemed tax exempt. At first glance, such an attempt might appear a rather natural act by a monarchy looking to bolster its finances, but it is important to recognize that for centuries, from one reign to the next, kings almost instinctively built a state and shaped society around the principle of privilege. As the monarchy grew beyond its medieval borders, as it extended its financial reach past the lands of the royal domain to seize revenue from taxes, the sale of offices, and loans, it reinforced the inequalities of feudal society by producing a regime of fiscal privilege that sharpened economic and social distinctions between elites and commoners. By the age of Louis XIV, society was saturated with fiscal privilege.

Approaching the seemingly chaotic world of the royal finances from different perspectives, William Beik, Daniel Dessert, and James Collins have all shown that Louis XIV secured the stability of the absolutist state by sustaining a financial alliance with elites in which tax revenue was extracted from lower orders of society and was redistributed (by means of pensions, interest payments, military

---

[1] Quoted in P. K. O'Brien and P. A. Hunt, "The Rise of a Fiscal State in England, 1485–1815," *Historical Journal* 66 (1993), p. 130.

outlays, and outright gifts) up the social hierarchy to tax-exempt courtiers, nobles, office-holders, and royal creditors.[2] Given that royal budgets in wartime could be worth as much as a fifth of the kingdom's total grain production and an eighth of its gross national product, and that as much as a third to a half of the kingdom's currency was pumped through the royal treasury, the scale of that redistribution was massive.[3] According to Beik, the monarchy was "in charge of the largest economic enterprise in the country: drawing money from the land, channeling it to well positioned notables on every level along the way, attracting it back from these same people along with their own landed revenues in the form of loans and advances, and redistributing what reached the court back again to armies, officers, creditors and courtiers."[4] Thus the Sun King did not simply dazzle the aristocracy into obedience with grandiose court ceremony; he convinced elites of the value of a strong monarchy by perfecting a type of welfare state for the privileged. This regime of privilege, which was under construction long before Louis XIV and which continued to shape French society until the collapse of the Old Regime, forms the background against which changes in eighteenth-century taxation and political culture must be understood.

STORIES OF FISCAL PRIVILEGE

We can view the world of privilege through the window of the *taille*, the main direct tax in France from the fifteenth century to the French Revolution. The most remarkable feature of this tax was the number of individuals who did not have to pay it. Clergymen, courtiers, nobles, military officers, magistrates and lesser office-holders, professors, doctors, state administrators and employees, as well as residents of entire provinces and towns all enjoyed at least partial exemption from the *taille*. In fact, almost anyone who was not

---

[2] William Beik, *Absolutism and Society in Seventeenth-Century France: State Power and Provincial Aristocracy in Languedoc* (Cambridge, 1985); Daniel Dessert, *Argent, pouvoir, et société au Grand Siècle* (Paris, 1984); and James Collins, *Classes, Estates, and Order in Early Modern Brittany* (Cambridge, 1994). See also Philip Hoffman, "Early Modern France, 1450–1700," in *Fiscal Crises, Liberty, and Representative Government, 1450–1789*, ed. Philip Hoffman and Kathryn Norberg (Stanford, CA, 1994), pp. 226–52.

[3] Emmanuel Le Roy Ladurie, *L'Ancien Régime, 1610–1715* (Paris, 1991), p. 125.

[4] William Beik, "A Social Interpretation of the reign of Louis XIV," in *L'état ou le roi: Les fondations de la modernité monarchique en France (XIVe–XVIIe siècles)*, ed. Neithard Bulst, Robert Descimon, and Alain Guerreau (Paris, 1996), p. 156.

a peasant managed to avoid paying some portion of the tax. How did fiscal privilege come to be spread so widely, and on what grounds did the privileges of so many groups rest?

The privileges of the clergy and the nobility were rooted in the medieval notion that society was divided into three distinct orders, each serving a particular function. The endurance of this myth over the centuries and in the face of profound social change is striking. At the turn of the first millennium, Adalbero, chancellor of France, described the society in which he lived in simple terms: "Here below some pray, others fight, still others work." In 1610 Charles Loyseau began his elaborate analysis of the corporate order in much the same way: "Some are devoted particularly to the service of God; others to the preservation of the State by arms; still others to the task of feeding and maintaining it by peaceful labors. These are our three orders or Estates General of France, the Clergy, the Nobility, and the Third Estate."[5] And, as late as 1776, the parlement of Paris still found it useful to remind Louis XVI that

every man in the kingdom is your subject, all are obliged to contribute to the needs of the State. But in this contribution one always finds order and harmony. The personal service of the clergy is to fulfill all the functions regarding instruction and religious worship, and to contribute to the relief of the unfortunate by means of its alms. The noble devotes his blood for the defense of the State and assists the sovereign with its council. The last class of the nation, which is not able to render such distinguished services to the State, discharges its duty to it through tributes, industry and physical work ... These institutions are not those which chance has formed and that time can change.[6]

The structure of the *taille* clearly reflected this tripartite division of society. When Charles VII introduced a permanent *taille* in 1439 he exempted the clergy and the nobility and let the tax fall entirely on the third estate. In the fifteenth, sixteenth, and seventeenth centuries, as the weight of the *taille* increased and as generations of commoners were inscribed in the tax rolls, liability to the *taille* became as much a sign of low birth as were other visible markers such as dress, speech, and manner. In legal treatises and administrative correspondence the very word *"taillable"* (payer of the *taille*)

---

[5] Quoted in Georges Duby, *The Three Orders: Feudal Society Imagined*, trans. Arthur Goldhammer (Chicago, 1978), pp. 1 and 13.
[6] Quoted in François Hincker, *Les français devant l'impôt sous l'ancien régime* (Paris, 1971), pp. 95–6.

became synonymous with *"roturier"* (commoner). According to Richelieu, this fiscal-social symbolism was so ingrained in the minds of the French that he believed it unwise to relieve "the common people" of their tax burdens, since "they would lose the mark of their subjection and consequently the awareness of their station. Thus being free from paying tribute, they would consider themselves exempted from obedience."[7]

Just as paying the *taille* indicated the low birth of commoners, exemption from it distinguished the high status of the clergy and nobility. As a 1641 royal declaration explained, the monarchy bestowed the clergy's privilege of tax exemption to show "the respect that we carry for the dignity of the church, and by the consideration of the title and rank that we attach to it, as well as to distinguish [clergymen] from the condition of our other subjects."[8] The clergy understood its exemption in much the same terms. "The most significant mark of honor which places the church of this province above the common people is exemption from the *taille*," observed the clergy of Normandy in 1634. Norman nobles saw in tax privileges the same "mark of honor" when in 1616 they stated that taxation would "shamefully subject them to obligations unworthy of [their] condition."[9]

It was not simply assumed that clerics and nobles were above tax-paying. That belief was sustained through a set of stories that justified their tax exemptions and explained why the first two orders should be treated differently from the third. Permeating the collective consciousness of Old Regime society, these stories provided the symbolic foundation for the perpetuation of privilege and the persistence of inequality in the direct tax system. As the estate that declared the order of the universe, the clergy easily justified its special place in it by making two claims. It argued that the spiritual functions of the church – disseminating the word of God, administering the sacraments, and assisting in the passage of souls from this world to the next – allowed clergymen, including those descending from noble lineages, to avoid royal military service and, by extension, to be exempt from war subsidies such as the *taille*. Secondly, the

[7] *The Political Testament of Cardinal Richelieu*, trans. Henry Bertram Hill (Madison, WI, 1961), p. 31.
[8] AN, AD IX 470, no. 10, Declaration of 24 July 1641.
[9] Quoted in Edmond Esmonin, *La taille en Normandie au temps de Colbert, 1661–1683* (1913; reprint, Geneva, 1978), p. 196.

clergy based its claim to tax exemption on the idea that the church was merely the "usufructuary" of God's property, meaning that it was entitled to the fruits of property it claimed not to possess. The wealth produced by sacred property was itself sacred and, as such, could be used only for the specific purposes of saving souls and caring for the poor. The Assembly of the Clergy repeated an old theme when it stated in 1750 that its exemption was "founded in the nature and destination of our wealth, which is consecrated to God, and of which his ministers alone can be the stewards and dispensers."[10] In short, the crown was not to meddle with God's property.

The nobility, for its part, claimed its exemption was deserved because the order already served the monarchy by fighting.[11] Military service was tantamount to a "tax in blood" that rendered payment of the *taille* redundant. Was there any question that fighting on behalf of the king outweighed venal contributions to the state? Could there be a greater service to the crown than that of losing or, at least, risking life on the battlefield? Lebret, an officer of the *cour des aides* of Rouen in the 1590s, certainly did not think so:

Of all the professions that contribute the most to the public good, that of the military seems to merit one of the first ranks . . . ; this is why men of this profession have at all times deserved to be honored by many distinguished privileges, especially exemption and immunity from all tributes and taxes . . . ; The truth is that they pay to the republic a rather big tribute by consecrating their blood and their life to serve it, risking hazards and perils on a daily basis.[12]

In addition to putting their sons in harm's way, noble parents incurred the costs of outfitting sons for war and providing them with a proper military education, which could be extremely heavy burdens for less wealthy members of the order.[13]

Thus, while spiritual service and sacred property legitimized the privileges of the first estate, military service and expense justified the privileges of the second. As monarch after monarch honored the

---

[10] Quoted in Marcel Marion, *Dictionnaire des institutions de la France aux XVIIe et XVIIIe siècles* (Paris, 1923), p. 102.

[11] In feudal society, holders of fiefs also served the crown by judging disputes between their vassals, but it was military service that justified tax exemption. John Bell Henneman, "Nobility, Privilege and Fiscal Politics in Late Medieval France," *FHS* 13 (Spring, 1983), pp. 1–17.

[12] Quoted in Esmonin, *La taille en Normandie*, p. 199.

[13] Jean Meyer, "Un problème mal posé: La noblesse pauvre – L'exemple breton au xviiie siècle," *Revue d'histoire moderne et contemporaine* 18 (April–June, 1971), pp. 161–88.

tax-exempt status of both estates, exemptions and the stories of
privilege embedded in them hardened into law, particularly for the
clergy, which made sure that kings periodically issued decrees
certifying its privileges. By the eighteenth century the clergy's
exemptions rested on an indisputable legal record. Even Necker, not
least among the Old Regime's reform-minded statesmen, admitted
in 1778 that although "it is certainly in the *taillables'* interests to see
privileges restrained within the most narrow limits, it is equally just
not to remove a privilege of the clergy which is founded on Laws."[14]
At the end of the Old Regime the tax privileges of the clergy and the
nobility were considered old legal rights.

Lest we ourselves fall prey to the myth of the three orders, it is
important to remember that clerics and nobles were not the only
subjects permitted to drink at the fountain of privilege.[15] On the
contrary, during the early modern period the fountain overflowed,
its waters pouring down the social hierarchy and across the French
landscape. Many privileges were scarcely feudal at all (notwithstand-
ing the wishes of those who possessed them), being the recent
creations of a state that granted exemption from the *taille* to
countless office-holders, state employees, and residents of particular
cities and provinces who had no claims whatsoever to nobility or the
ecclesiastical profession. From the sixteenth century on, the distribution of privilege matched less and less the simplistic feudal image
of a three-tiered society composed of prayers, warriors, and workers,
and conformed more and more to a society of myriad corps. Guilds,
municipalities, provinces, and above all the groups of royal office-
holders that, drawing their members from the ranks of the third
estate, proliferated in the judicial and financial branches of the state
received fiscal privileges that had once been reserved for the first two
orders. Privilege stratified.

In light of the monarchy's constant hunger for tax revenue, it may
seem paradoxical that it steadily widened the field of privilege. Why
would kings seeking to increase tax revenues distribute tax privileges
so lavishly? The answer is that privilege was useful. In order to
secure territory, the monarchy used privilege to ensure the obedience
of residents living in important cities. A letter confirming the early
exemption of the city of Tours from the *taille* in 1492 made it clear

---

[14] AD Calvados, C 4396, letter to Esmangart, intendant of Caen, 20 February 1778.
[15] I borrow this metaphor from Hilton Root, *The Fountain of Privilege: Political Foundations of
Markets in Old Regime France and England* (Berkeley, CA, 1994).

that the crown was only too happy to accept the "courtesy, gracious-ness, service, and obedience" of the residents of Tours in exchange for "privileges, freedoms, liberties, and exemptions." The same privilege also facilitated the integration of provinces into the kingdom. When a monarch proudly patched a new province onto the kingdom's border, he often granted it privileges that preserved its administrative and financial autonomy. In 1750 the provincial estates of Provence defended the province against the fiscal intrusions of Louis XV by reminding the king that "the maintenance" of the old laws "was the principal condition of the union of Provence with your Crown." "The reciprocal agreements" made between Provence and Charles, comte d'Anjou, in 1486 assured that Provence would unite itself with France "under the expressed condition that the privileges, Liberties, conventions, Laws, Customs, rights, statutes, administra-tion, and the way of life of the province would not be violated or infringed upon." Although the crown sometimes employed military force to obtain the obedience of cities and provinces, it was much easier to keep their allegiance by bestowing privileges.[16]

Besides securing and expanding territory, the monarchy used privilege to build an immense administrative and judicial edifice. The growth of royal office-holders and administrators in early modern France was nothing short of staggering. From 1515 to 1665 the number of royal offices jumped from 4,041 to at least 46,047, a figure that would soar again during the second half of Louis XIV's reign when he flooded the market for offices in an attempt to raise money for his last two great wars. The rise of venality leveled off after the War of Spanish Succession to reach some 60,000 or more offices by 1789, each of which provided privileges for the owner and his family.[17] The ranks of lower-level administrators also prolifer-ated, particularly in the quasi-private indirect tax farms. The General Farms of the eighteenth century employed some 30,000 persons, all of whom (with their families) benefited in some measure from exemption from the *taille*.[18] By attaching privileges such as tax

---

[16] AN, AD IX 470, no. 1, letter of February 1492; AN, K 900, no. 24, Remonstrances of the estates of Provence, 1750.

[17] Pierre Chaunu, "L'Etat," in *Histoire économique et sociale de France*, ed. Fernand Braudel and Ernest Labrousse (Paris, 1977), I, pp. 193–4; David Bien, "Old Regime Origins," p. 55. For a recent overview, see William Doyle, *Venality: The Sale of Offices in Eighteenth-Century France* (Oxford, 1996).

[18] Vida Azimi, *Un modèle administratif de L'Ancien Régime: Les Commis de la ferme générale et de la régie générale des aides* (Paris, 1987), p. 33.

exemption to offices and administrative posts, the monarchy made them more valuable and lured tens of thousands of individuals into state service. Officers staffed busier royal courts and employees of the tax farms collected increasingly substantial sums of money for the royal treasury. The loss of tax revenue resulting from the spread of privilege among minor administrative positions was offset by the gain in judicial and bureaucratic work.

In adorning offices with privileges, however, the crown was looking to attract more than professional labor. It sought to draw capital as well. Offices, after all, were purchased by advancing large sums of money to the crown in return for which officers received privileges, including enhanced social status, interest payments (*gages*), the right to exercise and collect fees from the functions of their office, and, of course, tax exemption. In a few cases this last privilege was of particular importance. According to a 1680 declaration, minor offices in the Royal Household were bought "not so much for serving at court as for acquiring a title of exemption."[19] But most offices were purchased for a combination of privileges, as advertisements for vacant offices made clear.[20] Whatever the motives of buyers, their investments fueled a brisk trade in offices that commodified and strengthened fiscal privilege. This was certainly true in the sixteenth and seventeenth centuries when sales boomed, but it was even true of the eighteenth century when investments in office became heavier as officers loaned more of their own capital to the crown, supplementing it with investments from outside creditors who were not necessarily officers themselves.

This deepening of lines of credit, which affected not only office-holders but nearly all members of the kingdom's numerous corporate bodies (guilds, municipalities, provincial estates, and the clergy), led to a further entrenchment of privilege. As the monarchy's dependence on this relatively low-cost system of credit grew, the prospect of reform receded ever further from the realm of political possibility. When, for instance, Louis XV moved to revoke the tax privileges of the clergy in 1725 and 1749, the Assembly of the Clergy warned that, if its tax immunities were removed, the clergy's own creditors would no longer invest in the church, and the church, in turn, would no longer be able to provide loans to the monarchy.

---

[19] Quoted in Esmonin, *La taille en Normandie*, p. 245.
[20] Doyle, *Venality*, pp. 155–7.

Unveiled threats like these were usually enough to ward off the most enthusiastic financial reformers and to set the state back on its familiar course of preserving the privileges of its creditors. As David Bien concluded, "French kings, far from struggling against privilege, found in it a resource they could not live without."[21]

The stories office-holders told in defense of privilege rested on two different yet complementary conceptions of their offices. As investors in office, they saw their immunity from the *taille* as part of a proprietary contract with the crown. When Louis xv in 1765 threatened to suspend the tax privileges associated with lower-level financial offices, the officers of the *élection* courts of Normandy understood the king to be breaking the contract by which they had agreed to invest in office. They complained to the finance minister that royal law since 1360 had granted exemption to those who owned their exact type of office, and from this they concluded that the tax privilege was "attached" to their offices and should, therefore, be treated as their personal property. The officers owned their tax privileges in the same way that they owned their offices, and the monarchy, as the retailer of such property, could not renege on the transaction. Besides emphasizing the notion of contract, the same officers argued that the prestige and function of their offices set them above the common mass of taxpayers. Their privileges were "less profitable than honorable," they explained, and "this suspension degrades and debases their offices." To be subjected to the very tax over which they were the "judge" provoked exclamations of shame and outrage: "What humiliation ... ! What a strange reversal of the Rules!"[22] Similar outrage was voiced by Pierre Charles de Cognet, a *procureur du roy* at the *vicomté* court of Pontorson, who discovered in 1772 that he had been placed on the rolls of the *taille*; "when the king created such offices, he intended that his officers be distinguished from commoners. It is therefore quite disgraceful to find himself placed on the tax rolls ... The supplicant [in that case] would be right to say that his status and that of a day laborer would be equal."[23] Fiscal equality was "shameful," remarked the president of the *présidial* court of Troyes in 1758, because "the public" was

---

[21] Bien, "Old Regime Origins," p. 41. The remarks of the clergy are found in AN, K 900, nos. 22 and 24, Remonstrances of September 1725 and 24 August 1749.

[22] AD Calvados, C 4521 bis, letter from the officers of the *élections* of Normandy to L'Averdy, 14 February 1765. Exemption was also believed to make financial officers disinterested.

[23] AD Calvados, C 4676, no. 18, petition to the intendant of Caen, 23 June 1772.

accustomed "to bestow its esteem on all offices in proportion as they lift those holding them out of the ordinary class of citizens through exemption from the public burdens."[24]

There is little doubt that, by extending privilege beyond clergy and nobility, the kings of early modern France gained greater financial, bureaucratic, and territorial strength than their medieval predecessors. But they also swelled the ranks of the privileged. Supported by a confusing array of justifications, from contracts and rights to service and status, individuals up and down the social hierarchy benefited from tax exemption. Non-noble postmasters and royal gardeners, urban artisans and bourgeois shopkeepers, and magistrates and tax collectors joined the ranks of nobles (many of whom never fought) and clergymen (some of whom perhaps rarely prayed) to form a broadly based social group that enjoyed fiscal privilege. What the history of the *taille* tells us is clear: monarchy and privilege grew together.

To be sure, the kings and administrators who perpetuated privilege were not entirely comfortable with the regime they were creating. Troubled by the way the *taille* sapped the peasantry and frustrated by the social limits of the levy, the crown made several efforts to reform the tax in the seventeenth and eighteenth centuries, none of which, however, fundamentally restructured the regime of privilege.[25] From the fifteenth century to the Revolution the *taille* never ceased being a highly visible manifestation of privilege as clerics, nobles, city-dwellers, residents of particular provinces, and a throng of office-holders were spared the public humiliation of full liability. As Dessert concluded from his study of seventeenth-century royal finances,

---

[24] Quoted in Doyle, *Venality*, p. 152. Royal legislation itself reinforced these ideas. The *arrêt du conseil* of 8 October 1658 was one of many decrees that defended the tax privileges of officers (in this case officers in the *maréchaussée*) against the encroachments of local tax collectors by explaining that it was not right "to put principal officers of the Crown on the same level with the most abject commoners." AN, AD IX 470, no. 15.

[25] According to Mireille Touzery, *L'invention de l'impôt sur le revenu: la taille tarifée 1715–1789* (Paris, 1994), the *taille tarifée* was put into effect in the generality of Paris late in the eighteenth century, but it never presumed to reach the wealth of the privileged. (Indeed, it scarcely made the *taille* fairer for those liable to it). Nor did the *charrue* rule make any serious inroads into the income of the privileged. The widely ignored rule held that nobles, bourgeois, and officers who directly oversaw the work on their land were to pay the *taille* on the part of their estate that exceeded a certain number of *charrues* (four *charrues* for nobles, two for officers, and one for bourgeois). A *charrue* varied from 50 to 100 acres depending on local definitions.

The state, by virtue of its finances and the whole system secreted by them, was imprisoned by the ties of dependence upon society which its own system had generated. Any attempt to change or challenge the fiscal system, even in the interests of the state, implied a challenge to the society upon which the self-same state was based. Therein lies one of the most serious contradictions in the ancien régime.[26]

This contradiction between a regime of privilege that served the state and the state's own attempt to change that regime would become all the more acute in the eighteenth century when the crown designed new taxes that, in principle, disregarded privilege altogether. These taxes were more than just fiscal innovations. They represented a direct challenge to a society laden with privilege and suggested the possibility of an entirely new relationship between state and society.

FISCAL–MILITARY RIVALRY AND THE ESTABLISHMENT OF
UNIVERSAL TAXES

After the famine of 1693–4 crippled the collection of the *taille*, Louis XIV established the *capitation* (1695–8; 1701–90), the first direct tax in France designed to strike all royal subjects no matter where they stood in the social hierarchy of the kingdom. After another disastrous harvest in 1709–10 he created a second universal tax, the *dixième* (1710–17, 1733–7 and 1741–9; and, renamed the *vingtième*, 1749–90).[27] Stretching from city to city, from the southern provinces to northern ones, and from peasants to princes, these taxes were meant to traverse centuries-old geographic, social, and legal boundaries of privilege and impose a new kind of equality among royal subjects.

Why would the crown weaken the privileges of the most powerful subjects in the kingdom and risk losing their loyalty? The correspondence between finance ministers and kings provides an unequivocal answer: military ambition. The penchant of European rulers for winning glory at arms and expanding the territory of their states should not be underestimated. Early modern Europe experienced what one could describe as a preindustrial arms race in which fiscal strength was as essential to military power as advances in strategy and technology. As battles were fought on the high seas and in distant colonies as well as on the European continent, and as armies

---

[26] Quoted in Peter Robert Campbell, *The Ancien Régime in France* (Oxford, 1988), p. 66.
[27] One could add the *cinquantième* (1725–7), which was universal as well.

grew spectacularly in size and required increasingly intensive training and more elaborate supply networks, the costs of war skyrocketed and rulers everywhere scrambled to find revenue. From 1695 to 1789, during a kind of second Hundred Years War with Britain, the kings of France were so desperate for money that they sought to tap the well-protected wealth of the privileged.[28]

From their inception, universal taxes were associated with international military and fiscal rivalry. Both taxes were created during the second half of Louis XIV's reign when the king, no longer personally leading his armies into battle, withdrew to his bureaux where he and his finance ministers devised ways to raise money for his last two great wars, those of the League of Augsburg and the Spanish Succession. Exploiting a set of wartime expedients known as "extraordinary affairs," the crown forced office-holders to invest more capital in their offices, created and hawked new offices by the thousands, mortgaged years of future tax revenues, borrowed hundreds of millions of livres through the sale of bonds and the use of promissory notes, manipulated the currency no fewer than forty-three times, and increased indirect taxes while establishing new direct ones.[29]

Buried among these "extraordinary" expedients, most of which were extraordinary only in their scale, we find the *capitation*, a tax established in 1695 in the middle of the War of the League of Augsburg. The financial demands of that war, fought by the largest French army of the century if not the entire Old Regime,[30] were enormous, and in 1694 Pontchartrain, the minister of finance, informed provincial intendants that the king was looking for new ways to finance it: "among the many expedients that have been considered to provide for the expenses of war, a general *capitation* on all subjects has been proposed to the king." Although new to France, he continued, the *capitation* was already being used in "many neighboring states, and the emperor recently instituted it in his hereditary states."[31] Having witnessed his principal enemy, the Holy Roman Emperor, establish a *capitation*, Louis XIV followed suit, and

---

[28] On early modern European military rivalry, see Geoffrey Parker, *The Military Revolution: Military Innovation and the Rise of the West, 1500–1800* (Cambridge, 1988).

[29] The number of manipulations in currency is from François Crouzet, *La grande inflation. La monnaie en France de Louis XVI à Napoléan* (Paris, 1993), p. 22.

[30] John Lynn, "Recalculating French Army Growth during the *Grand Siècle*, 1610–1715," *FHS* 18 (Fall, 1994), p. 903.

[31] BN, Ms. Fr. 8852, fos. 83–4, letter of 31 October 1694.

in January 1695, facing the exhaustion of credit and low returns from the *taille*, he announced that the only means to sustain the war was to establish a tax on "all our Subjects without any distinction."[32] Thus was born the *capitation*, a child of war and fiscal competition.

The *dixième* was established to pay for war too, this time the War of the Spanish Succession. The finance minister, Desmaretz, informed the intendants in 1710 that the *dixième* was needed urgently since "the King is counting on this revenue for the expense of the war, and His Majesty wants to have his armies enter the military campaign in good time."[33] Years later Desmaretz explained to the Regent how the *dixième* came to be instituted: "it was necessary to secure an annual fund during the war, which did not at all burden the revenues of the king, as did every other extraordinary means of revenue of which we had made use previously: we were able to find only an expedient [which taxed] the revenue of *all* the capital and *all* the wealth."[34] Desmaretz did not have to look far for a model of that new sort of expedient. As the declaration establishing the *dixième* stated, France's enemies "levy by way of taxes on land greater sums each year than the Dixième for which we are determined to ask."[35] The enemy in mind of course was England, which had imposed a land tax on rental income since 1692 at a rate, in principle, of 20 percent. There is also reason to believe, according to Richard Bonney, that Desmaretz modeled the *dixième* on taxes in Artois, Flanders, and Holland.[36] Thus, once again, in the midst of war and famine, scrutinizing the tax systems of neighboring enemies, Louis XIV attempted to overcome burdensome credit arrangements by imposing a new universal direct tax. Although a few officials dreamed naively that universal taxes would absorb the morass of debt that swamped the extraordinary finances, the *dixième* was merely used to service some of the royal debt and open the way for a fresh round of borrowing.[37]

---

[32] AN, AD IX 81, no. 107, Declaration of 18 January 1695.

[33] AN, G-7 1138, circular to intendants, 30 October 1710.

[34] Nicolas Desmaretz, *Mémoire sur l'administration des Finances* (n.p., n.d.), p. 23; the emphasis is mine.

[35] AN, AD IX 400, no. 84, Declaration of 14 October 1710.

[36] Richard Bonney, "'Le Secret de Leurs Familles': The Fiscal and Social Limits of Louis XIV's *Dixième*," *French History* 7 (1993), p. 392.

[37] On the *dixième* and the restoration of credit, see AN, G-7 1138, *caisse* of the *dixième*; and Gary McCollim, "The Formation of Fiscal Policy in the Reign of Louis XIV: The Example of Nicolas Desmaretz, Controller General of Finances (1708–1715)," PhD thesis, Ohio State University (1979), pp. 306 and 322–3.

The *dixième* was so critical to France's military position that Desmaretz attributed the peace of 1714 to it. He claimed that France's ability to impose the tax forced its enemies to negotiate:

the enemies of France were convinced that the establishment of it would be impossible; but having seen that every subject lent themselves to the needs of the State, . . . they saw the *dixième* as an inexhaustible resource for the war. It can be said that this is one of the principal considerations which forced the enemies to make peace: they themselves are rather explicit about this, so there is no reason to doubt it.[38]

Once the long War of the Spanish Succession ceased, fiscal–military competition among European states shifted toward debt reduction, because a well-managed debt signaled that a country could borrow easily in the event of another war. In 1715, in the aftermath of the war, Desmaretz became a fiscal spy of sorts and found that other countries were using universal taxes to pay off their debts. He reported to Louis XIV,

I have informed myself of what is practiced in Germany, Holland, and England to pay off their debts. The decrees and placards from these places reveal that their means consist wholly in taxing all their wealth for a great number of years, the revenue from which is designated to the payments of the debts contracted for the war.[39]

Months later the king announced that the *capitation* and the *dixième*, supposedly temporary wartime expedients, would be prolonged.

Whereas the *capitation* was prolonged indefinitely, the *dixième* was revoked in 1717, only to be reestablished between 1733 and 1737, during the War of the Polish Succession, and between 1741 and 1749, during the War of the Austrian Succession. When peace came in 1749, however, the *dixième* did not disappear but was reborn under the name *vingtième* to become a permanent part of the state's fiscal structure as the *capitation* had long been.

No longer having to worry about the establishment or reestablishment of universal taxes, finance ministers in the second half of the eighteenth century, confronting new wars, set their minds to increasing them. In 1759, seeking to meet the costs of the Seven Years War, Silhouette advised Louis XV that from a military point of view it would be wiser to raise taxes than to keep borrowing: "all operations of credit today would only produce the disastrous effect of unveiling

---

[38] Desmaretz, *Mémoire*, p. 23.
[39] AN, K 886, no. 23, *Mémoire au Roi*, 1715.

[the state's] powerlessness to our enemies, and of making peace more difficult. It is therefore only in the augmentation of revenues that we are permitted to look for resources."[40] The following year the king doubled the *capitation* on privileged subjects and increased the *vingtième* by a half. When Silhouette fell from power, his successor, Bertin, tried to prolong these tax increases for the duration of the war, reminding Miromesnil, the first president of the parlement of Rouen who was resisting the increases, that such taxes had once brought about great diplomatic triumphs: "let us not forget what happened in 1710; everyone knows that the zeal with which every subject supported the establishment of the *dixième* made a great impression on our enemies." In the same manner, Bertin insisted, the court's immediate consent to tax increases would "give some weight to our plenipotentiaries in their negotiations."[41] The finance minister got his way, and the increases remained in place until the end of the war.

During the last three decades of the Old Regime, as the debt that resulted from the Seven Years War and the costs of the War of American Independence burdened royal finances, ministers of state found that it was not enough simply to increase universal taxes. They had to be levied more equally. In 1768 Moreau de Beaumont, an intendant of finance, and L'Averdy, the minister of finance, informed Louis XV that they were studying "forms of taxation in every state in Europe." Based on reports of French ambassadors in more than thirty European countries, the comparative study showed that although taxes were used to "make the nation respected outside [its borders] . . . , the principal goal, and the most worthwhile, is to make the distribution of taxation as equal, and therefore, as little onerous as possible."[42] Looking for ways to finance the War of American Independence, Necker expressed the same sentiment: "among all the resources of the Royal Treasury, the most sure is without a doubt proportional equality of taxation since this is the most intelligent way to soften the common burden and provide the means to further increase taxation."[43] By the end of the Old Regime

[40] AN, K 883, no. 5, Mémoire sur la situation des finances, August 1759.

[41] P. Le Verdier, ed., *Correspondance politique et administrative de Miromesnil premier président du parlement de Normandie*, 5 vols. (Paris, 1899–1903), II, pp. 2–10, Bertin to Miromesnil, 27 July 1761.

[42] Jean-Louis Moreau de Beaumont, *Mémoires concernant les impositions et droits en Europe*, 4 vols. (Paris, 1768), avertissement. The original draft is located in AN, K 879, no. 1.

[43] AN, K 885, no. 5, Mémoire donné au Roy par M. Necker en 1778.

ministers of state considered equality as well as universality of taxation crucial to sustaining the nation's international standing.

It is clear, then, that the development of universal taxes in France was rooted in a Europe-wide martial culture. But what kind of impact did these new taxes have on politics and society *inside* the kingdom of France? Just as the post-war arms race of the twentieth century had important consequences for the domestic politics of its participants, the fiscal–military rivalry of the eighteenth century helped to create distinctive political cultures among the states involved.[44] In the French case we can begin to take the measure of these consequences by recognizing that the monarchy refashioned its ideology and bureaucracy in its effort to impose universal taxes. Louis XIV and his successors not only changed the ways in which they articulated their demands to the public; they altered the administrative forms by which they intervened in society.

PERSUADING THE PUBLIC: THE CROWN'S OWN STORIES

To impose universal taxes, the crown had to justify rearranging the very regime of privilege it had helped build. This was no small matter, since the success or failure of the taxes depended largely on the public's disposition. Even ministers of finance of the most "absolute" kings were very much aware of the force of public opinion: "whether [the *capitation*] is good or bad," Pontchartrain confided to Harlay, the first president of the *parlement* of Paris, "must ultimately be put to the public judgment."[45] A negative judgment could make a tax extremely difficult to collect. Yet kings were not powerless before the judgment of the public, for they knew that they could influence it by expressing themselves in public ceremonies and statements. "The Frenchman wants to be flattered, roused; he must be given a kind of spectacle to inspire him through his vanity," suggested Miromesnil, who believed that overcoming resistance to taxation was a simple matter of persuading the public. "Why irritate the spirit of a nation which is easy to lead, but to which the master must speak, always sure of being heard, even adored, when he wants."[46]

---

[44] For the British example, see John Brewer, *The Sinews of Power: War, Money and the English State, 1688–1783* (Cambridge, MA, 1990); and Linda Colley, *Britons: Forging the Nation, 1707–1837* (New Haven, CT, 1992).
[45] BN, Ms. Fr. 17430, fo. 81, letter of 17 January 1695.
[46] Le Verdier, *Miromesnil*, II, p. 22, letter to Bertin, 31 July 1761.

To speak to the people about finances, kings preferred above all the medium of the royal decree. Launched toward the public from behind the dark veil of secrecy that cloaked the royal finances, the decree momentarily illuminated the will of the king and the financial conditions and needs of the kingdom. According to Jacques Necker, who perhaps knew best how public opinion operated in the eighteenth century, the decree was a form of expression "particular to the French Government."

[In France,] where national assemblies do not exist, and where, nevertheless, the laws of the Prince need to be registered by the sovereign Courts; in France, where those in power must take the character of the nation into account, and where state ministers themselves feel at each moment the need for public approval, it is believed essential to explain the purpose behind the wishes of the monarch, as these wishes manifest themselves to the people, whether by edicts or by simple *arrêts du conseil* of the Prince. This responsibility, so politic and so just, is especially applicable to laws of finance.[47]

More recently, Michèle Fogel has explained that the royal decree, posted before the eye of the public, "was treated not only as a medium of its contents, a practical function, but foremost as a sign of the royal presence, a symbolic function, which is conveyed in the decree's presentation."[48] The formal way in which the king was introduced, the capitalization of words that referred to his person (such as "HIS MAJESTY"), and the use of allegorical figures at the head of laws endowed decrees with a tone of authority. But a spectacle of authority was not sufficient. The principles on which decrees were based had to be conveyed convincingly, especially if those principles or the policies based on them ran against the grain of popular opinion. Again we turn to Miromesnil, who asked the finance minister,

How many people do we find who cannot arrange facts in their mind, and who, further, are affected only by their own problems and find themselves little disposed to giving the necessary attention to that which truly concerns the public good? The people of this category know and hear only public clamors, and we must admit that in every order they compose the greatest number. Yet it is to this great number, monsieur, that we must speak; it is they who we must persuade.[49]

---

[47] Jacques Necker, *De l'administration des finances de la France*, 3 vols. (Paris, 1784), I, p. lxxi.
[48] Michèle Fogel, *Les cérémonies de l'information dans la France du XVIe au XVIIIe siècle* (Paris, 1989), pp. 107–8.
[49] Le Verdier, *Miromesnil*, II, p. 14, letter of 31 July 1761.

To persuade this great majority, kings placed eloquent preambles at the head of laws and worded the body of decrees very carefully, making universal tax edicts, declarations, and *arrêts* key sources for understanding how the crown characterized its challenge to privilege.[50] Before we interpret legislative rhetoric, however, it is worth pausing to consider the social parameters of the public to which decrees appealed. Broadly construed, any individual who read royal decrees was part of the public. As Habermas emphasized, "the addressees" of printed decrees "became 'the public' in the proper sense" inasmuch as they were being hailed by the crown.[51] Thus the dimensions of the public can be measured by following the paths of decrees once they were released from the confines of royal administration.

The breadth of the public reached depended on the law in question. The most important decrees, such as edicts and declarations, were sent first to sovereign courts of justice to be reviewed by magistrates who, insofar as they critically examined the royal council's decrees, constituted a small but important public connected symbolically to the larger one through the ritual of reviewing laws with "the doors open, and the people present." Edicts and declarations were more widely publicized after the courts registered them and employed printers to make large broadsheets that were then posted in public areas, such as marketplaces, main squares, court houses, street corners, and churches. (Such broadsheets were so ubiquitous that Louis-Sébastian Mercier could claim that they improved the literacy of Parisians). Lesser decrees that had not been sent to the courts, *arrêts du conseil* for instance, were printed by royal presses and distributed directly by provincial intendants, who posted them in public places, especially on the doors of parish churches; they were also read aloud at the end of mass to make the literate and illiterate alike aware of them.[52] Finally, laws were published in newspapers and sold by booksellers and street peddlers. Several

---

[50] The preamble took on special didactic significance during the Enlightenment. In Bertin's 1763 land tax edict Turgot saw "a very good opportunity to develop, in a preamble, the true principles of taxation, and to prepare men's minds for them. There is reason to believe that in six years these seeds will germinate, and that truths, which are today little known, will become popular." Gustave Schelle, ed., *Oeuvres de Turgot et documents le concernant*, 5 vols. (Paris, 1913–23), II, p. 254. Rousseau, too, saw in preambles a golden opportunity for rulers to speak to the public, as he stressed in *Discours sur l'économie politique* (reprint, Paris, 1990), p. 67.

[51] Habermas, *Public Sphere*, p. 21.

[52] AD Calvados, C 5942, letter from Labrisse to subdelegates, 12 August 1749.

foreign periodicals printed French laws, as did royally sponsored newspapers such as the Paris *Gazette*. After mid-century, provincial journals carried the news of royal laws to a growing readership, including people who did not live in towns (and therefore did not see many broadsheets), such as curés and gentlemen residing in châteaux.[53] Thus by readings, placards, or newspapers the texts of laws reached an extremely broad public in the eighteenth century, so broad that Malesherbes, president of the *cour des aides* of Paris, could comment in 1775 that, since "knowledge now spreads itself by way of print, Laws written today are known by everyone."[54]

In communicating to this broad public, universal tax decrees vacillated in tone between the bold and the defensive. As the *Gazette d'Amsterdam* commented in 1695 on the *capitation* declaration that first unveiled the crown's vision of a kingdom of taxpayers, the king speaks, on the one hand, as a "master who appears to have no need of his peoples' consent, ... but it seems, on the other hand, that this monarch speaks to them as if he is asking, and trying to persuade at the same time he commands."[55] The same was true of tax decrees after 1695; the crown consistently made demands and offered justifications in the same breath. The two motifs of command and persuasion are worth sorting out.

In commanding subjects to pay the *capitation* and the *dixième/vingtième*, the crown referred first to the principle of universality and added over the century a more and more explicit vocabulary of equality. The declaration of 1695 made Louis XIV's claims quite clear: "We wish that none of our subjects, whatever quality and condition they be, Ecclesiastic, Secular or Regular, Noble, Military or other, shall be exempt from the *Capitation*." All royal subjects "without any distinction" were expected to pay.[56] Stated concisely in this founding declaration, the principle of universality ran through all the legislation that followed. After 1695, however, Louis XIV began to stress the principle of equality alongside that of universality.

---

[53] *Annonces, affiches, et avis divers de la Haute et Basse Normandie* (Rouen, July 1762), Prospectus, p. 5.

[54] *Mémoires pour servir à l'histoire du droit public de la France en matières d'impôts* (Brussels, 1779), remonstrances of 6 May 1775. On the publicity of law, see Michel Antoine, *Le conseil du roi sous le règne de Louis XV* (Geneva, 1970), pp. 543–62; Edmond Esmonin, *Etudes sur la France des XVII et XVIII Siècles* (Paris, 1964), pp. 174–86; and Fogel, *Cérémonies de l'information*, pp. 26–42.

[55] Quoted in A. M. de Boislisle, ed., *Mémoires de Saint-Simon* (Paris, 1879), II, p. 465.

[56] AN, AD IX 81, no. 107, Déclaration pour l'Establissement de la Capitation, 18 January 1695.

Reestablishing the *capitation*, the declaration of 1701 explained that, in order to make the burden more bearable, the distribution of the tax would be "as equal as it is able to be." Likewise, the *dixième* of 1710, levied on "every property owner, noble or commoner, privileged or nonprivileged," was to be spread "with equality." An earlier draft of this declaration read that the tax was to be spread with "equity and justice," but a high official struck the phrase and wrote "with equality" above it. While we can only speculate on the thoughts that passed through the official's mind as he revised the text, it is reasonable to infer that he understood equality to mean something more than justice. Justice and equity implied fairness and balance; equality implied that taxpayers would be assessed according to a uniform tax rate and would pay roughly the same share of their income.[57]

The language of equality became stronger under Louis XV and Louis XVI. The declaration of 1749, which established the *vingtième*, explained that this tax was preferable to others "by the consideration that there is none other more just and more equal because it is distributed on each and all of our subjects in proportion to their wealth and property." In 1763 Louis XV attempted to institute a new land tax to redress the "arbitrariness and inequality in the distribution of taxes," and by the late 1770s Louis XVI (or, more precisely, Necker) was discussing equality and justice in taxation as principles of natural law. The *arrêt* of 2 November 1777, which sought to reform the administration of the *vingtième*, insisted that "the Laws of Justice and of equality" must be maintained by the king; to tax unfairly would only "introduce a new kind of privilege" into the system of finances. The royal theme of fiscal equality remained vital down to the final days of the Old Regime. On 5 May 1789, at the opening session of the Estates-General, Necker announced to the nation: "Among the improvements which concern every inhabitant of the

---

[57] AN, AD IX 81, no. 129, Déclaration du Roy pour l'Etablissement de la Capitation Générale, 12 March 1701; AN, AD IX 400, no. 84, Déclaration du Roi pour la Levée du Dixième du Revenu des Biens du Royaume, 14 October 1710; the early draft of the *dixième* edict is located in AN, G-7 1138–1139, Papiers concernant l'arangement du mois d'octobre 1710. While early on the specific meaning of equality went unstated, officials later in the century explicitly associated equality with a flat tax rate. Terray, for instance, understood equality to mean that "Every owner of capital, rich and poor, must contribute as much as possible in the same proportion." AN, H-1 1463, no. 115, letter from Terray to Fontette, 11 January 1773.

kingdom, we must rank first the establishment of principles which should assure an equal distribution of taxes."[58]

Breaking three centuries of tradition, the crown's demand for universal and equal taxation required a powerful rhetoric of justification. To counter the stories of privilege that had legitimized tax exemptions, the crown developed its own stories over the eighteenth century. Three themes appear again and again: that universal taxes would provide relief for the people; that they would strengthen the defense of the kingdom; and that they would fund the debt. Decrees elaborated the first of these themes by casting the king as a benevolent ruler seeking to ease the suffering of his people by cutting taxes such as the *taille* that struck the poorer classes. The declaration of 1710 promised that revenues from the new *dixième* would allow the crown "to grant to our peoples a reduction in the *Taille* of a fifth for next year." In more dramatic language, the declaration of 1749 assured the public that "by giving us the ability to diminish or abolish successively many dues and taxes … the fruit [of the *vingtième*] will be the real relief of our peoples," and the edict of 1771, which prolonged the *vingtième* indefinitely, promised "the reduction of taxes which are the most onerous to the indigent." The monarchy's language of benevolence and hope, typified by the ubiquitous phrase "relief of the people," never waned.[59]

But concern for the people did not explain why extra taxes were needed in the first place. To convince the public that supplemental taxes were absolutely necessary, monarchs emphasized the military vulnerability of the kingdom, warning the public about aggressive foreign powers and evoking images of the king as protector. The preamble of the *capitation* declaration of 1695 opened with this discussion of the War of the League of Augsburg:

Since the glory of our State, and the prosperity with which heaven has blessed our Reign, has excited against us the envy of a part of the Powers of Europe, and committed them to form a league to make war unjustly against us; … We hope to make known to all Europe that the strengths of France are inexhaustible when they are well managed, and that We have a certain resource in the heart of our subjects, and in the zeal that they have for the service of their King, and for the glory of the French Nation. With

58 AN, AD IX 401, no. 187, Edit du Roi, May 1749; AN, AD + 958, Déclaration du Roy, 21 November 1763; AN, AD IX 492, no. 37, arrêt du conseil, 2 November 1777; *Réimpression de L'Ancien Moniteur* (Paris, 1847), I, p. 16.
59 AN, AD IX 400, no. 84, Déclaration du Roi, 14 October 1710; AN, AD IX 401, no. 187, Edit du Roi, May 1749; AN, AD IX 492, no. 24, Edit du Roi, November 1771.

such confidence, We have decided, in order to put ourselves in a position to sustain the expenses of war for as long as the blindness of our Enemies leads them to refuse Peace, to establish a general Capitation.''[60]

Since various powers in Europe had joined forces to wage war "unjustly" against France, Louis XIV called on his subjects to make known to Europe that French subjects supported their king and nation. The interesting feature of the preamble (besides the precocious use of the term "nation") is that this call to military duty did not summon all loyal subjects to arms: it asked them to open their purses instead.

The declaration developed the theme of fiscal service in its specific appeals to the clergy and nobility. To the clergy Louis XIV said: "We are persuaded the Ecclesiastics will submit willingly to this tax ... ; their profession preventing them from serving in our armies, where most of them would be called by their birth, they can at present only contribute in this way to the defense of the State."[61] The king asked for a gift "proportioned to the needs of the State."

The nobility, on the other hand, were expected to pay outright: "We do not doubt that the nobility of our kingdom, which risks its life every day, and which sheds its blood so generously for our service and for the support of the State, will sacrifice with the same devotion such a light share of its revenues as that to which the tax on Gentlemen will be set."[62] Here we see Louis XIV extending the idiom of personal military service, which had long been used in a compelling manner to staff the army, to the area of taxation as well. If the nobility sacrificed their lives fighting for the crown, surely they would not object to a light tax that was to be put to the same ends. In fact, the spirit of service for which the nobility was renowned and in the name of which it generously shed its blood would no doubt make nobles eager taxpayers. Louis XIV stretched the second order's military obligations, adding war finance to its traditional role of fighting. That military service justified the nobility's exemption from the *taille* did not matter. This was an entirely new kind of tax.

The portrayal of the king as defender of a besieged kingdom who required the fiscal service of all his subjects continued in the decrees of the eighteenth century. In 1701 "jealous Princes" who resented France's power were responsible for the War of the Spanish Succes-

---

[60] AN, AD IX 81, no. 107, Déclaration du Roy, 18 January 1695.
[61] Ibid.   [62] Ibid.

sion and, therefore, the reestablishment of the *capitation*. In 1710 "the interest of those who want to perpetuate war and make peace impossible" had prevailed in European affairs; Louis XIV established the *dixième*. In 1741 the royal council explained to the public that "circumstances have forced us" to prepare for the War of the Austrian Succession; Louis XV reestablished the *dixième*. From the middle of the eighteenth century, by which time both universal taxes were firmly in place, the same logic of military defense justified increasing them. During the Seven Years War, Louis XV tripled the *capitation* and the *vingtième* because of a war that "justice and honor made indispensable." In 1782, in the throes of the War of American Independence, Louis XVI tripled the *vingtième* again, stating that "We are able to procure Peace to our Peoples only by opposing our Enemies with the resources that we are always sure to find in the zeal and love of our subjects."[63]

Military justifications had their limits, however. The crown, after all, continued to levy universal taxes in times of peace. How did the crown explain the need for extraordinary taxes when there were no aggressive foreign powers to blame? The monarchy claimed that additional revenue was needed for the debt. Initially cited as a secondary concern, debt later eclipsed war to become the principal justification for universal taxes. When the *capitation* was introduced in 1695, Louis XIV promised that the tax would replace the expedients of borrowing altogether. According to the declaration of 1695, the idea of extinguishing such "extraordinary" expedients was originally suggested by the provincial estates of Languedoc: the estates "proposed this aid [the *capitation*] to us, and indicated the reasons which should make it preferable to every other extraordinary means." Embracing this suggestion, the declaration pledged: "We even believe that if this collection succeeds ..., it will lead to the ending of the extraordinary affairs to which necessity forced us to have recourse." Since much of the revenue from extraordinary affairs came from loans that were forced on the privileged, it is easy to understand why such a promise may have had public appeal. Office-holders compelled to make further placements of capital in their offices or to buy up newly created offices, for example, were no

---

[63] AN, AD IX 81, no. 129, Déclaration du Roy, 12 March 1701; AN, AD IX 400, no. 84, Déclaration du Roi, 14 October 1710; AN, AD IX 401, no. 1, Déclaration du Roy, 29 August 1741; AN, AD IX 492, no. 7, Déclaration du Roi, 16 June 1761; AN, AD IX 492, no. 48, Edit du Roi, July 1782.

doubt interested in a tax that would end such vexing practices. By promising to rid France of "extraordinary" fiscal expedients, Louis XIV was hoping to gain support for the *capitation*.[64]

Of course the *capitation* never replaced the *affaires extraordinaires*. Borrowing continued at the same furious pace, and it soon became obvious that universal taxes, far from extinguishing the debt, made it possible for kings to borrow more and to service even larger debts. The rhetorical link between debt service and this new form of direct taxation was forged in eighteenth-century tax decrees, all of which explained that universal taxes were badly needed to help service – not reimburse – the debt by funding payments of interest to royal creditors. Universal taxes, in other words, kept the kingdom safe from bankruptcy.

It was in these terms that Louis XIV explained why he could not keep his promise to abolish the *capitation* and the *dixième* after the War of the Spanish Succession. The preamble to the declaration of 1715 declared:

In order to have our people taste the fruits of this peace so desired, We had intended to abolish the *Capitation*, and even the *Dixième* ...; but after the examination of the immense debts that We have been forced to contract during two consecutive wars, ... We have seen with pain that We would not yet be able to fulfill, according to our wishes, the fair expectation of our people, nor the promise that we had made ... If these two taxes were abolished, We would not be able to avoid neglecting the agreements that We made with those who furnished their wealth for the expenses of war.[65]

Turning the public's attention from war to debt, Louis XIV claimed he still needed the extra tax revenue.

Invoking the debt to justify universal taxation (in particular the *vingtième*) became commonplace from mid-century on. In 1749, after

---

[64] AN, AD IX 81, no. 107, Déclaration du Roy, 18 January 1695. The widespread if naive belief that the *capitation* would replace "extraordinary" borrowing was disseminated by the finance minister himself in a letter of 31 October 1694 in which he informed intendants that "If the product of the *capitation* is as considerable as we hope, it would consequently be able to bring to an end other extraordinary affairs that are imposed every day which fall directly or indirectly on the nobility." BN, Ms. Fr. 8852, fos. 83–4. The intendant of Caen later recalled that he had told Pontchartrain that he was quite favorable to the idea of a *capitation*, "but," he added, "one of the principal conditions that I informed him should facilitate this tax was to remove all the extraordinary fiscal expedients." F. Baudry, ed., *Mémoires de Nicolas-Joseph Foucault* (Paris, 1862), p. 309. For examples of other intendants who believed that the *capitation* would replace extraordinary affairs, see A. M. de Boislisle, ed., *Correspondance des contrôleurs généraux des finances avec les intendants des provinces, 1683–1715* (Paris, 1874–97), I, nos. 1387 and 1397.

[65] AN, AD IX 81, no. 167, Déclaration du Roi, 9 July 1715.

the War of the Austrian Succession, Louis XV converted the *dixième* to the *vingtième*, explaining that the new peacetime tax was necessary for the "liberation of the State" from debt, and in 1767 he invoked the specter of bankruptcy to prolong the same tax: "It is impossible for us to deprive ourselves of any revenue, without running the risk of suspending some of the loans We have contracted, an act which would concern the fortune of a considerable portion of our subjects." Even in the middle of the War of American Independence, which was financed primarily by loans, Louis XVI declared that he was "forced" to prolong the two *vingtièmes* because "the interest of the debts that we were obliged to contract to provide money for the costs of war" had "consumed most of our savings." By the time of the American war, demands for tax revenue were refracted entirely through the need to service the debt, rather than to pay for war directly, in effect distancing the taxpayer from the duty to military service that had once been the chief emphasis of wartime tax decrees.[66]

Naturally, when the American war was over, ministers of Louis XVI continued to stress the need for taxpayers to save France from a ruinous bankruptcy. A budget drawn by Loménie de Brienne and published by the royal press in 1788 stated simply that the state must find the needed revenue "in the correct distribution of a tax ... or fail to pay a part of its financial commitments (the idea of which alone will always be revolting)."[67] By publicizing the question of debt management, the monarchy hoped to make its debts a national concern requiring a truly national solution. Only universal and equal taxation, the monarchy told the public, would allow the nation to honor its obligations to creditors. The rhetoric that justified universal taxes had shifted from military service to debt service.

FROM COURTS AND COMMUNITIES TO ADMINISTRATORS
AND INDIVIDUALS

No matter the language of decrees, no matter how the crown was portrayed to the public, Louis XIV and his successors understood that universal taxes could not be instituted effectively without redesigning

---

[66] AN, AD IX 401, no. 87, Edit du Roi, May 1749; AN, AD IX 492, no. 20, Edit du Roi, June 1767; AN, AD IX 492, no. 42, Edit du Roi, February 1780.
[67] [Étienne Charles Loménie de Brienne], *Compte rendu au roi, au mois de mars 1788, et publié parses ordres* (Paris, 1788).

the kingdom's tax administration. Royal rhetoric could counter stories of privilege but it could not combat the concrete forms of power that underlay those stories. Nobles, for example, were not exempt from the *taille* merely because they provided military service to the crown. They were also exempt because they could easily rebuff the demands of local tax collectors. Collectors of the *taille*, usually peasants drawn from the local village, were no match for nobles who carried weapons and dominated local judicial and economic institutions. If the crown's ideological claim to fiscal equality was to be realized, it required sturdy bureaucratic support.

The methods used to levy the *taille* developed in a period when state power rested heavily on the cooperation of judicial and communal institutions. Lacking a modern bureaucracy but needing money, the late medieval and early modern state tended to treat individuals as members of corporate groups (towns, parishes, guilds, courts, the church, etc.), impose collective burdens on them, and let each group sort out the details of raising the money. When disputes arose among or within these groups, or when fiscal laws needed to be enforced, the monarchy depended on the intervention of an intricate set of local and regional courts. Exercising administrative as well as judicial authority, magistrates were expected to act on behalf of the crown to restore order and impose law. In the seventeenth century the crown continued to rely on this corporate "state of justice" but, when officers proved reluctant to enforce royal orders, the crown covered the state of justice with a thin layer of centralized administration that was more responsive to the will of the royal council. Over the course of the eighteenth century that layer thickened and became increasingly capable of exercising control over individuals without the mediation of corporate groups. It was this administration, meager by modern standards but substantial for the day, that was charged with overseeing universal taxes. To assess the scope of this change, let us compare the older administration of the *taille* with that of the newer universal taxes.

In the *pays d'élections*, the vast territory which stretched across most of the kingdom's generalities, courts and communities were essential to the levy of the *taille*. In the sixteenth century, finance ministers fixed the annual global sum of the *taille* according to economic reports from *trésoriers de France* (officers in the *bureaux des finances*), and divided the sum among the generalities. In each generality the *trésoriers* distributed the *taille* among several *élection* districts, and in each district the *élus* (officers of the *élection* court) distributed the tax among the parishes. After each parish was assigned a lump sum of money, parishioners subject to the *taille* gathered in a village assembly and elected assessors and collectors to draw a roll distributing the tax among heads of household and to collect the revenue. Once the lump sum was collected and remitted to the tax receiver, the parish was relieved of its debt. Thus the *taille* was a collective tax. Individuals paid it of course, but they did so as debtors to a parish that owed a collective debt. This is why royal officials often used the word *redevables* or "debtors" to refer to individual payers of the *taille*.

In the seventeenth century, from 1642 to 1648 but especially from Colbert on, the royal council began to send intendants to the provinces with specific orders to oversee the operations of the *bureaux des finances* and *élections*, and to correct, in the words of one opinionated intendant, "all the injustices, mistakes, and oppressions that the subjects of the King can suffer from the officers and ministers of justice by their corruption, negligence, [and] ignorance."[68] Although intendants owned venal offices (most commonly that of *maître des requêtes*), they were discharged to the generalities by means of revocable commissions, which gave the royal council the power to recall them if they were insubordinate or incompetent. This assured the council some control over intendants even if they were not always the uncompromising stalwarts of absolutism that many historians have made them out to be.

In the case of the *taille*, the authority of intendants was quite thorough in certain areas yet limited in others. It was thorough with respect to the distribution of the *taille*. Once settled in his generality, the intendant, with the assistance of the now subordinate *trésoriers de France* and *élus*, furnished economic reports to the finance minister and distributed the *taille* among the *élection* districts of the generality and among the parishes of each *élection*. But two fundamental characteristics of the *taille* endured: the tax remained collective and financial courts retained full jurisdiction over the disputes it provoked.

Disputes over the *taille* involved entire communities and, if severe

---

[68] BN, Ms. Fr. 21812, d'Aube, Mémoire concernant les intendants départis (1738). For the establishment of provincial intendants, see Richard Bonney, *Political Change in France under Richelieu and Mazarin, 1624–1661* (Oxford, 1978); and James Collins, *Fiscal Limits of Absolutism: Direct Taxation in Early Seventeenth-Century France* (Berkeley, CA, 1988).

enough, were refereed by courts. Since any reduction in an individual assessment meant a corresponding increase for the rest of the village, a payer of the *taille* who wanted to contest his or her tax appealed first to the village assembly. If the village could not resolve an internal conflict, or if the conflict involved more than one village or a large sum of money, the case went before the local *élection* court and, on appeal, to the regional *cour des aides*, the highest tax courts in the realm. At each level of contestation, disputes were true communal events: at the village level, heads of peasant households gathered in assemblies, listened to claims, weighed the testimony of neighbors, friends, and enemies, and settled conflicts; when cases went to trial, courtrooms were filled with the faces and voices of local judges, lawyers, plaintiffs, witnesses, heads of community, and parish collectors.

The corporate and judicial character of the administration of the *taille* is well illustrated by the case of the widow Elizabeth Vignon, a resident of the parish of Ivetot in the generality of Caen. On 19 June 1747 Vignon petitioned the intendant of Caen, complaining that she had been taxed at 59 livres and 12 sols for 60 *verges* (15 acres) of land when she owned only 43 *verges* (10.75 acres), and implored his "Equity" to reduce the assessment by 17 livres. The intendant's response to the petition is revealing. He immediately referred the case to the *élection* of Valognes, recognizing that the dispute was outside his jurisdiction. It was understood that, short of the extreme case of rebellion, all conflicts over the *taille* were to be handled by the courts.[69]

On Sunday, 2 July, a royal sergeant from Valognes, Jean Ruette, entered the parish of Ivetot. He waited for the parishioners to come out of church, asked them to assemble themselves in the adjacent cemetery, "as was the custom when making proclamations and all public requests," and summoned all inhabitants who paid the *taille* to the *élection* court in Valognes on 11 July.[70] The following

---

[69] AD Calvados, C 4698, no. 51, Vignon dossier. The restraint exercised by royal administrators in this respect is remarkable. In 1764 a customs employee of the city of Paris named Flaux claimed he was unjustly subject to the *taille* for land he owned in Morville near Valognes. Asked to investigate the matter by the intendant, the subdelegate of Valognes replied that Flaux was justified in his complaint, "but reducing the assessment on the roll would exceed the power of Monsieur the intendant. [Flaux's] complaint is absolutely under the jurisdiction of *élus* and of the *cour des Aydes*." AD Calvados, C 4393, reports of 18 September and 14 October 1764.

[70] AD Calvados, C 4697, no. 50, report of Jean Ruette, 2 July 1741.

Sunday, two days before the hearing, the parishioners of Ivetot decided to assemble and deliberate on Vignon's claim. Since she had never been taxed for more than 43 *verges*, the village assembly decided "in a unanimous voice" that the demands of her request were "just and true."[71] When the hearing was called to order on 11 July, Vignon, assisted by her counsel, immediately invoked the deliberation of the village assembly. "The inhabitants have expressed their will," she argued, and that will unequivocally demanded the reduction of her tax. When the collectors of the parish, six in all, were called to testify, however, they claimed that the legal action taken by Vignon did not conform to regulations. Contrary to the widow's testimony, the collectors contended that the *taille* was assessed not according to the size and worth of land but on the basis of "common knowledge" of her wealth. Moreover, they insisted that, since the *taille* was collective, they were not allowed to reduce an individual assessment without adjusting all the other assessments. When the court met again the following week, Vignon restated her argument, saying that the case of the collectors, "opposed to the reason of natural Equity," was "all the more poorly founded since the majority of the inhabitants condemned the injustice of the collectors."[72]

In the end, Vignon lost the case on a technicality (she did not contest the tax soon enough after it was assessed), but the episode illustrates the roles played by courts and communities in the administration of the *taille*. Not only did Vignon argue her case before the *élection* court, but her argument itself was based on a decision taken by the assembly of her village. Although the intendant received the initial petition, he had nothing whatsoever to do with the case.

When Louis XIV established the *capitation*, he deliberately bypassed the jurisdiction of courts and village assemblies to get at the individual privileged taxpayer. Under the pretext of needing a faster and less costly system of taxation, the declaration of 1695 invested *commissaires départis*, administrators commissioned by the royal council, with "all Jurisdiction" over the tax and prohibited "all our other Courts and Judges" from intervening. In practice courts did oversee the part of the *capitation* that fell on *taillables*, but the

---

[71] AD Calvados, C 4698, no. 56, transcript of the village assembly of Ivetot, 9 July 1741.
[72] AD Calvados, C 4698, no. 60, transcript of the *élection* of Valognes, 11 July 1741.

privileged confronted an entirely different administration, one composed of commissioned administrators, notably provincial intendants, whose authority emanated directly from the royal council.[73]
When the *dixième* was established, the jurisdiction of *commissaires* was
extended further to cover the whole of the tax, excluding the courts
even from matters regarding property-owning *taillables* who paid
the *dixième* (and later the *vingtième*). Louis XIV and his successors
went well beyond the institutions of the corporate state of justice to
entrust universal taxes to revocable commissioned agents of the
crown.

Nowhere was the difference between the administration of the
taille and that of universal taxes more marked than in the ways
disputes were resolved. Since universal taxes were not levied collectively as communal debt and therefore did not implicate village
assemblies or courts of law, disputes over their assessment involved
only the king and the individual taxpayer, who was no longer called
a "debtor" but a "contributor" (*contribuable*), the word revolutionaries would adopt for taxpayer.[74] As d'Ormesson, the intendant of finance charged with universal taxes, explained, individuals
contesting universal taxes, unlike those contesting the *taille*, were not
challenging other members of their community who shared a
common debt. Instead, they were challenging "the King himself."
When an individual failed to pay a universal tax, "it is the King who
loses. It is for this reason that His Majesty reserved the right to judge
contestations, that He entrusted the drawing of the tax rolls to his
council or to commissioners of his council, and that He wanted the
accounts to be rendered to them."[75] To the exclusion of the
community and the magistrature, royal administrators and individual universal taxpayers met head on. Subjects who wanted to
contest a universal tax had to send a petition directly to the
intendant, who would then decide the matter and issue a notice
which informed the supplicant of the decision. On appeal the case

---

[73] Indeed, the close connection between intendants and the royal council was a hallmark of
the new tax. After intendants drafted the *capitation* rolls of the nobility and other privileged
subjects, they rushed them to Paris to be signed by the king and council before using them
to levy the tax. No other tax roll in the kingdom was authorized in this way.

[74] "Each property owner is a *contribuable*," Terray wrote in reference to the *vingtième*, "which is
to say he is isolated from others." AN, H-1 1463, letter of 6 May 1772. When speaking of
universal taxes, the word "tax" likewise shifted from *impôt* to *contribution*. One intendant of
finance said he preferred *contribution* because it resonated with the idea of public utility. AN,
H-1 1463, no. 122, letter from d'Ailly to Fontette, 1 April 1774.

[75] AN, K 900, no. 35, report of d'Ormesson of July 1765.

went straight to the royal council (or, to be precise, to an intendant of finance or the controller-general).[76] No village assemblies or courtrooms were necessary to resolve conflict; the king's administrators "heard" disputes, though now only in the metaphorical sense, and dispensed justice from their desks. As this new administrative and individualistic system of managing contestation was laid on top of the older one, the monarchy established a field of direct contact between taxpayers and royal agents.

Since the power of the magistrature rested in its ability to intervene in specific areas of conflict, barring courts from hearing disputes delivered a painful blow to the judiciary. In an age when courts of law were accustomed to exercising administrative authority and when the lawsuit was the predominant form of contestation, the structure of the *capitation* and *dixième/vingtième* constituted a significant innovation. It is true that the shift in jurisdiction from courts to what Tocqueville identified as "administrative justice" had been going on for some time; in the seventeenth century the crown was known to withdraw certain cases from the courts to bring them before the royal council.[77] But the withdrawal of cases, known as *évocations*, occurred sporadically and in special circumstances, such as when royal officials were charged with misconduct. When the crown granted administrators the right to judge disputes over universal taxes, it in effect institutionalized the *évocation*, making it a permanent part of everyday administration. As a matter of procedure, all disputes were to be decided by royal administrators or the royal council itself.

Snubbed by this challenge, the *cour des aides* of Paris led a sustained counterattack beginning in 1756 when it protested that "[i]t is at the expense of these august Laws [the laws of your Kingdom] that the jurisdiction over contestations arising from the *Vingtième* and the *Capitation* has been taken away from well-ordered Tribunals, and that the only alternative for those of your Subjects who believed themselves wronged is to submit to an unfair tax or to find recourse

---

[76] The lack of deliberation on appeals in council confirms the thesis of Michel Antoine that decisions ostensibly emanating from the council were in fact made by individual ministers of state and their staffs, specifically, in matters of universal taxes, the controller-general and a designated intendant of finance. Antoine, *Conseil du roi*; Françoise Mosser, *Les intendants des finances au XVIIIe siècle: Les Lefèvre d'Ormesson et le "département des impositions" (1715–1777)* (Geneva, 1978), pp. 140–5.

[77] David Parker, "Sovereignty, Absolutism, and the Function of the Law in Seventeenth-Century France," *Past and Present* 129 (1989), pp. 36–74.

in the authority of the one who is the author of it, by asking him to reverse his own work." The court cannot yield "the right to exclusive jurisdiction over contestations which regard it," seeing that this right is "inherent in its constitution and its essence."[78] In 1760 the court moved beyond lodging complaints to order intendants to deposit the tax rolls of the two universal taxes in every *élection* court in its jurisdiction so that the lower courts could start hearing cases immediately. Whether one sees in this bold assertion of authority an attempt by the court to reclaim lost jurisdictional powers or an effort to pursue the monarchy onto the new terrain of universal tax administration, Louis XV was able to thwart the efforts of the *cour des aides* with remarkable ease. The royal council quashed the court's rulings with a set of *arrêts du conseil*, and intendants of Paris and other generalities which lay within the jurisdiction of the Paris *cour des aides* refused to relinquish the tax rolls. Although magistrates all over the kingdom continued to protest against what they understood to be a usurpation of their rights, the regime of administrative justice was too well installed to be seized by the courts.[79]

The shift in jurisdiction from courts to commissioned adminis-trators coincided with a dramatic growth in the size and power of intendancies. The intendancy of the generality of Caen is a typical enough example. At the beginning of the eighteenth century the intendant of Caen could count on the assistance of nine recently installed subdelegates and a secretary or two. By the 1780s, the intendant managed eleven subdelegates, thirteen secretaries and clerks, three lawyers (on a consultative basis), and a subordinate *vingtième* bureau composed of a director, eleven controllers, and six clerks, all of whom were responsible for investigating the wealth of taxpayers, revising the rolls according to new information, and supervising hundreds of parish *préposés* whom, unlike the collectors of the *taille*, the intendant had a right to appoint and dismiss.[80]

To pay for the expansion of the intendancy of Caen and that of

---

[78] *Mémoires pour servir à l'histoire du droit public*, remonstrances of 14 September 1756, pp. 4–15.

[79] AN, AD IX 491, no. 186, and 492, no. 11, *arrêts du conseil* of 4 December 1760 and 24 January 1762. The crown did concede, in 1761, the right of courts to adjudicate disputes over the *capitation* on *taillables*.

[80] AD Calvados, C 4703, no. 54, and C 5945; and Jacqueline Musset, *L'intendance de Caen: structure, fonctionnement et administration sous l'intendant Esmangart, 1775–1783* (Condé-sur-Noireau, 1985), part I. For the proliferation of subdelegates, see Julien Riccomard, "Les subdélégués des intendants aux XVIIe et XVIIIe siècles," *L'information historique* 24 (1962), pp. 139–48, 190–5, and (1963), pp. 1–7; and Michel Antoine, *Le dur métier du roi* (Paris, 1986), pp. 61–80 and 125–80.

others as well, intendants throughout the kingdom subsidized the official funds allotted them, which remained astonishingly low, with unofficial funds skimmed from the revenue of the *capitation*. In the early 1760s intendants officially received 16,470 livres each for their salary and anywhere from 3,000 to 8,000 livres for costs of administration; subdelegates were paid out of pocket by the intendant, as were secretaries, who were understood to serve in a personal not a public capacity.[81] Unofficially, however, the funds available to intendants soared in the second half of the century as intendants began to divert revenue from the *capitation* to increase their financial resources as much as four times over. In 1772 twenty-one intendants in the *pays d'élections* spent no less than 1,108,347 livres in "free funds of the *capitation*" on salary bonuses for themselves and their staffs, administrative projects such as drawing tax rolls, and public works and aid programs, which ranged from reconstructing city squares to providing compensation to peasants injured while laboring under the royal *corvée*.[82] These funds were obtained and spent "unofficially" insofar as the *chambres des comptes*, the courts that inspected tax receipts and guarded against the misappropriation of revenue, were not informed of their existence or provided with accounts. Monitored only by the finance minister and an intendant of finance (with greater attention after 1765), the secretly used tax revenue boosted the administrative capacity of the intendancy and, in turn, better equipped it to levy taxes.

Intendants dipped into these funds to compensate subdelegates, who drew the *capitation* rolls for the privileged, and directors and controllers of the *dixième/vingtième*, who investigated the wealth of property-owners. Apportioning the *dixième/vingtième* became a particularly laborious and expensive enterprise – in 1786 the intendant of Caen disbursed more than 25,000 livres in salary to the director and controllers of the generality – because, unlike the *taille* and *capitation*, the *dixième/vingtième* was based on declarations of wealth which, notoriously inaccurate since they were submitted by property-owners themselves, had to be verified.[83] The very idea of

---

[81] AN, G-7 1909–1914, contracts between crown and receivers-general.
[82] AN, 144 AP 114, dossier 1, Fonds libres de la *capitation*, 1772. For a detailed breakdown of the use of "fonds libres," see my "*Liberté, Egalité, Fiscalité*: Taxation, Privilege, and Political Culture in Eighteenth-Century France," PhD thesis, University of Michigan (1994), appendix A.
[83] AD Calvados C 6518, salaries and bonuses for the *vingtième* director and controllers of Caen.

disclosing one's wealth to royal authorities offended property-owners, as Bâville, intendant of Languedoc, explained. The typical French taxpayer felt "an extreme repugnance for declaring his wealth and revealing the secret of his family. This is such an extreme demand, and so contrary to the spirit of the nation, that nothing more unbearable could happen [to anyone]."[84] Small wonder that when the *dixième* was first established from 1710 to 1717 declarations of wealth were not always forthcoming and, even when they were submitted, intendants and subdelegates did little to verify them.[85]

By the second half of the eighteenth century, however, intendants, subdelegates, and increasing numbers of directors and controllers of the *vingtième* (some of whom were now trained in special schools in Amiens, Orléans, and Metz) were uncovering with greater ease what Saint-Simon, referring to the patrimonial wealth of nobles, called "the secret of their families." Several means of gathering information on property were available. The easiest method, used in assessing the *taille*, was to ask people about the wealth of their neighbors. Although most neighbors knew enough to remain silent when the tax assessor came around, some did provide valuable information. One subdelegate, investigating the property of a certain Madame de Coulvains, reported to the intendant: "if we are to believe common knowledge (*la notoriété public*), we should not put much faith in her declaration of wealth because people claim that she has a lot of capital invested with people who pay her interest ... the entire public claims she has a lot of money."[86] It was also easy to estimate roughly the value of offices, a form of property that was common among the privileged, since the crown itself created and sold offices and knew something about who owned them and how much they were worth.[87]

The knowledge gained from loose-lipped neighbors and the value of office fell far short of what was needed if administrators were going to the levy the *vingtième* effectively. Much more effective were the "verifications" of personal declarations of property. Verifications represented the cutting edge of royal fiscal administration, and their

---

[84] Boislisle, *Correspondance*, II, no. 891, Bâville to Chamillart, 11 October 1705.
[85] Bonney, "Le secret," pp. 400–5.
[86] AD Calvados, C 4678, no. 69, letter of 26 November 1772.
[87] Intendants of Caen had access to information on all the major offices in the generality's courts of justice. For details on minor officers, they solicited information from tax receivers who knew the value of offices because they were responsible for paying *gages*.

sophistication would shock any historian who, like myself, hesitates to use the word bureaucracy to describe the institutions of the Old Regime. From the early 1750s to the Maupeou coup of 1771 verifications were in general limited to investigating the property of individuals who had petitioned the intendant for reductions in their tax assessments, but from 1772 to 1782 the field of operations of the *vingtième* bureau broadened as controllers and directors, no longer restricting their work to petitioners and encouraged by merit-based salaries, began reassessing the property of taxpayers at large.[88] Systematically going after landowners with large holdings, controllers measured estates, noted the type and quality of the land, asked tenant-farmers to surrender their leases (in order to get information on rental values), and scoured the supposedly confidential *bureaux du contrôle*. As part of the royal domain, *bureaux du contrôle* were established in 1693 to certify the authenticity of (and of course collect fees on) notarial acts and documents used in court, including marriage contracts, wills and testaments, statements of inheritance, real estate titles, titles of office, bills of sale, leases, and other papers relating to property transactions. One need not be a social historian to appreciate the value of such documents for investigations into wealth and income. To access the records of the *bureaux du contrôle* was to enter the secret world of family property.

Thus, in addition to handling tax disputes, royal administrators forged new methods of estimating income and assessing individual taxpayers according to their ability to pay. They also transformed practices of collection. The chain of collection for the *taille* began at the bottom with local parish collectors, peasants elected by their village assemblies, and moved upward to tax receivers who received revenue from the collectors in a given *élection* district, to receivers-general, wealthy and powerful financiers who received money from a generality's district receivers. To collect the *capitation* from the privileged, the crown passed over the lowest rung of collectors to charge the task to the district tax receivers, who were of much higher social status. Since there were far too few receivers to collect the *dixième/vingtième* as well, intendants appointed *préposés* in each parish after more or less careful consideration. In their social standing

---

[88] The number and quality of verifications conducted by controllers and directors were monitored closely by the intendant, who adjusted their salaries accordingly. See AD Calvados, C 5945, correspondence on the payment of directors and controllers.

préposés were not all that much more distinguished than collectors, despite the fact that intendants tried to find qualified men, but *préposés* were far more accountable; intendants did not have to deal with the village assembly to revoke or replace them.[89] Judging by the personnel alone, then, payers of universal taxes confronted a more powerful collection system than did payers of the *taille*.

If taxpayers refused to pay, several means of coercion were available to the crown. When collectors of the *taille* encountered difficulties in recovering the parish tax debt, *élection* courts often intervened by ordering the wealthiest *taillables* of the parish, under the threat of imprisonment, to carry the burden of the communal debt and pay what their neighbors could not. This practice, known as *contrainte solidaire*, could not, however, be applied to universal taxes, which were levied on individuals.[90] To put pressure on individuals who were slow to pay their *capitation* and *vingtième*, tax receivers sometimes solicited individual constraints that, like collective ones, sanctioned the seizure of property by sergeants of the *élection* court. Intendants also imposed "military garrisons," which, in contrast to court-imposed seizures of property, were handled exclusively by subdelegates. Subdelegates ordered soldiers (retired, invalid soldiers in the case of the generality of Caen) to lodge themselves at the homes of delinquent taxpayers until all their back taxes were paid. In the interim, the taxpayer had to feed the soldier and pay a daily fine.[91]

Neither military garrisons nor judicial constraints spared the privileged. Occasionally, noblemen like a certain de Passay residing in the town of Mortain, who refused to pay the *dixième* and harassed royal administrators, were thrown in prison.[92] More commonly the property of high-ranking individuals was subject to seizure. On the morning of 22 March 1721, carrying orders from the local *élection* court, a sergeant entered the house of Mont Collardin, a relatively poor noble who had not paid his 12 livres of *capitation*, and seized a

---

[89] Finding that many collectors of the *taille* were illiterate, Turgot, as intendant of Limoges, asked local curés to persuade "intelligent individuals" to become *préposés* of the *vingtième* by offering fiscal exemptions and incentives. Schelle, *Turgot*, V, p. 179, circular to curés, 23 September 1762.

[90] On *contrainte solidaire*, see Hilton Root, *Peasants and King in Burgundy: Agrarian Foundations of French Absolutism* (Berkeley, 1987), ch. 6. For tax collection and coercion, see Jean Villain, *Les contestations fiscales sous l'ancien régime dans les pays d'élections de taille personelle* (Paris, 1943).

[91] AD Calvados, C 6044, letters from subdelegates and tax receivers comparing military garrisons to judicial constraints, 1780.

[92] AN, G-7 218, no. 160, letter from de La Briffe to Desmaretz, 3 August 1712.

dozen pewter plates.[93] In 1780 the goods belonging to the much wealthier *president à mortier* of the parlement of Bordeaux, Nicolas-Pierre de Pichard, were hauled away from two of his estates after he had for several years failed to pay his servants' *capitation* and the *vingtième* on his town house and estates.[94]

But the monarchy could not afford – in symbolic or financial terms – to force every defiant subject to pay taxes. It was the *threat* of coercion and punishment, rather than coercion and punishment themselves, that compelled subjects to pay. "People would not pay taxes if they did not fear the severity of coercion," one intendant stated flatly; it was best to make an example out of a few egregious cases, another explained, and "intimidate" the rest.[95] To this end, the intendants of Caen used the free funds of the *capitation* to publicize via large printed broadsheets the penalties inflicted on particularly unruly taxpayers. "Displayed and posted everywhere," one such broadsheet told the tale of a *préposé* of the *vingtième* who on the morning of 7 June 1759 went to collect 33 livres from Pierre Béatrix, seigneur de Saint-Martin, a nobleman living near St. Lo.[96] Saint-Martin, who refused to pay the *préposé* after an exchange of words, became "furious like a lion" and advanced toward the *préposé* "with brandished sword in hand . . . and placed it near the collector's stomach, at a distance of around half a foot, with the intention of running it through his body." Holding his sword to the *préposé*'s belly, the noble tauntingly commanded him to seize his property. "With hat still in hand," the *préposé* declined and fled. Although the nobleman succeeded in chasing away the tax collector, his victory was short-lived, for the *préposé* took recourse in writing a letter of complaint to the intendant, the very letter that was posted. At the end of the letter the *préposé* asked, "Is not this conduct on the part of Saint-Martin most reprehensible and worthy of punishment?" The broadsheet publicized the intendant's answer: Saint-Martin was to pay a 50 livre fine and was warned that any other "misdeed" or "malicious speech" to *préposés* of the *vingtième* would result in his imprisonment and a 500 livre fine. No doubt

---

[93] AD Calvados, C 4681 no. 65, report on Mont Collardin. Examples of seizures of crockery and livestock abound in AD Calvados C 4681, 4683, and 4690.

[94] William Doyle, *The Parlement of Bordeaux and the End of the Old Regime, 1771–1790* (New York, 1974), p. 61.

[95] AN, H-1 1463, no. 69, letter from Fontette to Terray, 2 July 1772; BN, Ms. Fr. 21812, d'Aube, Mémoire concernant les intendants départis (1738).

[96] AD Calvados, C 5295, ordinance of 21 August 1759.

broadsheets like these made other nobles think twice before brandishing their swords before collectors.[97]

Preceded by a series of rebellions that culminated in the Fronde, and followed by the critical spirit of the Enlightenment, the long reign of Louis XIV is often singled out as the apogee of French "absolutism." The Sun King instilled fear in European rulers, restored order to the French kingdom, added luster to the crown, and built a stronger institutional foundation for the state. But it would be unwise to exaggerate the power of Louis XIV: pointing to the factional conflicts, popular uprisings, famine, financial exhaustion, and military defeats of his reign, several historians have quite rightly put this famous king and the "absolutism" his name evokes in the proper context of the society, institutions, and culture of his day.[98] Similarly, we ought not to treat his reign in isolation. As this chapter emphasizes, the fiscal and administrative innovations of Louis XIV, many of which were introduced as mere temporary expedients, continued to develop throughout the eighteenth century under his less illustrious successors. The state not only "remained" after him, as Louis said it would on his deathbed ("I am going, the State remains"); it expanded in ways that would have seemed remarkable – and extremely appealing – to him. In this respect, it is worth considering the reign of Louis XIV not as the climax of absolutism but as the beginning of a new and ultimately revolutionary stage of state formation, a stage during which contradictions in the system of royal finance came to the fore.

It is undeniable that, from the reign of Louis XIV to the Revolution, the French monarchy sustained an elaborate regime of fiscal privilege in return for the loyalty – and capital – of elites. However, it is equally clear that, as a result of fiscal–military competition with other European states, the monarchy introduced universal taxes that, in principle, traversed the boundaries of privilege that divided

---

[97] Posted on the door of the parish church or on street corners, broadsheets recounted stories of property-owners threatening, insulting, and often beating collectors of the *vingtième* (and their family members) during or after seizures of property. Punishment normally consisted of the payment of back taxes, a fine of up to 100 livres, and the threat of imprisonment and a fine of 500 livres in case of future misconduct.

[98] Books that recognize the strength of Louis XIV without exaggerating the modernity of his rule include: Pierre Goubert, *Louis XIV and Twenty Million Frenchmen*, trans. Anne Carter (New York, 1970); Roger Mettam, *Power and Faction in Louis XIV's France* (London, 1988); Jay Smith, *The Culture of Merit: Nobility, Royal Service, and the Making of Absolute Monarchy in France, 1600–1789* (Ann Arbor, MI, 1996); Dessert, *Argent*; Beik, *Absolutism*; and James Collins, *The State in Early Modern France* (Cambridge, 1995).

the geographic, social, and legal landscape of France. Heralded by a new rhetoric of fiscal equality that increasingly put debt service before military service, and levied by a centralized administration capable of targeting individuals as well as groups, universal taxes raised the possibility of a new form of rule. The crown had grafted a fragile yet strikingly modern branch of fiscal administration onto the still dominant regime of corporate privilege.

Did these ideological and bureaucratic transformations change the ways in which subjects interacted with and perceived the monarchy? Did the creation of new forms of direct taxation have anything to do with the changes in eighteenth-century political culture to which so many historians allude? It would be hasty to try to answer these questions without first knowing who in fact ended up paying new direct taxes in the century before the French Revolution.

CHAPTER 2

A kingdom of taxpayers

"It is Our will that none of our Subjects of whatever quality and condition that they be, Ecclesiastic, Secular or Regular, Noble, Military or otherwise, shall be exempt from the said *Capitation.*"

– Declaration of 18 January 1695

"We command that all owners of property, nobles or commoners, privileged or nonprivileged, will pay the *Dixième.*"

– Declaration of 14 October 1710

The ideological and bureaucratic stance of the monarchy from 1695 to 1790 suggests it was intent upon raising more tax revenue by transcending structures of privilege and shifting the burden of taxation onto privileged elites. Did the crown succeed? Sometimes the simplest questions are the most difficult to answer. The main obstacle to any decisive response has always been the lack of sources: in the eighteenth century, fires both accidental and deliberate at the *chambre des comptes* and *cour des aides* burned a substantial body of fiscal documents; during the Revolution, when the National Archives were organized, whatever documents that remained were scattered among several different archival series; and in 1871 the fires of the Paris Commune consumed the holdings of the ministry of finances and the *cour des comptes.* Because documents do not always survive history in the making, the historian who seeks to reconstruct the direct tax system (or any other part of the royal finances) in the eighteenth century must be content to piece together bits of evidence and read an image across the lacunae of a puzzle that will never be complete.[1]

In the early twentieth century Marcel Marion attempted just such a reconstruction and produced several works on taxation that, taken

---

[1] For the history of financial archives in France, see Boislisle, *Correspondance*, I, Avant-Propos.

together, served as the definitive thesis for generations.[2] Marion argued consistently that the privileged blocked royal efforts to tax them and deflected the tax burden onto the poor. Forcing the crown to resort to ruinous loans and to rely upon an inefficient, arbitrary, and patently unfair system of taxation, the privileged brought on the royal bankruptcy that triggered the Revolution as well as the social resentment that fueled its radicalism. Marion's work was a tour de force and in the decades that followed few historians dared to take up the problem of taxation, let alone challenge Marion. In 1947 Lucien Febvre, the great editor of *Annales*, remarked upon the paucity of study on taxation and used the pages of his influential journal to issue a public call for research:

We are anxious to draw again the attention of all – historians, but also experts and above all ordinary citizens – to this problem of taxation which is not at all studied. *Never studied.* I mean to say as it should be and differently from Marion's way. Rare are the historians who have the courage to penetrate the brambly thickets of public finance, and to begin to clear the terrain. Some powerful blows are necessary.[3]

To study taxation as it should be studied and not "à la Marion" meant, for Febvre, to analyze the social distribution of taxation with the aid of statistical evidence, to treat taxation as a function of social and economic fluctuations, to consider the attitudes surrounding taxation, and to provide economists and other social scientists with the rich example of the past. No small order, but Febvre's exhortation has borne fruit. Since the 1960s our understanding of eighteenth-century French taxation and state finance has vastly improved, thanks to the growth of two historical subfields: social history and financial and economic history.

Financial and economic historians have penetrated the "brambly thickets" of French finances to gain a better understanding of the relationship between state and society. In 1963, in the midst of debate between Marxist and Revisionist historians, C. B. A. Behrens published a provocative article, "Nobles, Privileges, and Taxes in France at the End of the Ancien Régime," in which she argued that nobles in France not only paid taxes in the eighteenth century but

---

[2] Among his many influential books are: *Histoire financière de la France depuis 1715: I, 1715–1789* (Paris, 1919); *Les impôts directs sous l'ancien régime, principalement au XVIIIe siècle* (Paris, 1910); and *Machault d'Arnouville, étude sur l'histoire du contrôle général des finances de 1749 à 1754* (Paris, 1892).

[3] Lucien Febvre, preface to "De la constituante à Napoléan: Les vicissitudes de l'impôt indirect," *Annales* (January–March 1947), p. 17.

paid comparatively high rates of taxation with respect to other European elites. The nobility, she insisted, was not the selfish privileged caste that Tocqueville, Marion, and Behrens' Marxist colleagues had made it out to be, and whatever privileges it did enjoy it shared generously with the bourgeoisie, a social group hardly immune to exemptions under the Old Regime. No one could contest Behrens' assertion that the urban third estate possessed a goodly share of direct tax privileges (though it could easily be argued that it paid much heavier indirect taxes), but Behrens' controversial assertion about the nobility, based on anecdotal evidence, drew fire from Gerald Cavanaugh, who deployed anecdotal evidence of his own to show that nobles evaded payment of the taxes for which they were assessed. Although Behrens admitted that more evidence was necessary to decide the issue, her thesis won the wide approval of the Revisionist camp. In a Revisionist textbook that has become a standard, William Doyle appraised the debate by saying that "Cavanaugh's criticisms, which seem valid, nevertheless do not diminish the importance of Behrens' ideas in opening up the question of the nobility." Indeed, Behrens had raised a crucial problem even if her evidence had shortcomings.[4]

More evidence on taxation would come in the 1970s and 1980s and not just of the anecdotal kind. John Bosher, Peter Mathias and Patrick O'Brien, Alain Guéry, Michel Morineau, and James Riley provided statistical data on, and detailed descriptions of, eighteenth-century French taxes, and all save Bosher raised once again the possibility that the privileged paid more in direct taxes than was once thought. Further, a few scholars focused attention on the creation of universal taxes under the reign of Louis XIV. Guéry as well as François Bluche and J.-F. Solnon considered the ways in which the tariff of the *capitation* reflected or challenged the traditional social hierarchy of France, while Richard Bonney treated the administration of the *dixième* in the years immediately after its

---

[4] Behrens, "Nobles, Privileges, and Taxes"; Gerald Cavanaugh, "Nobles, Privileges and Taxes in France: A Revision Reviewed," *FHS* (fall, 1974), pp. 681–92; Behrens, "A Revision Defended"; Doyle, *Origins*, p. 17 and p. 216, n. 37. A debate preceding but similar to that between Behrens and Cavanaugh unfolded in France between Georges Lizerand and Robert Schnerb. The French debate focused less on fiscal inequality among social classes, which was assumed by both sides, and more on the geographical distribution of direct taxes. Georges Lizerand, "Observations sur l'impôt foncier sous l'ancien régime," *RHES* 36 (1958), pp. 18–44; and Robert Schnerb, "La répartition des impôts directs à la fin de l'Ancien Régime," *RHES* 38 (1960), pp. 129–45.

establishment. All of these studies enhanced our understanding of the scale of royal revenues and expenditures, the size of deficits, the methods of debt management, the thin line between private and public finances, and the overall weight of taxation. Yet none furnished any hard evidence on the extent to which different social groups were actually taxed: Bosher led us through the venal labyrinth of tax collection but did not investigate the sources of revenue on which it was based; Bonney, Riley, Morineau, and Mathias and O'Brien furnished national aggregate figures on taxation which, while illuminating other aspects of state finance, revealed little about the social distribution of the tax burden (though Bonney did cite administrative correspondence suggesting that the nobility was able to dodge the first *dixième*); and Guéry and Bluche and Solnon analyzed the social and intellectual implications of the tariff of the *capitation*, not its actual levy. All these historians provided rich qualitative descriptions of taxation, but their inability to measure its distribution made them, in the memorable words of Mathias and O'Brien, reluctant "to traverse the minefield of French historiography on this topic of social incidence."[5]

The second area in which the study of taxation became important was that of social history, particularly the kind of social history associated with the *Annales* project. Here the goal was not to analyze the sinews of the French state but to describe the demographic and social structure of a locality, region, or group, and, in this, tax rolls proved to be a crucial source. Rather than working from national records, social historians unearthed local tax rolls from the archives to determine the size, composition, migration patterns, and wealth of various social groups. By the 1970s tax rolls had become a staple of French doctoral theses in social history, and for studies of

---

[5] Peter Mathias and Patrick O'Brien, "Taxation in Britain and France, 1715–1810," *Journal of European Economic History* 5 (1976), pp. 601–50; John Bosher, *French Finances, 1770–1795: From Business to Bureaucracy* (Cambridge, 1970); Michel Morineau, "Budgets de l'Etat et gestion des finances royales en France au dix-huitième siècle," *Revue Historique* 264 (1980), pp. 289–336; James Riley, *The Seven Years War and the Old Regime in France: The Economic and Financial Toll* (Princeton, NJ, 1986); James Riley, "French Finances, 1727–1768," *JMH* 59 (1987), pp. 209–43; Alain Guéry, "Etat, classification sociale et compromis sous Louis XIV: la capitation de 1695," *Annales* 41 (1986), pp. 1041–60; Alain Guéry, "Les finances de la monarchie française sous l'ancien régime," *Annales*, 33 (1978), pp. 216–39; F. Bluche and J.-F. Solnon, *La véritable hierarchie sociale de l'ancienne France: le tarif de la première capitation, 1695* (Geneva, 1983); Bonney, "Le secret". The general books on the history of taxation (J. J. Clamageran, *Histoire de l'impôt en France*, 3 vols. (Paris, 1867–76); Gabriel Ardant, *Histoire de l'impôt* (Paris, 1971); François Hincker, *Les français devant l'impôt sous l'ancien régime* (Paris, 1971)) provide even less evidence on the social incidence of universal taxes.

eighteenth-century society the rolls of the *capitation* and the *vingtième*, more complete and detailed than those of the *taille*, were particularly useful.[6] A cursory examination of the *capitation* and *vingtième* rolls as presented in some of these social histories does suggest that the taxes struck the privileged, as Behrens originally contended, but the fiscal historian must approach such tax rolls with extreme caution. Although they reveal invaluable information on tax assessments (the amount of money individuals were expected to pay), tax rolls tell us nothing about actual tax payments because they account neither for the sums of money that tax receivers were unable to collect nor for the reductions in assessments that were granted to taxpayers. If the evasion of taxes was as rampant as Cavanaugh and others claim, then the rolls would be highly misleading.

Still, the studies of financial and social historians are of great importance when combined with other sorts of evidence. Building on what we know of national trends in French finances and on the details buried in tax rolls, this chapter uses a fresh set of archival sources, notably the *états au vrai* (accounts of tax receivers), to measure the tax payments of various privileged and nonprivileged groups over the whole of the eighteenth century and to consider the extent to which taxes tapped the income of the privileged. I will argue that universal taxes struck the privileged with some force: nobles, office-holders, residents of privileged cities and provinces, and to a lesser extent clergymen were paying far more in taxes than has been supposed, and evidence suggests that some privileged groups experienced increasingly heavy fiscal pressure as the Old Regime neared its fall. At the same time, this chapter maintains that taxing the privileged did nothing to lighten the weight of taxation on the nonprivileged. On the contrary, peasants and villagers were forced to pay new universal taxes in addition to the taxes they had always paid, both of which weighed heavily on commoners over the century. Thus, while the eighteenth-century crown imposed direct taxes on the privileged for the first time, it simultaneously continued to exert heavy fiscal pressure on commoners.

---

[6] Among the works of social history that use *capitation* and *vingtième* rolls are the following seminal studies: Jean-Claude Perrot, *Genèse d'une ville moderne: Caen au XVIIIe siècle*, 2 vols. (Paris, 1975); Jean Meyer, *La noblesse bretonne au XVIIIe siècle*, 2 vols. (1966; reprint, Paris, 1985); T. J. A. Le Goff, *Vannes and Its Region: A Study of Town and Country in Eighteenth-Century France* (Oxford, 1981); and Guy Chaussinand-Nogaret, *The French Nobility in the Eighteenth Century: From Feudalism to Enlightenment*, trans. William Doyle (Cambridge, 1985).

Although this two-part argument is simple enough, demonstrating its validity is more complicated, given the loss of archival documentation, the idiosyncratic classification of extant evidence, and the apparently Byzantine methods by which the crown levied taxes. But the royal finances were not hopelessly chaotic and enough records have survived to tell a coherent story. The fact that taxes were rarely levied according to the general principles spelled out in decrees should not daunt us, since the expedients, exceptions, and seemingly irregular practices that made the levy of taxes possible had a logic all their own. It is that logic which this chapter aims to uncover as we watch the monarchy cast its fiscal net across the varied social and legal terrain of eighteenth-century France.

It is best to begin with a sketch of the global growth of universal taxes over the century. In 1695, the first year of its levy, the *capitation* raised 21.4 million livres and by 1789 doubled to 42.8 million livres. The *dixième/vingtième*, for its part, yielded around 22 million in its early years and grew to over 60 million livres in 1789, probably reaching as high as 75 million livres from 1783 to 1786 when it was tripled. By any measure these were heavy sums, but it is important to put them in the wider context of the budget. Although nominally total French tax revenues more than doubled over the eighteenth century, the real tax burden (taking inflation and population growth into account) edged up only slightly after having skyrocketed in the previous century.[7] At first glance the two universal taxes do not stand out as a particularly important factor in sustaining the eighteenth-century tax load. They declined from 30 percent of the total tax yield in 1715 to 22 percent in 1789, reflecting a general fall in the relative weight of direct taxation to indirect taxation. Direct tax revenue shrank from 44 percent of the budget to 35 percent between 1726 and 1788 and indirect tax revenue grew from 50 percent to 57 percent.[8]

Yet, while the proportion of direct to indirect taxes dropped, an unmistakable change was taking place within the area of direct

---

[7] Riley, "French Finances"; Guéry, "Les finances de la monarchie française," p. 227; Morineau, "Budgets de l'Etat," p. 319; Mathias and O'Brien, "Taxation in Britain and France"; Hoffman, "Early Modern France," pp. 237–40.

[8] Morineau, "Budgets de l'Etat," p. 314. In my calculations for indirect taxes I have included the revenue from the royal domain. If the domain is excluded, indirect taxation held at just under 50 percent. See Bossenga, "Taxes". For indirect taxes, see Y. Durand, *Les fermiers généraux au dix-huitième siècle* (Paris, 1971); and George Mathews, *The Royal General Farms in Eighteenth-Century France* (New York, 1958).

taxation as the *taille*, the centuries-old tax on commoners, gave way to universal taxes. In 1695 the *capitation* increased the total yield of direct taxes by more than one-half; the *taille* of that year, instead of comprising virtually the whole of the direct tax burden as in the past, amounted to 64.3 percent of the burden while the *capitation* represented the remaining 35.7 percent. In 1715, five years after the *dixième* was established, the two universal taxes together amounted to 55.4 percent of the direct tax yield as the *taille* dipped to 44.6 percent. This trend continued gradually over the century, so that by 1789 the *taille* had shrunk to 41.8 percent of the total direct tax burden while the *capitation* and the *vingtième* climbed to 58.2 percent, and this last figure was higher still from 1783 to 1786. On the eve of the Revolution, universal taxes combined to raise far more revenue than the *taille* itself.[9]

Thus, although direct taxation declined relative to the rest of the budget, it appears to have undergone a significant change in form. The first step in gauging the scale of that change is to consider the legislation that guided the levy of universal taxes. According to the declarations establishing it, the *capitation*, as its name suggests, was to be a head tax on every subject of the kingdom, with the exception of clerics (who were expected to make a voluntary contribution in its place), wives and children possessing no independent wealth, *taillables* whose assessments were less than 40 sols, and the begging poor. To assess individuals, royal administrators were to use a tariff attached to the declaration which classified over 500 types of royal subjects. The tariff situated these types according to title, birth, office, profession, and wealth into a graduated scale of twenty-two brackets, with tax assessments ranging from 2,000 livres to 1 livre. What struck contemporaries about the tariff was that its hierarchy was ordered on the basis of wealth and not just birth. The *Gazette d'Amsterdam* remarked in 1695 that the establishment of the *capitation* "has already produced a new arrangement of subjects into twenty-two classes, in which the order of the nobility finds itself confused with commoners, some of the latter being elevated by the caprice of

---

[9] Early figures for the total revenue of the *capitation* are located in AN, G-7 1132–1133, and AN, KK 355, nos. 453–75. Early figures for the total revenue of the *dixième* are in AN, G-7 1138–1139, and Bonney, "Le secret," p. 415. The 1715 tax revenues are from AN, K 886, no. 12, Revenus ordinaires du Roy de l'année 1715. Figures for 1788 and 1789 are available in [Brienne], *Compte rendu*; and AN, AD IX 552, *Compte générale des revenus et des dépenses fixés au premier de Mai 1789* (Paris, 1789).

their fortune to the honor of the first class."[10] Indeed, the very first class of the tariff, taxed at the grand sum of 2,000 livres, included not only the dauphin and princes of the blood, but also ministers of state and farmers-general whose family lineages could be far from illustrious. Merely classifying these officials with the highest-ranking members of the titled nobility seemed scandalous. Equally astonishing, the tariff ranked certain types of nobles as far down as the nineteenth bracket, which included "gentlemen having neither fief nor château," who were to pay a mere 6 livres.

The tariff is such a rich document that it has tempted some historians to use it as a window onto French society. In their book on the "true" hierarchy of the Old Regime, Bluche and Solnon stated categorically that, "[a]fter three centuries, the tariff of 1695 remains without a doubt the most interesting attempt to classify the hierarchy of old regime French society."[11] Claiming that the tariff reflects a kingdom in transition from a society of orders to one of classes, the authors interpreted such oddities as the high ranking of financiers and royal officers as a sign that the social standing of wealthy state officials was on the rise. Guéry has rightly challenged this interpretation, however, by asking whether or not the tariff was intended to mirror social hierarchy in the first place.[12] It was, after all, designed for the purpose of raising revenue, not portraying the social order, and, looked at in this light, it is not surprising that wealthy subjects were placed in high tax brackets or that so many royal officers and financiers appear in the tariff's upper ranks. Since they depended on the crown for their income, officers and financiers made for vulnerable prey, as the periodic use of *chambres de justice* demonstrate.[13] The crown not only knew the worth of offices and financial positions, but it could pressure their occupants into paying taxes by threatening to withhold money that was due them. More than reflecting changes in society, the tariff shows the willingness of Louis XIV to play with traditional conceptions of hierarchy in his search for revenue.

---

[10] Quoted in Boislisle, *Mémoires de Saint Simon*, II, p. 464. Likewise, a book on the *capitation* of the royal court printed between 1695 and 1698 stated, "It is extraordinary that in the King's Household, and in other Royal Households, officers of distinction who possess the highest posts of the Crown find themselves confused with an infinite number of low officers." BN, Ms. Fr. 14080, *Capitation de la Cour.*

[11] Bluche and Solnon, *Véritable hierarchie*, p. 20.   [12] Guéry, "Etat".

[13] *Chambres de justice* were special legal inquiries into the mishandling of royal funds by financiers. By forcing financiers to pay heavy fines, the crown could, in effect, retrieve some of the money that "corrupt" financiers had gained during their service.

Unfortunately, the tariff is no more trustworthy as a document of fiscal history than it is of social history. Bowing to pressures of practicality, administrators discarded the tariff for all but courtiers and office-holders, employing their own methods of assessing the *capitation* on the privileged, such as estimating revenue from agriculture and bonds, discovering the size of familial inheritances, and counting the number of domestics that privileged taxpayers retained. In some cases the *capitation* betrayed its very name and was not levied as a head tax at all; certain provinces, courts of law, municipalities, guilds, and parishes, for example, were often assigned collective sums and given great leeway in raising the money. The lesson is that legislation can be very misleading. The practice of levying the *capitation* often violated the letter of the law if not its spirit as well.

The *dixième/vingtième* strayed from its founding principles too. The declaration of 1710 decreed that all "*propriétaires*" must submit declarations of wealth to administrators, who would levy a tax of 10 percent on net revenue (or 5 percent later, when the *dixième* became the *vingtième*). Using the declarations, administrators were supposed to levy the tax on every form of property and income: land, seigneurial dues, houses, offices, professional earnings, business profits, interest on investments, pensions, professional fees, and taxes levied by guilds and cities. But administrators of the *dixième/vingtième* often disregarded the guidelines set by legislation. Royal princes who did not submit declarations of wealth or let administrators assess their property negotiated payments with the royal council. And certain kinds of liquid income that were difficult to assess were scarcely touched by the tax, including the easily-hidden paper notes that composed the great fortunes of overseas merchants. In the end, administrators had to modify the laws regarding the *capitation* and the *dixième/vingtième* to fit the social and administrative realities of their day.

In practice the royal council imposed the two taxes by partitioning the kingdom into large geographic and social pieces. Geographically, the crown divided France into two territories, the *pays d'élections* and the *pays d'états*.[14] Residents of provinces that were *pays d'états* enjoyed the right to assemble in representative institutions, to negotiate tax burdens with the crown, and to collect their own taxes, whereas in

---

[14] One could add a third territory called the *pays conquis*, a cluster of provinces along the northeastern border of the kingdom, some of which boasted estates and paid taxes according to local custom.

the *pays d'élections* intendants levied universal taxes directly on the inhabitants of their generality. Beyond this basic territorial division, the crown targeted for taxation four groups that had long held direct tax privileges: royal courtiers; residents of the city of Paris; officers in the army, navy, and magistrature; and the clergy. Since every region or group paid the *dixième/vingtième* and *capitation* in a distinctive way, it is worth treating each one separately before drawing conclusions about the evolution of direct taxation in the century to the Revolution.

UNIVERSAL TAXATION IN THE *PAYS D'ÉLECTIONS*

The question of who paid universal taxes in the provinces of the *pays d'élections* is particularly important because residents there, having no right to assemble in estates to represent their interests to the king, were less able to resist the administrative and fiscal initiatives of the crown. It comes as no surprise, then, that the monarchy directed much of its project to establish new forms of taxation toward this large area, covering three-fifths of France, that Tocqueville called the kingdom's "nucleus."[15] To get at the incidence of universal taxes there, the most reliable sources are *états au vrai*, accounts drafted by tax receivers two or three years after the annual process of collection began for submission to the royal council and *chambres des comptes*. In drawing *états au vrai*, tax receivers had to account for *all* the money on the tax rolls: the amount collected or "recovered" from the rolls, the amount provincial intendants granted in tax reductions, and the amount that could not be collected from insolvent or obdurate taxpayers.

In the case of the *capitation*, which we will address first, receivers divided their accounts according to the different social groups subject to the tax, initially separating revenue collected from the mass of *taillables* (commoners who paid the *taille*) from that of the privileged subjects who enjoyed at least partial exemption from the *taille*. Figure 2.1 shows this breakdown in Caen, one of the twenty generalities that composed the *pays d'élections*, in the years for which evidence exists. Data from several other generalities confirm that the development of the tax in Caen was fairly typical.[16]

---

[15] Tocqueville, *Old Régime*, p. 33.

[16] Figures on the *capitation* and *vingtième* in other generalities are available in Kwass, "*Liberté, Egalité, Fiscalité*," appendix B. See the generalities for which the evidence is most complete:

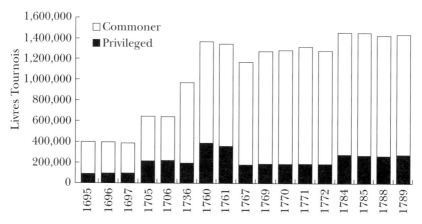

Figure 2.1   The *capitation* paid by privileged and commoner in the generality of Caen

Figure 2.1 clarifies several aspects of the *capitation*.[17] Although the *capitation* did raise revenue from 1695 to 1698, it became much heavier for the privileged when it was reintroduced at the beginning of the eighteenth century. From 1705 to 1736 the tax grew because of increased levies on commoners, but in 1760, with costs of the Seven Years War running high, the *capitation* on the privileged in effect doubled. After the war, during the late 1760s and early 1770s, the global tax yield declined slightly because of reductions in payments by the privileged, but by the 1780s the privileged were paying more, pushing the tax to its highest levels. Although commoners paid most of the tax by far throughout the century (their proportional burden ranging from a low of 66.6 percent in 1706 to a high of 86.3 percent in 1771), the privileged were not untouched.[18]

This picture needs to be nuanced by taking population and

Alençon, Amiens, Bourdeaux, Bourges, Grenoble, La Rochelle, Limoges, Moulins, Orléans, Paris, and Rouen.

[17] The data used in figures 2.1 to 2.6 on the *capitation* in the generality of Caen were compiled from: AN, G-7 1132–1133, *états au vrai* for the *capitation* under Louis XIV; AN, P 5269, 5270, and 5271, *capitation* rolls and *états au vrai* for the 1780s; AD Calvados, C 4524–4535, 4619, 4625, 4628, 4631, 4632, 4634–4665, 4701–4712, and 8104–8119, *capitation* rolls and *états au vrai*. The figures for 1789 are estimations from AN, AD IX, 390a, *Compte rendu par le commission intermédiaire provinciale de Basse Normandie* (Caen, 1790).

[18] Much of the increase in the *capitation* over the century can be traced to legislation. The 10 percent hike from 1705 (which became 20 percent from 1748), the permanent 1773 augmentation of 400,000 livres on the *pays d'élections* (imposed to offset the costs of canal-

inflation into account. Population growth was relatively slow in the generality of Caen, increasing 18 percent over the century to 705,000 souls in 1778–87. The surge in the first sixty-five years of the *capitation*, then, far outpaced the rise in population, making for a dramatic per capita increase in the tax. During the last three decades of the Old Regime, however, the growth rate of population exceeded that of the *capitation*, so easing the burden of the tax, especially on commoners, whose ranks grew more quickly. Dividing the population into privileged and nonprivileged groups reveals that privileged taxpayers and their families, who comprised at most 10.2 percent of the population, paid a moderate share of the tax, varying from highs of 33.4 percent and 26.2 percent in 1706 and 1761 respectively to a low of 13.9 percent in 1772; in the 1780s the privileged paid 18 percent or 19 percent of the tax. This was a high proportion of the tax relative to other generalities such as Alençon (where the privileged paid 9.2 percent), Bourges (7.4 percent), and Limoges (5.6 percent – no wonder Turgot complained!), but the privileged of Riom paid 14.8 percent and those of Amiens as much as 20.6 percent.[19] In Caen the privileged always paid a proportion of the tax that was larger than their fraction of the population, but commoners, as we shall see, contributed much greater shares of their income.[20]

Inflation had more of an effect on the weight of the *capitation* than did the rise in population. According to the price indices of James Riley and Jean-Claude Perrot,[21] Caen and France in general experienced only modest inflation from the stabilization of the livre in 1726 to the early 1760s, which means that the remarkable increase in the burden on the privileged during the Seven Years War was altogether real. From the conclusion of the war in 1763 to

---

building in Picardy and Burgundy), and the increase of 2.5 percent from 1776 in the jurisdiction of the parlement of Paris for the reconstruction of a palace were all established by *arrêts du conseil*. The 50 percent rise in the tariff in 1701 and the doubling and tripling of the tax on the privileged during the Seven Years War were instituted by royal declaration. It was also possible for finance ministers to avoid issuing legislation and to impose gradual increases by administrative order, as they did in the case of the *taille*.

[19] Kwass, "*Liberté, Egalité, Fiscalité*," appendix B.

[20] Figures for the total population of the generality of Caen are from Jacques Dupâquier, ed., *Histoire de la population française* (Paris, 1988), II, pp. 76–7. To determine the size of the population of the privileged, I took the number of privileged in the *capitation* rolls for 1784 and multiplied by four to count family members. On the assertion that the number of commoners grew faster than the number of privileged, see Riley, *Seven Years War*, p. 49, and the discussion of the size of the nobility below.

[21] Perrot, *Genèse*, II, pp. 760–61; and Riley, *Seven Years War*, pp. 9–12.

1771, however, the price of grain and other commodities soared by
as much as 50 percent, while the *capitation* remained relatively even,
making the tax much lighter in real terms. Indeed, for those who
were fortunate enough to bring large surpluses of grain to market
in this period, the *capitation* must have felt quite mild. But prices
stabilized or declined after 1771 and languished into the 1780s,
when small increases were imposed in the *capitation* of the privileged. On balance, inflation did not weaken the *capitation* before the
mid-1760s, but thereafter it rendered the tax less impressive even if
the increased burden on the privileged in the mid-1780s was real
enough.

Let us now turn directly to the privileged. Who exactly were "the
privileged" anyway? Within this category the *capitation* was subdi-
vided among four groups: nobles (who with their families formed
approximately 0.8 percent of the total population of the generality of
Caen), officers of justice (0.6 percent), *privilégiés* (0.9 percent), and the
bourgeoisie (7.9 percent). Figure 2.2 demonstrates the extent to
which the tax struck each privileged group. It is evident that the
nobility and the bourgeoisie – the former small and wealthy, the
latter by far the most populous – paid most of the *capitation* on the
privileged. And it is now possible to note that, whereas all privileged
groups paid the increases in the early 1760s, the nobility and to a
greater extent the bourgeoisie supported the increases in the 1780s.
To see more clearly how the tax struck individual members of each
group, it is best to treat one group at a time.

Figure 2.3 shows the evolution of the *capitation* on the nobility and
includes both the totals of the tax rolls and the amounts of money
paid in years for which evidence exists. (In this figure, as in those
that follow, the absence of columns representing "taxes paid" reflects
lack of evidence, not nonpayment). First, this figure demonstrates
that there was a difference between the total of assessments on the
tax rolls and the sums that were actually collected. The discrepancy
between these two figures was due mostly to the reductions (*décharges
et modérations*) that intendants granted to taxpayers who had petitioned against their assessment, and partially to the money that tax
receivers were simply unable to collect (*nonvaleurs*).[22] We will look at
the politics of petitioning for tax reductions in chapter 3, but for the

---

[22] *Décharges et modérations* typically made up over 90 percent of the discrepancy between total
assessments and total payments, while *nonvaleurs* constituted the remainder.

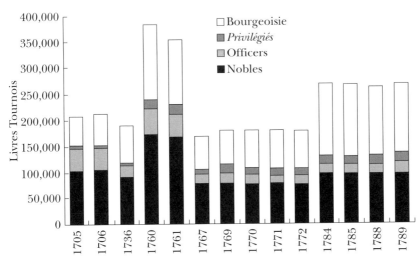

Figure 2.2   The *capitation* on the privileged in the generality of Caen

KWASS Fig. 2.2

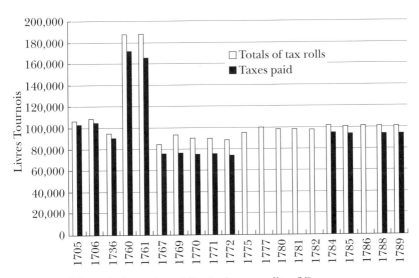

Figure 2.3   The *capitation* on the nobility in the generality of Caen

moment it suffices to say that, despite adjustments in assessments and problems in collection, receivers were able to collect most of the tax, even during the Seven Years War when the *capitation* doubled. Never doubled again, the tax declined precipitously in the late 1760s and early 1770s, but nobles – especially wealthier ones[23] – did see their assessments rise from 1772 into the 1780s, and evidence for the years 1784, 1785, 1788, and 1789 shows that those higher assessments led to increases in payments. The nobles of Caen were not alone in confronting higher assessments in the 1780s, as their counterparts in Bordeaux, Bourges, Grenoble, Limoges, and Orléans experienced a similar rise in the *capitation*.[24]

How much did the average noble in the generality of Caen pay? By dividing the total amount paid by the number of nobles on the tax rolls, we can determine that for the years 1769, 1770, 1772, 1784, 1785, 1788, and 1789 the average noble paid, respectively, in livres: 42.5, 42.4, 44.0, 63.8, 63.6, 63.1, and 62.7. The 20-livre increase from the 1770s to the 1780s, paralleled in Grenoble and Limoges, resulted from rising assessments and a marked decline in the number of nobles on the tax rolls, a decline that meant the average noble could count on fewer and fewer of his peers to help him support the increasing burden.[25] Moving beyond averages, which reveal little about a group as stratified as the French nobility, we discover that there was a broad range of payments among the 1,500 to 1,800 nobles listed in the rolls. Situated at the summit of the order, the wealthiest seigneurs and titled nobility paid several hundred livres or more; in 1781 the seigneur de Querqueville, a great landowner, paid a *capitation* of 1,062 livres, the equivalent of 271 bushels of wheat or 18 milking cows, a heavy sum by any measure. Much more common were middling seigneurs like Robert Gosselin D'Anissy, seigneur de Quesnay, who paid 232 livres in 1734, or even Joseph Martin, a squire, who paid 27 livres in 1736. At the low end of the scale the poorest squires or their widows paid

[23] Mohamed El Kordi demonstrates that these increases struck wealthier nobles harder than poorer ones. *Bayeux aux xviie et xviiie siècles: contribution à l'histoire urbaine de la France* (Paris, 1970), pp. 52–3.

[24] Kwass, "*Liberté, Egalité, Fiscalité*," appendix B.

[25] The number of entries in the rolls fell steadily from 1,782 in 1769 to 1,496 in 1789. (Most entries represented the male head of a family, but some included groups of family members, such as widows and children, who had received an inheritance). Guy Lemarchand and Jean Meyer have also noticed that the nobility was shrinking, especially in the second half of the eighteenth century. For possible explanations, see Guy Lemarchand, *La fin de féodalisme dans le pays de Caux* (Paris, 1989), pp. 317–20.

as little as 3 or 4 livres a year.[26] The degree to which the *capitation* struck noble income is difficult to determine – we will make a more thorough attempt with the *vingtième* – but a tax rate of 1.5 percent, given on a noble *capitation* roll for the *élection* of Vire, is a reasonable estimate.[27] This was hardly a burdensome rate, but the nobility's keen awareness of its privileges made it heavy enough to be felt.

In addition to the nobility, the *capitation* struck officers of justice who, though generally non-noble, enjoyed tax privileges by virtue of the offices they held in over fifty mid- to lower-level courts scattered throughout the generality.[28] No hard evidence exists for the *capitation* on officers in Caen from 1695 to 1698 (probably because they were lumped with the nobility), but the declaration of 1701 thanked officers "who in the last war contributed so generously to the support of the state."[29] In the beginning of the eighteenth century, intendants followed the instructions of the 1701 declaration and assessed officers by adding 50 percent to the rates of the tariff of 1695, which bracketed office-holders according to the prestige and value of their offices. By 1736 the tariff had been jettisoned and officers were paying far less than before. During the Seven Years War, however, assessments doubled (even tripled for certain financial officers), and officers paid their highest *capitation* of the century. After the war the tax dropped dramatically, but in 1769 the old method of assessing officers by adding 50 percent to the original tariff was reinstituted.[30] Assessments soared once again yet, as figure 2.4 demonstrates, officers did not actually pay

[26] AD Calvados, C 4622, 4678, no. 7, and 4675, no. 3, petitions from de Querqueville, d'Anissy, and Joseph Martin. Wheat and livestock equivalents are based on Perrot, *Genèse*, II, p. 1029; and Georges d'Avenel, *Histoire économique de la propriété, des salaires, et de tous les prix* (reprint, New York, 1969), IV, p. 92. Olwen Hufton gives the scale of assessments for nobles residing in the town of Bayeux: among eighty noble families, the wealthiest were assessed from 300 to 500 livres (twice as much as the wealthiest commoner), the middling from 20 to 250 livres (on a par with wealthy bourgeois), and the poorest seventeen households (almost a quarter of the group) from 20 livres on down. Olwen Hufton, *Bayeux in the Late Eighteenth Century: A Social Study* (Oxford, 1967), ch. 2.

[27] The rate of 1.5 percent (from AD Calvados, C 4636, no. 1) is not far from the 1.2 percent estimate made by the intendant of Caen in the early 1780s (AD Calvados, C 4703, no. 73, Observations).

[28] Courts included *bailliages, élections, hautes justices, vicomtés, eaux et forêts*, and *amirautés*; 90 percent of officers of justice in Bayeux were of non-noble origin. El Kordi, *Bayeux*, p. 57.

[29] AN, AD IX 81, no. 129, Déclaration du Roy, 12 March 1701.

[30] It is not clear who was responsible for the reestablishment of the tariff. Royal officials later attributed it to Terray but Terray entered office in December 1769, too late to draw that year's tax rolls. Was it the work of d'Invau or an early product of Maupeou?

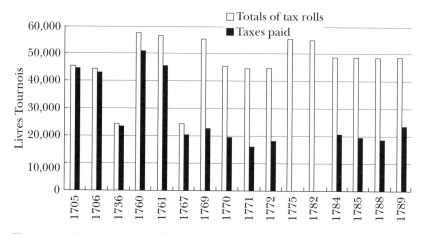

Figure 2.4   The *capitation* on officers of justice in the generality of Caen

more. The same intendants who raised assessments on officers proceeded to grant considerable reductions to those whom they had just assessed.

Why did intendants bother to increase assessments on officers of justice only to turn around and lower them? Esmangard, the intendant of Caen, explained that he and other intendants were following a deliberate policy laid out by Terray:

The purpose of M. l'abbé Terray, in adopting this practice [of raising assessments and distributing reductions] was wise and useful to the service of the king. He knew that for many years, officers of the *Bailliages*, *Présidiaux*, and even subordinate courts had affected, in some provinces, a kind of independence which infrequent contacts with commissioned administrators seemed to permit. How many times has it happened that officers have refused to give intendants clarifications asked of them by order of the royal council, whether having to do with criminal trials, sentences in police matters, or purely civil trials? It is certain that the tie that M. L'Abbé Terray has sought to reestablish produced in part the effect that he desired.[31]

By raising the assessments of officers and then forcing them to

---

[31] BN, JdF 1444, fos. 85–94, letter from Esmangard to Necker, 31 October 1781. In a letter to Fontette, Terray instructed the intendant to fix assessments of officers according to the tariff "without making any mention of reductions. This will give you more liberty to distribute reductions that His Majesty would like to grant." AD Calvados, C 4525, letter of 2 October 1771.

petition for reductions, intendants were pressuring officers to be more cooperative. Naturally, magistrates in the sovereign courts objected to this practice; "Deign, Sire," remonstrated the *cour des aides* of Paris in 1775, "to state if it is true that each year in a lot of towns all Officers of Justice are subject to a *Capitation* stronger than that which they can be made to pay, which forces them to come ask a grace from the Intendant, and thus puts them in a state of absolute dependence on this Magistrate." But such protests did little to change what had already become an administrative routine by the time Terray fell from power. During the two decades between 1769 and the Revolution, the crown forced officers of justice in Caen and throughout the *pays d'élections* to ingratiate themselves with intendants or face sharply higher taxes.[32]

Individual officers of justice ended up paying varying amounts of *capitation*. For the 1,100 or 1,200 officers of justice in Caen, the average *capitation* payment, between 18 and 21 livres from 1769 to 1789, seems moderate enough. The average was low compared with that for officers in Limoges and Grenoble, who paid annually around 35 livres in *capitation* in the 1780s, but averages for Caen are deceiving because clerks and officers in the lowest courts paid hardly anything while important officers in higher courts paid quite a bit. At the upper end of the scale we find officers like Jean Timoleau le Portier who as a *conseiller du roi* at the *bailliage* court of Caen in 1789 paid 44 livres, a sum that exceeded the 36 livres of *gages* that he received annually, much like an interest payment on his investment in the office. An officer of the same court, Pierre Quedrue, who had paid a light *capitation* of 16 livres before purchasing his office, was obliged to pay 58 livres as a *receveur des consignations*. And when Pierre Simon de Mallou, a *procureur du roi* at the *élection* of Caen, went to the tax receiver's office to obtain what he thought was going to be 276 livres of *gages*, he discovered to his dismay that the tax receiver had withheld 162 livres for his *capitation* of 1787, 1788, and 1789.[33] These were not inconsequential sums for officers of mid- or lower-level

[32] Elisabeth Badinter, ed., *Les "Remontrances" de Malesherbes, 1771–1775* (Paris, 1985), p. 239. In a letter of 14 April 1777 Necker told Esmangard to maintain the use of the tariff in assessing officers, but to moderate assessments to what officers had paid before the tariff was reinstated. He explained that this would accustom officers and prospective buyers of office to the tariff. AD Calvados, C 4703, no. 30. See also BN, JdF 1448, fo. 95, Mémoire sur le compte rendu de Necker.

[33] AD Calvados, C 8110, petitions from le Portier and de Mallou; AD Calvados, C 4682, no. 28, petition of 29 July 1776 from Quedrue.

courts, many of whom were not particularly wealthy and were easily put off by such exactions. Emphasizing the trials of lower office-holders who saw their *gages* evaporate, William Doyle cites the *procureur du roi* of the *bailliage* of Macon who complained of the debts that the company was forced to contract and the "matchless rigour" of the *capitation*, both of which rendered the vacant offices of the court "contemptible and unsaleable." Likewise, the magistrates of the *bailliage* of Sézanne, alluding no doubt to the new tariff system from 1769, complained that the rise in the *capitation* was "so extraordinary that several among them are paying certainly more than they would have paid in *taille*."[34]

Besides nobles and officers, a third category of privileged taxpayers existed called the *privilégiés*. Although in common par-lance a *privilégié* could mean any privileged subject, royal adminis-trators used the term more specifically to refer to two groups: men who were neither noble nor acting officers of justice but whose positions or occupations endowed them or their widows with exemptions from the *taille*, and employees of the General Farms, the company that collected indirect taxes for the king.[35] In the generality of Caen the first group numbered about 200, including retired and active army officers (such as non-noble *chevaliers de Saint-Louis*), militia captains, retired officers of justice, officers of the Royal Household (many *gardes du roi*), doctors, professors of law and medicine, clergymen without benefices, clerks of the church, moneychangers, and various royal administrators such as post-masters, subdelegates, *vingtième* controllers, and officials working for the royal domain and the service of roads and bridges. On average these individuals or their widows paid approximately 20 livres a year; in the 1780s, for instance, postmasters were assessed at 18 livres and doctors as high as 42 livres. The second group, the throng of employees of the General Farms who gathered taxes on tobacco, salt, wine, and other goods, numbered as many as 1,300 to 1,400 in the generality of Caen alone. Under instructions from the intendant, heads of the General Farms drew the tax rolls for their

---

[34] Doyle, *Venality*, pp. 186–90.
[35] From 1701 to 1769 the *privilégiés* were comprised strictly of employees of the General Farms. From 1769 to 1775 tax receivers lumped the other privileged individuals with the employees, but after 1775 the two groups were separated from one another. That tax officials had trouble classifying the *privilégiés* shows how this large group fit into neither the noble elite nor the mass of commoners.

employees, scaling the tax progressively according to salary. While employees enjoying the highest annual salaries, above 1,000 livres, were taxed at slightly over 3 percent of their salary at the end of the century, those with the lowest salaries (50 to 400 livres) paid around 1 percent. Thus, simple "guards" paid under 4 livres, "directors" over 100 livres. In 1785 the average *capitation* paid by employees was a little more than 7 livres.[36]

The final and by far the largest privileged group was the bourgeoisie, a category that encompassed the residents of the generality's twelve biggest towns, all of which benefited from some sort of privilege with regard to the *taille*.[37] Figure 2.5 illustrates the evolution of the *capitation* on this group. It is no surprise that the *capitation* on the bourgeoisie, like that on the rest of the privileged, jumped during the Seven Years War. But, after returning to pre-war levels, the tax took a dramatic leap in 1781, the reason for which is clear. In 1781 towns began to pay an additional 66,000 livres in *capitation* to help pay the *cazernement*, a tax of 250,000 livres for the quartering of troops that had previously been levied solely on *taillables*. This additional tax extended to no other privileged group but the bourgeoisie.[38]

Each town was responsible for apportioning the *capitation* among its residents. Intendants informed city officials what they owed and let them (in conjunction with subdelegates in some cases) distribute the tax on individuals.[39] Because city-dwelling nobles, officers of justice, and *privilégiés* were placed on separate rolls, the urban elite was conspicuously absent from the rolls of the bourgeoisie. Merchants with high *capitations* did appear of course, but the majority of bourgeois tax rolls were filled with countless small

---

[36] AN, P 5270–5271, rolls and *états au vrai* for the *capitation* in the generality of Caen.
[37] The towns were Caen, Bayeux, St. Lo, Thorigny, Valognes, Cherbourg, Coutances, Granville, Avranches, Pontorson, Vire, and Condé sur Noireau. Cherbourg and Granville had been completely exempt from the *taille* since the middle of the fifteenth century; land outside these towns owned by the bourgeoisie was half exempt. Caen, Bayeux, Valognes, and others paid the *taille* but exercised the privilege of using revenue from cities' customs duties to do it, allowing city-dwellers to avoid paying the *taille* as a direct tax on their personal wealth. Caen paid its entire *taille* of 29,900 livres in this fashion. AD Calvados, C 4392, report on "villes franches et tarifées," 30 May 1759.
[38] AD C 4703, no. 75, mémoire from the office of the intendant.
[39] In 1757 the intendant further delegated the responsibility of levying the *capitation* on guild-members to the guilds themselves in order to establish "equality in the distribution [of the tax], and diminish injustices, complaints, and petitions." AD Calvados, C 4565, no. 1. In 1757, 48 guilds in the city of Caen, totaling 2,943 members, were subject to a *capitation* of 11,055 livres. AD Calvados, C 4564, *capitation* rolls for the guilds in the city of Caen.

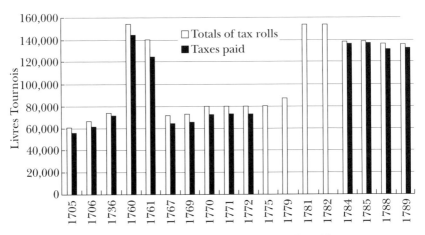

Figure 2.5　The *capitation* on the bourgeoisie in the generality of Caen

assessments. In the 1780s the rolls for the city of Caen, the largest city of the generality, listed over 5,000 individuals, whose payments added up to 60,000 livres. While day-laborers, some of whom earned less than 1 *livre* a day, paid 1 or 2 livres a year, bakers, surgeons, and small shopkeepers paid up to 20 livres. Nicolas Vaussard, a butcher, complained that he would rather pay 3 percent of his meager income than the 4 livres and 16 sols of *capitation* he was paying.[40]

On the whole, then, the privileged nobles, officers, *privilégiés*, and bourgeois of Caen confronted a mildly burdensome *capitation* in the eighteenth century. But the fact that they were now contributing lightly to the direct tax levy in no way translated into tax relief for rural commoners. On the contrary, for peasants and villagers the *capitation* was but an addition to the *taille*, which imposed an already heavy tax burden. Because it struck those who were least in a position to resist it, the *taille* had long provided the crown with an expedient means of increasing revenue. "Although many other [taxes] had been less onerous, and less harmful to the prosperity of the kingdom," Necker confessed in the declaration of 13 February 1780, the *taille* kept increasing because it was "the

[40] AD Calvados, C 4549–4554, *capitation* rolls for the city of Caen; AD Calvados, C 4567, petition by Vaussard. For a more detailed discussion of the *capitation* and the city of Caen, see Perrot, *Genèse*, I, pp. 342–7.

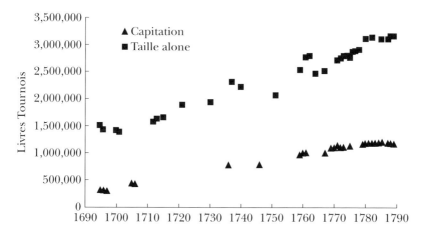

Figure 2.6   The *capitation* and the *taille* on commoners in the generality of Caen

easiest and fastest resource."[41] As figure 2.6 illustrates, both the *taille* and the *capitation* increased steadily on those unprotected by privilege.[42]

In 1695 commoners paid 315,153 livres of *capitation*, a 21 percent surcharge on the *taille*. By 1789 the *capitation* on commoners had increased to 1,168,768 livres, adding 37 percent to a *taille* that had itself doubled, bringing the total *taille* and *capitation* on commoners to 4,320,862 livres. If we estimate the number of households that paid the *taille* in the generality at 150,000 in the late eighteenth century, the combined weight of the *taille* and *capitation* on an average household was approximately 29 livres a year – a considerable sum relative to income.[43] In the neighboring pays de Caux, for example, *taillables* were paying 12 percent to 30 percent of their net income for the *taille* and *capitation*.[44] Further south in the Aunis, a poor day-laborer paid, in 1763, 12 livres in *taille*,

[41] AN, AD IX 82, no. 86. As the declaration explained, one reason for the rise of the *taille* was that administrators kept adding local taxes to it. By 1780 half of the *taille* was in reality a composite of supposedly temporary provincial taxes that were used to pay for public works and other expenses such as the *gages* of office-holders.

[42] Data on the *taille* are from AN, G-7 215–217; and AD Calvados, C 4389–4398.

[43] The figure of 29 livres for *taille* and *capitation* squares with evidence for the *taille* in Jean Lethuillier, *Le Calvados dans la Révolution* (Paris, 1990), pp. 357–69, and matches Morineau's estimate that the average head of household paid an annual *taille* of 20 livres at the end of the Old Regime. Morineau, "Budgets de l'Etat," p. 321.

[44] Lemarchand, *Fin de féodalisme*, pp. 346–63. I have reworked Lemarchand's figures by

capitation, and other direct taxes out of a total gross revenue of 183 livres, but if we subtract his expenses for the bare essentials – rent, food, firewood, and clothing – the taxes mounted to 20 percent of the remaining income.[45] These rates of taxation far exceeded those the privileged confronted when paying the *capitation* and *vingtième*. There were exceptional cases like that of Charles Alphonse de Cotelle, an owner of a fief in Coutances who in 1702 was assessed for the *capitation* as a noble at 42 livres. Because de Cotelle had always paid less, 34 livres, for the *taille* and *capitation* when classified as a commoner, he asked to be placed back on the rolls of the *taille*.[46] But few privileged subjects cared to follow de Cotelle's example. They knew that the same kings who were now obliging elites to pay direct taxes exerted much heavier fiscal pressure on the nonprivileged.

Although the *dixième* and *vingtième* in the *pays d'élections* developed differently from the *capitation*, their incidence suggests similar conclusions. Figure 2.7 shows how the two taxes evolved over the eighteenth century in Caen.[47] Note that, unlike the collection of the *capitation*, which sometimes lagged well behind assessments, royal administrators recovered virtually all the assessments on the *vingtième* rolls. In the years for which there is evidence for both tax rolls and actual payments, the discrepancy between the two is minimal, even when the tax was on the rise. Property-owners were eager for tax reductions, as in the case of the *capitation*, but intendants were far less likely to grant abatements in the *vingtième*. Rejecting the pleas of petitioners, intendants stood firm, confident in the justice of the tax.

A much heavier tax than the *capitation*, the *vingtième* rose and fell with legislation that doubled and tripled it. Between 1756 and 1789 a second *vingtième* was added to the first, and from 1760 to 1763 and again from 1783 to 1786 a third *vingtième* was added to the first two. The effects of these doublings and triplings are quite noticeable in

---

subtracting rental costs from gross revenue in order to calculate the rate of the *taille* and *capitation* on net income.

[45] Michel Morineau, "Budgets populaires en France au xviiie siècle," *RHES* 50, no. 2 (1972), pp. 225–6.

[46] AD Calvados, C 4688.

[47] Data for the *vingtième* in the generality of Caen were compiled from AN, G-7 1138–1140; AN, P 5270–5271; AD Calvados, C 4398, no. 27, C 5898 and C 5964–5967; and Yves Préel, *L'impôt direct au XVIIIe siècle: les vingtièmes dans la généralité de Caen* (Caen, 1939), p. 222.

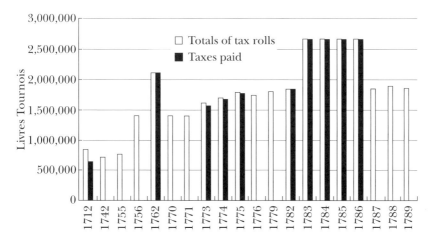

Figure 2.7   The *dixième* and *vingtième* in the generality of Caen

the chart. But the chart reveals other kinds of increases as well. Although the *dixième*, a 10 percent tax on income, was converted in 1749 to a *vingtième*, a 5 percent tax, the rolls of the tax did not decline in accordance with the reduction in the rate. In the early 1750s the finance minister, Machault, made every effort to have intendants revise the rolls, verify old declarations of wealth, and seek new declarations from those who had managed previously to evade the tax. Whereas in many generalities, Bordeaux for one, such efforts were largely ineffectual, in Caen the single *vingtième* eventually measured up to the *dixième*.[48] The other significant increase not related to a doubling or tripling of the tax was the 30 percent rise from 1771 to 1782, which was the result of an administrative campaign to verify and raise the assessments of the two *vingtièmes* in place. From 1783 to 1786 increases in assessments stopped but a third *vingtième* was imposed, bringing the tax to its highest point before the events of the Prerevolution.

The campaign to raise *vingtième* assessments from 1771 to 1782, one of the few institutional legacies of the Maupeou coup, merits a closer

---

[48] Other generalities such as Bourges also underwent a round of verifications, making the *vingtième* worth more than half the *dixième*. In 1752 the *vingtième* yielded globally 28.7 million livres, 68 percent of the *dixième* of 1749. Riley, *Seven Years War*, p. 56; Marion, *Impôts directs*, p. 352.

look. In 1771 the chancellor of France, René-Nicolas de Maupeou, launched his famous attack on the parlements, the highest law courts in the realm, abolishing three of them and substantially remodeling the rest. In the aftermath of this coup Terray wasted no time in submitting to the new parlements and *conseils supérieurs* the edict of November 1771, which prolonged the first *vingtième* indefinitely and the second until 1781.[49] The edict also declared that, in response to the price inflation, which had augmented royal expenses and "improved landed income in greater proportion to that of the growth of taxes," the crown intended to levy the *vingtième* according to the edict of May 1749, which stipulated that the assessments of the tax accurately reflect levels of income. Terray inserted this seemingly harmless reference to the edict of 1749 to provide a pretext for a wholesale revision of *vingtième* assessments, which he believed no longer matched the income of taxpayers. To appreciate the ambition of Terray's plan one has to remember that, in many cases, property-owners were paying the *vingtième* on the basis of declarations of wealth submitted as far back as 1749 or even 1741 or 1733. Such declarations, scarcely trustworthy at the time of submission, were by 1771 entirely inadequate. Underscoring the nature of this problem, d'Ormesson, an influential intendant of finance under Terray, insisted that the time had come for the state to get at the "publicly known and acknowledged augmentation that all landowners have experienced in their revenue since 1764 when the commerce in grain expanded." Thanks to the liberalization of the grain trade in 1763–4, grain prices and agricultural profits soared but, d'Ormesson bemoaned, the resistance of the parlements to readjusting the *vingtième* had enjoyed "a great success." Even during the Seven Years War when the tax was doubled and tripled, parlements insisted that the assessments themselves remained untouched and after the war, as the tax fell steeply, this stipulation warded off attempts to revise the rolls. The success of the parlements from 1763 to November 1771 "accustomed the Peoples to believe that the *vingtièmes* must not at all undergo an increase. The more landed revenues augmented during this period, the more dear this conviction became to property owners."[50]

Terray's plan was to make the *vingtième* the basis for a true land tax

---

[49] AN, AD IX 492, no. 24, Edit du roi, November 1771.
[50] AN, H-1 1463, no. 7, *mémoire* on taxation by d'Ormesson.

distributed "with the greatest equality possible."[51] Instead of a general increase in the tax, which would be "unfair since the inequality in the present assessments would grow even more," Terray wanted to "know the true product of the property subject to the tax" and to reapportion the tax accordingly.[52] To get at information on income he instructed intendants to examine several sources of information: tax rolls that parishes secretly composed in order to pay for church repairs and poor relief, the rolls of the *taille*, leases for the ecclesiastical land tax (*dîme*), and ordinary rental leases. A still "more effective" method was to conduct "verifications" of declarations of wealth by measuring land, a lengthy but thorough process.

This was not the first time verifications had been ordered. Rarely used during the first three *dixièmes*, a wave of verifications was conducted in the early 1750s following the creation of Machault's *vingtième*. The memory of this round of increases was still fresh in the minds of the *parlementaires* of Rouen when they stipulated, upon registering the second *vingtième* in 1756, that the two taxes be collected on the basis of the "present rolls." Verifications proceeded anyway as controllers continued to make use of the *bureaux du contrôle*, where notarial contracts, leases, and documents used in civil trials were deposited, but such investigations were generally restricted to cases in which property-owners had petitioned against their assessments. In 1762 the parlement prohibited agents of the intendant from going through confidential records in the *bureaux du contrôle*, but it was not until the following year that the court was able to halt verifications altogether. The parlement's *arrêt de défense* of 18 August 1763 threatened to prosecute any official who augmented the assessments of the *vingtième* rolls and, in case that was insufficient, the president of the court used his influence with the finance minister to restrain one particularly zealous controller who was "digging up information in notarial offices, in the bureau du controlle, and even in private homes."[53] After 1763, verifications waned in Caen and across the *pays d'élections*, for the parlement of Paris had also prohibited the rolls from being touched, making Terray's sudden

---

[51] AN, H-1 1463, no. 115, letter from Terray to Fontette, 11 January 1773.
[52] AN, H-1 1463, no. 53, letter from Terray to Fontette, 3 May 1772; AN, H-1 1463, no. 18, circular from Terray to intendants of the *pays d'élections*, 6 May 1772.
[53] Le Verdier, *Miromesnil*, II, p. 240, letter of 29 June 1763.

full-scale revivification of the procedure in 1771 all the more
alarming.

The intendant of Caen, Fontette, was at first reluctant to follow
Terray's orders but when the minister revealed his long-term goal of
reestablishing the *vingtième* along the lines of current levels of income,
Fontette became decidedly enthusiastic, instructing directors, controllers, and parish *préposés* to investigate the property of taxpayers
and revise the rolls. On his own initiative Fontette ordered controllers to check the property of wealthier taxpayers (those with more
than 1,000 livres of revenue), before looking over the rest of the rolls.
He urged his assistants to be thorough in their work and tactful in
their relations with taxpayers (reminding them to exhibit the "polite-
ness that one expects from a man who has received a good
education") and asked the finance minister for an additional 25 to 30
commissaires.[54] If property-owners wanted to contest their new reassessments, Fontette welcomed their petitions as long as they documented their claims. Petitions in fact provided an easy way to learn
about the wealth of taxpayers: "The goal [of discovering wealth] can
be fulfilled by simply requiring that all petitioners provide detailed
mémoires, titles, leases and other documentation. Each increased
assessment will give rise to a petition, and the multiplicity of petitions
will allow intelligent state employees to conduct a general verification of most of the parishes."[55] Those who did not complain about
the increases, on the other hand, were presumed to be taxed at the
right level. In 1775 the director of the *vingtième* for the generality of
Caen informed the intendant that "[m]any assessments [that were]
doubled in 1773 did not provoke complaints. The silence of the
taxpayer who withholds records proves that he fears an investigation."[56]

One of the most intriguing features of Terray's campaign to raise
the *vingtième* is that it survived him. Although his successor, Turgot,
promised Louis XVI that he would not raise taxes, fearing that
further increases in the *vingtième* would undermine the confidence of
taxpayers in the crown, evidence suggests that verifications did not

[54] AN, H-1 1463, no. 72, letter from Fontette to controllers; AN, H-1 1463, no. 112, instructions
     for *commissaires* of the *vingtième*. The request was denied on the grounds that it would only
     agitate people "and arm them against the investigations we want to make." AN, H-1 1463,
     no. 65, letter from d'Ormesson to Fontette, June 1772.
[55] AN, H-1 1463, no. 35, letter from Fontette to Terray, 17 February 1772.
[56] Quoted in Préel, *L'impôt direct*, p. 113.

slow down between 1774 and 1776.[57] In 1777 when Necker came to power, he not only embraced the policy of verification but expanded it significantly. Necker may have raised the money for the American war by floating loans but he was at the same time very interested in improving the *vingtième*, so much so that his *arrêt* of 2 November 1777 declared that all lands that had not been reassessed since 1771 were going to be verified by intendants and their staffs with the aid of "notable landowners" and collectors from each parish. Moreover, verifications would no longer pinpoint individuals but would cover entire parishes through a "public" procedure in which parishioners participated.[58] The *arrêt* of 2 November went into effect immediately and verifications under Necker, recorded in large well-organized workbooks, reached an astonishing level of sophistication that made earlier verifications look amateurish. Thus verifications continued from 1771 through 1782 as the ministry of finances passed from Terray to Turgot to Necker. During this period, royal administrators verified more than one-fifth (22 percent) of the parishes of the *pays d'élections*, increasing the *vingtième* of this vast area by one-quarter. Normandy's augmentation was a little higher than average: the 30 percent increase in Caen was matched by a 28.6 percent rise in the generality of Rouen where the province's parlement sat.[59]

So the *vingtième* rose, but swings in the tax shed little light on its social incidence. The *vingtième* and its continuously renewed 20 percent supplement was a tax of 6 percent (or 11 percent and 16 percent when doubled and tripled) on net income from three sources: industry, offices, and land.[60] The tax on industry, which fell on members of guilds as well as individuals earning professional and commercial income, was levied simply as an addition to the *capitation*,

[57] Schelle, *Turgot*, IV, p. 351, letter to the intendant of Bordeaux, 18 October 1775.
[58] AN, AD IX 492, no. 37, *arrêt du conseil* of 2 November 1777.
[59] Augustin Rioche, *De l'administration des vingtièmes sous l'ancien regime* (Paris, 1904), p. 109. The 22 percent increase in the tax in the *pays d'élections* is recorded in BN, JdF 1448, nos. 34–37. The figure for the generality of Rouen is based on data from AD Seine-Maritime, C 481–486, *états au vrai* for the *vingtième*.
[60] In principle the *vingtième* also struck the capital of private creditors. Borrowers were supposed to withhold the tax from interest payments to lenders and to forward the sum retained, along with the borrowers' own *vingtième*, to tax collectors. A ruling upholding this practice by the *bailliage* of Rouen suggests that at least one disgruntled creditor had brought the issue before the court and lost. *Annonces*, 20 August 1762 and 8 October 1762. Another piece of evidence comes from the pen of the merchant Paul-François Depont who told his son, "Your brother could easily borrow at six percent by draft [*billet*] but without deducting the *vingtième* tax." Robert Forster, *Merchants, Landlords, Magistrates: The Depont Family in Eighteenth-Century France* (Baltimore, MD, 1980), p. 71.

amounting to an extra 1 or 2 livres for artisans or 5 to 10 livres for small shop owners. The *vingtième* on offices struck all officers who earned money from service fees (as opposed to *gages*), such as notaries, clerks, and the countless petty officials who possessed the right to collect dues at the marketplace. Certainly, more prestigious officers were subject to the *vingtième* but they paid through a separate withholding tax on the interest their office accrued. All in all, the *vingtième* on industry and offices amounted to a tiny fraction of the tax, a mere 2 percent to 3 percent in Caen.[61]

The bulk of the tax fell on landowners – but which landowners, privileged or nonprivileged, noble or commoner? Although no evidence is available for the generality of Caen as a whole, Mohamed El Kordi, who has analyzed the *vingtième* rolls of 1750 for the *élection* of Bayeux (one of nine *élections* in the generality of Caen), has found that nobles, representing around 7 percent of landowners, carried 30 percent to 75 percent of the *vingtième* burden in the great majority of parishes. In slightly more than half of the parishes, the nobility's share was fixed at 50 percent to 90 percent of the total parish assessment, and in certain parishes in the *élections* of Bayeux and Caen where the seigneur was the sole landowner he paid the entire *vingtième* for the parish. Such was the case with Jean-Robert Gosselin de Manneville, a gentleman whose family not only paid the *dixième* and *vingtième* for the whole parish of Manneville from 1734 to 1789 but watched its tax rise from 310 livres to 800 livres.[62] This is suggestive evidence, indicating that the nobility supported a principal share of the tax, but to find more complete data on *vingtième* payments for whole generalities (rather than *vingtième* assessments for particular parishes or *élections*), we have to look beyond Caen to Limoges and Bourges, the only two generalities for which tax receivers divided their accounts into the categories of privileged and nonprivileged. (Why certain receivers of Limoges and Bourges drew their accounts in this exceptional manner I have no idea, but I am grateful for the fastidiousness).

In both Limoges and Bourges the nobility was more thinly spread

---

[61] AN, P 5271, *états au vrai* for the *vingtième* in the generality of Caen.

[62] El Kordi, *Bayeux*, pp. 48–9; AD Calvados, C 5631, *vingtième* rolls for the parish of Manneville. It is possible that landlords such as Manneville passed some of the *vingtième* to their tenants by way of higher rents, but it is equally likely that tenants passed the *taille* on to landlords in the form of lower rents. Because there is no way of determining how taxes figured into informal rental arrangements, I have left the problem out of my discussion.

than in Caen, but their cases are revealing nevertheless. During the 1770s and early 1780s the privileged of Limoges (nobles, officers of justice, and *privilégiés*) represented slightly more than 0.5 percent of the total population but paid 28 percent of the *vingtième* on land, their individual payments averaging around 250 livres. In Bourges the privileged represented the same small fraction of the population but their contribution was even greater, reaching 43 percent of the *vingtième* on land in the 1770s. There, the privileged paid on average 335 livres a year. Such averages mask the innumerable small payments of less well-off privileged subjects as well as the occasional large annual payments of well over 1,000 livres from wealthy nobles.[63]

Thus, the privileged in Caen and elsewhere were paying a large share of the *vingtième* at the end of the Old Regime, a far higher share than they paid of the *capitation*. The crucial question, however, is whether the tax struck the income of the privileged in any substantial way. It is possible after all that the privileged were wealthy enough to have paid substantial proportions of the total *vingtième* without the tax making an important inroad into their income. Tax rates of 11 percent or 16 percent, heavy for the time, were indeed applied but they were imposed on suspected revenue, which, based often on taxpayers' own declarations of property, was far below the level of real revenue.

The gap between suspected and real revenue is terribly difficult to measure because social historians tend to base their estimates of real income on tax rolls, an obviously flawed use of evidence for our purposes. The better method is to compare the leases of property-owners with revenue listed on the tax rolls. Jean-Claude Perrot made such comparisons for property in the city of Caen and found that the ratio of suspected net revenue to real net revenue was 75 percent, although he later revised that figure to 45 percent.[64] If we apply Perrot's more conservative figure to the ostensible rates of the

---

[63] Averages were calculated by dividing the total *vingtième* payment of the privileged by the number of privileged in the *capitation* rolls. AN, P 5195 (Bourges) and 5416–5417 bis (Limoges). The employees of the indirect tax farms and the residents of towns exempt from the *taille*, which swelled the ranks of the privileged in Caen, appear to have been counted as commoners in the *vingtième* accounts for these two generalities. My estimates of total population for the two generalities are from Dupâquier, *Population française*, II, pp. 76–7.

[64] Perrot's original estimate of 75 percent is in "Introduction à l'emploi des registres fiscaux en histoire sociale: L'exemple de Caen au XVIIIe siècle," *Annales de Normandie* (1966), p. 42, n. 30. He revised this estimate in *Genèse*, II, pp. 609–13.

vingtième (11 percent and 16 percent), we find that the true rates were 4.9 percent when the tax was doubled and 7.2 percent when tripled. Like Perrot's findings, my own research, based on a small sample of six landowners from different parts of the generality of Caen, suggests that although the ratio of suspected revenue to real revenue varied widely – some property-owners hid most of their rental income while others paid taxes on as much as 80 percent of it – it averaged 65 percent, which means that property-owners were paying, respectively, 7.1 percent and 10.4 percent of their landed revenue when the *vingtième* was doubled and tripled.[65] These were significant rates indeed when we recall that a century earlier the very idea of a direct tax on privileged landowners was inconceivable.

Weighing the impact of the *vingtième* in terms of average tax rates is slightly misleading, because it glosses over a well-defined pattern in the application of the tax. Besides poorer landowners with little to hide, those paying higher rates for the *vingtième* were frequently well-off landowners, whether noble or commoner, whose estates had been selected for verification by controllers.[66] It is clear that those whose property had been verified experienced sudden, heavy increases in their tax rate. For example, in 1767 a certain Charles Adrien Danisy, seigneur of the parish of Merville, rented his lands for 6,800 livres a year. Since 1754 he had been paying his *vingtième* on the basis of only 2,000 livres of revenue, a vast underassessment. In 1771, however, his revenue was reevaluated at 5,500 livres, driving

---

[65] I came to the figure of 65 percent by first calculating the ratio of suspected income to rental income as stated in leases, which was 73 percent, and then revising this downward to account for non-rented land exploited directly by property-owners. I made the conservative assumption that non-rented land was assessed at half its true value and amounted to one-third of the land on estates. The leases of the six landowners (Lair, d'Hermerel de Cleronde, Dudouet, Danisy de Merville, Gosselin, and Bourdon de Grandmont) are located in AD Calvados, C 9388–9389, and 9869, records of the *bureaux du contrôle* for the *élections* of Bayeux and Caen. The *vingtième* rolls for the six landowners are found, respectively, in AD Calvados, C 5395, 5342, 5396, 5635, 5594, and 5722. There are problems, of course, with using leases in this way since some leases may not have been registered in the bureaux and others may have been artificially low as landlords were known to draft leases that omitted *pots de vin* (under-the-table rental supplements). But examining leases is still one of the better methods of determining the annual rental value of land, which was precisely what the *vingtième* was meant to tax.

[66] The governor of Normandy, d'Harcourt, and the intendant of Caen, Fontette, were to serve as examples to other wealthy landowners by undergoing verifications themselves. Célestin Hippeau, ed., *Le gouvernement de Normandie au XVIIe et au XVIIIe siècle*, 9 vols. (Caen, 1863–70), v, pp. 83–4, letter from Terray to d'Harcourt, 20 June 1772; AD Calvados, C 5909, verification of a d'Harcourt estate, 21 February 1774; AD Calvados, C 5901, Fontette's petition of 11 January 1776.

his tax assessment up to 605 livres, or 8.8 percent of his rental income. In this case the verification succeeded in capturing a much greater proportion of the nobleman's income. Similarly, René Louis Fermond de Clermonde, a councilor in the parlement of Rouen, leased land he owned in the parish of Couvert in 1762 for 1,900 livres a year. Although his suspected income from this property was only 1,200 livres between 1751 to 1772, it jumped to 1,800 livres after two verifications in 1773 and 1774. Of course, by 1774 Clermonde had probably raised his rent by as much as one-half, like so many landowners at the time, but it must have been clear to him and others that the chase was on. In the 1770s, as leases turned over, landowners in Normandy and elsewhere jacked up their rents in order to profit from the rise in prices that had begun in the mid-1760s. The use of verifications after 1771 and the tripling of the tax in the 1780s made sure that the crown captured a portion of land-owners' rising incomes.[67]

Thus, if the *vingtième* did make important inroads into the income of the privileged, it did so in large part because of the effectiveness of verifications, in particular the verifications practiced during Necker's tenure as finance minister. There are plenty of examples of effective verifications under Terray and Turgot, but it was Necker who raised the practice of verification to the level of an administrative science, and the results were impressive. After Necker redesigned the pro-cedures of verification in 1777, large landowners such as Alexandre Augustin de Saffray hid precious little from the controllers who visited their parishes. Saffray was a moderately wealthy noble who owned a large seigneurial estate in Engranville, a parish selected for verification by the assiduous controller of the *élection* of Bayeux, Le Blanc. In the summer of 1780 the controller toured the parish with the collectors of the *taille* and the *vingtième* and four "notable land-owners," who had been chosen by the village assembly under Le Blanc's orders. Together they surveyed the property of each of the parish's forty-nine landowners, evaluating the extent of the land, its type (arable, pasture, or meadow), and its quality (good, mediocre,

---

[67] The steep rise in Norman rents is documented in El Kordi, *Bayeux*, pp. 358–9; Lemarchand, *Fin de féodalisme*, p. 292; Perrot, *Genèse*, II, pp. 795–7; and Jean-Pierre Chaline, "Les biens des hospices de Rouen: recherches sur les fermages normands du xviiie siècle au xxe siècle," *RHES* (1968), pp. 194–6. For the rise in rents on a national scale, see David Weir, "Les crises économiques et les origines de la révolution française," *Annales* 46 (1991), pp. 927–9.

or bad), before asking each landowner to sign a new declaration of property.

Then, without consulting the notables, Le Blanc calculated the monetary value of such holdings based on information from sixteen "non-suspect" leases he had obtained from various tenants in the parish. Using the leases to draw a tariff of annual rental values per acre for nine possible types of land – arable, pasture, and meadow of good, mediocre, and bad quality – he applied the tariff to the signed evaluations he had procured in consultation with the notables. All this activity did not bode well for Saffray, who, like many seigneurs, owned most of the land in his parish. When the tax roll was finally complete, its first four pages were devoted exclusively to Saffray's assessment, which was divided into seventeen parts: three rented farms, eleven tracts of land (eight of which were rented), a château, a garden, and seigneurial dues. To determine the annual net revenue of Saffray's rental properties, the controller consulted tenants' leases, carefully checking each lease against his own estimations; for non-rental property, he simply applied his tariff to the size, type, and quality of land and calculated its rental value. The new estimate of Saffray's net revenue mounted to 9,595 livres, an increase of 2,395 livres (or 33 percent) on his previous estimate. This reassessment raised his tax for 1781 from 792 livres to 1,055 livres, and would push it up to 1,535 livres from 1783 to 1786 when a third *vingtième* was imposed.

Given the thoroughness of the verification, it is likely that these sums were not too far below the targeted 11 percent and 16 percent of his landed revenue.[68] If Saffray was distressed by his new assessment, at least he could find plenty of fellow seigneurs with whom to commiserate. Since more than one-fifth of the *pays d'élections* was verified in this way, and since controllers were concentrating their efforts on larger landowners, most nobles probably knew a friend or neighbor who had undergone a verification, if they had not experienced one themselves.

Evidence from Caen, Bourges, and Limoges suggests, then, that the *vingtième*, much more than the *capitation*, succeeded in striking the wealth of privileged landowners. If the *capitation* drew only one

---

[68] Saffray may have been hiding other, more liquid forms of property such as private or state bonds, but noble landowners in this area received the great majority of their income from the land, farmhouses, mills, and presses they rented or managed themselves. El Kordi, *Bayeux*, p. 255.

percent, more or less, of income, the *vingtième*, when doubled and tripled in the second half of the eighteenth century, struck landed income at rates as high as 7 percent to 10 percent, or possibly more in the case of landowners whose estates had been verified from 1771 to 1782 by particularly enthusiastic controllers and who then paid a triple *vingtième* in the 1780s. For the period, such rates of taxation constituted a major inroad into the income of the privileged. At the same time, however, over half the *vingtième* fell on the nonprivileged who were already paying the *taille*, which brings us back to the conclusion that, although universal taxes struck the privileged of the *pays d'élections* with some force, especially late in the century, they also added great weight to the tax load shouldered by commoners, especially wealthier land-holding commoners, the *laboureurs*, who had long paid the bulk of direct taxation.[69] Eighteenth-century direct taxation may have expanded to include the privileged, but in no way did it relieve nonprivileged members of the third estate of their burden.

UNIVERSAL TAXATION IN THE *PAYS D'ÉTATS*

Outside the *pays d'élections* the system of direct taxation was far less uniform. In the *pays d'états*, provinces possessed governing institutions – provincial estates – which claimed immunity from royal taxes and exercised the privilege of levying taxes of their own. Over the course of the seventeenth century, the estates that managed to escape suppression by the Bourbons, including those of Languedoc, Brittany, Burgundy, and Provence, began to make financial contributions to the monarchy in the form of *dons gratuits*, or "voluntary gifts." The use of the word "gift" was deliberate. Offering "gifts" in the place of taxes signified that the provinces' claims to tax exemption were still valid and that their jealously guarded provincial liberties remained uncompromised even as they advanced money to the royal treasury.

---

[69] James Collins has shown that in the early seventeenth century the top quartile of the tax rolls bore most (two-thirds to four-fifths) of the direct tax burden and the top two quartiles paid almost all of the tax. Collins, *Fiscal Limits*, pp. 173–7. This trend seems to have continued in the eighteenth century. A published budget of a well-off land-owning commoner in the generality of Paris reveals that in 1787–8 he paid 61 percent of his gross revenue in direct taxes: the *taille* and *corvée* tax took 37 percent, the *capitation* 14 percent, and the *vingtième* 10 percent. *Tableau des impositions que supporte une propriété de 6,122 livres dans la province de l'Isle de France* (n.p., n.d.).

Long after negotiations over the size and payment of *dons gratuits* became routine, the fiction of the gift lived on.

When the *capitation* and the *dixième* were introduced, however, a second kind of fiscal arrangement evolved, known as the *abonnement*, in which the pretenses of gift-giving were stripped away. Paying taxes in the form of *abonnements*, lump sums of money raised by estates and remitted to the crown in lieu of royal taxes, was still a privilege – the provinces of the *pays d'élections*, lacking estates, could not pay this way – but it was a privilege that, symbolically at least, brought the *pays d'états* one step closer to outright royal taxation. The term *abonnement* in no way alluded to the idea of a gift.

Compared with the methods of taxation in the *pays d'élections*, *abonnements* had certain advantages for both the provinces and the crown. Even though provincial estates could not claim that in paying an *abonnement* they were bestowing a gift, they at least retained the right to negotiate the terms of the *abonnement* with the royal council and, more importantly, to raise the money needed to fulfill the king's demands. Estates themselves levied the taxes and floated the loans that covered the costs of *abonnements*, keeping royal tax officials outside provincial borders and leaving the institutional power of estates intact. There were advantages for the crown too, advantages that Marion, who saw in *abonnements* the utter capitulation of the crown to provincial power, failed to emphasize.[70] For the crown, *abonnements* guaranteed a payment of a fixed sum of money by a certain date, all at no administrative cost. Lebret, the intendant of Brittany, may have been exaggerating when he said that *abonnements* drew more money from the province than full royal taxation would have, but they did represent a valuable resource for a monarchy that was consistently short of revenue.[71]

On occasion the crown grew frustrated with this arrangement and refused to accept *abonnements*, believing that it could raise more money if it ignored provincial privileges and levied taxes directly on the *pays d'états*. From 1715 to 1734, for example, provincial intendants levied the *capitation* in Brittany, and in 1750 Machault d'Arnouville, the controller-general who played the hero for Marion, announced that the *pays d'états* would not be granted the right to pay the *vingtième* by way of *abonnement*. How many contemporary observers there must

---

[70] Marion, *Histoire financière*, I, p. 37.
[71] AN, H-1 347, doss. 1, no. 11, letter to Bertin, 16 April 1760.

have been like the lawyer Edmond Barbier who at first interpreted Machault's gesture as only a threat "to intimidate" provincial estates and thereby "draw more considerable *abonnements*."[72] But Machault was serious, it turned out, and from 1750 to 1755 the *vingtième* was imposed in the *pays d'états* by royal officials who composed new tax rolls and oversaw collection. In this brief period of half a decade the tax privileges of the *pays d'états* were revoked, forcing independent provinces such as Languedoc and Brittany to function more like those of the *pays d'élections*. By 1756, however, after Machault had fallen from power and France had drifted back to war, *abonnements* for the first and newly added second *vingtième* were renewed and hawked to provincial estates willing to pay hard cash for tax bargains. Machault's short experiment with the abolition of *abonnements* was to be the last and only credible threat to this method of paying universal taxes.

Figures 2.8 and 2.9 show the weight of taxation in Brittany[73] and Languedoc,[74] the two largest and most powerful provinces of the *pays d'états*. Behind the steady progression of taxation in both provinces lay the addition of the *capitation* at the end of the seventeenth century, its increase at the beginning of the eighteenth century, the creation of the *dixième*, and finally the doubling and tripling of the *vingtième*. In both regions taxation peaked when the *vingtième* was tripled, during the Seven Years War (1760–3) and after the American war (1783–6). Less obvious is the increase (or lack of decline) from 1750 to 1755 when the *dixième* was ostensibly cut in half by the introduction of a single *vingtième*, whereas in fact the *vingtième* generated far more than half the *dixième*, thanks to Machault's effort to revise assessments. Compare the revenue of the *dixième* of 1747 in Brittany or of 1734 in Languedoc with that of the two *vingtièmes* of 1757 in Brittany or of 1768 in Languedoc; the two *vingtièmes* tower above the single *dixième*. The other half-hidden jump occurred in

---

[72] Edmond Barbier, *Chronique de la régence et du règne de Louis XV, 1718–1763*, 8 vols. (Paris, 1857–8), IV, p. 415.

[73] Data for Brittany were compiled from: AN, AD IX 491, no. 119; AN, H-1 345–347; AN, H-1 527; AN, H-1 550–551; BN, JdF 1448, fos. 34–37; [Brienne], *Compte rendu*; L. Guihenneuc, *Etude sur la capitation proprement dite dans la province de Bretagne de 1695 à 1788* (Rennes, 1905), pp. 34–6; and Henri Fréville, *L'intendance de Bretagne (1689–1790)*, 3 vols. (Rennes, 1953). The voluntary gift in this figure represents its annual worth, that is half the gift given every two years.

[74] Data for Languedoc were compiled from: AN, AD IX 400, no. 192, and 491, no. 107; AN, H-1 748/284, 870–871, 898, 1093, no. 138; BN, JdF 1448, fos. 34–37; and Marcel Marion, *Dictionnaire des institutions de la France* (1923; reprint, Paris, 1989), p. 324.

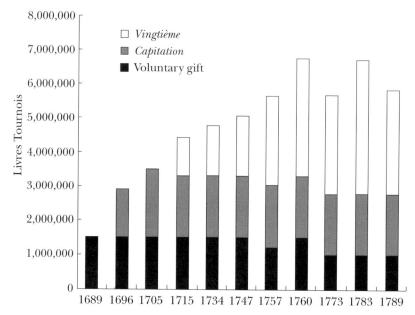

Figure 2.8   Taxes on Brittany

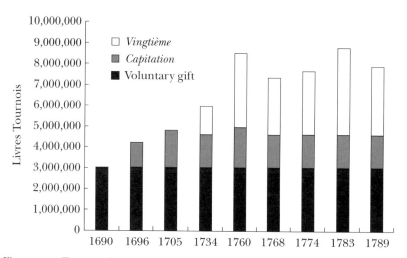

Figure 2.9   Taxes on Languedoc

1772 as Terray squeezed a one-ninth increase in the *vingtième abonnement* from both provinces under the threat of extending the verification campaign under way in the *pays d'élections* to the *pays d'états*. This small jump is visible in figure 2.9 when one compares the data for 1768 with those for 1774.

If we back away from short-term swings and take a long-term view, it becomes clear that over the century the provinces could claim that less and less of their contribution to the crown was a gift. This was especially true for Brittany, where the voluntary gift came to represent only a fraction of the province's total tax payment. The estates of Brittany and Languedoc managed to maintain much provincial autonomy by paying *abonnements* instead of unconditional royal taxes but, as the figures demonstrate, they did so at higher and higher prices. By 1789, for the voluntary gift, *capitation*, and *vingtième*, Languedoc was paying around 8,000,000 livres a year, Brittany around 6,000,000. Although the provinces of the *pays d'états* paid lighter royal taxes than those of the *pays d'élections*, almost everyone except the most ardent reformers expected them to. What is significant is that the fiscal load grew with universal taxes, permitting the crown at least to keep even with or at times surpass the rise in inflation.[75]

Figures 2.8 and 2.9, admittedly, do not reflect the true tax burden. Usually the crown allowed estates to hold in reserve a portion of the *abonnement* provided that it was used for reducing the debts of the provinces. That is, the crown let estates use money they had raised for royal taxes to manage their own provincial debts. Kings deliberately let this tax revenue slip from their hands because they borrowed from estates at relatively low rates of interest and wanted to make sure that the financial standing of estates would allow these bodies to continue to borrow from provincial creditors and to lend to the crown. Since estates loaned kings much of the money that estates themselves borrowed, it was as important for the crown to have estates service their debt as it was to tax them. Some examples will illustrate the utility of this technique. In 1767 Louis XV agreed to let half of Languedoc's *capitation* of 2,000,000 livres be used to

---

[75] Other *pays d'états* fit the same pattern. See AN, H-1 29 (Artois); AN, H-1 1231 (Provence); and AN, H-1 141 (Burgundy).

amortize a debt that the estates had incurred earlier in order to raise money for a 10,000,000 livre loan to the king. The finance minister, l'Averdy, believed it was wiser to permit some tax revenue to stay in the province than to force the province further into debt. This way he could continue to borrow in the future. Sometimes, in a kind of circular logic common in royal finance, the crown agreed to let part of *abonnements* be used to pay off debts that the estates had accrued earlier to pay previous *abonnements*. In 1789, for example, half of Languedoc's *abonnement* of 1,600,000 livres for the *capitation* was set aside to reimburse creditors who had loaned money to the estates for the purpose of paying previous *abonnements*.[76]

Finances in Brittany followed a similar pattern. Brittany's *capitation* of 1748, for example, was 1,800,000 livres; but 300,000 livres of it was designated for the payment of interest on a 4,000,000 livre loan taken out by the estates. The estates had previously borrowed the 4,000,000 livres to lend to Louis XV to dissuade him from imposing a ten-year, 20 percent increase in the *capitation*.[77] In this case the crown was letting the province buy off a long-term tax increase in return for an immediate loan. Recognizing that the resulting provincial debt had to be serviced, Louis XV allowed the estates to keep some of the 1748 *abonnement*. Thus, *abonnements* were designed not only to tax the provinces, but to make sure that estates remained solvent and able to borrow and lend in the future.

No matter what proportion of *abonnements* went directly to the royal treasury or was siphoned off to provincial creditors, estates had to raise money to pay for them and did so by levying taxes on the residents of their province. Given their personal status and place of residence, elites of the *pays d'états* were in a sense doubly privileged and it is interesting to see if they experienced universal taxes in a similar fashion to their counterparts in the *pays d'élections*. The tax rolls of the *capitation* in Brittany suggest that privileged individuals were touched by the tax, but only very lightly. The rolls for the nobility fluctuated between 100,000 and 125,000 livres, making its share of the tax in 1745 a mere 6.6 percent, or 10.5 percent if the payments of members of the parlement and *chambre des comptes* are added. The small proportion of the Breton *capitation*

---

[76] AN, E 2345, *arrêt du conseil* of 7 June 1767; AN, H-1 748/284, records of the estates of Languedoc.

[77] AN, H-1 551, no. 17, records of the estates of Brittany.

paid by nobles of the province was reflected in their light individual assessments. In 1710 no less than 38 percent of the nobility were assessed below 10 livres; 30 percent were assessed from 11 to 50 livres; 22 percent from 51 to 100 livres; and the top 9 percent at above 100 livres. The average assessment in 1750 was 36 livres, a modest sum that became smaller still after significant reductions were granted.[78] The *vingtième* in Brittany, by contrast, struck the nobility much harder. In the early 1750s the nobility paid 32 percent of the total *vingtième*, a proportion that, according to Jean Meyer, accurately reflected the amount of land it owned in the province. And during this period, when the average noble payment was around 160 livres, assessments seem to have risen for the wealthiest nobles, at least in the diocese of Saint-Malo. T. J. A. Le Goff's study of Vannes provides a sense of the range in payments. Of the twenty-nine nobles in the parish of Sarzeau all but one were assessed above 100 livres for the single *vingtième* of 1754. Eight were assessed between 500 and 999 livres, seven between 1,000 and 4,999 livres, and three at over 5,000 livres. Assessments for the third estate, in contrast, clustered between 10 and 100 livres. Lest one object that nobles escaped their assessments by using their influence to obtain reductions, Meyer points out that moderations in the *vingtième* came to less than 1 percent of the total tax.[79]

Like their peers in Brittany, nobles in Languedoc did not evade the *vingtième*. In 1783 when the *vingtième* was tripled, for example, nobles were assessed at 606,448 livres, or 14.5 percent of the tax. If, for the same year, we combine all the categories except commoners, this group accounted for slightly over 40 percent of the total of the tax rolls. Figure 2.10 displays these proportions.[80] I have found no evidence for the total amount of *capitation* paid by the nobility of Languedoc, but Robert Forster provides some excellent examples of how the *capitation* and the *vingtième* fell on the income of noble landowners outside Toulouse. In 1750 the marquis d'Escoulaubre owned and administered seven farms, which produced a revenue of 6,720 livres. Since a small part of his estate spread onto "common" land (in Languedoc around 90 percent of land was common and subject to the *taille* even if owned by nobles), the marquis paid a

---

[78] Meyer, "La noblesse pauvre," p. 186; Meyer, *Noblesse bretonne*, I, pp. 8–24; and Guihenneuc, *Etude sur la capitation*, pp. 36 and 163–4.
[79] Meyer, *Noblesse bretonne*, II, pp. 640–50; Le Goff, *Vannes and Its Region*, p. 183.
[80] AN, H-1 748/272.

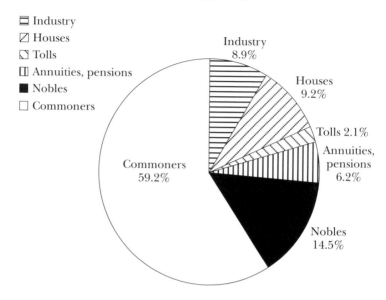

⊟ Industry
☒ Houses
▧ Tolls
⊞ Annuities, pensions
■ Nobles
☐ Commoners

Industry
8.9%

Houses
9.2%

Tolls 2.1%

Annuities,
pensions
6.2%

Commoners
59.2%

Nobles
14.5%

Figure 2.10   The rolls of the *vingtième* in Languedoc in 1783

taille of 240 livres in addition to a *capitation* of 136 livres and a
vingtième of 209 livres, making his total tax 585 livres, or 8.7 percent
of his revenue.[81] The marquis' tax burden, moreover, was relatively
light compared with that of other prominent noble landowners.
The average tax payment from a sample of twenty large estates was
around 15 percent of estate revenue, a considerable proportion
indeed. Forster also furnishes evidence on the incidence of noble
taxation in Burgundy, another important province in the *pays d'états*.
On one very large estate the duc de Saulx-Tavanes paid, for the
triple *vingtième* of 1786, 8.6 percent of his gross revenue or, if we
subtract wages and repairs, 10.1 percent of his net revenue; in 1788
when only two *vingtièmes* were in place, the duke paid taxes on the
order of 6 percent of his total revenue. These figures fall well below

---

[81] Robert Forster, *The Nobility of Toulouse in the Eighteenth Century: A Social and Economic Study*
(Baltimore, MD, 1960), pp. 33–4 and 185–8. To his credit, Forster is one of the few social
historians who estimates landed revenue according to family records, a more accurate
source than tax rolls. Comparing declarations of revenue submitted by two payers of the
vingtième with revenue they recorded in their private accounts, Forster found that one
undervalued his estate by one-third and the other by a little more than two-thirds.

the nominal rates of 11 percent and 16 percent for the two and three *vingtièmes* and their supplement, but they do suggest that in the *pays d'états* taxes were, by early modern standards, making important inroads into the income of the privileged.[82]

The impact of universal taxes on the *pays d'états* was significant. Not only did they increase the total tax burden of Languedoc, Brittany, and other provinces, they raised taxes on the privileged residing in those provinces. (In this respect the *vingtième* proved far more effective than the *capitation*). But again it must be observed that commoners as a group still paid more taxes and no doubt higher tax rates than the privileged. Commoners in Languedoc and Brittany supported, respectively, 60 percent and 68 percent of the *vingtième*, and a much higher share of the *capitation*. The pattern is unmistakable: as in the *pays d'élections*, universal taxes did reach the privileged but only added to the fiscal pressure on commoners.

UNIVERSAL TAXES ON TARGETED PRIVILEGED GROUPS

Besides spreading the tax burden across the vast territory of the *pays d'états* and *pays d'élections*, the monarchy singled out four particular privileged groups: royal courtiers; residents of the city of Paris; officers in the army, navy, and magistrature; and the clergy. Let us start with the center of privilege under the Old Regime, the royal court.

The very purpose of the court was to maintain the fidelity of the kingdom's most powerful subjects by giving them prestigious positions in the Royal Household, luxurious pensions, and access to the drama of royal ceremony. Before 1695 the courtiers who basked in the privileges of Versailles never suffered the embarrassment of being approached by a tax collector. But with the introduction of the *capitation*, Louis XIV began taking money away from those to whom he was distributing it. Sensing the difficulty of such an enterprise, the royal council charged itself with the task of taxing the court and proceeded with mixed results. Although the *capitation* on the court proved difficult to collect, courtiers paid over 700,000 livres a year for the first three years of the tax, a sum greater than that levied on

---

[82] Robert Forster, *The House of Saulx-Tavanes: Versailles and Burgundy 1700–1830* (Baltimore, MD, 1971), pp. 90–1 and 140–1 (my calculations assume that "taxes" in table II.5 refers to the *vingtième* as is implied on p. 90).

entire generalities. In 1703 the court paid just over 1,000,000 livres, and in 1762, when the rolls were doubled, the figure reached 1,339,702 livres. Later the total tapered off to about 800,000 a year in the 1770s, and 700,000 in 1789.[83]

On top of the *capitation* courtiers had to pay the *dixième*, a 10 percent withholding tax on their pensions. In 1770 Terray restructured the *dixième* on pensions by instituting higher tax brackets for those with larger pensions. Whereas the lowest pensions still underwent a reduction of 10 percent, pensions above 2,400 livres, the highest bracket, had to pay three *dixièmes*, or 30 percent. In 1787 two more brackets were added, so that the highest tax rate, levied on pensions above 20,000 livres, reached 40 percent. Taxing pensions worked: in 1777 the *dixièmes* withheld 3,000,000 livres, and in 1788, with the new upper brackets installed, the royal treasury withheld 5,000,000 livres from a total of 27,000,000 livres in pensions.[84]

One might also include under the category of taxes on the royal court the *vingtième* that princes were forced to pay on their estates. Like provinces that were *pays d'états*, princes escaped rigorous modes of assessment by agreeing to pay *abonnements* instead. Of course the *abonnements* did not reflect the true value of their enormous tracts of land, but the tax was far from nominal and was paid without resistance. In 1788 the *abonnements* of princes added up to 188,700 livres, not an insignificant sum considering the fact that it was paid by only six individuals.[85]

Some examples will show what all these different sorts of taxes meant to individual courtiers and members of the royal family. The marquis de Briges, who served Louis XVI as first equerry of the royal household, paid a *capitation* of 2,700 livres, to which were added withholding taxes for the *dixième* in the amount of 6,300 livres (300 livres of which were withheld from 3,000 livres in *gages* from his office and 6,000 livres of which were cut from 20,000 livres in pensions). Not including the *vingtième* on his landed estates, then, he

[83] AN, G-7 1132–1133; AN, F-4 1077, 1078, 1079, and 1082; and AN, D VI 9, nos. 68 and 80. By withholding the *capitation* directly from financial gifts to courtiers, Turgot facilitated the collection of the tax. Schelle, *Turgot*, IV, p. 293.

[84] AN, F-4 1082, royal treasury account of 1777; [Brienne], *Compte rendu*.

[85] Although in 1710 the duc d'Orléans was assessed at 120,000 livres for the *dixième*, he never paid anything close to that. In 1788 the duke paid an *abonnement* of 44,000 livres. AN, G-7 1138–1139; [Brienne], *Compte rendu*.

paid 9,000 livres in taxes.[86] The prince of Condé paid much more. Of the 220,000 livres of pensions granted to him, 110,000 were subject to three *dixièmes* (the remainder was exempt as an expense of war), and he paid a *vingtième abonnement* of 40,000 livres on his estate, making his total tax contribution 77,000 livres.[87] As one of the richest men in the kingdom, 77,000 livres in taxes might not have disturbed Condé's personal finances, but it is interesting that even wealthy princes owed the king some portion of their revenue.

Office-holders throughout the kingdom were also vulnerable to withholding taxes. We have already seen how the *capitation* and the *vingtième* struck officers in Caen, but our discussion did not include magistrates of high-level courts whose withholding taxes do not always show up in tax rolls or receipts. These taxes do appear, however, in accounts known as *états des finances*, a type of civil list for venal office-holders that reveals how the crown was able to seize money from the privileged before it even reached their pockets. Every year tax receivers set aside part of the revenue from the *taille* to be distributed to officers who, having advanced capital to the king to purchase their offices, expected to receive *gages*. In the generality of Caen in 1789, for example, 246,659 livres of *taille* (around 7 percent of the total yield of the tax) was earmarked for officers. The movement of such a sum from commoners to officers demonstrates clearly how the crown was redistributing wealth up the social hierarchy. But before that money reached the officers, it was taxed, as receivers withheld 23,846 livres for the *dixième* and 31,111 livres for the *capitation*, leaving 191,702 livres (77.7 percent of the initial sum) for officers. Individual office-holders experienced this reduction directly. Jean François, a *trésorier de France* at the *bureau des finances* of Caen, saw his *gages* decline considerably from 2,348 livres to 1,898 livres, a reduction of almost one-fifth.[88]

This kind of taxation struck the highest courts in the kingdom, including the parlement of Rouen, Normandy's most important judicial body. The parlement of Rouen nominally received 204,361 livres in *gages* for the year 1786, but 40,570 livres (19.9 percent) were deducted for the *capitation* and 21,116 livres for the *dixième* (another

---

[86] AN, O-1 729 and 657, no. 423. The payment of the *dixième* as a withholding tax did not exempt one from the *vingtième* in one's place of residence. Alternatively, because the *capitation* was a head tax (and should therefore be paid only once), intendants deducted money withheld for the tax from residential assessments.

[87] AN, F-4 1945; [Brienne], *Compte rendu*.   [88] AN, P 5267, *états des finances* for Caen, 1782.

10.3 percent).[89] Louis François de Pontcarré, the first president of the court, witnessed the evaporation of his *gages* from 4,125 livres to 1,912 livres and 10 sols, after the crown withheld 412 livres and 10 sols for his *dixième* and 1,800 livres for his *capitation*. The *gages* of many lesser officers such as Jacques de la Cour, a *conseiller clerc*, were completely absorbed by withholding taxes, leaving them with no payment whatsoever. Taxes also whittled down the *gages* of the *secrétaires du roi* in the chancellery of the court, who had invested enormous sums in their offices; François Doré de Bariville's *gages* of 2,750 livres shrank to 2,290, reducing the interest he was earning on his investment from 5 percent to 4 percent.

Such reductions pressed upon magistrates across the kingdom from Bordeaux to Rennes to Paris.[90] In case after case, the monarchy used universal taxes to pare down its payment of *gages* and, in effect, cut the rate of interest at which it borrowed from officers. The marquis d'Argenson called this "tempered venality."[91]

For individuals who received salaries from the monarchy, the *capitation* and *dixième* in the form of withholding taxes simply reduced their income. Nearly everyone on the state payroll saw their allowances diminish: provincial intendants, financiers, employees in the indirect tax administration, engineers in the king's roads and bridges corps, even officers in the army and navy. The heads of the General Farms, who made great fortunes from collecting the crown's indirect taxes, paid almost 500,000 livres in their own taxes to the king.[92] And officers in the army and navy, for their part, paid from 1,000,000 to 1,500,000 livres a year through withholding taxes on their salaries in the last decades of the Old Regime. For a cavalry officer like the comte de Tocqueville, this meant that his pay for the year of 1774, originally 590 livres, would be reduced by 10 percent for the *dixième*, and by 48 livres for the *capitation*.[93]

---

[89] AN, P 5764, *états des finances* for Rouen, 1786.

[90] Doyle, *Parlement of Bordeaux*, pp. 40–1; Meyer, *Noblesse bretonne*, II, pp. 950–1; François Bluche, *Les magistrats du parlement de Paris au XVIIIe siècle* (2nd edn., Paris, 1986), p. 125.

[91] René-Louis d'Argenson, *Considérations sur le gouvernement ancien et présent de la France* (Amsterdam, 1764), p. 195. The monarchy implicitly equated withholding taxes with a cut in interest rates when it exempted from the *dixième* certain *gages* that had already been slashed by decree. For further discussion of the practice of withholding taxes from *gages*, see David Bien, "Offices, Corps, and a System of State Credit: The Uses of Privilege under the Ancien Régime," in *Political Culture*, ed. Keith Baker (Oxford, 1987), pp. 108–9; Doyle, *Venality*, pp. 198–201; and McCollim, "Fiscal Policy," p. 324.

[92] Schelle, *Turgot*, IV, p. 310.

[93] AN, F-4 1077, treasury account for 1762; Charles-Joseph Mathon de la Cour, *Collection de*

If by the eighteenth century the monarchy had built a welfare state for the privileged, the *capitation* and the *dixième*, functioning as withholding taxes, worked to trim the extraordinary sums of money it was doling out. Although the crown continued to redistribute money to pensioners, officers, financiers, and administrators, it also began to tax these expenditures as a matter of administrative routine. The monarchy was giving conspicuously with one hand while taking discreetly with the other.

In levying universal taxes the crown also targeted the city of Paris, treading on a privilege originating in 1449, when Paris was granted exemption from the *taille*. Although the city occasionally advanced "gifts" to the crown and paid infamously high rates of indirect taxation, Paris, an island of privilege surrounded by the kingdom's most heavily taxed countryside, did not experience permanent direct royal taxation until the introduction of universal taxes.[94] Changing the geography of privilege by turning Parisians into direct taxpayers, the *capitation* on Paris yielded 1,536,090 livres in 1701 and climbed by the end of the eighteenth century to upwards of 2,000,000 livres a year, a sum tantamount to the contributions of two generalities or a whole province.[95]

As figure 2.11 illustrates, six different groups and institutions paid the tax.[96] Assessed according to the rental values of homes and apartments, the Parisian bourgeoisie, composed of the city's well-established heads of household, furnished the bulk of the tax revenue. Then came the guilds, whose members paid almost a quarter of the tax, followed by royal financiers, officers of the lower-level courts, administrators who worked in the indirect tax bureaucracy, and the University of Paris.

Parisians paid the *vingtième* as well, which ultimately exceeded the *capitation* in the final decades of the Old Regime. Royal budgets in the 1770s put the capital's *vingtième* at 2,500,000 to 3,000,000 livres; in 1789 the rolls of the *vingtième* mounted to 3,805,950 livres and by 10

---

comptes rendus, pièces authentiques, états et tableaux concernant les finances de France (Lausanne, 1788), budget of 1775; AD Calvados, C 4695, no. 58, petition from Tocqueville, 21 November 1774.

[94] Robert Descimon, "Paris on the Eve of Saint Bartholomew: Taxation, Privilege, and Social Geography," in *Cities and Social Change in Early Modern France*, ed. Philip Benedict (London, 1989), pp. 69–80.

[95] AN, G-7 1134, *capitation* accounts for the city of Paris, 1701; AN, F-4 1078, royal treasury receipts of 1772. In November 1790 the committee of finance reported that the city had paid 1,704,476 livres by the tenth of that month out of a total imposition of 2,897,780 livres for the year 1789. AN, D VI 9.

[96] AN, G-7 1134.

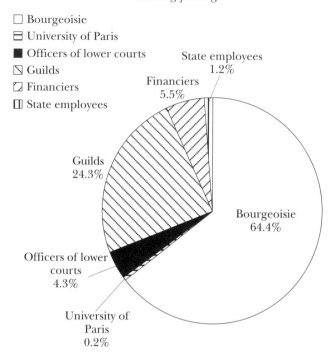

□ Bourgeoisie
目 University of Paris
■ Officers of lower courts
◩ Guilds
▨ Financiers
⊞ State employees

State employees
1.2%

Financiers
5.5%

Guilds
24.3%

Bourgeoisie
64.4%

Officers of lower
courts
4.3%

University of
Paris
0.2%

Figure 2.11   The *capitation* paid by the city of Paris in 1701

November 1790 nearly 70 percent of the tax had been collected.[97] Despite confusion in the administration of both taxes, the *capitation* and the *vingtième*, totaling roughly 4,500,000 livres at the end of the century, eroded the capital's precious direct tax privileges and augmented a fiscal burden already weighed down with indirect taxes.[98]

Of all the privileged groups targeted for taxation by the crown the clergy was the wealthiest, owning nearly 10 percent of the kingdom's land but comprising less than 1 percent of the population, and was by far the best organized, holding general assemblies convoked by the king at least every five years. Did universal taxes touch the clergy

[97] AN, F-4 1079 and 1082, royal treasury receipts of 1773 and 1774. Figures for 1789 are located in AN, D VI 9, report by the committee of finance, 10 November 1790.
[98] The peculiar administration of the two taxes in Paris merits a comment. The *prévôt des marchands* administered the *capitation* on the bourgeoisie and the *vingtième* on property, offices and fees, and the labor of men and women outside the guilds. The *lieutenant général* of police administered the *capitation* and *vingtième* on the guilds, assigning each institution a collective sum and allowing guild leaders to distribute and collect the tax on fellow members.

too? First, we must distinguish between the "clergy of France" and the "clergy of the frontiers," each of which experienced taxation differently. Unlike the clergy of France, the clergy of the frontiers, consisting of several dioceses added to the kingdom since 1561, had no central representative body through which it could address the king.[99] Thus, when the *capitation* was established, each diocese offered a separate *abonnement* in order to avoid being assessed by royal administrators. In 1697 these sums amounted to 333,000 livres and never climbed much higher than that. The *abonnements* for the *vingtième* on the clergy of the frontiers, however, rose from a mere 25,300 livres in 1710 to 635,000 livres in 1774. Whatever claims could be made regarding its exemption from the *taille*, the clergy of the frontier could not escape the new taxation of the eighteenth century, especially the *vingtième*.[100]

The question of taxation and the clergy of France is more complicated. From the sixteenth to the eighteenth century there were three layers to the clergy's financial obligations to the crown.[101] The earliest layer, formed in the sixteenth century, was the annual grant of revenue that was drawn from the *décimes*, a tax levied by the church on benefices. This grant was given to the crown to service *rentes* (bonds) issued by the city of Paris in return for assurances that the monarchy would step up its struggle against heretics. A second layer was added in the early seventeenth century during the Thirty Years War when the clergy began to provide *dons gratuits*, voluntary gifts that were much larger than the earlier grants. The remittance of voluntary gifts, which lightened after the war, became a matter of financial routine during the first half of Louis XIV's personal rule.

---

[99] Dioceses belonging to the clergy of the frontiers included Arras, Cambrai, Tournay, Ypres, St. Omer, Metz, Toul, Verdun, Besançon, Boulogne, Strasbourg, Basle, Spire, Constance, and Roussillon. In the figures that follow I include the order of Malte in this category.

[100] AN, G-7 1132–1133, and 1138–1139; Mathon de la Cour, *Comptes rendus*, budget of 1774. In times of war, clergymen along the border were more than willing to pay taxes in return for protection. Caught in the crossfire of the War of the Spanish Succession, the archbishop of Cambrai asked the finance minister to pressure clergymen to pay their *capitation* and to use the revenue to prevent the enemy from burning down the countryside. Boislisle, *Correspondance*, II, no. 1162, letter of 20 December 1706.

[101] The following discussion is based on Claude Michaud, "La participation du clergé de France aux dépenses de la monarchie à la fin de l'ancien régime," in *Etat, Finances, et Economie pendant la Revolution Française* (Paris, 1991), pp. 3–10; Robin Briggs, *Communities of Belief: Cultural and Social Tension in Early Modern France* (Oxford, 1989), ch. 5; and Norman Ravitch, *Sword and Mitre: Government and Episcopate in France and England in the Age of Aristocracy* (The Hague, 1966), ch. 5.

With the advent of the *capitation* and the threat of universal taxation a third layer of fiscal obligation appeared. Louis XIV never intended to make clergymen pay the new head tax but he did use its creation to squeeze additional aid from them. In the first circular on the *capitation* sent to the intendants, the finance minister explained: "Although his Majesty excepts ecclesiastics from the *capitation*, please include them in the census that you will make so that his Majesty can better know the extent of the grace that he is bestowing upon them."[102] The price of that "grace" came to 4,000,000 livres a year, which, in addition to its voluntary gifts, the clergy paid from 1696 to 1698 and again from 1701 to 1710 as an "extraordinary aid in place of the *capitation*."[103] The clergy's annual contribution of 4,000,000 was far from negligible, as it represented nearly one-fifth of the global weight of the tax. In 1710, however, after Louis XIV began selling exemptions from the *capitation* for six times its annual assessment, the clergy laid down the enormous sum of 24,000,000 livres and purchased complete exemption from the tax. After that payment the clergy never made any contributions to the crown that were linked explicitly to the *capitation*.

Likewise, the clergy of France never paid any sums of money that were linked in name to the *dixième/vingtième*, but the clergy's gifts were implicitly tied to the tax. Immediately after creating the *dixième*, Louis XIV entered into negotiations with the clergy and the two parties settled on the contract of 13 July 1711 which stated that, despite the "general" nature of the *dixième*, "His Majesty, attentive to the privileges of the clergy, has not included it in the declaration which orders its levy." In return for such attentiveness to privilege, the contract stipulated that the clergy would present the crown with a voluntary gift of 8,000,000 livres to be paid over a few years.[104]

Compared with paying the taxes in full, the purchase of exemption from the *capitation* and the *dixième*, totaling 32,000,000 livres, turned out to be a bargain over the long run. But the figure of 32,000,000 does not account for increases in voluntary gifts that were later extorted from the clergy after monarchs repeated the threat to revoke the orders' tax-exempt status. Although the value of such increases is impossible to determine, we can see qualitatively

[102] BN, Ms. Fr. 8852, fo. 84, letter of 31 October 1694.
[103] AN, Z-1P 10, the tax roll for the diocese of Paris.
[104] AN, AD IX 400, Contrat entre le Roy et le Clergé, 13 July 1711.

how this fiscal technique was used by looking at the register of the
royal council for 1715, the year the crown revoked a number of
exemptions from the *capitation* it had sold in 1709 to various
provinces, office-holders, and other willing individuals.[105] In 1715
the clergy was told that its exemption, too, was going to be
abolished. Since other groups who had bought exemption were
being taxed anew, the register of the council explained, "it seems
likewise appropriate to re-impose the *capitation* on the clergy who
purchased exemption from it at the same time as the others." This
statement seems straightforward enough – the council was seeking
to tax the clergy again – but, as the heading in the register reveals,
the statement was written with another purpose in mind, that of
"sounding out the clergy on a new voluntary gift." A month after
the council leveled the threat of taxation, the clergy responded by
insisting, on the one hand, that its members "cannot be included in
the rolls of the *capitation*," and offering, with the other, a new much
larger gift of 12,000,000 livres, which the council graciously
accepted "as in the past."[106] The threat of imposing the *dixième/
vingtième* was also repeated at mid-century by Machault and again
in 1788, when the exemption from the tax was in fact revoked and
the clergy all but withdrew its gift. As soon as Louis XVI issued
decisive orders to subject the land owned by the clergy to a direct
tax replacing the *vingtième*, carrying out what had always remained
just a threat, the clergy snubbed the king by offering him the most
meager gift of the century, 1,800,000 livres, a mere fraction of its
usual payment. Why pay for an exemption that would no longer be
honored?

Buoyed by the threat of direct taxation, the clergy's voluntary
gifts in the eighteenth century were not all that small. From 1660 to
1690 the quinquennial voluntary gift had ranged from 2,200,000 to
3,000,000, with the exception of 4,500,000 in 1675, and had
averaged annually from 440,000 livres to 600,000 livres.[107] From
1690 to 1785 the frequency of gifts increased, as did their size,
which now ranged from 4,000,000 to 18,000,000 livres, averaging
around 3,500,000 livres a year or, depending on which estimate of
the clergy's revenues one chooses, 2 percent to 5 percent of the

---

[105] In 1709, taxpayers were given the opportunity to purchase royal bonds, in the amount of
six times their annual *capitation*, in exchange for complete exemption from the tax. The
resulting sell-off of the *capitation* is depicted on the jacket cover of this book.
[106] AN, G-7 1849, first register, pp. 4 and 48.   [107] Briggs, *Communities of Belief*, p. 195.

church's income.[108] To finance its voluntary gifts, or, more precisely, the loans that were contracted to pay its gifts, the clergy (like provincial estates) levied an internal tax, the *décimes*, which fell on all members of the Gallican church who held a benefice, from wealthy bishops down to poor curés. After the reforms of 1755–60, the tax rate was strikingly progressive: the greatest *bénéficiers* were taxed at the rate of 25 percent and the smallest at 6 percent. The progressiveness of the tax received praise from such reformers as Necker and Brienne, but it is important to remember that that rate was applied to self-declared statements of income which, like those used for the *vingtième*, did not always reflect real income. According to Norman Ravitch, wealthier ecclesiastics holding the most lucrative positions were able to hide much of their income, whereas the well-known income of curés was less likely to be undervalued.[109] As a result, clerical taxation was not as progressive as it looked on paper. The most that can be said is that it became less regressive after mid-century.

Thus, despite the clergy's claim that it was merely offering gifts to the crown, clergymen both high and low did experience internal forms of taxation that loosely paralleled royal taxation. For the clergy the important distinction was that it administered its own taxes, though there is some evidence that this privilege was also beginning to be challenged at the local level, at least in the generality of Caen. From 1770 the intendants of Caen levied a special land tax to raise revenue for public works projects and for the reimbursement of landowners whose property had been appropriated by the monarchy in order to build roads. The tax produced 150,000 to 200,000 livres annually and officials of the church, as landowners, paid a good part of it. In Bayeux, where clergymen made up 8 percent of the city's property-owners, they paid 15 percent of the tax. Although the clergy, with no pretext of gift-giving, paid this tax every year after 1770, the intendant insisted that "the privileges of the clergy remained intact" because the tax was regional and was used to fund public works that actually boosted the value of the clergy's own land. This small land tax in Caen appears to be unique, but it suggests ways in which the justification of public utility could be used

---

[108] Marion, *Dictionnaire*, p. 105; Michaud, "Participation du clergé," p. 4; Ravitch, *Sword and Mitre*, p. 168.

[109] Ravitch, *Sword and Mitre*, pp. 175–91.

at the local level to undermine ecclesiastical privileges at the end of the Old Regime.[110]

By all accounts the century of Enlightenment did not experience the dramatic rise in taxation that the *Grand Siècle* had, but it did sustain and even slightly increase levels of real per capita taxation as inflation rose and the population grew. The monarchy was able to keep pace with inflation and population growth by increasing indirect taxes, squeezing more revenue from the royal domain late in the century, and creating new direct taxes. Although the full story of the royal domain remains to be told,[111] and whereas indirect taxes shot up but did not change form, direct taxes rose only moderately but were transformed to intervene in society in new ways. Levied in addition to the *taille*, whose per capita real weight leveled in the eighteenth century, the *capitation* and the *dixième/vingtième* widened the monarchy's fiscal reach to include formerly tax-exempt groups such as the nobility, officers of justice, royal officials and employees, and residents of privileged cities and provinces. Moreover, the tax burden and the administrative intrusion that accompanied it increased in the second half of the century in three waves: the first in the early 1760s during the Seven Years War when universal taxes were doubled and tripled; the second beginning in the 1770s when Terray initiated three reforms that would remain in place until the fall of the Old Regime, namely the reinstallment of the *capitation* tariff on officers, the restructuring of the *dixième* on pensions, and, above all, the verification of the *vingtième* on landowners; and the third in the 1780s when the *vingtième* was once again tripled and the *capitation* on the nobility increased. The impact of these increases was deepest in the *pays d'élections*, where nobles paid several hundred livres for the *vingtième* at rates that rose as high as 7–10 percent of their landed revenue. In the *pays d'états*, ending an era in which "gifts" alone were advanced to the crown, the *capitation* and the *vingtième* not only penetrated privileged provinces but struck privileged individuals who resided there.

Besides levying universal taxes in the provinces, the crown more

---

[110] AN, AD IX 390a, *Compte rendu*, part II, ch. 2; AN, H-1 1463, no. 69, letter from Fontette to Terray, 2 July 1772; AN, F-5 I 1, provincial finances; and El Kordi, *Bayeux*, pp. 44–5.
[111] The rise in revenue from the royal domain is indicated in Morineau, "Budgets de l'Etat," p. 314. Doyle describes the monarchy's campaign to reassert its domanial rights in *Parlement of Bordeaux*, ch. 16.

or less successfully targeted a number of traditionally privileged groups. Courtiers and office-holders confronted withholding taxes that shrank the size of pensions and reduced the rate of interest earned on investments in office, while residents of Paris found that the monarchy was closing a critical gap in the geography of direct tax privileges. The attempt to tax the clergy was the least successful. Ostensibly, the clergy of France paid no royal taxes at all, but the possibility of extending the *capitation* and the *dixième/ vingtième* to the clergy pressured it to provide gifts that, if small relative to the income of the church, were not negligible given the passing of religious war. Besides the taxes they paid internally to fund these gifts, clergymen (in Caen at least) also contributed to local taxes.

With the introduction of universal taxes in the eighteenth century came the birth of a new type of royal subject: the individual privileged taxpayer who, at least partially exempt from the *taille*, nonetheless made significant tax contributions directly to the crown. To be sure, the advent of this oxymoronic creature heralded neither the coming of fiscal equality nor a resolution to the monarchy's fiscal crises: commoners continued to pay higher tax rates and to bear the lion's share of the direct tax burden amidst rising rents and declining real wages; and the royal finances continued to operate on the edge of bankruptcy as the tax revenue that flowed toward the throne was absorbed by the holders of royal debt and the expenses of war. But the fact that elites paid far and away more direct taxes than they ever had, and that such taxes made important inroads into their income and forced them into immediate contact with royal fiscal agents, does suggest that France was entering a new and final stage of absolutism, which disturbed the "symbiotic relationship" between privilege and the state that defined so much of the Old Regime.[112] Paradoxically, the same monarchy that continued throughout the eighteenth century to draw tax revenue from commoners and to redistribute it to privileged nobles, officers, and creditors also began to tax those same elites with greater and greater effectiveness.

This disturbance in the regime of privilege, however slight it may seem to modern eyes, was strong enough to have profound political consequences. In its ongoing search for tax revenue, the eighteenth-

---

[112] The phrase is from Bien, "System of State Credit," p. 92.

century monarchy was now confronting a kingdom of taxpayers, and the contestation that ensued produced ideas and rhetoric that helped to undermine the legitimacy of absolutism and, ultimately, of aristocracy.

PART TWO

The politics of taxation and the language of dispute

Petitioning for "justice": tax disputes in the administrative sphere

"Necessity is the cause of taxes. The king's justice presides over their distribution. None of his subjects will have recourse to it in vain."

– Joseph Marie Terray[1]

"The taxpayer is able to compare his tax to that of another taxpayer and, if he notices an unfair proportion . . . , or if the burden is not equal or justly distributed, he cries of injustice."

– Marie-François Lefevre d'Ormesson[2]

Universal taxes were not imposed without provoking dispute. Although eighteenth-century universal taxpayers were less likely than their seventeenth-century ancestors to join in popular revolt, they did vigorously contest their taxes and engage the crown in constant negotiation. At one level, powerful corporate bodies, such as the Assembly of the Clergy, provincial estates, and parlements, clashed with the crown on a well-lit and much-studied public stage. These dramatic spectacles of conflict drew commentary from *philosophes*, sparked controversy at court and throughout the provinces, and captured the attention of taxpayers everywhere. Below this public stage, however, was another level of dispute about which we know very little. In the murkier world of day-to-day administration all sorts of individuals and groups contested their taxes as a matter of simple routine. Although less spectacular than their public counterparts, contestations that took place within the confines of royal administration reveal much more about the ways in which ordinary subjects negotiated with the crown.

This chapter will eavesdrop on such negotiations, listening to the

[1] AN, H-1 1463, letter to Duchatel, first president of the *conseil supérieur* of Bayeux, 8 March 1772.
[2] AN, H-1 1463, no. 7, *mémoire* on taxation, 1772.

dialogue between, on the one hand, discontented taxpayers who were moved to draft petitions and, on the other, royal administrators (usually provincial intendants) who were placed in the difficult position of having to placate taxpayers without sacrificing too much of the crown's revenue. To get at the first side of this dialogue, we will explore the rhetorical strategies employed by the legions of privileged taxpayers who attempted to persuade royal administrators to bestow "justice" on them either by freeing them entirely from the *capitation* and *dixième/vingtième* or, at least, by significantly reducing their tax assessments. The petitions betray rich patterns of language in which various formulas were used, words emphasized, stories told, and emotions conveyed. The other side of the dialogue, responses to petitions, also followed a certain logic, as administrators sometimes reduced assessments but only rarely bestowed the full measure of justice that petitioners were seeking.

PETITIONS AND THE CLAMOR FOR JUSTICE

As described in chapter 1, the monarchy barred universal taxpayers from pursuing grievances in courts of law. *Taillables* who wanted to contest their *taille* and *capitation* assessments continued to do so in village assemblies and local courts, but privileged payers of the *capitation* and all payers of the *dixième/vingtième* were to contest their assessments through the administrative channels that the monarchy left open to them. Echoing national decrees, Vastan, intendant of Caen, issued an ordinance in 1735 reminding taxpayers that, "for those who can establish that they are taxed beyond a just proportion of their income ..., we have always left a way open to lodge appeals against our decisions."[3] That "way open" was through the petition (*requête*). A common mode of initiating legal action or of asking favors from those in positions of authority, the petition was already a familiar mode of recourse, and universal taxpayers made good use of it. Every year thousands of petitions streamed into administrative offices in all quarters of France: Parisians petitioned the *prévot des marchands* and the lieutenant of police; courtiers petitioned the finance minister; and provincial taxpayers petitioned estates and intendants. Everywhere the scale of petitioning was considerable, substantiating Christian Jouhaud's observation that, whereas revolts

---

[3] AD Calvados, C 4713, ordinance of 25 May 1735.

under the Old Regime were episodic, breaking out in specific times and places, "contestation, to the contrary, [was] everywhere."[4] Far below the parlements' famous remonstrances, taxpayers spoke to the crown (or at least its agents) in a purely administrative sphere.

Rarely more than a page or two hand-written by the taxpayer, petitions from residents of the generality of Caen to the intendant, and from courtiers to finance ministers, varied widely in the audacity of their claims. In general, petitioners did not challenge the crown's right to impose the *capitation* or the *dixième/vingtième*, although Pontchartrain had worried about that possibility before he established the *capitation*.[5] The historian searching petitions for bold assertions of rights and privileges, political tirades, and invectives against the king will be sorely disappointed. Until the creation of a provincial assembly in Caen in 1787 liberated their quills, petitioners only sporadically made rash statements, characterizing universal taxes as "arbitrary" or a source of "oppression."[6] In 1745, for example, a lawyer named Coudray, denouncing the municipal officers of the city of Vire for imposing a *capitation* that was "willfully unfair," bluntly told the intendant that the officers "should not pride themselves on such despotism."[7] And under the cover of anonymity one taxpayer dared send a letter to Desmaretz stating that the administration of the *dixième* reduced the French to "slavery": "we would be a thousand times happier in Turkey than in France."[8]

There were great risks in petitioning aggressively, however, since petitioners who expressed hostility violated the unspoken rules of deference on which the petitioning process was based. Offending the intendant only made matters worse, as the example of François de Launay makes abundantly clear. In his petition to the intendant of Caen, Launay, a bailiff in Bayeux, claimed that the subdelegate of Bayeux, Martel, over-taxed him deliberately. Martel, Launay explained, was his "principal enemy" who, from "vengeance," wanted to "crush [him] under the weight of his authority." Launay complained boldly that his own *capitation* had been raised to 75 livres, whereas Martel barely taxed other, more important individuals:

---

[4] Christian Jouhaud, "Révoltes et contestations d'Ancien Régime," in *Histoire de la France*, eds. André Burguière and Jacques Revel (Paris, 1990), p. 19.

[5] BN, Ms. Fr. 8852, fos. 83–4, letter from Pontchartrain to Lebret, 31 October 1694.

[6] AD Calvados, C 4695, no. 32, petition of l'Etourny, August 1736; and C 4686, no. 5, petition of Doûrie, 12 October 1734.

[7] AD Calvados, C 6517, petition of 8 September 1745.

[8] AN, G-7 1138, letter of 10 October 1712.

"considerably wealthy nobles who own carriages and the first officers of the city pay only ten or twenty livres at most."[9] Nor did the subdelegate himself pay his fair share, Launay asserted, claiming that out of 10,000 livres of income Martel paid only 30 livres of *capitation* and was therefore enjoying illegitimate privileges.[10] After all, everyone was supposed to pay his or her share of the tax; "even *monseigneur* the chancellor and all the ministers of state presently pay the *capitation* and the *dixième*." Having accused the subdelegate of malice and corruption, Launay ended his petition by requesting that his own tax be reduced.

Even more offensive than the tone of Launay's petition was the manner in which he submitted it to the intendant, Guynet. In a letter to the finance minister, Guynet described the petitioner's behavior in the following terms: "filled with venom against the subdelegate," Launay had "the insolence to bring me the petition in the *hôtel de ville* of Bayeux, where I was in a meeting concerning the city's affairs."

I told him to leave and that I was not there to examine his petition. He threw it rudely on my desk. While he was leaving, I told him that I would punish him for his insolence. Three hours later, he returned to resubmit his petition. His extremely arrogant attitude scandalized everyone. As I knew him to be impudent and argumentative, I told him that since I was leaving to see you, I would have the honor of giving you an account of his conduct and that his petition would be decided on the basis of that account. With the same insolence, he answered that he would see you before I would.[11]

To prove that Launay's insolence was dangerous, Guynet intercepted private letters that the bailiff had written to his wife. In one letter Launay wrote that he was expecting a change in government that would limit the minister of finance to one voice among many in the royal council. Consequently, "the intendants will no longer be kings as in the past. In the future one will be heard and judged by competent people with a full knowledge of the facts." Guynet fulminated to Desmaretz that such language could not be tolerated, for, if Launay went unpunished, "the authority of the intendant and

---

[9] AN, G-7 219, no. 225, petition to Guynet, 30 March 1715.
[10] There was truth to Launay's charge that subdelegates enjoyed tax privileges – too much truth for his own good. See AD Calvados, C 4679, letter from Montagutt to Fontette, 9 December 1768.
[11] AN, G-7 219, no. 227, letter from Guynet to Desmaretz, 23 May 1715. It was not uncommon for well-placed taxpayers to petition over the heads of provincial intendants to intendants of finance or the finance minister, but these officials usually supported the intendant's ruling.

the subdelegate would certainly fall." Deeming him "seditious" and "mutinous," Desmaretz instructed the lieutenant-general of police to issue *lettres de cachet* for Launay's imprisonment.[12]

Aware of cases like Launay's, most petitioners knew that "seditious speech never helped a cause."[13] Rather than expressing resentment towards administrators or other taxpayers, petitioners were far more likely to blame "excessive" tax assessments on "secret enemies" or to assign no explicit blame at all. Deference, not defiance, set the tone of the petitions, as the estate manager for the duc de Boüillon understood when he suggested that the duke, in petitioning against his *dixième*, address the intendant not as "monsieur" but as "monseigneur," a title reserved for the highest nobility.[14] But we should guard against interpreting such acts of deference as a sign of complete powerlessness. Deference had its uses. Petitioners of all kinds, notes James Scott, tend to "clothe their resistance and defiance in ritualisms of subordination that serve both to disguise their purposes and to provide them with a ready route of retreat that may often soften the consequences of a possible failure."[15] This was certainly the case with universal taxpayers who, lest their petitions fail, did not want to offend the official who fixed their assessments.

Deference was built into the very structure of petitions, whose beginnings and endings conformed to rhetorical formulas that scarcely changed over the century. Petitions began by formally addressing the intendant and respectfully listing his various titles, seigneuries, and offices. Then came the phrase *"supplie humblement"* ("begs humbly"), which stressed the submissiveness of petitioners by characterizing them as supplicants, followed by the petitioner's name, social rank or profession, and place of residence. After introducing themselves, petitioners wrote *"et vous remontre que"* (literally, "and shows you again that") or, less frequently, *et vous represente que* or *et vous expose que*, phrases that opened the way for petitioners to make their particular case. The use of the verb *"remontrer"* expressed the juridical concept that all recourse against a legal act must be

---

[12] AN, G-7 219, nos. 221 and 231, letters of 19 July 1715 and 6 September 1715.
[13] AN, R-2 501, anonymous letter relating to a tax dispute in the *vicomté* of Turenne, 3 July 1734.
[14] AN, R-2 501, letter of 17 November 1734.
[15] James Scott, *Domination and the Arts of Resistance: Hidden Transcripts* (New Haven, CT, 1990), pp. 96 and 101.

heard first in the presence of the original author of that act.[16] Petitioners claimed to be "*re*-showing" and "*re*-presenting" their cases because the administrators to whom they appealed had set the petitioners' assessments in the first place.

In the same way that "*remontrer*" framed the opening of petitions, an appeal to "*justice*" usually closed them. After arguing for consideration and providing the details of their cases, many subjects told intendants that "to have recourse to Your Justice" was their last hope. The term "Your Justice," or the occasionally employed "Your Equity," "Your Religion," or "Your Kindness," suggests that the quality of justice, or equity, religion, or kindness inhered in the person of the intendant who, once aware of the particular circumstances of the petitioner, would naturally correct the injustice at hand. Petitioners also spoke of the intendant's capacity "to do justice" by responding favorably to their pleas. Lower my tax "and you will be doing justice," taxpayers liked to write before they signed their names at the bottom of petitions. In this more active form, justice was less a personal quality than an act to be performed by the intendant in his capacity as both a magistrate and an administrator.

Whether formulated as a trait or a course of action, justice rather than rights was on the minds of petitioners, a finding not all that astonishing since the monarchy had long been portrayed as the source and dispenser of all justice. "All justice emanates from the king," wrote the jurist Antoine Loisel.[17] And behind the king's justice was God's, as Jean Domat expressed to Louis XIV: "Sire, as God makes kings to take his place above men, he elevates them to this rank, and puts the empire of justice in their hands, only for the purpose of his own rule."[18] Descending from the heavens to mortals through the rule of monarchs, justice touched all affairs of state, not least the royal finances, as the depiction of the figure of justice at the head of tax decrees suggests. When taxpayers asked for justice they were demanding something that the crown had always said it would provide.

In seeking justice, taxpayers made different kinds of arguments.[19]

---

[16] On this principle of legal recourse, which applied to the "remonstrances" of the sovereign courts as well, see Villain, *Contestations fiscales*, ch. 6.

[17] Quoted in Emile Littré, ed., *Dictionnaire de la langue française* (Paris, 1957), p. 1350.

[18] Jean Domat, *Les loix civiles dans leur ordre naturel*, 3 vols. (Paris, 1689–94), I, preface.

[19] That these arguments were their own and not those of legal counselors is evidenced by the poor handwriting and prose of petitions. Of the hundreds of appeals I read, only one gave any obvious sign of the assistance of a lawyer or notary.

In the case of the *dixième/vingtième*, justice was a rather technical affair, a matter of making sure that tax assessments did not exceed a legally defined percentage of income. Petitioners filled their appeals with details and documentation on the value of their personal property and simply tried to show that their income was not as high as the tax roll indicated. The petition of Gervais Francord Antoine L'Hote, sieur du Londel, a *secrétaire du roi* residing in Caen, was quite typical. In 1742, when the *dixième* was reestablished, Londel petitioned the intendant and explained that in 1733, even though he had declared that his revenue was no more than 2,550 livres, he had been assessed at 510 livres, 20 percent of his declared revenue. Believing himself overcharged, he had submitted a petition to Vastan, the former intendant, who in turn had reduced his tax to 300 livres, a sum he paid annually until 1737 when the *dixième* was abolished. Now, in 1742, finding his tax assessed anew at 400 livres, Londel argued that his revenue was still 2,550 livres and that his *dixième* should therefore be only a tenth of that. To support his claim he gave a brief history of the value of his land which, according to a lease enclosed with the petition, was rented in 1707 for 2,550 livres a year. In 1735, he added, he rented half the land for 1,200 livres and worked the other half himself to earn an additional 1,350 livres, again making the total revenue 2,550 livres. His 400-livre assessment, therefore, was excessive. The intendant looked over the petition and referred it to the director of the *dixième*, who investigated the case and advised the intendant to reassess Londel's revenue at 3,400 livres. The intendant followed the advice and reduced his *dixième* from 400 to 340 livres. Justice was done, though we have no way of knowing whether Londel believed it had been done satisfactorily.[20]

Petitions against the *capitation* were far more colorful than those against the *dixième/vingtième*. Because the rules governing the assessment of the *capitation* were so vague – the head tax was levied on the basis of an ill-defined combination of wealth and social position – petitioners mustered all kinds of arguments on their behalf. Income was always a point of contention as it was in *vingtième* petitions, but payers of the *capitation* also invoked a bewildering array of pleas, complaints, and short autobiographies to argue that they were

---

[20] AD Calvados, C 5284, petition of 3 April 1742.

overcharged. Within this disorderly litany of appeal there were patterns in the way certain taxpayers articulated their claims.

Nobles at court and in the provinces tended to organize their petitions around the theme of military service and the personal and familial costs associated with it. In a petition drafted at court in 1711 the duc de Mortemart wrote to Desmaretz of the "debts which he is obliged to pay to serve in the king's army" and which kept him from making simple purchases such as a carriage for his wife.[21] Likewise, the princess d'Harcourt explained in 1706 that she had spent all her money on her children's military adventures: "my son alone cost me more than 40,000 francs this year because I bought him a regiment and put his company in order."[22] Nobles in the provinces might not have spent so much outfitting their sons for royal service but what they did spend could certainly strain the less well-off among them.[23] Bernadin François Cadot, marquis de Sebeville, former *maître de camp* and *chevalier* of the order of St. Louis, informed the intendant of Caen in 1736 that "he" – petitioners normally referred to themselves in the third person – "served in the king's army during the preceding wars for 24 consecutive years." When his health no longer permitted him to serve, he retired from service, "but the expenses [which had been] necessary to maintain his rank threw his financial affairs into disarray." He, like his father before him, had ruined himself by serving the king. Cadot then claimed he could not pay a *capitation* as high as 300 livres and told the intendant that he hoped to obtain "the justice which rules all your conduct." The plea worked; the intendant lowered the tax to 200 livres for that year, but Cadot would have to petition again the following year.[24]

In their stories of military service nobles emphasized personal sacrifices alongside financial ones. In 1788 one nobleman, Hugen, recounted how he lost his eyesight in Louisiana; "this misfortune is a consequence of service in the colonies where, to maintain peace and union with savage nations, he was obliged to live with them."[25] Had

[21] AN, G-7 1135, petition of 20 December 1711. Desmaretz agreed to lower his *capitation* from 3,300 livres a year, the rate for dukes, to 2,200 livres a year, the rate for the *premier gentilhomme de la chambre du Roi*.
[22] Chamillart reduced her *capitation* from 1,500 to 1,000 livres a year. AN, G-7 1134, petition of 25 May 1706. Evidence from later in the century suggests that little had changed in the ways courtiers petitioned. In 1788 the petitions for exemptions from the *dixième* on royal pensions were filled with similar arguments about military service. AN, O-1 657, no. 423.
[23] Meyer, "La noblesse pauvre."
[24] AD Calvados, C 4685, no. 60, petition of 20 December 1736.
[25] AD Calvados, C 8104. His request for exemption was denied.

not a gentleman who lived among "savages" and lost an eye serving in distant colonies already met his obligations to the king? Adding to the chorus of appeal, René François de Vaubovel explained that he sacrificed "with pain his youth and his fortune in the service of His Majesty."[26]

By recounting the sacrifices their families made for the monarchy, in livres spent, limbs lost, and lives taken, nobles of the sword were combating a new form of obligation – direct taxation – with an older, more familiar one – military service. Though they were reluctant to put it in such stark terms, nobles argued that because they had gone to extraordinary lengths to meet the call for true service to the crown, they should be relieved of the supplementary fiscal demand of the *capitation*.

Beyond the nobility it is difficult to see parallels between the rhetoric of petitions and the social status of petitioners. It is true that officers of justice tended to speak of public service and the financial burden of their offices, just as bourgeois often discussed the problems of slow business and low wages, but the more marked differences in the type of rhetoric used in petitions lay in the ways in which taxpayers characterized the kind of justice they were seeking. All taxpayers, noble and otherwise, sought "justice," but they implicitly referred to two different senses of the word: personal justice and distributive justice.

Personal justice emanated from the person to whom the petition appealed and was to be bestowed directly upon supplicants without reference to other taxpayers. In most cases such justice was characterized as purely gratuitous, as a kind of grace or charity that sprang from the heart of the administrator. Less frequently, petitioners believed that personal justice was something that was owed them, not unlike the "commutative justice" defined by the *Encyclopédie* as "this virtue and this part of administration which aims to render to each that which belongs to each ... like when it is a matter of paying the value of something which has been provided."[27] Nobles who meticulously recorded their service in petitions, for example, were implicitly claiming that they were owed a tax exemption or at least a reduction. But whether gratuitous or owed,

---

[26] AD Calvados, C 4675 no. 26, petition of December 1770. His *capitation* was reduced from 18 livres to 9 livres.

[27] Denis Diderot and Jean Le Rond d'Alembert, eds., *Encyclopédie, ou Dictionnaire raisonné des sciences, des arts, et des métiers*, 35 vols. (Neufchatel, 1751–1780), IX, p. 94.

personal justice invoked only the relationship between the petitioner and the crown and never the triangular relationship among the crown, the petitioner, and other taxpayers.

Examples of appeals to personal justice abound. Countless taxpayers presented themselves as desperate supplicants, submitting tales of unredeemable debts, dire poverty, debilitating sickness (usually gout), old age, natural disasters (fires, hail storms, agricultural epidemics), burdensome large families, and secret enemies. Even the high nobility with positions at court did not shrink from supplicating themselves before the monarchy and asking for the "protection" of the controller-general. Owing 13,950 livres for several years of the *capitation*, the prince of Guemené begged the minister for his "justice" and "grace," claiming that the tax was "excessive … in relation to his meager wealth, his large family of twelve children, and the considerable debts on his inheritance which he was obliged to pay."[28] Further down the social scale lesser nobles recounted the difficulties of living according to their rank, while officers of justice complained of meager *gages* and fees. Pierre Charles de Cognet, a *procureur du roi* in the *vicomté* court of Pontorson, recounted that he could not walk owing to "the sad effects of gout," a sickness that made it impossible for him to earn fees from his office. Having just enough money for his family's subsistence, he could not afford to provide an education for his children and, by implication, sustain their social status. The final sentence of his petition reveals the highly personal nature of his appeal and the extent to which grace and justice could overlap: "By granting him this grace, the supplicant will be obliged to pray to heaven for the preservation of Your Greatness."[29] The most desperate pleas for personal justice came from the urban poor, people like Georges Borel and his wife of the town of Bayeux, who stated that they had no money with which to pay their *capitation* of 4 livres. Having sold everything except "the miserable bed on which the supplicants sleep," they lived in constant fear of prison, for they were unable to pay their rent and could afford only bread. "These facts," Borel

---

[28] From a 59,559 livre inheritance from the late princess, he had to pay 13,842 livres in *rentes constitués*, 6,000 livres in pensions, 7,500 livres for estate maintenance, and 15,000 livres to his son, leaving him roughly 17,000 livres to support his family and to live according to his rank. Chamillart decided that if the prince paid for his arrears for 1705 and 1706 and continued to pay 2,250 livres a year, "we will no longer speak of the past." AN, G-7 1134, petition of 19 July 1706.

[29] AD Calvados, C 4676, no. 18, petition of 23 June 1772.

wrote, "which are common knowledge oblige him to take recourse in Your Equity."[30] Borel's story was repeated by a chorus of widows living, they said, on the edge of subsistence.

Not all petitioners believed that justice was merely personal, consisting of rescuing the unfortunate. Instead of portraying themselves as desperate supplicants, many taxpayers, knowing full well that taxes were not simply imposed on individuals but distributed among various groups of subjects, used justice in its distributive sense to complain of being treated unfairly. At the center of distributive justice was the comparison. As the *Encyclopédie* defined it, "distributive justice" was spread in "geometric proportion, that is to say, by comparison of one person and one fact with another."[31] D'Ormesson put it less abstractly: "the taxpayer is able to compare his tax to that of another taxpayer and, if he notices an unfair proportion . . . , or if the burden is not equal or justly distributed, he cries of injustice."[32] Behind seemingly formulaic appeals for distributive justice lay specific comparisons, validating the dictum of contemporary philosophers that "[j]ustice may consist of generalities, but injustice – even if widespread – is always localized."[33]

Sometimes the locality of injustice took geographic form as neighbors sized up each other's wealth and tax burden. Anne du Chastel explained in 1702 that as a widow she received an inheritance of only 325 livres a year, a fact to which her curé attested, but when she heard that her *capitation* would be 104 livres she figured she had been put on the "tax rolls of the rich." "Equity" demanded that her tax be lowered since people "in her neighborhood" enjoying 2,000 livres of income were not obliged to pay such "heavy sums."[34]

Yet for the most part comparisons were "localized" in another, not necessarily geographical, sense in their tendency to conform to the corporate structures of early modern French society. Despite the fact that universal tax decrees reflected the individualist language of Enlightenment reform, the taxes themselves were often levied

[30] AD Calvados, C 4680, no. 2, petition of 12 October 1734. The intendant lowered their *capitation* from 4 livres to 2 livres.
[31] Diderot, *Encyclopédie*, II, p. 94.
[32] AN, H-1 1463, no. 7, mémoire on taxation, 1772.
[33] Robert Solomon, *A Passion for Justice: Emotions and the Origins of the Social Contract* (Reading, MA, 1990), p. 251; Michael Walzer, *Spheres of Justice* (New York, 1983).
[34] AD Calvados, C 4686, no. 3, petition of 11 March 1702. Occasionally, the geographic perspective of the comparison extended well beyond the locality. Nobleman Phillippe Blanchard assured the intendant that "there is no other gentlemen in the province more surcharged than he." AD Calvados, C 4698, no. 27, petition of September 1736.

collectively on such corporate bodies as families, guilds, law courts, cities, and provinces, and it was within these corps that individual petitioners situated themselves. Corps provided a framework for comparisons, a context within which injustices were perceived and from which appeals were issued. If justice tends to be perceived and measured within discrete spheres, such spheres in Old Regime France corresponded to the myriad corps and collectivities that composed society.

"A nation is only a composite of many families," observed Diderot.[35] Families were the most basic economic, social, and legal unit of society, and it makes sense that petitioners mentioned them more than any other collectivity. To a large extent one's relation to one's family determined one's relation to the state. Children, for instance, used their membership in the family as a pretext to escape taxation, because only the head of each household was legally obliged to pay the family's taxes. Young men claimed exemption by arguing that they were but "sons of the family" or the "youngest of the family." Daughters made the same case. Three sisters from the city of Vire – Marie, Françoise, and Marguerite Coquard – argued that "as daughters, the supplicants should not be made to pay the *capitation*." Living with their mother, maintaining no household of their own, and facing a collective *capitation* of 60 livres, the three sisters shrewdly suggested that their brother be made to pay for them.[36]

Relations between husbands and wives were no less an issue. Married women who owned property independently of their husbands were expected to pay their own *capitation*. When Françoise Binet was taxed separately, her husband explained to the intendant that their property was "common," enclosing their marriage contract to prove it.[37] Conversely, Catherine Berot petitioned to make clear that, having been "forced to take letters of separation" from her husband after he had fallen into bankruptcy, she could not be held accountable for his tax arrears. Claiming she had only 400 livres of income for the subsistence of her husband, child, and

---

[35] Quoted in Villain, *Contestations fiscales*, ch. 6.

[36] On the advice of the municipal officers of Vire, the intendant rejected their petition. The declaration of 1701, the officers pointed out, stated that daughters who possess property or who engage in their own business are subject to the *capitation*. Further, the officers explained that the youngest sister had just entered a marriage which brought her "a prodigious fortune." AD Calvados, C 4700, no. 54, petition of 1782.

[37] AD Calvados, C 4685, no. 20, petition of 9 April 1702. The intendant decided to tax them jointly and to lower their assessment.

herself, Berot asked the intendant to lower the *capitation* from 28 to 4 livres.[38] Finally, André Joseph de Bellemare, like so many men, saw his *capitation* increase the year he was married. He petitioned the intendant, stressing the financial insignificance of his marriage, for in choosing his wife he "followed his inclination and his taste rather than his [financial] interest."[39]

Equally fundamental but more complicated than family relations was the problem of inheritance. Administrators followed lines of inheritance closely, trying to apportion the *capitation* in relation to changing patterns of property-holding, but taxpayers often complained that the administrators had been mistaken in their assumptions about who had inherited what. The case of Jacques Augustin Louis le Danois, *conseiller du roi* at the *présidial* court of Caen, was typical. He said he was surprised to see his *capitation* increase so suddenly; "If this is because the *capitation* of his father, who died six months ago, was added on to his own," there had been a grave "injustice" committed. Since his father's widow received the bulk of the inheritance as custom dictates, he suggested that "his father's *capitation* should be shifted onto the widow, his stepmother."[40] Other taxpayers claimed that their inheritance was not as bountiful as it appeared, as did Jacques Louis de Marguerie, a noble from Bayeux, who detailed the pensions he was obligated to pay to family members from his inheritance.[41] Still others, like Nicolas de la Chambe, bemoaned the debts attached to their inheritances, claiming that the inheritance was so "completely burdened with debt" that it was not worth the taxes assessed on it.[42] Many individuals who inherited debt- and tax-ridden property simply renounced their inheritance altogether.

When applied to smoldering familial tensions the spark of taxation could ignite intense disputes. After her grandmother died, for example, Marie Bernard, a women of modest means living in the city of Caen, shared with her grandfather her grandmother's

[38] AD Calvados, C 4696, no. 1, petition of 3 July 1734. The intendant lowered her tax but only to 22 livres.

[39] AD Calvados, C 4682, no. 19, petition of 3 July 1736. Similarly, Lombay, an officer of the *bailliage* of Valognes, complained that his marriage was being used as a "pretext to augment his *capitation*" from 5 livres to 25 livres but "the revenue that his wife brought to him was not at all considerable enough to justify such a large increase." AD Calvados, C 4696, no. 3.

[40] AD Calvados, C 4682, no. 17, petition of 2 July 1736.

[41] AD Calvados, C 4678, no. 49, petition of 30 August 1751.

[42] BN, Ms. Fr. 11906, no. 224, petition of 6 July 1750.

inheritance and the *capitation* of 8 livres associated with it.[43] She and her grandfather split the tax evenly between them. When her grandfather died, he left his inheritance to his nephew, Jacques Gallet, who also inherited the 4 livres of *capitation* that his uncle used to pay. Upon receiving his inheritance, however, Jacques Gallet petitioned to be discharged of the tax, a request the intendant reviewed favorably, relieving Gallet of his 4 livre *capitation* and placing the sum onto the tax of Marie Bernard. When Bernard was informed that she now owed the full 8 livres, she asserted that "this was not fair since Jacques Gallet profited from his uncle's full inheritance" and deliberately misrepresented the facts of the case in his petition, which she had managed to acquire. Gallet may have lived with his aged uncle to help him with his craft of making candlesticks, but, Bernard told the intendant,

the way Gallet presents this in his petition, he was acting out of charity, as if his uncle would have fallen sick and suffered miserably had he not been helped ... This is a false statement ... Jacques Gallet himself needed help, having just become a master candlestick maker. His uncle left him a good business and a house.

Bernard also denounced Gallet for not telling the whole truth about the inheritance:

Jacques Gallet did not give all the facts. He says that his uncle had received an inheritance from his wife of only 350 livres and the ownership of a small house. The supplicant has the honor to inform Your Greatness that this little house can be rented for at least 50 livres a year ... Nor does he say in his petition that his uncle received more than 500 livres in furniture and money, in addition to the 350 livres mentioned above.

Since Jacques Gallet inherited his uncle's property, and since his uncle was taxed "jointly" with the supplicant, Bernard concluded that "he cannot refuse to pay his part of this *capitation*." Make him pay half the tax, she implored the intendant, "and you will be doing justice."[44]

There was similar bitterness between the brothers Campion, who inherited their father's *capitation* along with his property. Charles François de Campion, the younger son, explained that, while he normally paid 6 livres 12 sols of *capitation* under his own name, he was notified that he also owed, collectively with his brother, a

---

[43] AD Calvados, C 4694, no. 13, petition of August 1734.
[44] The intendant refused her request but reduced her *capitation* from 8 livres to 7 livres.

capitation of 74 livres under the heading of "inheritors of François de Campion." Charles asked if it were possible to divide the sum in half so that he and his older brother could pay it individually. He explained,

He had been forced to undergo too many contestations with his brother. The supplicant was prepared to give up all his interests, whatever they might be, in order to procure peace. [But] not having been able to find in his brother the sentiments of conciliation he desired, the supplicant ... found himself charged with the total amount of the collective tax without any hope of compensation.

The intendant was fully persuaded and ordered that the two brothers each be taxed half, "without any *solidité* between them."[45]

When asking for "justice," Charles de Campion, Marie Bernard, and countless others were clearly referring to distributive justice. They petitioned by calling attention to what they understood to be an injustice in the way the *capitation* was being distributed within their family. Aggravating what were already sensitive questions of familial inheritance, the duc d'Harcourt explained, taxes troubled families because they assigned a value to wealth that was "always different from the value that family members assigned to it, and this hindered the division of inheritances and other family affairs."[46] By measuring and assessing wealth, income, and exchanges of property from a perspective outside the family, the crown often contradicted the delicate proprietary arrangements and evaluations that had been made privately within the family.

Families were only one kind of corps in which membership served as the basis for comparison. The royal court was another, and at each level in the hierarchy of the court taxpayers looked carefully around them, craning their necks to see what their peers were paying. The prince of Montbazon began his petition by stating that the king had "the kindness to lower to modest sums the *capitations* of Monsieur le duc d'Elbeuf, Monsieur le duc de Guiche, Monsieur le duc de Sully, Monsieur le duc de Foye, ... and many others." The prince asked for the same consideration, "being a lot worse in his

---

[45] AD Calvados, C 4688, no. 22, petition of 20 June 1736. Examples of bickering brothers could easily be multiplied. Jean Lottin, an *avocat du roi* at the *bailliage* of Avranche, complained that his brothers were more favorably treated because "he is without question more poor than his brothers, and yet he alone has been assessed for the entire sum that their father had trouble paying." AD Calvados, C 4676, no. 29, petition of 18 July 1772.

[46] Hippeau, *Gouvernement de Normandie*, V, pp. 100–3, letter from d'Harcourt to Bertin, 28 October 1772.

affairs than any of them."[47] And, just as the prince compared his tax with those who belonged to the highest tier of the court, lower-level officers who staffed the court made comparisons among themselves. The nine *valets de garde robe* of the duc d'Orléans specified that they were taxed at 40 livres each but that the duke's *valets de chambre*, who received 100 livres of *gages* more than they, paid a *capitation* of only 30 livres each.[48] In the competitive arena of the court the *capitation* became yet another device for measuring the favors granted to one's peers.

Outside the court, royal office-holders made similar kinds of comparisons, always measuring their taxes against those of their colleagues. In the *élection* court of Bayeux, Jean Baptiste Louis Abry, a *receveur des tailles*, asked to have his *capitation* reduced from 80 to 50 livres, "the same sum" paid by "his colleague," Beaumont, a fellow *receveur des tailles*.[49] Baubigny, a *procureur* of the *bailliage* of Avranches, claimed that he was unfairly charged with "the highest tax assessment of all his colleagues" in the court.[50]

Central to many comparisons was the amount of *gages* officers received. In 1779 the *avocats généraux* of the parlement of Dijon complained that they were assessed at 120 livres each while the councilors of the *grand chambre*, who enjoyed the same *gages*, paid only 80 livres. Even more striking, they insisted, was the fact that the *procureur-général*, who received no less than 6,000 livres in appointments, was taxed at 120 livres, the same sum they were paying.[51] Likewise, the clerks of the *bureau des finances* of Alençon demonstrated with precise arithmetic why "justice" was "due" them. The chief clerk, Champré Cherbonnier, petitioned both the intendant of Alençon and the controller-general, explaining that *trésoriers* of the court had unfairly assessed the clerks' *capitation* at 549 livres a year. While clerks received only 367 livres of gages, "each *trésorier* has 2,000 livres of gages and some have three or four [thousand livres]."

---

[47] AN, G-7 1134, petition of 18 March 1704. Chamillart lowered his tax from 1,500 livres to 1,000 livres.

[48] AN, G-7 1134, petition of 12 November 1702. The logic of the nine *valets* was not denied; their tax was lowered to 30 livres each. The secretary of the French Academy employed the same logic when requesting that the academy's pensions be exempt from the withholding tax on pensions. Since the academy of *belles Lettres* had been exempted, the secretary asked for "the same favor." AN, O-1 657, no. 423.

[49] AD Calvados, C 4679, petition of 6 December 1734. Vastan reduced it to 60 livres.

[50] AD Calvados, C 4676, no. 14, petition of 6 October 1770. His *capitation* was reduced from 18 to 12 livres.

[51] AN, H-1 173, no. 88.

Since the *trésoriers* did not pay a proportionally higher tax, Cherbon-nier asserted, it was truly an injustice "to burden the clerks ... more than the *trésoriers*."[52] Sometimes comparisons extended to entire courts of law, as one court petitioned collectively to complain that other courts were being treated more favorably. The syndic of the parlement of Dijon wrote to d'Ormesson in 1772 about the relative weight of his court's tax burden and that of the parlement of Besançon. "If there should be a difference [in *capitation*] between them and us, it should be in our favor, since the *gages* of their councilors are 2,400 livres and ours are 2,000 livres."[53]

Another common frame of reference for comparison was the city or town. Charles Vuinard of Bayeux claimed his *capitation* was "exorbitant relative to other bourgeois of the city," just as Blondel, a resident of Avranches, protested that he was taxed both as a bourgeois of the city and as an employee of the indirect tax administration. "And what is more painful for the supplicant," Blondel emphasized, "is that in this same city of Avranches there are many employees who have property in the city like he does, but who are not at all imposed like he is for the *capitation* on the bourgeoisie."[54]

Often whole towns, like courts, compared their collective tax burden to that of other cities. In 1787 the neighboring cities of Valognes and Cherbourg engaged in a bitter struggle over how the *capitation* was going to be assessed.[55] The municipal officers of Valognes claimed that the city of Cherbourg had expanded rapidly since the crown began building an enormous shipyard there. While Cherbourg prospered, the officers told the intendant, their "unfortu-nate" city was experiencing depopulation and economic stagnation. They asserted that their city's *capitation* "is not only exorbitant, but it is disproportionate to those of other cities in your generality."

Meanwhile, as the intendant considered raising the *capitation* on Cherbourg, the mayor and *échevins* of that city tried to persuade him that this was not fair either. Claiming that the naval yard was being built along the coast and not, as thought, in their city, they named several rural parishes, some as far as 50 leagues from Cherbourg, where work was being done. The city of Cherbourg was not in fact

---

[52] AN, G-7 1134, petition of 1704.
[53] AN, H-1 173, no. 78, letter of 3 December 1772.
[54] AD Calvados, C 4680, no. 3, petition of 1 August 1734.
[55] AD Calvados, C 4711, nos. 77–87, and C 8118.

swelling in population. "To the contrary," the officials insisted, the parishes "depopulate us," as shopkeepers and artisans leave the city to go live on the coast: "We therefore lose all these taxpayers, taxpayers which the syndics of rural parishes will not fail to include in their tax rolls." This was an open invitation for the intendant to increase taxes on the countryside rather than on the city. The rest of the petition was written "to respond to the complaints lodged by *messieurs* of Valognes, who claim that many of their inhabitants are deserting their city and coming to ours." "It is true," the officials of Cherbourg admitted, that many of their day-laborers and workers have come here, "but they are all poor" and cannot pay much in taxes, "while on the other hand many of our well-off bourgeois have gone from our city to Valognes." The mayor and *échevins* concluded that their city was not "in a position to support any increases in taxation."

On 14 June the municipal officers of Valognes reiterated in no uncertain terms that the prosperous city of Cherbourg should shoulder some of Valognes' tax burden. The municipal officers assured the intendant that, although they were making comparisons between their city and Cherbourg, their intentions were not hostile:

It is not at all, *monseigneur,* with an envious eye that we see our neighbors grow rich, but they should help those who are overtaxed and who do not have the same opportunities to improve their fortune. If we take Cherbourg as an object of comparison, we do not at all do so out of jealousy. But since the overall tax cannot be decreased at this time, it is necessary to redistribute it more equally, and Cherbourg has more leeway . . . ; we know that to oblige our fellow citizens and to render justice to them is a true pleasure for you.

The municipal officers of Valognes conceived of the injustice committed against them in the wider context of Cherbourg's good fortune.

If we take a closer look at cities, we see that cities themselves were composed of corps in which disputes often arose. Just as the intendant informed municipal officers of the lump sum owed by their city, the municipal officers of Caen informed guild officials of their lump sum contributions. Guild officials, in turn, drew the tax rolls for the guilds, a task that frequently provoked disputes among guild members. Nicolas Vaussard and Marie Cornet, members of the butchers' guild in the city of Caen, said that "drawing the *capitation* rolls in their guild always caused discord, division, and contestation among them."⁵⁶ In 1757 fourteen workers from the stocking-makers' guild of Caen collectively petitioned the intendant, complaining that the masters of the guild were taxing them unfairly. The "unfortunate workers," who reaped none of the guild's profits and had to struggle just "to feed themselves," were made to pay "at least half of the guild's *capitation*." "The masters alone," they demanded, "should be charged; they alone profit from their work; they alone are in a position to pay the tax." In this case, journeymen were using their right to petition in order to defend themselves against more powerful masters.⁵⁷

The countryside had corporate-like structures as well. Like the guilds in the city, rural seigneuries were made up of unequal members, seigneurs and vassals. (The term "vassal" referred to anyone who owed dues to the seigneur, whether a peasant or a tenant-farmer). Since the *dixième/vingtième* was supposed to be levied on all forms of revenue, including feudal dues, it touched the seigneury directly, aggravating the often poor relations between seigneurs and vassals, both of whom now disputed how the royal tax should fall on feudal dues. The origins of these disputes go back to the declaration of 1741, which instructed all debtors who paid annual *rentes* (interest payments) to creditors to withhold the *dixième* on their *rentes* and forward the sum to the crown as part of the debtor's own tax payments. This practice assured the crown that when the *dixième* was assessed on borrowed capital, the lender (who owned the capital), not the borrower, would ultimately pay the tax. Taking their cue from legislation, vassals began withholding the *dixième/vingtième* from their seigneurial dues, which they evidently saw as a type of *rente*. On 13 October 1750 the crown intervened by issuing an *arrêt du conseil* that prohibited vassals from withholding the *vingtième* from their dues and announced that, instead, seigneurs were to declare their seigneurial dues as income to be subjected to the *vingtième*. Vassals could deduct their seigneurial dues from their taxable income but they had to pay them in full. The crown was still interested in taxing seigneurs, only now it wanted to do it directly.

Ignoring the *arrêt*, vassals continued to withhold a percentage of

---

⁵⁶ AD Calvados, C 4567, petition from Nicolas Vaussard and Marie Cornet, 1761(?).
⁵⁷ The stocking-makers' guild was composed of 139 masters and 557 journeymen, who collectively owed a *capitation* of 1,200 livres, 501 livres of which were assigned to the journeymen. The intendant lowered the sum to 301 livres. AD Calvados, C 4585, petition of 14 May 1757.

their dues after 1750, a practice that became a serious point of contention within the seigneury. On 18 May 1761, Louis XV had to issue a second *arrêt* reiterating that of 1750 because of "frequent contestations" over this matter, but this second *arrêt* seems to have had as little effect as the first.[58] Peasants persisted in retaining their dues and seigneurs continued to pursue them in the courts, which generally found in favor of seigneurs. (Although they involved the *vingtième*, these cases also concerned the nonpayment of seigneurial dues and were therefore under the jurisdiction of the courts). Pitted against seigneurs who found sympathetic listeners in local officers of justice, some peasants brought their grievances before the finance ministry. In 1773, after the seigneur of the parish of Acqueville near Cherbourg took his vassals to court (first the seigneurial court and then the *bailliage*) for not paying their seigneurial dues in full, the community of Acqueville collectively petitioned the controller-general. Paying the dues in full, wrote Jean Le Vanfre, the community's deputy, "overturns every principle of law and equity . . . [and] is contrary to the rule prescribed by His Majesty who intends and ordains that the *dixième*, *vingtième*, and other royal taxes be imposed on owners of property and not on debtors." The new system, he went on, "becomes abusive because poor citizens find themselves overburdened with royal taxes that they do not owe."[59]

Seigneurs, on the other hand, asked administrators to make vassals pay their dues in full. On 1 May 1766 the abbé de Mathon, seigneur de Fresville, reminded the intendant that the law forbade vassals from withholding royal taxes. He claimed that his mother had declared the seigneurial dues as income in 1734 and, to prove this to his vassals, he had asked the director of the *vingtième* to furnish a copy of his mother's declaration of wealth. But the director refused, and word of this refusal strengthened the vassal's resolve: "Having been informed of the difficulty in showing them that his mother had listed the income from seigneurial dues in her declaration of wealth, the vassals of Fresville have refused to pay their debts with more boldness than before." Ultimately, Mathon's petition was unsuccessful. Upon checking the declaration of wealth, the intendant learned that Mathon's mother had not in fact declared her

[58] AD Calvados, C 5294, *arrêt du conseil* of 18 May 1761.
[59] Terray referred the case to d'Ormesson who, reversing his earlier position of 1769, rejected the petition but urged the vassals to subtract their dues from their taxable income. AD Calvados, C 5908, petition of 28 April 1773, and C 5942, letter of 21 December 1769.

seigneurial dues as income. The intendant told the abbé that he could either make a new declaration of wealth or allow his vassals to continue making deductions on their dues.[60]

Vassals against seigneurs, workers against masters, cities against cities, townspeople against townspeople, courts against courts, officers against officers, brother against brother: the comparisons in petitions reveal unequivocally that the boundaries of discrete spheres of justice in the Old Regime were based on the corporate structure of early modern French society.[61] Although the sharp divisions that show up within and between corps did not take on the dimensions of a crisis, they do demonstrate that ordinary taxpayers believed that universal taxes were being distributed unfairly. Sometimes, as in the cases of vassals and seigneurs or of journeymen and masters, that sense of unfairness had a social component and added to tensions that arose between parties who played highly unequal roles in processes of economic production. More commonly, perceptions of injustice arose between siblings, colleagues, and men and women of roughly the same social rank, all of whom used universal taxes as a type of measuring stick to claim that their counterparts were receiving more favorable treatment from the state. Veiled by tones of deference, a feeling of injustice and frustration permeated petitions.

ADMINISTRATIVE JUSTICE

Intendants responded to this clamor for justice as effectively as they could, believing that they were placed in the provinces as representatives of both the king to the people and the people to the king. "If I am a servant of the King who must execute his orders," Fontette, intendant of Caen, wrote in 1772, "I am no less a servant of the Province who must make the execution of those orders more gentle and mild."[62] This role was particularly important in matters of taxation, Necker told Esmangard, Fontette's successor; "No one knows better than you ... the interests of the taxpayers of your generality and how to reconcile them with the interests of the

---

[60] AD Calvados, C 5904, petition of 1 May 1766.
[61] We could also add Frenchmen against non-Frenchmen to this list of conflict, since landowners in the Cerdagne, to the protest of village communities, identified themselves as Spaniards in order to exempt themselves from the *capitation*. Peter Sahlins, *Boundaries: The Making of France and Spain in the Pyrenees* (Berkeley, CA, 1989), pp. 81–4 and 154–5.
[62] AN, H-1 1463, no. 42, letter of 9 April 1772.

King."[63] Intendants had to find a way to draw as much money as possible from their generality without fomenting too much resentment. They had walked this narrow line when initially assessing each individual's taxes but, knowing that assessments were not perfect, they accepted petitions against those assessments and were willing to consider making adjustments. If taxpayers responded with few petitions, this was taken as a favorable sign; in 1782 the municipal officers of the town of Vire said that the paucity of petitions received from residents was "testimony" to the "charity and justice of monseigneur the intendant."[64] If, on the other hand, petitions flooded administrative bureaux, this indicated that the demands of the crown might be either too burdensome or too unfairly distributed. In 1783 the intendant received a wave of petitions against the *capitation* from nobles residing in the generality, a dangerous sign of discontent that prompted an investigation. Justifying the length of his *mémoire* on this matter, one administrator wrote, "we thought it necessary to enter into all this detail because we were informed that nobles are murmuring a lot against their tax of 1783."[65]

Two ways to avoid murmurs of this kind were generally unavailable to intendants. The first was to draft a petition to the controller-general, asking him to lower the global sum of a tax on their generality. If taxes were simply too high, wrote one intendant, "the intendant must make some sort of objection to the minister charged with the administration of finances."[66] These pleas could be moderately successful in the case of the *taille*, the global sum of which underwent small annual diminutions every year depending on the generality's economic condition, but for the *capitation* and the *vingtième* such general reductions were rarely forthcoming. The other obvious way to calm disgruntled taxpayers would have been to grant in full the demands put forward in their petitions, yet this was not a viable option either, for finance ministers pressured intendants to limit their generosity.

Prohibited from slashing the global sum of universal taxes and

---

[63] AD Calvados, C 4703, no. 30, letter from Necker to Esmangard, 14 April 1777.
[64] AD Calvados, C 4700, no. 54.
[65] AD Calvados, C 4526, La capitation des nobles.
[66] BN, Ms. Fr. 21812, fo. 601. When such objections were made they sounded a lot like the petitions that individuals submitted to intendants. The sharp increases in the *vingtième* in 1772 forced Fontette to make "representations on behalf of the taxpayers of my generality," who "are not treated ... as favorably as those of the *pays d'états*," a policy that violated "principles of distributive justice." AN, H-1 1463, no. 35, letter of 17 February 1772.

unable to grant petitioners all they were asking for, intendants and their assistants were forced to sift through hundreds of petitions to determine when to make compromises and when to hold firm. Intendants referred petitions against the *dixième/vingtième* to the director, who, aided by controllers, investigated petitioners' claims and suggested how the intendant might respond. Petitions against the *capitation* were referred to subdelegates or tax receivers, who checked the validity of their contents and offered counsel to the intendant. Following the advice of his subordinates, the intendant either rejected petitions outright or allocated reductions, attempting to silence murmurs while providing the king with revenue.

How often and how much did intendants concede to petitioners? With regard to the *vingtième*, they gave in rarely and sparingly, as figure 2.7 illustrated. If tax receivers were able to collect nearly the full amount of assessments on the tax rolls, however, this was certainly not due to any shortage of contestation. Petitions against the *dixième/vingtième* clogged intendancies in the early 1710s, mid-1730s, early 1740s, and early 1750s, and from 1772 to 1782, periods in which the tax was established, reestablished, or reformed, occasioning new submissions of declarations of wealth and fresh rounds of verifications of those declarations. When taxpayers discovered that their *dixième/vingtième* was assessed on official estimates of revenue that exceeded the estimates they had disclosed in their own declarations of wealth, they were likely to make an appeal. Even during the period from 1763 to 1771 when no new declarations of wealth were solicited and few assessments were touched, Fontette estimated that he had rejected no fewer than 1,000 petitions for reductions in the *vingtième* submitted by the property-owners of his generality.[67] From 1772 to 1782, when verifications were conducted on an unprecedented scale, leading to upward swings in assessments, petitions from landowners, including such notables as former intendants, magistrates of sovereign courts, and titled aristocrats, overwhelmed intendants and *vingtième* directors and controllers. Esmangard counted as many as 387 requests waiting for responses in 1780.[68]

[67] AN, H-1 1463, no. 102, letter to Terray, 16 November 1772.
[68] AD Calvados, C 5945, *mémoire* on controllers, 1780. Other intendancies drew large numbers of petitions against the *dixième/vingtième* as well. That of Auvergne, which in 1713 confronted an "infinite number of requests," received over 900 petitions in 1734. Bonney, "Le secret," p. 401; and Abel Poitrineau, *La vie rurale en Basse-Auvergne au XVIIIe siècle (1726–1789)* (Paris, 1965), p. 365.

Rulings on petitions for reductions in the *dixième/vingtième* were generally unfavorable. Investigations were often delayed – half the petitions in 1780 received no consideration at all because controllers did not have the time to get to them – obliging petitioners to pay the full amount of their assessment until they received notification. As they waited for a ruling, many petitioners thought that their petitions had been lost or willfully ignored. And when requests did receive prompt consideration they were likely to be rejected on the basis of insufficient documentation. Petitioners had to prove, by providing valid estate documents, that their income was lower than estimated, a feat that seldom occurred.

A dispute between one noble landowner, d'Ecramville, and Fontette suggests the rigor with which even ultimately successful petitions were treated. In 1773, when the official estimate of the revenue on which his *vingtième* assessment was based shot up from 9,555 to 12,940 livres after a verification of his estate, d'Ecramville petitioned the intendant, Fontette, who responded that he could do nothing for the nobleman until he submitted copies of leases on his land. For months the petitioner refused, preferring to appeal over Fontette's head to d'Ormesson, intendant of finance. After Fontette told d'Ecramville that his "threat" of continually soliciting d'Ormesson until the tax was lowered was "uncalled for" and that "there are many other taxpayers who are in your position, but who conduct themselves decently," d'Ecramville finally turned in his leases with a new petition which asked that his *vingtième* be assessed on 10,261 livres of income instead of 12,940 livres.[69] Making a rare concession, the intendant granted the request in part and fixed the noble's *vingtième* on the basis of 10,600 livres of income, a sum higher than the original estimate but lower than the verification assessment. In this case, d'Ecramville had to submit detailed documentary evidence to obtain a reduction in his *vingtième*, a step most petitioners were not prepared to take.

It was much easier for taxpayers to convince intendants to reduce the *capitation*. Tables 3.1 to 3.4 show how different social groups in the generality of Caen fared in their attempts to persuade administrators "to do justice."[70] The tables also show the number of

[69] AD Calvados, C 5900, letters from d'Ecramville to the intendant, 3 October 1773, and from the intendant to d'Ecramville, 7 October 1773. AD Calvados, C 5900, petition of 19 January 1774.

[70] Tables 3.1 to 3.4 were compiled from AD Calvados, C 4704–4712, 4524–4535, and 8104–8119. I found no evidence for years other than those listed in the tables.

Table 3.1. *The* capitation *and the nobility: reductions and failures to pay*

Year	Number given reductions	Total amount of reductions (livres)	Average reduction (livres)	Number who did not pay	Total amount unpaid (livres)	Average amount unpaid (livres)
1736	153	4,162	27.20	18	162	9.00
1760	172	14,644	85.14	27	1,380	51.11
1761	210	21,168	100.80	41	1,458	35.56
1767	114	8,144	71.44	40	839	20.98
1769	197	14,213	72.15	70	3,243	46.33
1770	180	12,932	71.84	71	3,049	42.94
1771	184	12,881	70.01	51	1,563	30.65
1772	192	12,510	65.16	46	2,205	47.93
1788	129	6,964	53.98	–	522	–

Table 3.2. *The* capitation *and officers of justice: reductions and failures to pay*

Year	Number given reductions	Total amount of reductions (livres)	Average reduction (livres)	Number who did not pay	Total amount unpaid (livres)	Average amount unpaid (livres)
1736	41	619	15.10	26	531	20.42
1760	152	5,816	38.26	40	963	24.08
1761	205	10,035	48.95	43	1,093	25.42
1767	90	3,528	39.20	59	699	11.85
1769	–	31,077	–	90	1,848	20.53
1770	350	21,916	62.62	75	4,016	53.55
1771	376	23,359	62.13	97	5,154	53.13
1772	395	23,232	58.82	63	3,318	52.67
1788	386	29,292	75.89	–	833	–

individuals who did not pay their *capitation* and the amount of tax money that the crown was unable to collect.

These tables tell us a number of things about the scale and form of contestation over the *capitation*. Most striking is the number of privileged subjects who petitioned against, and received reductions in, the tax. In a typical year such as 1771 no fewer than 936 nobles,

Table 3.3. *The capitation and the* privilégiés: *reductions and failures to pay*

Year	Number given reductions	Total amount of reductions (livres)	Average reduction (livres)	Number who did not pay	Total amount unpaid (livres)	Average amount unpaid (livres)
1736	2	33	16.50	2	14	7.00
1760	33	698	21.15	1	6	6.00
1761	53	1,063	20.06	3	125	41.67
1767	5	107	21.40	2	49	24.50
1769	107	2,080	19.44	11	219	19.91
1770	114	2,884	25.30	13	426	32.77
1771	50	1,673	33.46	12	547	45.58
1772	–	1,853	–	–	514	–
1788	37	1,411	38.14	–	36	–

Table 3.4. *The capitation and the bourgeoisie: reductions and failures to pay*

Year	Number given reductions	Total amount of reductions (livres)	Average reduction (livres)	Number who did not pay	Total amount unpaid (livres)	Average amount unpaid (livres)
1736	171	1,009	5.90	612	1,623	2.65
1760	414	6,086	14.70	620	3,885	6.27
1761	1650	12,286	7.45	795	3,226	4.06
1767	182	6,589	36.20	489	1,417	2.90
1769	236	4,272	18.10	768	3,139	4.09
1770	253	5,535	21.88	685	2,520	3.68
1771	326	4,429	13.59	569	3,113	5.47
1772	313	4,970	15.88	415	2,736	6.59
1788	194	2,246	11.58	–	2,986	–

officers, *privilégiés*, and bourgeois benefited in some measure from petitioning the intendant of Caen. One reason the number of petitions was so high was that tax reductions, when granted, did not always change the assessments on the tax rolls in a permanent way, forcing even successful petitioners to petition year after year with little assurance that they would be accorded the same favor from one year to the next.[71] The sheer number of petitions and reductions throughout the eighteenth century suggests that the *capitation* brought the privileged into regular contact with intendants on a broad scale. Thus, for many privileged, the intendant was not some distant abstract figure representing the authority of the royal council but an administrator who raised or lowered their tax and responded to their requests on an annual basis.

Outright rejections of petitions against the *capitation*, which unfortunately cannot be tallied with certainty, appear to have been exceptional, since intendants were willing to provide, at the very least, small token reductions in the tax. Why contestation over the *capitation* was more likely to result in compromise than that over the *dixième/vingtième* is no mystery. Whereas *dixième/vingtième* assessments were based either on self-declared statements of income or on relatively careful investigations, assessments for the *capitation* were imposed without the taxpayers' participation and were based on weaker knowledge gathered by fewer administrators. The *capitation* was therefore apt to be seen as arbitrary. Moreover, the definition of what the *capitation* was meant to tax – persons or property, status or wealth, or some combination of them – was exceedingly vague compared with the *vingtième* and thus tended to draw contestation from taxpayers who believed that they were surcharged. But, by remaining flexible and bending to the will of taxpayers, the crown prevented itself from pushing too many of them to the point at which they would refuse payment altogether.

Not that all taxpayers received the same degree of consideration. There were patterns in the frequency with which different social groups petitioned and in the way intendants answered their appeals. As table 3.1 shows, nobles were active and fairly successful petitioners. Of the 1,676 nobles on the *capitation* rolls in 1772, at least 192 (over 11 percent) were able to obtain a reduction in their assessment. On average, nobles received higher reductions than any other group, their reductions peaking in 1761 (when the tax was doubled) at slightly more than 100 livres, but they were assessed at higher levels than other groups and, within the nobility, those who received larger abatements had contested heavier assessments. The marquis de Sebeville, for example, obtained a reduction of 100

---

[71] The petition of Jean Bonnaventure du Jardin, seigneur de Biville, was rejected just a year after it had been accepted. AD Calvados, C 4695, no. 13, petition of September 1736.

livres in 1736 but his tax assessment of 300 livres was comparatively high.[72]

Although nobles enjoyed the largest reductions, the most active petitioners by far were officers of justice, who petitioned in droves during the tax hikes of the early 1760s and the increases after 1769. Of the 1,157 officers on the 1772 tax rolls, no fewer than 395 – more than one-third of all officers! – were granted reductions averaging 60 livres. For hundreds of officers in Caen (and thousands throughout the kingdom), supplicating intendants became a humiliating routine that continued down to the Revolution. The *privilégiés*, who also petitioned in great numbers after the tax increase of 1769, received smaller reductions than officers but were not taxed as highly in the first place.

The bourgeoisie, taxed the lightest per capita, received hundreds of small reductions. In 1788 the intendant gave municipal officers of Caen over 2,000 livres to relieve "the infinite number of wretched souls who . . . burden me with requests."[73] More impressive than the number of reductions granted to this group was the extremely high number of bourgeois who failed to pay their *capitation*. The incidence of nonpayment, which was relatively low among nobles, officers, and *privilégiés*, stands out among townspeople, although it does not follow from this that townspeople were particularly defiant of the monarchy. The records of searches in the homes of delinquent taxpayers suggest that utter poverty prevented a large segment of town residents from paying the *capitation*.

What moved intendants to make concessions to petitioners? In some cases petitioners used their social stature or that of well-placed friends to influence the rulings of intendants. Marcel Marion attributed the failure of universal taxes and the chronic financial instability of the eighteenth-century monarchy to just such abuses of influence, and, more recently, Guy Chaussinand-Nogaret argued that nobles could easily pressure intendants to lower their taxes,

---

[72] AD Calvados, C 4685, no. 60, petition of 20 December 1736. Although statistics cannot be compiled for nobles at court, impressionistic evidence suggests that they were also successful in obtaining reductions and negotiating the payment of arrears. The prince of Isenghein received a 750 livre reduction in his *capitation* of 2,250 livres "under the condition that he pays what he owes," namely three years of *capitation* arrears worth 6,750 livres. AN, G-7 1134, petition of 1706.

[73] Quoted in Perrot, *Genèse*, I, p. 140. Intendants throughout the kingdom were swamped with petitions from cities. More than one-fourth of the residents of Lyons petitioned against the *capitation* every year. BN, JdF 1444, fos. 95–8, letter from intendant of Lyons to Fleury, 8 November 1781.

quoting the boast of the duc d'Orléans, "I make arrangements with the intendants and pay nearly what I want."[74] To be sure, there were times when intendants capitulated to the pressure of their social peers and superiors, as the example of a noble army officer named Briqueville illustrates. Having been informed that his *capitation* of 1752 had risen, Briqueville petitioned the intendant, La Briffe, asking to be spared the increase. When La Briffe promptly rejected his request, the nobleman solicited the help of a patron, Geoffroy-Macé Camus de Pontcarré, the first president of the *parlement* of Rouen and one of the most powerful individuals in Normandy, who wrote on behalf of Briqueville to ask La Briffe to lower the nobleman's *capitation*. The intendant balked, defending his original decision by emphasizing to the first president that Briqueville's assessment could easily have been yet higher given his income; "Thus, I do not see that he has reason to complain to me." Not wanting to be a party to the manipulations of Pontcarré, the intendant informed him, with some cynicism, that if the magistrate was absolutely resolved to see his client's tax lowered, he would completely relinquish his jurisdiction over the matter.

If, however, these reasons and considerations do not strike you [as legitimate], monsieur, I will leave you to be the master and to determine yourself the *capitation* of Monsieur de Briqueville; I ask you only to consider the fact that I will be obliged to reimpose the amount you remove [from Briqueville's tax] on poor unfortunate subjects who are already overtaxed.

Since becoming "master" of his client's tax would have constituted an egregious usurpation of the intendant's authority, Pontcarré declined the invitation, as La Briffe had probably expected. Instead the president reiterated his wish to have the intendant lower the tax: "I expect this from your friendship and even more from your ordinary justice." This time the intendant gave in, letting Pontcarré know that it was against his better judgment. Briqueville should pay the full amount, La Briffe said, but he would reduce it anyway "since you believe, monsieur, that Monsieur de Briqueville would be wronged by the original arrangement."[75] Although initially resistant to the pressure of Pontcarré, in the end the intendant acquiesced on account of his "friendship" with the first president.

It would be wrong to make too much of La Briffe's concession,

---

[74] Chaussinand-Nogaret, "Le fisc et les privilégiés sous l'ancien régime," in *La fiscalité et ses implications sociales en Italie et en France aux XVIIe et XVIIIe siècles* (Rome, 1980), p. 197.
[75] BN, Ms. Fr. 11906, fos. 238–243, letters of 30 May, 12 April, and 24 May 1752.

however. Few taxpayers, including nobles, were capable of soliciting the protection of a powerful patron like Pontcarré. In fact, intendants were more likely to appeal to their own protector, the finance minister, when attempting to subdue unruly nobles. But these cases, too, were rare. The fact is that most contestations were resolved without recourse to patrons.

This does not mean that intendants did not bear in mind the social background of petitioners. Clearly they did. In a *mémoire* on his intendancy, d'Aube suggested that administrators should consider the rank of the petitioner when assessing and granting reductions for the *capitation*.[76] The rules for assessing nobles echoed the very considerations that nobles themselves raised in petitions. The intendant, for instance, must account for the costs of educating and caring for children and of outfitting them for war: "it is necessary to consider, as a burden on the wealth of gentlemen, the notable expense that is made to maintain children in the service of the king and state." Since "a gentleman of very old and illustrious extraction" must be expected to spend a lot, his *capitation* should not be too heavy. D'Aube also argued that officers of justice who were too poor to live as honorably as they should ought to be given lighter assessments. The intendant had little to say about the *privilégiés* and the bourgeoisie, except that the former should be taxed according to the position that endowed them with privileges and the latter should be assessed without much variation between individuals. Administrators in Caen shared some of d'Aube's opinions. The subdelegate of Bayeux recommended a reduction in the *capitation* of one noble petitioner on the grounds that the supplicant had a lot of children, "for whom he provides a costly education."[77]

In responding to petitions for justice, however, administrators were far more concerned with levels of property and income than with social status. When evaluating pleas for personal justice, intendants remained flexible because they worried that petitioners were truly being overtaxed. After all, if the vivid descriptions of financial duress and hopeless circumstances evoked in petitions were real, if pleas for personal justice were legitimate, then to ignore them could allow discontent among taxpayers to grow to dangerous levels. In the words of Chorier, an historian living in the rebellious

---

[76] BN Ms. Fr. 21812, Mémoire concernant messieurs les intendants départis dans les differentes provinces et généralités du royaume (1738), pp. 575–607.
[77] AD Calvados, C 4678, no. 84, report of 25 January 1775.

seventeenth century, "He who speaks of desperation to his sovereign, threatens him."[78] Indeed, petitioners on the edge of despair were delivering an unspoken threat that the failure to redress injustices might sever, or at least weaken, the loyalty that bound them to the monarch. The possibility of revolt was enough to make administrators take petitions seriously.

To prevent perceptions of injustice from reaching dangerous proportions, intendants attempted to gain a better knowledge of the circumstances in which petitioners found themselves and to adjust the *capitation* according to their findings. They had already estimated the wealth of taxpayers when first drawing the tax rolls, but intendants knew better than anyone that their estimations were not exact, and so, upon receiving a petition, they immediately reconsidered the taxpayer's financial standing. Petitioners who could document their hardship by providing such materials as attestations of poverty signed by local curés were highly successful in obtaining reductions.[79] When adequate documentation was lacking, as was more often the case, administrators had to verify whether petitioners were really as badly off as they claimed. They consulted neighbors, checked legal documents deposed in the *bureaux du contrôle*, met with petitioners, observed the condition and furnishings of their houses and the number of domestics employed, and estimated the scale of their commercial or agricultural revenues. When the tax receiver for Coutances investigated the petition of nobleman Jacques Louvel, the receiver discovered that Louvel was, as he had claimed, a younger son with gout; but "as for his revenue," the receiver reported to the intendant, "I was informed by many persons of honor that he has eight or nine hundred livres of income." Based on this information, the intendant decided to lower Louvel's tax not from 60 to 6 livres, as Louvel requested, but to 40 livres instead.[80] In this instance considerations of wealth overrode the petitioner's personal tale of sickness.

---

[78] Quoted in Scott, *Domination*, p. 96.

[79] Besides testimony from curés, taxpayers provided documentation on *capitation* payments made outside their place of residence (such as at the royal court or in the army) to prompt intendants to reduce the *capitation* owed in Caen by the amount paid elsewhere. When no documentation was provided, petitions were rejected. For example, the *chevalier* de Gouet claimed that a higher *capitation* was imposed on him as an army officer than as a resident of the generality of Caen. "But he does not prove this, ... which is why the subdelegate believes that the petition should be rejected." AD Calvados, C 4678, no. 86.

[80] AD Calvados, C 4688, no. 3, petition of 28 September 1702.

They could also override technicalities in the law. Etienne Legeay, who complained that he was paying a "double *capitation*," 12 livres for being an employee of the salt tax administration and 10 livres as a bourgeois of Condé, asked for a "complete discharge" from the tax he paid as a bourgeois. Normally, the intendant would have exempted the employee from the city's *capitation*, since the declaration of 1701 stated that taxpayers assessed on more than one tax roll should pay only the highest assessment. But in this case, after a brief investigation, the intendant remarked that "the wife of the supplicant ... probably makes a profit on the *eaux de vie* that she sells at retail" so that "justice" did not permit him to give Legeay a full exemption. The discovery that Legeay's wife earned income allowed the intendant to skirt the law.[81]

When investigations into the wealth of taxpayers yielded little information, intendants made measured compromises. After looking into the affairs of Charles Feron, a lawyer who requested that his *capitation* for 1714 be lowered from 46 livres to the previous year's assessment of 6 livres, the tax receiver admitted that "he did not know the wealth or income of the supplicant." With no information to go on, the intendant met Feron half way and reduced his tax to 25 livres.[82]

If administrators responded to pleas for personal justice with some flexibility, they were also quite attentive to appeals for distributive justice. The fear that complaints of unfairness could spiral into a general outcry outweighed orders to curb the expensive habit of granting reductions to petitioners. In 1778 Necker urged Esmangard to limit the reductions given to officers of justice, insisting that "the *taillables*, being the class which contributes the most to the expenses of the state and particularly to this tax, should receive a higher proportion of the aid being distributed." The finance minister could not see "the reasons" for doling out big reductions to privileged officers when commoners needed relief. Esmangard replied flatly that he could not carry out the minister's orders. If he were to restrict reductions, "the officers would not fail to complain that they were being treated more severely than other taxpayers." Officers were sensitive enough to the intendant's distribution of justice that

---

[81] The intendant did moderate the tax from 10 to 3 livres, however. AD Calvados, C 4700, no. 38, petition of August 1737.
[82] AD Calvados, C 4682, petition of 4 December 1714.

he dared not provoke them by cutting back on annual diminutions.[83]

When petitioners compared their taxes with those of others, administrators carefully considered both sides of the comparison. Handling demands for distributive justice required a lot of information and a good sense of balance. The contestation between the cities of Cherbourg and Valognes led to a full reexamination of the economic conditions of both cities. Commenting on a petition from the municipal officers of Cherbourg regarding possible increases in their city's *capitation*, Beaulieu, a subdelegate, informed the intendant that it was "natural" for the officers to be "jealous of their neighbors" who have a lighter *capitation*:

But they should not have disguised the true state of their condition and have us believe that neighboring parishes have taken from them all the benefits [of the naval yard], benefits of which Cherbourg is really the center. This statement alone would make us doubt the sincerity of their petition. They admit that consumption, rents, and the number of newly built houses have all augmented. Is this not admitting that the place has undergone improvement?[84]

The subdelegate then hammered his point home. He informed the intendant that the economy and population of Cherbourg were far more substantial than those of Valognes and that, while the officers of Cherbourg bemoaned the fact that they were experiencing a scarcity of goods, Valognes and the rest of the district suffered from the same problem. He concluded, "for a long time I have seen with distress the disproportion of taxation between these two cities." Following the subdelegate's report, the intendant decided to reestablish "equilibrium" in the tax burden by lowering the *capitation* on Valognes and raising it on Cherbourg. Not knowing exactly how much the tax should be lowered and raised, the intendant again asked Beaulieu for advice. Beaulieu thought that if the tax on Valognes were reduced by 2,000 livres, and the one on Cherbourg were raised by the same amount, the two cities would be "nearly even." The intendant agreed.[85]

Equilibrium and evenness: these were the principles that guided administrators as they negotiated with petitioners who asked for distributive justice. Administrators hoped that if they applied such principles rigorously, the distribution of taxation would become

[83] AD Calvados, C 4703, nos. 39 and 41, letters of 6 March 1778 and 17 April 1778.
[84] AD Calvados, C 4711, no. 79, report from Beaulieu to Launay, 30 May 1787.
[85] AD Calvados, C 4711, nos. 81 and 82, letters of 30 June 1787 and 11 August 1787.

uniform and all comparable taxpayers would pay exactly the same amount. Such a project, however, tested the capacity of royal administration. Responding to a 1773 petition submitted by members of the parlement of Dijon who claimed that they were being taxed unfairly relative to members of other parlements, Terray ordered a thorough investigation into the distribution of the *capitation* on officers in all parlements. Only by reviewing the case in its full comparative dimension would the finance minister be "in a position to judge the protests made by the officers of the parlement of Dijon." Terray assigned the case to his assistant, Mesnard de Couichard, who, in turn, consulted d'Ormesson, the expert on the *capitation*. Believing that "the *capitation* of the courts should be uniform," d'Ormesson worked for weeks with Couichard to make sure that similar officers (from presidents to clerks) in different parlements were taxed the same amount. Exact uniformity could alone satisfy the parlement of Dijon and prevent further complaints and petitions. The relentless flow of petitions suggests that such uniformity was never achieved.[86]

Certain patterns in the way administrators responded to petitions are clearly identifiable. Administrators were remarkably inflexible in their handling of the *vingtième*. They rejected the great majority of the petitions they investigated and delayed ruling on those that they did not have the time to verify. The burden of proof fell overwhelmingly on petitioners, who could not, like disgruntled payers of the *capitation*, simply tell an unfortunate tale of misfortune or hardship, speak of their service to the king, or complain that other taxpayers were being treated more favorably. Petitioners against the *vingtième* had to demonstrate that their property produced less revenue than had been estimated, a challenge that few could meet. The justice that *vingtième* petitioners sought was, therefore, consistently denied throughout the century.

Alternatively, administrators were quite flexible when it came to the *capitation*. In responding to appeals for personal justice, intendants adjusted the assessments of those they believed to be truly overburdened or desperate and, in response to appeals for distributive justice, they attempted to balance the way the tax fell, weighing the burden of the petitioner's tax against that of taxpayers with whom the petitioner had compared him- or herself. No matter what

---

[86] AN, H-1 173, nos. 69–90.

sort of justice was evoked by petitioners, administrators rarely accorded them all they had asked for. The reductions that were granted in the *capitation* represented compromises, not complete concessions.

Blocked from pursuing justice in the courts, universal taxpayers directed their appeals to administrators in the form of written petitions, countless numbers of which coursed through the organs of state every year from 1695 to the Revolution. The language of petitions reveals much about the political attitudes of ordinary privileged and property-owning subjects who were now confronted with the monarchy's fiscal demands. By their very nature petitions were not apt to be explicitly hostile. Few privileged taxpayers used their appeals to cast aspersions on royal administrators, to challenge the right of the monarchy to impose taxes on the privileged, or to theorize about politics in the abstract. Unlike the rhetoric deployed by privileged subjects who found themselves caught in the rolls of the *taille*, the language of petitions against universal taxes rarely contained expressions of outrage and almost never raised the discussion of "rights." Petitioners chose instead to speak of justice.

Requests for justice in petitions against the *vingtième* contained tedious but precise discussions of revenues, expenses, and assessments – a modern administrative language for a relatively modern tax – and usually lacked any trace of anger at, or frustration with, the crown and its agents. No doubt such emotions existed, but they were not manifest in petitions.

Petitions for justice in the levy of the *capitation* were more varied. The petitions of nobles of the sword followed a distinct pattern as they recounted the experience and cost of military service, implying that nobles had met their personal obligations to the crown and, thus, the *capitation* was redundant and excessive. Beyond the special case of the nobility, petitioners in general employed one of two senses of justice: personal and distributive. Taxpayers seeking personal justice attempted to move the intendant by relating stories of desperation and tragedy; here, justice was often little more than charity or grace. Petitioners seeking distributive justice compared themselves with peers or social superiors who were supposedly paying a lighter tax; in this case, the word "justice" evoked principles of equity or equality to demand that intendants distribute the burden more fairly. Although it can hardly be said that the language of justice threatened the principles on which the monarchy was based – petitioners were trying to bend the will of the crown, not break it – appeals to distributive justice were not passive requests for royal paternalism, graciousness, or mercy. Rather, they implied that state administrators were balancing competing interests in a unfair and arbitrary manner.

Appeal by petition brought the privileged into direct and frequent contact with royal fiscal administration. That contact was, for *vingtième* petitioners, largely negative, as their pleas were repeatedly rejected or neglected by intendants confident in their evaluations of income. As the next chapter will show, such property-owners grew dissatisfied with the intendancy, the *vingtième* bureau, and the fiscal demands of the crown.

The effect of petitioning on privileged payers of the *capitation* is more difficult to assess. Hundreds upon hundreds went through the procedure of petitioning every year in the generality of Caen (tens of thousands went through it throughout the kingdom) and their efforts tended to result in compromises. How did the nobleman who already served the crown, the artisan who could barely feed his family, or the sister who believed her siblings were better treated feel when they learned that the intendant answered their requests by reducing the tax to a level above that for which they had pleaded? Apart from the rare show of exasperation, it is impossible to determine if they were satisfied with the intendant's ruling, upset that they did not get all they had asked for, or simply irked by having to go through the bureaucratic procedure. We do know that officers of justice resented their dependence on the intendant for tax reductions, and it is reasonable to assume that many nobles, for whom the process of petitioning was equally if not more humiliating, shared their sentiment. As for the desperate artisan or the ill-treated sister, he or she might have felt fortunate to receive some considera-tion or might have privately cursed the intendant for his stinginess or lack of equity. Certainly, the fact that so many taxpayers, year after year, showed administrators in painstaking detail exactly where injustices lay and gave clear expression to the idea that they were being treated unfairly does suggest a certain degree of frustration with fiscal administration. Although that frustration was cloaked by tones of deference and circulated silently within the confines of royal administration, disputes over taxation in the institutional sphere would give it an authoritative, public voice.

CHAPTER 4

Taking "liberty" to the public: tax disputes in the institutional sphere

"This reflection is as applicable to the clergy as it is to the Parlements, to the *pays d'états*, and to every corps which has prerogatives: the Government fears their irreverence; they fear its invasions; and in this battle of imagination, each often goes too far because there is no line demarcating suspicion and distrust."

– Jacques Necker[1]

"The ideas [of the parlement] had shocked beyond measure; and yet perhaps they would have been tolerated if they remained a secret between the magistrates and the crown. But nearly always printed, distributed in public, read avidly, and commented on in a hundred different ways, sometimes even before the royal court received them, they aroused in France a fermentation which was always growing and which rightfully worried the crown."

– Amable-Pierre Floquet[2]

To impose universal taxes the crown had to confront institutions as well as individuals. Indeed, when we shift our attention away from the administrative to the institutional sphere, a whole new level of dispute comes into focus. Here, conflict unfolded on a grand scale as the monarchy collided with the Assembly of the Clergy, provincial estates, and sovereign courts of law such as parlements, *chambres des comptes*, and *cours des aides*. All of these institutions contested the monarchy's fiscal demands and maneuvered to obstruct the royal will in ways that individual taxpayers could or dared not. Not only did institutions lay claim to broad geographical, administrative, and legal jurisdictions, they employed a language of protest that extended

[1] Necker, *De l'administration*, II, p. 335.
[2] Amable Floquet, *Histoire du parlement de Normandie*, 7 vols. (Rouen, 1840–3), VI, p. 402.

well beyond the deferential vocabulary found in administrative petitions. Institutions did more than solicit justice; they spoke defiantly of "despotism," "liberty," and the rights of the "citizen" and "nation." Where such words came from, why and how they were deployed, and what they meant in the context of tax disputes is the subject of this chapter.

This chapter will also examine the relationship between conflict over universal taxation and public opinion. Institutions did not silently convey their grievances to royal administrators as individual petitioners did. Rather, they deliberately publicized them in the form of dramatic political gestures, incendiary speeches, and printed statements of protest. Was the public paying attention? How did the publicity of disputes politicize the problem of taxation and shape the attitudes of taxpayers outside institutions?

We can observe the process through which taxation was politicized by focusing on a single institution, the parlement of Rouen. While institutions like the Assembly of the Clergy and provincial estates clashed with the crown in defense of their liberties and privileges, the parlements, the highest law courts in the realm, formulated the strongest and most far-reaching language of opposition to royal taxation. The parlement of Rouen, whose jurisdiction encompassed the three Norman generalities of Caen, Alençon, and Rouen, provides a particularly instructive example of judicial opposition for two reasons. First, because we are familiar with the incidence of taxation in the generalities of Caen and Rouen, we may map the evolution of parlementary rhetoric against actual fluctuations in the *capitation* and *vingtième*. Secondly, of the thirteen parlements, the one seated in Rouen was among the most vocal during the last decades of the Old Regime. The "grenadier" or "avante-garde" of the magistrature, as one royal minister called it, the parlement of Rouen expressed with great clarity many of the ideas that other parlements and certain provincial estates advanced more hesitantly.[3] The conspicuous quality of Rouen's resistance to taxation makes the court an interesting and lively case, especially when seen against the background of the activity of other courts. From the 1750s to the Revolution, in response to a stream of tax decrees and to particular surges in the *capitation* and *vingtième*, and under the pressure of a small but enthusiastic opposition party, the court modified

---

[3] Le Verdier, *Miromesnil*, VI, p. xiv, quotation of L'Averdy.

rhetoric it had already used in religious disputes to develop constitutional ideas that resonated with the privileged taxpayers of Normandy. In its attempt to fend off the advances of royal fiscal administration, the court familiarized the taxpaying public with a discourse that challenged the claims of absolute monarchy.

Until recently much of the history of eighteenth-century tax disputes between parlements and the crown was written by ardent partisans of either side. Partisans of the monarchy accused magistrates of cynically using the courts to protect their fiscal privileges by blocking promising royal initiatives to reform the tax system. Every time forward-looking ministers attempted to rationalize the tax system or equalize the tax burden, Marcel Marion wrote, "the egotistical and tyrannical caste" of magistrates put their retrograde interests before the interests of the people and the king, and impeded reform.[4] Other historians have taken the side of the magistrates, arguing that the parlements served as the last legal barrier to an excessively powerful and power-hungry throne. Without the staunch opposition of the parlements, the rule of law would have disintegrated, exposing royal subjects to the ravages of a relentlessly "authoritarian monarchy."[5] In their least careful moments, historians writing in each of these traditions have simply reformulated the arguments of the parlements or the crown, reenacting one side of a battle that raged more than two centuries ago.

More recent historiography has considered the parlements with greater detachment. Resisting moral judgments about the value of monarchical reform and parlementary resistance, a number of historians, mostly British, have looked more closely at the mechanics of parlementary politics: the negotiations between royal ministers and magistrates, the tactics of parties within parlements, the personal and collective motivations of judges, the influence of courtly intrigue on different parlementary factions, and the ways in which kings managed or mismanaged parlementary affairs.[6] Thanks to this

---

[4] Marion, *Histoire financière*, I, p. 183. Variations on this thesis have been sustained by, among others, Alfred Cobban, *A History of Modern France 1715–1789* (London, 1957); and Michel Antoine, *Louis XV* (Paris, 1989).

[5] Jean Egret, *Louis XV et l'opposition parlementaire* (Paris, 1970), pp. 133–9. A similar sympathetic portrait of the judges is drawn in Jules Flammermont, *Le chancelier Maupeou et les parlements* (Paris, 1883).

[6] Doyle's *Parlement of Bordeaux* was a turning point in this respect. Recent studies of Parisian judicial politics include: Peter Campbell, *Power and Politics in Old Regime France 1720–1745* (London, 1996); John Rogister, *Louis XV and the Parlement of Paris, 1737–1755* (Cambridge, 1995);

corpus of studies we now have a much more nuanced picture of Old Regime politics, especially the politics internal to and surrounding the parlement of Paris. But there is still disagreement over certain fundamental questions. Did conflicts between parlements and crown subvert the authority of the monarchy? To what extent did the parlements' invocation of despotism, national sovereignty, and liberty alter the nature of Old Regime politics? Did parlementary rhetoric influence the public to which the courts appealed? As British historians have focused on the complexities of parlementary politics, remaining characteristically cautious in their speculation about the ways in which the courts eroded royal authority, others have ascribed great potency to judicial discourse, believing it capable of such Herculean deeds as "desacralizing" the monarchy, legitimizing the influence of public opinion in government affairs, and disseminating the idea that sovereignty resided in the nation and not the king.[7]

This chapter synthesizes these two recent approaches – one emphasizing practice, the other rhetoric – by underscoring connections between transformations in state fiscal administration and changes in parlementary politics, by determining the meaning of parlementary rhetoric within the particular context of tax disputes, and by assessing the impact of such rhetoric on the attitudes of privileged taxpayers in general. An examination of the parlement of Rouen will help us move between technical questions about the way the law court functioned and larger concerns about the nature and influence of parlementary ideology.

THE CALM BEFORE THE STORM

The engagement of the parlement of Rouen in universal tax disputes followed a distinct evolution that can be divided roughly into three periods: 1695 to 1756, an era of relative calm; 1760 to 1764, years of intense legislative conflict; and 1771 to 1782, a decade marked by the

---

Julian Swann, *Politics and the Parlement of Paris under Louis XV, 1754–1774* (Cambridge, 1995); and Bailey Stone, *The Parlement of Paris, 1774–1789* (Chapel Hill, NC, 1981).

[7] For public opinion, see Baker, *Inventing*, ch. 8; and Bell, *Lawyers and Citizens*. For desacralization, see Van Kley, *Damiens Affair*, pp. 246–55; and Jeffery Merrick, *The Desacralization of the French Monarchy in the Eighteenth Century* (Baton Rouge, 1990). For national sovereignty, see Roger Bickart, *Les parlements et la notion de souveraineté nationale au XVIIIe siècle* (Paris, 1932); and Elie Carcassonne, *Montesquieu et le problème de la constitution française au XVIIIe siècle* (reprint, Geneva, 1970).

Maupeou coup and its legacy. In each period the crown presented the court with a train of universal tax decrees. Because "extraordinary" universal taxes (particularly the *dixième* and *vingtième*) were levied for fixed durations, they, unlike the "ordinary" and permanent *taille*, had to be reestablished, prolonged, or increased with new legislation – and that legislation, to be effective, had to be registered by the kingdom's parlements.

Before mid-century the parlements of Paris and the provinces generally, if grudgingly, accepted universal tax measures. From 1695 to 1756 the parlement of Rouen voluntarily registered all eight edicts and declarations establishing or reestablishing the *capitation*, the *cinquantième*, the *dixième*, and the *vingtième*.[8] It is true that when registering these decrees and thereby rendering them enforceable by the courts, magistrates voiced objections, or "remonstrances," in which they pointed out a given law's disadvantages or its incompatibility with existing law, but in this period remonstrances were surprisingly mild, focusing on technical matters such as the temporary duration of universal taxes (which were expected to terminate at the end of wars) and the application of specific articles in the laws. The strongest language against the *dixième*, appearing first in 1741, referred to the "abuses" of administrators who, estimating the wealth of taxpayers at "whatever price pleased them," rendered the tax "arbitrary." "Arbitrary" would eventually become a key word in parlementary protests against taxation, but during this early period the magistrates of Rouen had not yet associated the term with "despotism." And even if they had, few would have known about it since, before 1760, fiscal remonstrances were never printed for public consumption.

Conflict escalated in 1749 when the controller-general, Machault, converted the wartime *dixième* to a peacetime *vingtième*. The establishment of this first *vingtième*, which threatened to strike the clergy and revoke the *abonnements* previously arranged with provincial estates, caused major conflict with the clergy of France and the powerful estates of Languedoc and Brittany. Although the parlement of Paris, after mild objections, registered the edict of May 1749, the parle-

---

[8] AD Seine-Maritime, 1B 230, secret register of the parlement of Rouen, 21 and 26 November and 12 December 1710; 1B 5445, secret register, 26 November 1725; 1B 253, secret register, 18 January 1734; 1B 261, secret register, 14 November 1741; 1B 268, secret register, 9 and 16 July 1749; 1B 276, secret register, 15 November 1756. (No deliberations on the *capitation* appear in the secret registers for 1695 and 1701).

ments of Bordeaux, Aix, Rennes, Dijon, and Toulouse remonstrated and did not register the edict until *lettres de jussion*, royal orders commanding courts to register decrees without delay, moved them to transcribe the legislation into their registers. The parlement of Rouen was ambivalent. Echoing the language of individual administrative petitions, the magistrates of Rouen reminded the king that his subjects were living in extreme "misery" and that noble "warriors who ... risked their lives for the service of your majesty" would now return to their land only to find heavy tax obligations. The court also reiterated its protest against the methods by which the *dixième* had been administered, particularly the "harassment of directors and controllers" who ignored declarations of wealth and made "estimations [of property] at their will and by this means rendered the tax arbitrary." But the parlement deliberately undercut the power of these words by expressing its willingness to register the decree should the king order it to do so: "If our humble remonstrances are not heard and Your Majesty deigns to give us new orders for the registration of such an onerous edict, we will obey with the most respectful submission and we will be exonerated in the eyes of the peoples of this province who could reproach us for not having spoken of their exhaustion and their needs." Such an open solicitation for *lettres de jussion* revealed the utter flexibility of the court as well as the absence of any intention to print the remonstrances. In 1749 the court was ready to yield to the king's will as long as it could maintain its reputation of protecting those whom it claimed to represent.

Much more serious was the action the court would take when the crown, having drifted back to war in 1756, doubled the *vingtième*. By 1756 magistrates throughout the kingdom had learned that the *vingtième* was not as harmless as it first appeared. Since 1749 provincial directors and controllers, under direct orders from Machault, had been systematically revising the old *dixième* rolls by investigating the wealth of taxpayers. When the crown presented the edict of 7 July 1756 calling for a second *vingtième* to be levied during the war, several parlements put up a vigorous fight: Paris, led by a small Jansenist faction, refused to register the law, mounting its first public opposition to wartime taxation since the minority of Louis XIV; Besançon initiated the protracted conflict that would become known as the Besançon affair; the *cour des aides* of Paris began its own long campaign against the practice of "one single Magistrate," the intendant, having full power over the tax, and reclaimed the right of courts of law to judge contestations; and the parlements of Toulouse, Aix, Bordeaux, and Rouen lashed out against the "inquisition" and "caprice" of "these hidden agents," the controllers.[9] Emboldened by its successful ventures into the refusal of sacraments controversy of 1753 and the Grand Conseil affair of 1755–6, the parlement of Rouen took opposition a step further. Although it voluntarily registered the edict of 7 July to support the war, it stipulated in its registers that, "to prevent subjects from being exposed to a new tax through the arbitrary assessments of Controllers and Directors," the tax rolls were not be revised. It had requested as much in its remonstrances of 1741 and 1749 but it now inserted this proviso directly in its registers, giving it the force of law and making it possible to prosecute controllers who changed assessments. The assertiveness of this act caught the attention of the marquis d'Argenson who, ever alert to signs of political change, prophesied that "the provincial Parlements will go further than Paris; they will be the lost children of the magistrature."[10]

JANSENISTS AND TAXPAYERS, 1760–1764

The marquis was not to be disappointed. From 1760 to 1763, as the crown forced the parlements to register a series of hikes in the *capitation* and the *vingtième*, the scale, language, and publicity of fiscal dispute reached heights unprecedented since the Fronde of the mid-seventeenth century. The provincial parlements, led by Grenoble, Toulouse, and Rouen, exercised powerful methods of opposing royal fiscal legislation and employed a new vocabulary of resistance to taxation that was, for the first time, publicized widely in printed remonstrances. The decree that touched off this heated round of conflict was the edict of February 1760, which for two years added a third *vingtième* to the first two while doubling the *capitation* on the privileged (and only on the privileged) and tripling it on certain financial officers. The parlement of Rouen refused registration and issued extraordinarily antagonistic remonstrances that would set the linguistic framework for the court's opposition to taxation for the

---

[9] Swann, *Parlement of Paris*, ch. 6; Marion, *Histoire financière*, I, pp. 181–2; Rioche, *Vingtièmes*, p. 66.
[10] Quoted in Egret, *Louis XV*, p. 79.

remainder of the Old Regime. For this reason, the remonstrances of 10 May 1760 merit our close attention.[11]

At one level the remonstrances simply developed themes raised in previous remonstrances and in administrative petitions against universal taxes. They reiterated technical grievances about the costs of estate maintenance, complained about the arbitrariness and lack of "economy" in the tax system, and reproached the financiers who profited from it. The remonstrances also continued to stress the ways in which "every order" was harmed by taxes. Not only had high taxes pushed the misery and exhaustion of "the peoples" to extreme levels, but they made it increasingly difficult for magistrates and nobles to serve the crown professionally. Taxes "persecuted" a nobility whose chief obligation to the kingdom was military defense and "forced" magistrates to abandon the expensive duty of fighting oppression. "All orders of state groaned under the burdensome weight" of taxes, which "take from the rich the honest wealth that accords with their station and removes from the poor the subsistence that is owed all men."

At another level the magistrates used rhetoric that had been entirely absent from earlier remonstrances against taxation. They used words such as "despotism," "liberty," "citizen," "nation," and "estates" to conjure the image of a kingdom perched on the precipice of disaster. Explaining how the kingdom had arrived at such a state, the magistrates divided French history into three stages: a distant, ideal past; an intermediate period during which "finance" ruined France; and the present moment in which the king faced a choice between destroying the kingdom or restoring the old order. The first epoch, for which the magistrates gave no precise dates although they alluded to Francis I, was a Golden Age of estates, healthy citizens, and flourishing princes.

As long as the meeting of Estates lasted in France, the people, in the persons of its Deputies, shared in the estimation of public needs and knew the nature and extent of them: familiar with the nature and extent of its resources, it knew how to assess & pay its contributions. These [contributions] sufficed for even extraordinary expenses without diminishing the wealth of individuals. The Government flourished as did the Citizen: the

---

[11] AD Seine-Maritime, 1B 278, secret register of the parlement of Rouen, 10 May 1760. The printed version is entitled *Remontrances du parlement de Rouen au sujet de l'édit du mois du février dernier, & de la déclaration du 3 du même mois* (n. p., [1760]).

subject paid more willingly that which he paid without effort; the Prince received in full what was brought to him with economy.

In this era princes had sufficient revenue because the "Citizen," having participated in the administration of taxes, voluntarily paid them. Here lay the origin of a new definition of citizenship: the citizen was a subject who willfully taxed himself and contributed the sum to the prince.

Yet this Golden Age passed. "The order was reversed and taxes were collected without asking, so that, nothing being legal, all was arbitrary: old and venerable conventions, safeguards for the well-being of the State and the legitimate liberty of its members were eluded, scorned, and these sacred barriers, august monuments to our first existence, were crossed" to the point where the state "hardly recognized itself." These violations unleashed "a flood of taxes" that inundated the provinces. Such was history since the decline of estates.

To pass from history to theory, from past to present, the magistrates focused on the single agent of the kingdom's decline: finance. Note how the verb tense changes seamlessly from past to present in the following passage: "Finance, this worm-like eater of Citizen & State, attacked, overran, subjugated everything. Even legislation became its prey: to make laws, to revoke them; to create as to destroy, only it [finance] is consulted." Having asserted that finance degrades law, the remonstrances asked if the name "law" could even be applied to the confused mass of royal decrees put into effect without the consent of the nation. The parlement's answer was unambiguous: "The main attribute of a law is to be accepted. The right to accept is the right of the Nation." "Once the soul of the French Government," today this right is "exercised during the interval between Estates by those whom the Nation regards as depositories of legislation," namely the sovereign courts. This assertion of national sovereignty directly contradicted absolutist theory, which held that legislative authority resides exclusively in the prince. Although the magistrates admitted that the king could impose his will on the nation by forcing the courts to register decrees, they claimed that this practice was "vicious in its principle" and should be suppressed. In the absence of estates, the institutions that expressed the will of the nation, the sovereign courts must be allowed to step forward to give laws "a public character" without which laws were "nothing."

At this point in the remonstrances the word "despotism" appears in connection with the jurisdiction of intendants. Having raised the status of the parlement to that of a body that provisionally represents the nation, the remonstrances appealed directly to the king: "Can your Parlement, Sire, this august body born with the monarchy, be replaced by these indefinable Judges, who in the past were unknown to the nation, and who exist and act without principles?" After explaining that these new judges, the intendants, had been improperly granted the right to handle tax disputes, the magistrates declared that "despotism . . . is practiced everywhere in the name of the Prince." Despotism manifested itself in the growing number and weight of all kinds of taxes, but the remonstrances leveled their most serious charges against the *capitation* and *vingtième*, taxes that bypassed the jurisdiction of courts. The *capitation*, an "arbitrary tax" that could be increased by a simple letter from the controller-general to the intendant and that was not, as it was supposed to be, levied with the assistance of local nobles, was a "tax of servitude," a phrase probably borrowed from Montesquieu.[12] The *vingtième*, for its part, was construed as a grave threat to private property. If tripled, "the ownership of property that the laws of the nation maintain for the citizens would no longer be but an empty title." Was there a more blatant sign of the approach of despotism than utter disregard for private property?

The king, then, had to make a decision. He could impose the tax edict, a dire policy that would "risk losing and destroying everything." He could withdraw the edict and provide the kingdom with the relief he had promised. Or better yet he could overcome financial crisis by changing the constitutional structure of the kingdom and restoring defunct provincial estates. Although this last request for the estates of Normandy was suffused with deferential appeals to the king's paternal justice, it daringly compared two distinct political worlds: one with estates in which citizens taxed themselves and liberty thrived; and the other, without estates, in which citizens were victims, even slaves, of the tyranny of fiscal administration:

You are equally, Sire, the father of all your peoples: under this title they all

---

[12] Although Montesquieu was not cited, his comment that "the head tax is more natural to servitude" seems to have inspired the magistrates. Charles-Louis de Secondat, baron de Montesquieu, *De l'esprit des lois* (reprint, Paris, 1979), I, p. 364.

have an equal right to your royal protection. However, some contribute to the needs of the State by means of taxes that they distribute themselves; others fall prey to Financiers, & are the sad victims of the tyranny of their Agents. Why is it that having the same father, they have such different lots? Some, stripped of their rights, groan, as it were, in slavery: others, supported in these inviolable rights, still enjoy the liberty of children. Return to us, Sire, this precious liberty, return our Estates. You will make disappear these ruinous contestations that afflict the Citizen, these multiple evocations that remove from him his natural Judges, and these immense efforts that consume him fruitlessly for Your Majesty & for the Nation.

The magistrates promised that, once the estates were reinstituted, liberty would prevail and "joy would succeed alarm and complaint." But as long as the province was unable to represent itself in national or provincial estates, administrators would continue to impose and increase taxes arbitrarily, doing harm to privileged and nonprivileged citizens alike. On these grounds the parlement of Rouen refused to register the edict of February 1760 voluntarily.

This was strong language and it is worth pausing to consider its origins. The magistrates who drafted the remonstrances had certainly done their homework. Beyond the many legal treatises they had encountered while studying law at the University of Caen (or Paris), they seem to have been informed by a few very precise sources. Certain phrases appear to have been drawn from Montesquieu's *De l'esprit des lois*, such as the description of the *capitation* as a "tax of servitude" and the consistent self-definition of the courts as "depositories of the law."[13] The word "despotism" may have come from the same source or from Boulainvilliers, who used the term in his *Histoire de l'ancien gouvernement de France* (1727) and whose *État de la France* (1737) was cited in the remonstrances. The magistrates also appear to have been reading the remonstrances of the *cour des aides* of Paris, written by its president, Malesherbes, who in 1756 drew attention to the ways in which the royal council had usurped the jurisdiction of the courts in affairs relating to the *capitation* and the *vingtième*. Just as Malesherbes hinted in 1756 and would explicitly state in 1775, the magistrates of Rouen suggested that "despotism" sprang from the intendants and a throng of fiscal agents who were trespassing so far onto the jurisdiction of the courts that they threatened to replace them altogether.

---

[13] It is difficult to trace Montesquieu's influence because magistrates were reluctant to cite him before the Maupeou coup. Carcassonne, *Montesquieu*, pp. 113–14.

The most obvious source of the new constitutional language stemmed from the court's involvement in the Jansenist controversy. Although the vocabulary of despotism, liberty, and citizenship was new to fiscal contestation, the court had used it before, in 1753, when it attempted to prosecute priests who were denying sacraments to Jansenists, the Augustinians who were condemned by the papal bull *Unigenitus* in 1713. In May of 1753, mimicking colleagues in Paris with whom he corresponded, the Jansenist councilor Antoine-Augustin Thomas du Fossé, grandnephew of a well-known member of the abbey of Port-Royal, stood before his fellow magistrates of the parlement of Rouen and denounced a curé in the town of Verneuil for refusing to administer last rites to a dying Jansenist priest. The royal council, moving quickly to protect the curé from prosecution, evoked the case and admonished the court for intervening in matters beyond its jurisdiction. The court responded with two remarkable remonstrances, written by Fossé and his allies, which bear a strong resemblance to later tax remonstrances inasmuch as they character-ized the sacraments as a type of property that required protection from arbitrary authority or "despotism."[14] By claiming that the clergy, as "debtors," owed the sacraments and that the Jansenists as "citizens" possessed the "liberty" to receive them, the parlement turned a religious controversy into an affair of property and public order which fell more squarely within its jurisdiction. Further, the court justified its disobedience to the king, who had sided with the pro-*Unigenitus* episcopacy, by claiming that kings recognized the need "to put some kinds of limits on their own Power, to submit their wills to the inspection of enlightened and faithful Magistrates." As "depositories of Your Authority," the courts were "free" to use that authority according to "their own conscience" even if it forced them "to resist the Sovereign himself." This was a potent constitutional challenge to royal absolutism.

The connection between the development of constitutionalism and the controversy over Jansenism has been well demonstrated by Dale Van Kley, who has helped to move Jansenism from the wings of

[14] This discussion of the remonstrances of 14 August and 6 November 1753 is based on Olivier Chaline, *Godart de Belbeuf: le parlement, le roi et les Normands* (Luneray, 1996), pp. 383–98; Mathew Levinger, "La rhétorique protestaire du parlement de Rouen," *Annales* (May–June, 1990), pp. 591–7; and Floquet, *Parlement de Normandie*, VI, pp. 269–324. The characterization of sacraments as property is discussed in Merrick, *Desacralization*, chs. 4 and 5; and Merrick, "Conscience and Citizenship in Eighteenth-Century France," *Eighteenth-Century Studies* 21 (Fall, 1987), pp. 48–70.

religious history to the center stage of the debate over the origins of the Revolution. In the 1750s and early 1760s, Van Kley contends, Jansenist magistrates and their Gallican allies in the parlement of Paris were far more willing to defy the crown over issues of religious conscience than over mundane financial affairs. The oft-quoted words of the Parisian councilor Philippe Thomé are not to be denied:

a distinction had to be drawn between one's conscience in religious matters and that in purely human affairs; that in religious affairs one ought never to do a thing that one believed to be evil, because one owed obedience to God rather than to men; but that in purely human affairs [such as taxation], one was quits after having made the appropriate efforts to enlighten the sovereign on the inconveniences of the measure he wished to adopt.[15]

To those engaged in dramatic battles over salvation and religious "Truth," how urgent could the problem of royal fiscal administration be? During the Seven Years War the parlement of Paris consistently put its religious concerns above its fiscal ones, as it refrained from extreme protest against tax increases in exchange for greater influence over religious policy.

Yet if we look at the provinces during the period of the Seven Years War, they tell a rather different story. Jansenism may have had a hold on many Parisians and on a small but important faction within the parlement of Paris but it was much weaker in distant provincial capitals. The parlements of Besançon, Aix, and Grenoble, for example, were Gallican but hardly Jansenist, and throughout the eighteenth century they were far more sensitive to financial affairs than to religious ones. Even in Paris the problem of taxation could occasionally rival that of religion, as the Parisian lawyer Edmond Barbier confided to his diary in May 1763: "People no longer speak but of these [tax] edicts, each person talking about what he knows, which has totally made everyone forget about the Jesuits." Months later he regretted the renewal of the dispute with the Jesuits because "the most important affair is to lighten taxation, and yet find the means to pay the debts of the State which are considerable."[16] Further, judicial Jansenism, like all movements of opposition, did not survive its own successes. After the victory over the Jesuits in 1764, it

---

[15] Quoted in Van Kley, *Damiens Affair*, p. 101. Also quoted in Swann, *Parlement of Paris*, pp. 157–8; and Egret, *Louis XV*, p. 46.
[16] Barbier, *Chronique*, VIII, pp. 71 and 127.

could no longer remain a viable political force as secular issues such as taxation became predominant.

The interesting question is not whether religion or finance was the more significant issue – both were extremely important. The better question to pose is, how did the transition from the first issue to the second occur, and what did that transition mean for parlementary politics, ideology, and public opinion? To follow the bumpy road from religious to fiscal politics is to travel one step closer to the kinds of crises that would eventually bring down the Old Regime.

In Rouen, as elsewhere, the tie between Jansenist and fiscal opposition was above all biographical. The same Fossé who led the charge against the "despotism of the clergy" in 1753 and spearheaded the attack on the Jesuits in 1762 was also a member of the committees that drafted the remonstrances against the tax legislation of 1760, 1761, and 1763. Although it is unclear whether there was a coherent Jansenist party in the parlement of Rouen – Van Kley believes there was; Chaline insists there was not – Fossé did correspond with members of the Jansenist party in the parlement of Paris such as Adrien Le Paige, the lawyer who penned the influential *Lettres historiques sur le parlement de France* (1753–4), copies of which circulated among the more radical Norman magistrates.[17] Small wonder that the anti-tax remonstrances of 1760 resembled the anti-*Unigenitus* remonstrances of 1753.

The resemblance between the two documents, however, should not divert our attention from the ways in which the later remonstrances refashioned the rhetoric of judicial Jansenism. In 1760 the court transposed the language of the 1753 protest into the key of fiscal dispute, changing the meaning of that language in the process. Consider the examples of such words as despotism, citizen, and liberty. In both 1753 and 1760 the word "despotism" was invoked to condemn "arbitrary" authority, which was widely believed to be illegitimate. Theorists of absolutism, such as Jacques-Bénigne Bossuet, Louis XIV's court theologian, asserted that, although the authority of monarchs in France was absolute, it was not arbitrary as it was in Eastern monarchies. Absolute government in France, like that of all "civilized states," was limited by reason, divine and

[17] Dale Van Kley, *The Jansenists and the Expulsion of the Jesuits from France, 1757–1765* (New Haven, CT, 1975), pp. 175–7; Dale Van Kley, *The Religious Origins of the French Revolution: From Calvin to the Civil Constitution, 1560–1791* (New Haven, CT, 1996), p. 158, n. 49; Chaline, *Godart de Belbeuf,* p. 383; Le Verdier, *Miromesnil,* IV, p. 121, letter of 5 February 1766.

earthly law, and respect for life and property. Bossuet established this distinction between absolute and arbitrary authority in order to defend absolutism against its critics who, he thought, might try to confuse it with arbitrary government in order to make it sound "odious and unbearable."[18] Bossuet rightly anticipated eighteenth-century objections: the remonstrances of 1753 and 1760 both used the term "arbitrary" to imply that French absolutism was becoming dangerously erratic to the point of approaching "despotism."

But the two remonstrances did not offer the same critique of royal authority. Whereas the source of arbitrary authority in 1753 was the pro-*Unigenitus* clergy (and by implication the royal council whose policy protected that clergy), arbitrary authority in 1760 was rooted in the fiscal-administrative apparatus of state, composed of the controller-general, financiers, intendants, and a host of commissioned tax agents, all of whom transgressed the "sacred barriers" of old liberties and conventions. (Although the king was not part of this composite, he was expected to keep it under control). If in 1753 "despotism" resulted from a misguided religious policy pursued by the clergy and supported by the royal council, in 1760 it lurked in the very machinery of state which, by design, attacked property. That property, of course, no longer consisted of the divine sacraments denied to a religious minority but of the earthly fruits of thousands of property-owners across the province. The stakes had changed from the salvation of the few to the wealth of the many.

If the magistrates changed the meaning of despotism in 1760, they also modified the term "citizen." The word "citizen," meaning simply "subject" or "bourgeois of a city" in the early eighteenth century, was used in the context of the Jansenist controversy to refer more specifically to Catholics who possessed the right to receive sacraments.[19] In the remonstrances of 10 May 1760 magistrates changed the meaning of the word again to allude to taxpayers both past and present. The citizen-taxpayer of the past, who had participated in determining the weight and distribution of taxes and, consequently, paid them willingly as a tribute to the king, had become the contemporary citizen-taxpayer who found himself besieged by "finance" and deprived of proper legal recourse. Why

---

[18] Jacques-Bénigne Bossuet, *Politique tirée des propres paroles de l'Ecriture sainte*, ed. Jacques Le Brun (Geneva, 1967), pp. 92 and 291.

[19] Merrick, "Conscience and Citizenship," pp. 48–9; and Charlotte Wells, *Law and Citizenship in Early Modern France* (Baltimore, MD, 1995), ch. 5.

would the latter citizen willingly yield money to the king? Only the return of liberty could restore the security and generosity of the citizen.

Liberty, too, had multiple meanings. Although in both 1753 and 1760 the word was used to describe the freedom with which the parlement should rightfully be able to deliberate on and register royal decrees, other meanings of "liberty" changed as it migrated from religious to fiscal disputes. Instead of alluding to the liberty of the Catholic citizen to receive the sacraments, it now meant the freedom of citizens to contribute taxes voluntarily to the crown. It meant participating in the estimation of the needs of the state and the resources of the citizenry, fixing the proper scale and distribution of taxes, and willfully providing the sums to the king. In short, it meant the freedom to tax oneself. While historians are apt to equate Old Regime liberty with privilege, that definition does not fully obtain in this instance. To be sure, *parlementaires* sought to protect their own right to register decrees and to shield the privileged of Normandy from tax increases, but they pursued these narrow jurisdictional and fiscal goals by broadening the meaning of liberty. Never did the court invoke the term to claim that nobles and officers were exempt from the *capitation* and the *vingtième*.[20] Instead, liberty came to stand for the general principle of judicial consent to legislation and the freedom to participate in the levy of taxation.

The same tendency to pursue particularistic aims through abstract principle manifested itself in 1760 when the parlement spoke of the "nation" and "estates." Simply by referring to the "nation" and "estates," anti-tax remonstrances diverged sharply from earlier anti-*Unigenitus* protests, which did not include such words. The parlement of Rouen used the word "nation" for the first time in its remonstrances of 26 June 1756, when it objected to the royally sanctioned extension of the jurisdiction of the Grand Conseil by speaking vaguely of a "uniform and constant spirit of the Nation," but in 1760 the court went further by insisting that the parlement itself temporarily represented the nation when it reviewed and consented to royal decrees. Leaving aside the question of whether the nation in this context was Normandy or France – the famous "theory of

---

[20] Such a claim was rare among the sovereign courts. The exception that proves the rule was the parlement of Toulouse, which claimed in 1756 and 1757 that the *vingtième* violated feudal rights of tax exemption. Egret, *Louis XV*, p. 108; and Rioche, *Vingtièmes*, p. 66.

classes" confused the two entities – the magistrates asserted unequivocally that the nation possessed a share of legislative sovereignty.
The 1760 remonstrances stressed that the parlements borrowed
that sovereignty from "estates," which truly represented the nation.
Although the magistrates issued a specific call for the provincial
estates of Normandy at the end of the text, they used the word
"estates" without the modifying adjectives "general" or "provincial"
throughout to evoke a general form of government that was preferable to the arbitrary authority they believed they were experiencing.
Whereas the anti-*Unigenitus* remonstrances of 1753 were undoubtedly
bolder insofar as they justified the right of magistrates to resist the
will of the king, those of 1760 changed the composition of the rivalry
between parlement and royal council by adding a third institutional
pole, estates. In contrast to Parisian jurists such as Le Paige who
eschewed the tactic of calling for estates because it jeopardized the
jurisdictional integrity and constitutional claims of the Paris parlement – would not the Estates General overshadow the parlement? –
the magistrates of Rouen were prepared to run the risks of jurisdictional rivalry within Normandy in order to protect the province
from the fiscal-administrative intrusions of the crown. Besides, the
few provincial estates that had survived into the eighteenth century
provided a living, breathing example of government by estates that
was more compelling than any myth about the medieval origins of
the parlements. Although the question of estates had come up in
private correspondence among Parisian jurists, the parlement of
Rouen was the first court in the eighteenth century to speak boldly
and publicly of the possibility of their return.[21]

One last point of comparison between the remonstrances of 1753
and those of 1760 needs to be addressed: the medium in which both
found expression. Both texts were printed for the reading public.

---

[21] The parlement of Rouen did, in 1718, ask for the restoration of the estates of Normandy but
its request was not made public and did not discuss estates in the abstract. Before the
Maupeou coup, other sovereign courts to raise the issue of estates in their remonstrances
included: the parlements of Besançon (1757), Aix (1760), and Grenoble (1760), which alluded
to provincial estates but did not ask for them; and the *cour des aides* of Paris (1763) and the
parlement of Rennes (1764), which mentioned the Estates General. In Paris the Jansenist
magistrate Henri de Revol believed as early as 1757 that, in matters of taxation, only the
Estates General truly represented the nation, but Le Paige and many others would not
endorse this idea until the Maupeou coup. Van Kley, *Damiens Affair*, pp. 192–4; Van Kley,
Religious Origins, p. 209; Egret, *Louis XV*, pp. 127–30; Carcassonne, *Montesquieu*, p. 294; and
Monique Cubells, *La Provence des lumières. Les parlementaires d'Aix au XVIIIe siècle* (Paris, 1984),
pp. 272–4.

During the personal reign of Louis XIV (since 1673 at least) remonstrances remained in manuscript form and were never released as printed pamphlets.[22] The parlement of Paris began to leak remonstrances to publishers during the disputes over Jansenism of the 1720s and 1730s, as Jansenist lawyers and editors of the periodical *Nouvelles ecclésiastiques* printed their own appeals to the public.[23] In the 1750s, during the refusal of sacraments controversy and the Grand Conseil affair, the practice of printing texts was pursued with greater enthusiasm, so much so that the English visitor of Mably's *Des droits et devoirs du citoyen* (1758) could tell his French friend, "I have heard that the practice of publishing the *arrêts* and remonstrances of your parlements, introduced in the course of recent contestations, has been an occasion for you to think, reflect, and instruct yourselves."[24] Mably could use the plural "parlements" because, in the 1750s, provincial parlements eagerly joined Paris in printing their once confidential commentaries to the king. The parlement of Rouen began publishing its remonstrances in 1753, in the midst of the sacraments affair, and in 1760 first used the printing press to publicize remonstrances against taxation.[25] Once printed, remonstrances quickly found their way into pro-parlementary French-language foreign newspapers such as the *Gazette de Leyde* and, from 1762, were advertised in the book review section of Normandy's new newspaper.[26]

Precisely how remonstrances were leaked to presses is unclear; the *procureur-général* of the parlement certainly did his best to prevent them from straying beyond the private channel between court and royal council. Yet magistrates with access to the court's secret registers were evidently able to copy the statements from the registers and deliver them to printers. Barbier suggested in 1760 that the magistrates depended on "the good offices of the Jansenists" to turn the written word into print.[27] Barbier did not name names, but

---

[22] Michel Antoine, "Les remontrances des cours supérieures sous le règne de Louis XIV (1673–1715)," *Bibliothèque de l'École des Chartes* 151 (1993), pp. 93 and 98.
[23] Farge, *Subversive Words*, pp. 36–40; and Bell, *Lawyers and Citizens*, chs. 3 and 4.
[24] Quoted in Baker, *Inventing*, p. 89.
[25] The *Objets de remontrances* of 1759 were printed against the *subvention générale* and earlier fiscal remonstrances were later printed as part of collections of legal documents, but the first immediate printing of anti-tax remonstrances occurred, in Normandy, in 1760.
[26] Barbier, *Chronique*, VI, p. 336; D. Joynes, "The *Gazette de Leyde*: The Opposition Press and French Politics, 1750–1757," in *Press and Politics in Pre-Revolutionary France*, ed. Jack Censer and Jeremy Popkin (Berkeley, CA, 1987), pp. 141–2.
[27] Barbier, *Chronique*, VII, p. 282.

it is likely that the procedures first created for printing remonstrances against the "despotism of the clergy" in 1753 were the same as those used to publicize the "despotism" of fiscal administration in 1760. We know that the Jansenist lawyer, printer, and pamphleteer Pierre-Jacques Le Maître, who printed the parlement's rulings against the Jesuits in the early 1760s, assisted in the printing of tax protests in 1772.[28] It would not at all be rash to suggest that Jansenists familiar with the world of clandestine printing assisted magistrates in publicizing the remonstrances of 10 May 1760 as well.

The remonstrances of 10 May 1760, then, set down in print the principles of citizenship, liberty, national sovereignty, and government by estates that formed the basis of the Norman parlement's opposition to royal taxation in prerevolutionary France. As impressive as these remonstrances were, they were but the opening scene in a long drama that would last through the summer of 1760. It is worth examining the remainder of the dispute – and the quarrels of 1761 and 1763 – to get a closer look at factional politics within the parlement and at the broader relationship between the court and public opinion.

As printed copies of the remonstrances of 10 May 1760 reached Paris and Versailles, Bertin, the finance minister, and Miromesnil, the first president of the parlement of Rouen, discussed the best way to resolve a dispute that both believed was affecting public opinion. Bertin was primarily concerned with the damage that the publicity of remonstrances was doing to France's ability to borrow money needed to wage the Seven Years War: "our unfortunate habit of making remonstrances public, the kind of incredible fermentation in people's minds, does more good for our enemies than does their own success;... Tracts of many remonstrances or *arrêtés* on a *lit de justice*, disseminated in the cafés of London, have been more useful to Mr. Pitt than all the insults and scorn that their newspapers and rantings level against us." The publicity of the parlement's resistance, he said, was prompting Dutch, German, and Swiss financiers to lend money to England instead of France. The English government was currently experiencing some difficulty in floating a loan but it was determined to see it through, "due to the difficulties the new [French tax] edicts had suffered, especially at the hands of the parlement of Normandy."

28 André Doyon, *Un agent royaliste pendant la Révolution. Pierre-Jacques Le Maître (1790–1795)* (Paris, 1969), pp. 1–37.

Given all the fighting over taxes in France, European creditors believed it would be safer to invest in England.[29]

Miromesnil, who as first president served as an arbitrator between the royal council and his court, pleaded Bertin's case to the magistrates and asked them, to no avail, to register the edict of February 1760. The magistrates were simply too sensitive to tax increases. "The greatest number" of magistrates, the president surmised, resisted the edict because they "thought only of avoiding, if possible, the payment of new taxes." Following their "self-interest," they were "more attentive to themselves than to the people, whose name they use as a pretext." Aggravating the problem was a small group of fanatical magistrates, impervious to persuasion because "prejudice sees nothing and reasons even less," who wielded a degree of influence wholly out of proportion with its numbers. By intimidating moderate men who might otherwise have been persuaded to register the edict, the more radical magistrates were attempting to secure the intransigence of the parlement's collective will.[30]

Like Bertin, Miromesnil was concerned about public opinion but he cared less about international credit than about the ways in which the dispute was weakening the authority of the king at home. According to the first president, the oppositional faction in the parlement was leading the public against the throne: "The idea is spread in public with great care that the King does not know the least thing about what goes on, that he does not even know that people already pay two *vingtièmes*, that he never sees the remonstrances of the parlement, and that, finally, his ministers do everything without his participation."[31] Not everyone believed "these absurdities." "The magistrates are more persuaded of them than others, and that is what makes the remonstrances resemble acts of slander." The disparity between the negative image of the king that was being cultivated by the magistrates and the more benign image in the mind of the public rendered the remonstrances libelous. Miromesnil believed that certain magistrates wanted to prolong the dispute deliberately in order to "indispose the people" against the crown and to effect "a change in the form of government and a real diminution in the authority of the King."[32]

---

[29] Le Verdier, *Miromesnil*, I, p. 73, letter of 23 June 1760.
[30] Le Verdier, *Miromesnil*, I, pp. 92 and 95–6, letters to Bertin, 24 and 25 June 1760.
[31] Le Verdier, *Miromesnil*, I, p. 106, letter of 25 June 1760.
[32] Le Verdier, *Miromesnil*, I, pp. 129–30, letter of 10 July 1760.

To dissolve the bond being forged between the opposition faction in the court and the public, Miromesnil labored to negotiate a compromise between court and royal council. Unable to solicit a milder version of a letter from the chancellor that denounced the "dangerous principles" and "exaggerated facts" of the remonstrances (because the letter was divulged to the public by a careless postmaster), and unsuccessful in procuring from Bertin a reduction in the duration of the *vingtième*, Miromesnil put his trust in what he believed to be a foolproof solution to the recalcitrance of his court: good kingship. In June he began to arrange for a delegation of magistrates to deliver iterative remonstrances to the king himself. The king's reply, if delivered authoritatively, would instantly bring the rebellious judges into line. The first president was so taken with this idea that, with the precision worthy of a theatrical director, he instructed Bertin to stage the king's performance. His Majesty was not to let the chancellor speak on his behalf, as had happened during the delegation of 1753, nor was the king to read his lines from a piece of paper as he was prone to do, for then he seemed only to be saying what his ministers wanted him to say. Instead, the king would lift his head and speak directly to the magistrates. "It is necessary that the king show himself and appear to act by himself" in order to destroy "the belief shared by everyone that the king does not want to take the trouble to govern himself." By speaking forcefully and with the correct mixture of intimidation and love, Louis XV could convince the delegation that he was indeed ruling France and was himself commanding the court to register the tax increases. The supreme majesty of the king could end the whole affair: "one word alone from his mouth may resolve all these troubles and lead the parlement of Rouen back to obedience."[33]

Bertin agreed. At the end of July a delegation composed of the president and eight magistrates, iterative remonstrances in hand, was received in Versailles by Louis XV. The delegation handed the remonstrances to Louis, who passed them to Saint-Florentin, secretary for the province of Normandy, who read them aloud while the king listened with an unhappy expression on his face. Restating many of the themes broached in the remonstrances of 10 May, the iterative remonstrances insisted that the court was not exaggerating

---

[33] Le Verdier, *Miromesnil*, I, pp. 60–61, 67, 137, and 147, letters of 15 and 21 June, 18 and 19 July 1760.

the terrible condition of the province or advancing dangerous principles; that the *capitation*, an arbitrary tax entrusted to the will of one man (the controller-general), threatened to deliver a "fatal blow to the State and the Citizen"; and that the province of Normandy be granted "the liberty" to tax itself by means of estates, as the Norman charter intended. The new remonstrances made the additional claim that the act of free registration represented "the suffrage of the Peoples," a variation on the phrase "the liberty of suffrages" that would become something of a slogan in the tax disputes of the early 1760s. When Saint-Florentin finished reading, Louis XV said, "These remonstrances contain many things which should not be there. Wait at Versailles until I give you my orders."[34]

The deputation withdrew and spent the evening and next day visiting ministers of state, all of whom criticized the disrespectful tone of the remonstrances. Despite Fossé's wish to snub the finance minister by refusing his invitation, the delegation met with Bertin who explained in some detail that the reestablishment of the provincial estates of Normandy was not in the interests of the *parlementaires*. Not only would it be difficult to determine what form the estates would take, but the authority of the parlement would be "considerably diminished" by the recreation of a rival body. That the magistrates had to be told that estates were not in their interest is a measure of the gravity of tax disputes in this period. In the sixteenth and seventeenth centuries parlements never called for estates because they knew that such assemblies would shift authority away from the courts. The Norman magistrates were aware of the same possibility in 1760 – they had read Le Paige and knew of the power that parlements could obtain by claiming to be the sole representative of the nation – but their desire for the fiscal-administrative independence that estates would bring to the province outweighed the narrower interests of corporate jurisdiction.

On 3 August, after countless meetings and dinners, the deputation was summoned to the king's chamber. Following the directions of Miromesnil, Louis XV took center stage and declared: "I am your master, I should punish you for the audacity of your principles: return to Rouen, register my edicts without delay. I want to be obeyed. I am more occupied than you think with the relief of my

---

[34] AD Seine-Maritime, 1B 278, supplementary remonstrances of 26 July 1760. This description of the events at Versailles is based on Miromesnil's journal in Le Verdier, *Miromesnil*, I, pp. 173–94.

people and the way to attain it, and they will feel the effects of it. This is my response that I have written with my own hand." This was the kind of speech that Miromesnil believed would weaken the resolve of the magistrates. Barbier, for one, was impressed: this reply, "the strongest and firmest made in a long time ... is all the more interesting since it is written in the King's hand, which is not at all ordinary."[35]

The king's audience was not moved, however. Confounding Miromesnil's predictions, the delegation returned to Rouen and recounted their story to the entire parlement, which promptly adopted an *arrêté* stating that the king's order to register the edict "directly attacked ... the liberty of suffrages" and the parlement's "ability to deliberate." The experience of meeting the king had apparently done little to calm the spirit of the court.[36]

Intent on imposing tax increases, Louis XV would now have to resort to force. He ordered the maréchal de Luxembourg, governor of the province of Normandy, to command the court to register the edict. This forced registration was the first of many to come in the arena of universal taxes. On 8 August 1760 Luxembourg entered the parlement of Rouen and presented the first president with royal orders commanding the court to register the edict without delay. Miromesnil objected, asking the governor to withdraw from the chamber so that the court could exercise its right to deliberate freely before registration. When Luxembourg refused, the first president declared, "everything suggests that this company is hindered in its suffrages, the liberty of which forms the only existence of deliberating corps." If Luxembourg would not leave, Miromesnil and his company would withdraw and deliberate elsewhere. The first president then stood up to leave, signaling the magistrates to follow, but Luxembourg stopped him. Presenting special *lettres de cachet* from the king, he commanded the president and the *procureur-général* to stay while the rest of the men withdrew. In the empty hall the governor then dictated the edict to the clerk, who inscribed the words in the court's register. Under direct orders the president and the *procureur-général* signed the transcription, and the decree, now registered,

---

[35] Barbier, *Chronique*, VII, pp. 274–5.
[36] *Réponses du roi, lettres de jussion et de cachet, arrêtés et itératives remontrances du parlement à Rouen, au sujet de l'édit du mois de février dernier et de la déclaration du 3 du même mois* (n. p., n. d.); Floquet, *Parlement de Normandie*, VI, p. 385.

became law. Tax officials could now proceed to collect sharp increases in the *capitation* and the *vingtième* for two years.[37]

The following day the magistrates assembled to discuss their next move. When the proposal was made to concede victory to the crown by voluntarily registering the decree that had just been forcibly transcribed, those who resisted reconciliation "were transported into a fury." Despite the uproar, the measure passed narrowly by a margin of four votes – the count was thirty-six to thirty-two – and the parlement willingly registered the decree "to announce to the enemies of the king that there is nothing that his subjects would not sacrifice for the glory of his arms and for the defense of the nation." For Miromesnil the voluntary registration was like a "beautiful dream," inspiring him to boast privately to Bertin that, had the chancellor's initial letter to the court been less severe, he could have prevented the printing of the remonstrances of July.[38]

But Miromesnil still had much to worry about. The vote for voluntary registration was close and he believed that the party of opposition was getting stronger every day. Furious with those who had supported voluntary registration, party members, including many young men looking to make a name for themselves, "threw caution to the wind in their speeches" and intimidated otherwise reasonable magistrates. Even worse, they took their cause to the public, the very idea of which caused Miromesnil "to blush with embarrassment for the magistrature." Just days after certain magistrates publicly expressed their disapproval of the court's capitulation, "the most indecent verses" ridiculing the parlement ran through Rouen. Aware that the opposition party was successfully courting public opinion, the first president observed that "the people," by which he meant "individuals from every estate who are not well informed," "divides itself and floats" between the oppositional "hot-heads" and the more moderate judges.[39]

To this fractured public as well as to the king the parlement issued the last word in the dispute. The tax increases were registered, to be sure, but the court could not resist drafting a last set of remonstrances, written apparently by members of the opposition party who sat on the remonstrances committee. The remonstrances of 22

---

[37] Le Verdier, *Miromesnil*, I, pp. 200–1, n. 1; and Floquet, *Parlement de Normandie*, VI, pp. 386–7.
[38] Le Verdier, *Miromesnil*, I, p. 202, n. 1; I, pp. 203–4, letter of 10 August 1760; I, p. 214, letter to Lamoignon, 7 September 1760; Floquet, *Parlement de Normandie*, VI, pp. 390–1.
[39] Le Verdier, *Miromesnil*, I, p. 214, letter to Lamoignon, 7 September 1760.

August 1760 were similar to the two previous ones, though they gave more vivid expression to the humiliation experienced by "your most respectable Subjects" who had to beg intendants for justice in the *capitation*. More importantly, they gave the strongest statement to date on the impropriety of forced registrations, these "blows of illegal authority," these "military executions" which, violating "the liberty of suffrages which alone forms the existence of an essentially deliberative Body," "insert an appearance of consent into [the court's] records that it did not give." Although the magistrates abandoned the explicit call for provincial estates – perhaps their meeting with Bertin at Versailles had dashed their hopes – they nonetheless suggested that "citizens" be permitted to distribute a new single tax under the auspices of the *chambre des comptes* and *cour des aides* of Rouen. This shift in emphasis from estates to judicial consent would continue until 1771, when the call for estates would once again take precedence.[40]

The long conflict over the edict of February 1760 was followed by a minor dispute in 1761 and a full-scale crisis in 1763. The quarrel of 1761, as insignificant as it was, is worth examining briefly for the correspondence it generated between Bertin and Miromesnil, who further developed their ideas about kingship and public opinion.

With the tax hikes established by the edict of February 1760 due to expire at the end of 1761 and the crown still desperate to find money to finance the Seven Years War, the royal council issued the declaration of 16 June 1761, which prolonged increases in the *capitation* and the *vingtième* for two more years. Recalling how in 1710 Louis XIV forced his enemies to the peace table by creating the *dixième*, Bertin wanted the declaration of 16 June to be registered quickly in order "to give our diplomats some weight in their negotiations." But he feared that, in seeking tax increases, he would set off another round of public contestation that would only weaken France's ability to borrow. "What is this principle of credit so necessary to the State? It is confidence, and can confidence exist when Courts race to cast suspicions, disfavor, and even disgust on all the activities of the minister?" "By inundating the capital and the provinces with printed remonstrances and protests," the magistrates were weakening public confidence in the crown and chasing away credit. Thus Bertin had to find a way to impose the taxes without

[40] *Nouvelles remontrances du parlement de Normandie au roi* (n. p., [1760]).

creating a "scene that will spread in a week to the cafés of London and the newspapers of Holland." He considered presenting the magistrates with a memoir that described the king's financial needs but was afraid that the magistrates might print it and further weaken French credit. The only way to impose tax increases without damaging credit was to force the parlement to register the decree before it had time to draw up remonstrances.[41]

Miromesnil was sympathetic but feared that a sudden forced registration might provoke a more serious crisis. Again he placed his hopes in the revivification of the king's majesty. If, in 1710, Louis XIV had been able to draw additional support from his subjects, this was because he studied the character of the nation and led it with "magnificent speech." Perhaps Louis XV could do the same in 1761: "The Frenchman wants to be flattered, led; it is necessary to provide a kind of spectacle, to inspire his vanity. He naturally loves his King; he is sensitive to honor ... Why agitate the spirit of a nation that is easy to lead, but to which the master must speak, always sure to be heard, even adored, when he wants." The king must especially reach out to all those who have difficulty reasoning and who cannot see past their own troubles to discern the public good. "The persons of this class know and hear only public clamors, and we must admit that in every order they compose the greatest number. However, it is, Monsieur, to this great number that it is necessary to speak and to persuade, and this is precisely the area in which we least apply ourselves." Meanwhile, Miromesnil suggested that the king write a private letter to the court explaining why tax increases were so important. Louis XV followed his advice, and on 5 August, the day before the forced registration was due to take place, the parlement listened to a letter that graciously revealed the king's foreign policy and urged the magistrates to play a decisive role in bringing about a favorable conclusion to the war by accepting tax increases and "letting our enemies see that we are in condition to resist them."[42]

Once again the royal touch engineered by Miromesnil was not very successful. The letter did not convince the court to register the declaration voluntarily so that, on 6 August, the duc d'Harcourt, lieutenant-general of the province, had to force the court to register the decree, sanctioning tax increases for two more years. But the

---

[41] Le Verdier, *Miromesnil*, II, pp. 7–8 and 31, letters of 27 July and 3 August 1761.
[42] Le Verdier, *Miromesnil*, II, pp. X, 14, 22, letter of 31 July 1761.

king's letter may have kept tempers calm in the aftermath of the forced registration. In 1761 the opposition party was held in check.

Whatever restraint was exercised in 1760 and 1761 was completely abandoned in 1763, the year the Seven Years War ended. The treaty of Paris may have established peace among the European powers but it did little to resolve conflict within the French kingdom. On the contrary, several provincial parlements, with Rouen, Toulouse, and Grenoble in the lead, launched their fiercest campaign of opposition to the crown since the Fronde.[43] In Paris, Bachaumont praised the "beautiful Remonstrances" that showered the capital, reminding him of the "glorious days of the republics of Athens and Rome."[44] In Normandy, the opposition party gained the upper hand in the parlement and, amidst a flowering of British constitutional rhetoric, persuaded all 90 magistrates to resign.

The source of the conflict was the edict of April 1763 which, while allowing the third *vingtième* and second *capitation* to expire at the end of the year, prolonged the first *vingtième* indefinitely and the second until 1770, and declared the establishment of a *cadastre*, a kingdom-wide land survey that would be used for a wholesale redistribution of the *taille* and *vingtième*. The worth of every plot of land, large or small, was to be evaluated anew and systematically reassessed.[45] The edict was unacceptable to the magistrates of Rouen. With peace finally at hand the parlement expected a reduction of the tax load to at least pre-war levels, when only a single *vingtième* had been levied. And yet the crown was trying not only to prolong the second *vingtième* but to install an extensive administrative apparatus for a *cadastre*. Further, the magistrates were in no mood to acquiesce to royal demands. The edict was issued immediately after the parlement had succeeded in striking a major blow against the Jesuits, breaking up the order and closing its schools throughout Normandy, a victory that heightened the court's sense of political entitlement. According to Miromesnil, this was particularly true for Fossé and his Gallican allies who had led the charge against the Jesuits; "the new and incredible way in which people acted during the Jesuits affair has

---

[43] For an overview, see David Hudson, "The Parlementary Crisis of 1763 in France and Its Consequences," *Canadian Journal of History* 7 (1972), pp. 97–117.

[44] Louis Petit de Bachaumont, *Mémoires secrets pour servir à l'histoire de la république des lettres en France*, 31 vols. (London, 1777–89), I, pp. 300–1.

[45] AN, AD IX 492, no. 14, edict of April 1763. The edict also increased indirect taxes and prolonged both the 10 percent addition to the *dixième* withholding tax and the *don gratuit* levied on cities since 1759.

further boosted the confidence of the parlements, and now impassioned men believe proudly that there is no obstacle they cannot overcome."[46] Fresh from this triumphant campaign, the magistrates turned their attention to the new tax edict.

To understand the crisis of 1763, we must also recognize that the king's justification for the edict of April – that substantial tax revenue was needed to service the overwhelming debt amassed during the war – carried little weight with the parlement of Rouen. As Miromesnil repeatedly emphasized to the finance minister, the bulk of his colleagues' fortunes consisted of land, making them far less likely than Parisian *parlementaires*, who invested heavily in royal bonds, to agree to tax increases. Many land-owning provincial magistrates considered royal bankruptcy preferable to a tax burden laden with two *vingtièmes* and the promise of a *cadastre* that would expose undervalued assessments: "I hear many people who have no trouble saying that it would be better if the king suspended the payments of a great part of his creditors rather than burden the people [with taxes], the most part of these creditors not being beyond reproach."[47]

Recent research supports Miromesnil's speculation about the fortunes of his colleagues. The wealth of the magistrates of Rouen consisted largely of rural land (60–80 percent) and included only a small fraction of bonds (15 percent), most of which were private not royal, urban property, offices, furnishings, and liquid assets. Whereas the fortunes of the *parlementaires* of Rennes, Toulouse, Bordeaux, Besançon, Dijon, and Grenoble reveal the same predilection for landed real estate as those of Rouen, Parisian magistrates with diversified portfolios were more likely to be substantial creditors of the state.[48] This helps to explain why provincial parlements in general, and that of Rouen in particular, objected so stridently to the tax increases of 1763 even if it meant risking royal bankruptcy. Indeed, many provincial parlements urged Louis xv to tax bonds, slash interest rates, or suspend payments to creditors instead of taxing land.[49]

---

[46] Le Verdier, *Miromesnil*, II, p. 303, letter to Bertin, 8 August 1763.
[47] Le Verdier, *Miromesnil*, II, p. 227–8, letter of 15 June 1763.
[48] See Bailey Stone, *The French Parlements and the Crisis of the Old Regime* (Chapel Hill, NC, 1986), pp. 53–5; Paul Robinne, "Les magistrats du parlement de Normandie à la fin du XVIIIe siècle (1774–1790)," Thèse de l'École des Chartes (1967), pp. 156–8 and 187–236; Bluche, *Magistrats du parlement*, pp. 160–3; and Doyle, *Parlement of Bordeaux*, p. 58.
[49] Rouen, Bordeaux, Toulouse, and Besançon all made such suggestions. Le Verdier,

Perceived as indefensible, the edict of April 1763 strengthened the hand of the opposition party in the parlement of Rouen. A growing number of magistrates were willing to take extreme measures to express their hostility to the decree. On 7 July, when the commission charged with writing remonstrances met to discuss the edict, the possibility of resigning immediately arose. One member of the commission announced that if, as expected, their remonstrances had little effect and Louis XV ordered the governor to force the parlement to register the edict, he would resign. Fed up with ministers of state who burdened people with taxes in order to pay the pensions of their creatures, he believed it was time for the parlement to get in step with "the public," which had in 1760 thought the court "ridiculous" when it voluntarily registered the tax edict of February. Another member added that if the crown were to bypass the parlements every time they refused to register a decree, it would soon reduce them to the status of lower courts; he too suggested they resign in the face of yet another forced registration. Miromesnil feared that this party had greater ambitions. If it could convince the entire parlement of Rouen to resign, other parlements would follow, forcing the king not only to withdraw the edict but "to change the form of his government and submit the administration of finances to the examination of the courts."[50]

The court and the public, the first president observed anxiously, were leading each other toward this goal. On the one hand, public rumor informed the magistrates' opinions. Stories circulated that the king was about to waste millions of livres on the construction of royal palaces and that he was prepared to withdraw the new tax edict. "This public discourse which comes back to Messieurs of the parlement contributes greatly to their indisposition." On the other hand, the opposition party informally cultivated opinion outside the court, preparing it for political change. The more zealous magistrates "employed every possible resource to encourage the public to desire this revolution." Their loose talk "embittered" a people already tired of high taxes and directed resentment against the government. The result was a climate of opinion in which "all the

---

Miromesnil, I, p. 39, II, pp. 227–8, and III, p. 88; Doyle, *Parlement of Bordeaux*, p. 223; Marion, *Histoire financière*, I, pp. 233–5; and Jean Egret, *Le parlement de Dauphiné et les affaires publiques dans le deuxième moitié du XVIII siècle*, 2 vols. (Paris, 1942), I, pp. 234 and 242.

[50] Le Verdier, *Miromesnil*, II, pp. 247–9 and 258, letters from Miromesnil to Bertin, 7 and 11 July 1763.

orders of state expected tax relief and the reform of the State" and in which the king was reduced to "the simple role of an indifferent spectator."[51]

Into this charged atmosphere the parlement injected two texts: the *Objets de remontrances* of 16 July 1763, a preliminary list of the main points that would be addressed in impending remonstrances, and the remonstrances of 5 August 1763 themselves.[52] Both were printed immediately upon completion – the *Objets* appearing in Paris on 19 July before the king had even laid eyes on them – and both were announced in the Norman newspaper.[53] Like the remonstrances of 22 August 1760, those of 1763 suggested that a single tax replace the confusing array of existing taxes, and characterized parlements and estates as the nations' representative organs, the former enjoying the right, found in all states that were not "despotic," to register tax decrees freely, the latter providing the institutional means for the province to tax itself. The fear of a *cadastre*, however, drove the magistrates to formulate a more challenging defense of the right of property and emboldened them to ask the king to submit his budget. Responding directly to the specter of the "tyrannical domination" that would accompany a *cadastre* and its "legions of administrators," the remonstrances tightened what had been rather loose rhetorical linkages between property, liberty, and citizenship to form a coherent Lockian theory of state. The *Objets* declared:

That most of the taxes by which the People are burdened, attack, by the arbitrariness of their distribution, the natural and legitimate liberty of Citizens, and that all [taxes] taken together, strike a heavy blow at [that liberty], by making the right of property illusory in its effect: That this right which distinguishes the Freeman from the Serf, is anterior to the whole political establishment; that its preservation was the primary purpose of the institution of all civil authority.

The right of property superseded that of the king to tax: "The domain of the Citizen on his possessions is naturally unlimited; the right of the State on the property of its Subjects is fundamentally defined by its needs." If the state needed the citizen's property, it

---

[51] Le Verdier, *Miromesnil*, II, pp. 258–9 and 286–7, letters to Bertin, 11 July and 4 August 1763; III, p. 41, letter to L'Averdy, 24 December 1763.

[52] *Objets de remontrances, arrêtés par le parlement séant à Rouen ... le 16 juillet 1763* (n. p., [1763]); *Remontrances du parlement séant à Rouen, au roi, au sujet de l'édit et la déclaration du mois d'Avril dernier* (n. p., [1763]).

[53] Barbier, *Chronique*, VIII, pp. 90–1; *Annonces*, 22 July and 12 August 1763.

would have to demonstrate that need to the courts. The king would have to surrender his budget to the parlements.

The influence of British constitutional thought and practice on the magistrates was obvious to Bertin, who was determined to prevent the spread of such "Anglican principles."[54] The chancellor too rebuffed the magistrates' demand to see the budget and threw himself into the public debate by printing his own letter of reprimand: "Since when did Magistrates believe that they had the right to examine the king's conduct, cast worried looks on his administration, and explain in such a way as to make themselves heard, that under certain delicate circumstances, he must render account to them?" More disturbing than the content of the remonstrances was the fact that the magistrates undermined loyalty to the crown by publicizing them: "How were [the magistrates] able to make such declamations, the publicity of which, contrary to all rules, would weaken, if possible, the ties which attach the peoples to a King who has no other desire than to procure their happiness?"[55] The finance minister and the chancellor decided to end the affair by forcing the parlement of Rouen to register the edict.

On 18 August, the day before the magistrates were scheduled to take their annual vacation, d'Harcourt again entered the parlement to order the court to transcribe the edict into its registers. The now familiar ritual was carried out in the usual fashion but Miromesnil's speech, prepared that morning by the assembled magistrates, advanced the court's claim to share legislative sovereignty with the crown in the most explicit language. Railing against forced registrations that deprived the magistrates of "the liberty of their Deliberations," the court claimed that to approve royal decrees "blindly" was to deny the constitutional fact that the parlement "participated in the ministry of Legislation," a phrase remarkable enough for Barbier to note in his journal.[56] The parlement was asserting that it shared legislative sovereignty with the crown.

---

[54] Le Verdier, *Miromesnil*, II, p. 316, letter of 14 August 1763. These principles penetrated the parlement of Paris as well. In 1760 one Parisian magistrate drew an invidious comparison between England and France, pointing out that the English parliament approved extraordinary taxes annually, whereas the French parlements were expected to register increases in the *capitation* and the *vingtième* that lasted several years. Swann, *Parlement of Paris*, p. 187.

[55] *Lettre de M. Chancelier au parlement de Rouen, ou réponse aux remontrances de ce parlement* (n. p., n. d.).

[56] *Relation de ce qui s'est passé au Parlement séant à Rouen, au sujet des édits et déclarations du mois d'avril 1763* (n. p., [1763]); Barbier, *Chronique*, VIII, pp. 96–7.

D'Harcourt would have none of it of course, and ordered the transcription as he planned. But he made a tactical error when, upon leaving the chamber prematurely, he allowed the magistrates enough time to deliberate before they retired for vacation. In this final moment of the judicial year, as if to demonstrate that the court did indeed possess a share of legislative sovereignty, the opposition party, led by Fossé and Camus de Pontcarré de Viarme of the chamber of the *Enquêtes*, seized hold of the proceedings and opined that the court should deploy the most powerful weapon in its judicial arsenal, the *arrêt de défense*. An *arrêt de défense* was a ruling that would prohibit royal officials from executing the edict of April 1763 under the penalty of being prosecuted for misappropriating public funds. Even if the *arrêt* were not strictly enforced, its mere existence would interfere directly with the tax levy by intimidating tax assessors and collectors. Because such a resolution blatantly defied the will of the crown, many moderate magistrates believed that they either had no right to issue it or should not issue it for fear of royal retribution. But unlike in 1760 and 1761, when the opposition party was too weak to move the court to extreme measures, now the party prevailed – to the surprise and dismay of Miromesnil – and led the parlement to this most confrontational form of contestation. The influence of the most radical members of the corps was strong enough to carry the day and turn the parlement of Rouen into a model of resistance for other parlements such as Toulouse, which soon promulgated its own *arrêt de défense*.

As soon as the Norman *arrêt de défense* was issued, conflict turned into a battle over legislative publicity. Two contradictory legal rulings existed in the court's registers – the edict itself and the court's subsequent ruling that those who heeded the edict would be treated as criminals – and both the royal council and parlement set out to convince the lower courts and public that their ruling was the legitimate one. D'Harcourt ordered copies of the edict printed and posted in public places throughout the province under the watchful eye of royal troops, and attempted to prevent the lower courts and the public from even seeing the *arrêt de défense* by forbidding the printers' guild of Rouen to publish it. But he did not act fast enough. Its access to print temporarily impeded, the parlement swiftly drafted over 100 manuscript copies of the *arrêt* which it sent to lower courts and, under the cover of night, posted where broadsheets of the edict had been displayed. Although the *arrêts* were torn down by d'Harcourt's men, there was no doubt who was winning the publicity campaign as printed extracts of the forced registration and pamphlets providing sympathetic documentary accounts of the parlement's resistance swamped the city.

Frustrated with the parlement's disrespect, the royal council retaliated by having d'Harcourt force the registration of a new *arrêt du conseil* that nullified the parlement's resolutions. The royal council also issued another *arrêt* that prohibited the sale of the remonstrances of 5 August and chided the parlement for "the license and infidelity" with which it "betrayed the secret of this precious correspondence" with the throne.[57] And to express his personal displeasure with the court's disobedience, Louis XV ordered several magistrates to spend their vacation following the royal court at a distance and living in purgatorial exile, unable to return to their province yet forbidden to approach the king or even enter the towns of Versailles and Fontainebleau. Pro-parlementary pamphlets did not miss this opportunity to describe the miserable villages and rustic inns where the exiled were forced to stay among the likes of peddlers and poultry sellers.

By the time the parlement resumed its service in November, the public dimension of the dispute had raised the stakes. Each party, the parlement and the crown, had courted the public and put its honor on the line. With parlement back in session, they immediately exchanged rulings and entered into a showdown that would result in the magistrates' mass resignation. The parlement resolved to maintain the *arrêt de défense* and to draft iterative remonstrances stating that the *arrêts du conseil* of August, posted "with affectation throughout the entire kingdom" served "to degrade [the king's] parlement in the eyes of the public." The royal council riposted with an *arrêt* that denounced "a Company, which having overstepped the boundaries of the power entrusted to it, no longer follows but a phantom of independence"; the parlement's rulings were "detrimental to [the king's] authority and contrary to the obedience which is due to him."[58]

On 18 November, d'Harcourt entered the parlement to force the court both to register the new *arrêt du conseil* and to strike its own *arrêts* from the record. Yet again the ceremony of the forced registra-

---

[57] Barbier, *Chronique*, VIII, p. 99.
[58] *Précis de ce qui s'est passé au Parlement séant à Rouen, depuis la S. Martin jusques et y compris le 19 Novembre 1763* (n. p., [1763 or 1764]).

tion was performed but this time the ritual was followed by an extraordinary act. When they returned to chamber after the execution of the transcription, all 90 magistrates resigned. Justifying their resignation, they not only recited the slogan concerning "the liberty of suffrages" but claimed again that that they had been "degraded, debased in the eyes of the public." The parlement resigned, Miromesnil explained, because of the public humiliation inflicted by *arrêts du conseil* that, "printed and distributed not only throughout the province but in every city of the kingdom," insultingly characterized the magistrates as rebels. The parlement was left with little choice: "it had to oppose its master, or be dishonored in the mind of the public." It chose to oppose its master.[59]

The resignation of the parlement stirred the public with an inspiring spectacle of defiance: new documentary brochures, poems, and engravings were printed heralding the court's cause as crowds gathered in courtyards to catch glimpses of famous magistrates. For the crown, the resignation was a disaster that, by triggering the suspension of lower courts, threatened to bring the administration of justice to a halt. Seeking to coax the parlement back to its duties and to assuage other recalcitrant courts, Louis XV made two significant gestures that expressed a newfound desire to compromise with the courts. He replaced the edict of April 1763 with the declaration of 21 November 1763, which, while still insisting on the prolongation of the two *vingtièmes* and the establishment of a land survey, announced that the king was going "to consult" with the magistrature on matters of finance in order "to profit from [its] knowledge." Magistrates were asked to submit *mémoires* on how best to improve the administration of finances and reform taxation.[60] Secondly, to demonstrate just how willing the crown was to work with the parlements in financial matters, Louis XV replaced Bertin with a new controller-general, L'Averdy, who was drawn from the parlement of Paris. Important as they were, Miromesnil feared, these gestures would carry little weight with the magistrates of Rouen unless accompanied by other measures, notably a public retraction of the infamous *arrêts du conseil* that had humiliated the court, a concerted

---

[59] *Précis*; Floquet, *Parlement de Normandie*, VI, p. 565 and 573; Le Verdier, *Miromesnil*, III, pp. 65–7 and 115–18, letters to L'Averdy, 4 and 23 January 1764.

[60] AN, AD+ 958, Declaration of 21 November 1763. Some memoirs are located in AN, K 879, no. 5.

effort to lobby the leaders of the court's factions, and a meeting with the king in which the monarch must "speak and assert himself."[61]

In his effort to bring the parlement back into service, Miromesnil had to think hard – harder than ever before – about the factions that drove parlementary politics, and his correspondence during this period throws several parties into relief. Insofar as these relatively undisciplined factions overlapped they did not resemble modern political parties, but Miromesnil could discern distinctive patterns of thought and action among five groups. The three calmest factions – Miromesnil's "friends" who were willing to compromise with royal ministers but were "all very tranquil men ... who fear those who put heat in the affairs," a swing party of "limited men" who either mindlessly followed the noisiest faction or were too intimidated to speak against it, and a group of moderates led by Barthélemy-Thomas Le Couteulx – coincided to a considerable extent.[62] The two main opposition groups, which also overlapped, drew their strength from the first *Enquêtes* and consisted of the "hot-heads" led by Viarme and the Gallican (and possibly Jansenist) party led by Fossé. Viarme, who led the campaign for the *arrêt de défense*, had very personal reasons for opposing the crown. A relative of the two first presidents preceding Miromesnil, Viarme believed himself destined to occupy the prestigious position, but after being passed over in 1757 he turned against the new president. His youth and bitterness, Miromesnil noted, induced Viarme to accept the role of leader of the opposition. Fossé, head of the Gallican–Jansenist opposition and doyen of the *Enquêtes*, had led the charge against the refusal of sacraments in 1753 and the Jesuits in 1761–2, and, during the tax increases of the Seven Years War, had enthusiastically extended his antipathy from religious "despotism" to the "despotism" of the fiscal-administrative state.

Sensing the balance between the personal and ideological considerations that motivated faction leaders, Miromesnil spent much of the winter and spring courting Le Couteulx, Viarme, Fossé, and others. To Viarme he stressed that L'Averdy was in the process of cutting royal expenses and needed the support of the parlement to keep him in power. The same argument was made to Fossé and Le Couteulx on whom it had a great effect since both gentlemen

---

[61] Le Verdier, *Miromesnil*, III, p. 80, letter to L'Averdy, 10 January 1764.
[62] Le Verdier, *Miromesnil*, III, pp. 9, 70, and 88, letters to L'Averdy, 4, 7, and 11 January 1764.

happened to be related to L'Averdy. In fact, L'Averdy made direct personal appeals to both his relatives to enlist their support, demonstrating the advantages of having a man of the robe assume the office of finance minister. The appeal to family solidarity dulled the edge of Le Couteulx's resistance, but it did not prevent him from sticking to deeply held political principles. He believed that taxes were at wartime levels and thus too high, that the tax system was riddled with abuses, and that, before the court registered any new declaration, it would have to be assured that reforms would be made. "In the present circumstances," he wrote Miromesnil, "I speak as an Englishmen and I say: 'We want very much to pay, but first it is necessary to put our house in order.'" Even this moderate leader was not afraid to invoke English principles to criticize French taxation. Miromesnil replied that taxes were needed to stave off bankruptcy and that L'Averdy, who was a friend of the parlements, needed their support, an argument that seemed to carry some weight.

Although Miromesnil complained that certain magistrates "could try the patience of a saint," his attempts to reason with them could be quite successful. In less than two hours the first president convinced one councilor, whom he described as "sharp, fiery, and a sworn enemy of finance," to support the new declaration by persuading him of the "impossibility of destroying finance in one fell swoop and the necessity of enduring the pain of taxes."[63]

The capstone to Miromesnil's plan to restore the parlement involved an audience with the king. As in 1760, Miromesnil believed that good kingship would lead the court back into obedient service, although now he refrained from over-confident predictions about the power of the royal presence. If Miromesnil believed in 1760 that one word from the king's mouth would "reestablish everything in its natural order," he had since seen too much conflict to expect such a blissful result. Still, direct communication with Louis XV would have a practical effect. The *arrêt du conseil* reprimanding the court had aggravated fiscal conflict because the magistrates believed that it emanated from the council "and not the master," but the king could dispel this belief if he spoke to a parlementary deputation and entered into "enough detail to demonstrate that he is well in-

---

[63] Le Verdier, *Miromesnil*, III, pp. 91–4, letter to L'Averdy, 14 January 1764; III, p. 169, letter from Le Couteulx, 13 February 1764; III, pp. 172–5, letter to Le Couteulx, 15 February 1764.

formed."[64] Once again the plan was put into operation. In early March, a deputation from Rouen arrived at Versailles and met first with the finance minister, who said that the king was willing to revoke the *arrêts du conseil* that had so painfully humiliated the magistrates and to provide relief for his people by diverting tax revenue from the voluntary gift to the province's hospitals, which were in poor financial shape. In return, the court was expected to register the declaration of November 1763. The deal was sealed during a visit with Louis XV on 10 March 1764 in which the king spoke directly to the magistrates, as advised, and returned their letters of resignation.

Four days later, amidst banquets, orations, and the customary embraces of the Rouen fish-wives, the parlement reassembled to strike the infamous *arrêts du conseil* from their register and record the declaration of 21 November 1763. The declaration was duly transcribed as promised, but with the addition of the old proviso that royal officials were not to increase assessments of the *vingtième*. Having established the proviso in 1756 and reiterated it in 1760 and 1761, the court had proudly watched other parlements, including that of Paris, adopt it as their own in 1763. The judges were not about to let their guard down in 1764 when the specter of a *cadastre* still threatened.

The dispute should have ended there. But the publicity that had fueled it all along reignited it as the magistrates exploited the stipulation in the declaration that allowed them to submit memoirs on financial reform to the king. No sooner had the court returned to its duties than the magistrates began to disseminate printed memoirs on royal finance that were supposed to be remitted directly to Louis XV. The crown promptly declared the publication of the memoirs illegal, an act that provoked Morellet to write his famous treatise on the freedom to publish on the subject of royal administration.[65] A practical man, Miromesnil simply doubted that the crown could enforce such a restriction since his magistrates were "in general strongly inclined to have everything printed."[66] Eventually, L'Averdy struck a compromise with the court that restricted the jurisdiction of

<hr />

[64] Le Verdier, *Miromesnil*, III, pp. 65 and 82, letters to L'Averdy, 4 and 19 January 1764.

[65] Written in 1764, André Morellet's *Réflexions sur les avantages de la liberté d'écrire et d'imprimer sur les matières de l'administration* was published later in London in 1775. See also the reaction of Bachaumont, *Mémoires secrets*, II, p. 42.

[66] Le Verdier, *Miromesnil*, III, pp. 280–1, letter to L'Averdy, 27 May 1764.

the parlementary bureau that was charged with drawing the memoirs, but it is fitting that the tax dispute of 1763–4 ended in a battle over the printing of judicial texts.

On 19 August 1764, as Miromesnil was attempting to resolve the memoir affair, he wrote an extraordinary letter to L'Averdy, which analyzed the fiscal contestation that had shaken his court during the past few years and discussed the relationship between parlement, public opinion, and monarchy.[67] He suggested that the "zealous men" in the parlement, who led "limited men" by intimidating them and younger men by appealing to their desire for immortal glory, were deliberately seeking conflict with the crown, "hoping by this means to bring about a chimerical change in the form of government, to make themselves necessary, to dazzle the people, and to erect themselves its heroes." What made the zealots particularly effective, however, was their alliance with public opinion on which the strength of the parlement depended; the zealots fed off "the general indisposition of attitudes throughout the nation." To understand the roots of parlementary power, then, one had to look beyond the judges at the kinds of people to whom they were appealing. Miromesnil stressed repeatedly in his correspondence with royal ministers that, in the context of tax disputes over the *capitation* and the *vingtième*, "the people," "the nation," "the public," or, his favorite term, "the multitude" that followed parlementary affairs was composed of individuals "from every estate" and "every order."[68]

This semantic qualification was crucial to Miromesnil's analysis of parlementary politics. It was easy to understand why commoners supported the parlement's resistance to taxation, for commoners had always borne a heavy tax burden. But thanks to the dramatic increases in the *capitation* and the *vingtième*, he explained, the nobility was now behind the parlement as well: "the noble, who at bottom neither likes nor respects men of the robe, happily sees in them the people who exert pressure against royal authority in order to set him free from the taxes that he is forced to pay." (The clergy was also happy to see the magistrates preoccupy themselves with finance because it diverted their attention from ecclesiastical affairs.) Sustained by "all the publications with which the kingdom has been

<hr />

[67] Le Verdier, *Miromesnil*, III, pp. 341–56, letter of 19 August 1764.
[68] Le Verdier, *Miromesnil*, I, p. 214, letter to Lamoignon, 7 September 1760; II, p. 14, letter to Bertin, 31 July 1761; III, p. 259, letter to Bertin, 11 July 1763; III, p. 351, letter to L'Averdy, 19 August 1764.

inundated," disputes over universal taxes captured the attention of a broadly based public of elites and commoners, all of whom found tax increases repugnant. The fragile but important eighteenth-century alliance between the nobility and the magistrature that Franklin Ford observed some time ago was built partly in reaction to the steep tax increases on the privileged during the Seven Years War.

To reverse this development and tighten the loosening bonds between the people and the monarchy, Miromesnil proposed two changes in policy. The first was to avoid great blows of royal authority, which he believed were symptomatic of weak government and resulted in "a continual combat between a kind of despotism and anarchy." Instead of using heavy-handed methods against the parlements, such as the forced registrations that became common during universal tax disputes between 1760 and 1764, the government should apply even pressure on the courts and gradually cultivate their obedience. Managing the parlements in a firm yet less authoritarian and erratic manner would restore the healthy equilibrium between royal authority and respect for the law.

The second strategy was to steal the support of the public from the parlements by lowering taxes:

> The entire kingdom has its eyes on the parlements because the entire kingdom is tired of paying taxes, and because people expect from the invincible steadfastness of the Courts the reduction of taxes for which they long. To the extent that the burdens of the people diminish, the need that people think they have for the efforts of the parlements will diminish; the people will be less attached to them because it will no longer ask for its help; all wishes will turn toward the King, who will always be the dispenser of favors.

Having witnessed since 1760 several forced registrations, an *arrêt de défense*, exile, and resignation, Miromesnil no longer believed that the seemingly perpetual fiscal conflict in which the magistrates of Rouen engaged was a matter of poor relations with, or misconceptions of, the king. He never surrendered his great hope that the right royal gesture at the right moment could restore order, but he now realized with greater clarity that the problem of taxation ran deeper than personal rule and could be resolved only if the king beat the parlement at its own game, that is if he lowered taxes and thereby deflated the court's pretensions to protect the liberty of the people.

MAUPEOU AND BEYOND, 1771–1782

Taxes did dip immediately after the Seven Years War, restoring a degree of order in Normandy, but another crisis occurred in the 1770s as controllers of the *vingtième* began to reassess the wealth of landowners in Normandy and the rest of the *pays d'élections*. From 1771 to 1782 both the form and language of tax disputes changed dramatically. Magistrates sharpened their criticism of the arbitrary practices of commissioned tax officials to suggest that the state was veering out of control, once again sounding the call for estates, and, for one brief but revealing moment, resistance and complaint spread beyond the parlement of Rouen to privileged taxpayers at large, allowing the "public" to speak for itself.

In 1771, as a result of personal ambition as well as the mishandling of the Brittany affair, the chancellor of France, René Nicolas Charles Augustin de Maupeou, introduced a sweeping reform of the judicial order. He abolished three parlements, including that of Rouen, remodeled the rest, and established "superior councils" that replaced abolished parlements and intruded on the jurisdiction of surviving ones. In the eyes of many magistrates and their supporters, Maupeou's strike against the parlements violated the property of judicial office and delivered a devastating blow to the last counterweight to despotic government in France. "If arbitrary power can commit offenses, abolish offices, and confiscate property," the parlement of Rouen cautioned the king before its suppression, "then this is the end of the liberty of the people."[69] Tampering with judicial office provoked a general cry for the convocation of the Estates General, as a chorus of courts in the winter and spring of 1771, led first by the parlement of Rouen and then the Paris *cour des aides*, both of which had already solicited estates in the early 1760s, joined pamphleteers to demand that the king consult the Estates General.[70]

Judicial "reform," however, was not the only aspect of the Maupeou coup that raised the delicate issue of property and stirred political emotions. With the obstreperous parlements either removed or debased, Louis XV's finance minister, Terray, proceeded with a

---

[69] Durand Echeverria, *The Maupeou Revolution: A Study in the History of Libertarianism, France 1770–1774* (Baton Rouge, 1985), pp. 105–6.
[70] Other courts that called for the Estates General in 1771 included the parlements of Bordeaux, Toulouse, Rennes, and Dijon. The Paris parlement did not demand estates, though Parisian lawyers did.

plan to revamp the *vingtième*. Terray had already slashed interest payments to royal creditors, an act that did not deeply trouble land-owning provincial magistrates, but he was now anxious to impose tax increases. What a supreme moment of opportunity Terray must have seen in the aftermath of the chancellor's coup: no longer would royal tax decrees be subjected to lengthy legal battles; no longer would the parlements issue public rulings that denounced fiscal administration and contradicted royal legislation. No wonder the very first law of any significance to be presented to the remodeled parlements and the newly created superior councils was the edict of November 1771, which was far more aggressive than it appeared on the surface. Predictably, the edict prolonged the two *vingtièmes*, the first indefinitely and the second until 1781, but it also opened the way for heavy increases in *vingtième* assessments by declaring that the *vingtième* be levied following the terms of the edict of 1749 – that is, as a percentage of income. The explicit reference to the 1749 edict was designed as a pretext for overriding parlementary rulings that had for years prohibited adjustments in *vingtième* assessments. Since 1756 the parlement of Rouen had stipulated that the tax rolls must never be revised, and in 1763, fearing the creation of a *cadastre*, other courts joined with it in inserting this proviso into their own registers.

In 1771, however, Terray navigated his way around these provisos and launched an administrative campaign to get at the wealth of large landowners whose revenues had long outpaced their assess-ments. As soon as the new courts registered the edict of November, intendants throughout the *pays d'élections* ordered *vingtième* directors and controllers to verify tax rolls and reassess the landed elite. As chapter 2 demonstrated, this effort was far more effective than is usually thought, making the revision of the *vingtième* one of the most significant, if underemphasized, legacies of the Maupeou coup.[71] For landowners of the *pays d'élections*, the coup's most painful effect was the scrutiny of their land by controllers and the following sharp rise in their assessments.

Although parlements during and after the Maupeou coup were on the whole more docile, their collective resistance less coordinated, and their protests less apt to be printed, they remained confronta-

---

[71] To his credit, Doyle recognized that the *vingtième* reform was the crown's only major undertaking of the period but he did not have the evidence to measure its scale. "The Parlements of France and the Breakdown of the Old Regime," *FHS* 6 (Fall 1970), pp. 429–31; and Doyle, *Origins*, p. 75.

tional in the matter of taxation. Several restructured parlements remonstrated against the edict of November 1771 (Rennes and Bordeaux were particularly vocal), but nowhere did resistance take the shape it did in Normandy, where the parlement had been completely abolished. The abolition of the parlement left a void that taxpayers rushed to fill. Whereas in the 1760s the parlement directed oppositional rhetoric to the public, which was at best a passive audience that occasionally fed rumors to the judges, in 1772 sections of the public came to life to form a broad movement against the *vingtième*. Rising to fill the vacuum created by the parlement's dismissal, three groups – officers of justice, residents and officials of the city of Caen, and noble taxpayers from all over Normandy – organized new forms of protest and voiced their complaints in language resembling that of the parlement. Having paid close attention to the statements publicized by the parlement in earlier disputes and well aware that the court had several times specified that augmentations in *vingtième* assessments were prohibited – the parlementary proviso had been printed in the Norman newspaper since 1762 – individuals throughout Normandy demanded that the crown cease illegal tax increases, restore estates, and respect the liberty of citizens to tax themselves and live free from the excesses of a bureaucratic state.

Each of the three groups resisted the crown in a particular way. Officers of justice, who faced rising *capitation* as well as *vingtième* assessments, maneuvered to block the operations of controllers of the *vingtième*. In 1772, Léonard Radulph, the *procureur-général* of the new superior council of Bayeux, the supposedly submissive court established by Maupeou, went after an infamous *vingtième* controller named Le Blanc who, under orders from the intendant, had been reevaluating personal property in Bayeux for the purpose of increasing assessments. Radulph tracked down the ambulatory controller, compelled him to surrender the intendant's orders, which Radulph called "illegal," and threatened that, on the "first complaint" made against Le Blanc, the court would prosecute him "to the fullest."[72] Fearing that Radulph might indeed prosecute the controller and create a scandal that would jeopardize verifications throughout the province, Fontette, the intendant, promptly informed Terray of the affair. Terray thought the matter worthy of his personal attention

---

[72] AN, H-1 1463, no. 80, letter from Le Blanc to Fontette, 1 September 1772.

and sent a letter of reprimand to Radulph: "I am astonished," the finance minister scolded, "that before taking an action which can only frustrate procedures which the administration has judged appropriate, you did not express verbally or by writing your doubts and concerns to Monsieur Fontette." Terray explained that in the interests of imposing taxes "with justice and equality," the edict of November 1771, because it invoked the edict of 1749, permitted administrators to "travel throughout the parishes, executing the instructions that you have seen." Besides, the courts had never been allowed to intervene in matters regarding the *vingtième* and the *capitation.* "I hope that after this explanation," the minister concluded, "far from intimidating the administrators, you will sustain and protect them."[73]

Terray's strong words thwarted Radulph's efforts, but a similar dispute soon arose involving another controller of the *vingtième,* Aufray, who was meeting with syndics of the parishes of Mortain and instructing them to revise parish *vingtième* rolls according to more accurate information on the wealth of landowners. Alarmed by this activity, a lieutenant of the *élection* of Mortain, Thébault, went to speak to the syndics to explain that their actions were "illegal." Denouncing Aufray as a conspirator in a plot "to crush the people," the lieutenant seized the controller's instructions, ordered the syndics to stop cooperating with him, and exclaimed, "It will be a beautiful day when the parlements return." Aufray took immediate recourse in the intendant, emphasizing the damaging effects of Thébault's speech: "These remarks, spoken bombastically in the presence of the people by a judge fulfilling his duties, stirred their spirits. Without a doubt, my operations are going to encounter obstacles which would not have existed if Thébault had not imprudently harangued the people during these meetings."[74] Vouching for Aufray's character, Fontette brought the case to the attention of the finance minister, who, having just admonished Radulph in Bayeux, dealt firmly with Thébault. "If the minister allowed this to be tolerated," a *mémoire* from Terray's office stated, "it would set a bad example for all of Normandy, and we could no longer expect anything from this province which otherwise would have been very

[73] AN, H-1 1463, no. 81, letter from Terray to Radulph, 11 September 1772.
[74] AN, H-1 1463, no. 87, letter from Aufray to Fontette, 13 September 1772.

important and would have produced a considerable augmentation in revenues." Terray summoned Thébault to the royal court.[75]

The opposition of the courts to the crown's efforts to increase the *vingtième* was seconded by municipal officers and residents of the city of Caen. The mayor and *échevins* of Caen appealed to Terray and Bertin, now secretary of the province of Normandy, in language that mimicked the banished parlement. Calling their protests "remonstrances" written in the name of the "public good" on behalf of "every citizen of Lower Normandy," the municipal officers objected that current reassessments of the *vingtième* were "founded neither in law nor on the expressed will of the King." The increase in the tax, they continued, "will contribute to the misery of the poor by exhausting the resources of landowners."[76] That a handful of municipal officers dared to issue remonstrances on behalf of the citizens of Lower Normandy astonished the intendant. "It is remarkable indeed," Fontette said, "that a municipal body grounded in its community, a body which cannot even represent that community regarding a tax which is not collective, imagines that it can speak in the name of the entire province."[77] Fontette's observation suggests that something new was happening. While it was quite normal for the parlement to speak on behalf of the province and to discuss such general matters as the poor, the public good, and the improper deeds of royal administrators, it was "remarkable" that an ordinary municipal corps was asserting itself in this way.

It was equally remarkable that residents of the city of Caen acted on their own behalf to resist the *vingtième*. In the final months of 1772 many of Caen's most prominent inhabitants, among them titled nobility, pledged that instead of petitioning the intendant for reductions in the *vingtième* they would refuse to pay any increases, and, if their property were seized and put up for sale as a result, no one would purchase it. The leader of this movement was Jean-Robert Gosselin de Manneville, the former Jansenist mayor of Caen whose own *vingtième* rose, after a thorough verification, from 385 livres in 1771 to 550 livres in 1773.[78] A noble of the sword in regular correspondence with former members of the parlement of Rouen,

---

[75] AN, H-1 1463, no. 82, *mémoire* from the office of the controller-general.
[76] AN, H-1 1463, no. 51, letter from the municipal officers of Caen to Terray, 28 April 1772; Floquet, *Parlement de Normandie*, VI, p. 691.
[77] AN, H-1 1463, no. 74, letter to Terray, 15 August 1772.
[78] AD Calvados, C 5631, *vingtième* rolls for the parish of Manneville.

Manneville was always looking for ways to fight "the Administration," and during the city's tax revolt he never missed an opportunity to discourage fellow citizens from paying increases in the *vingtième*.[79] One day, in the office of Caen's tax receiver, upon overhearing a city resident complain that he had not yet received a response to a petition for a reduction in the *vingtième*, Manneville interrupted, "you cannot have [the reduction] because, to whom did you present your petition?" To the intendant, the man answered. "Well!" Manneville exclaimed, "the intendant does not have the right to give reductions because he does not have the right to impose the tax, and you couldn't be paying at a worse time." The zealous noble proceeded to persuade the petitioner and six or seven other people in the office not to pay their taxes. Twenty years after the refusal of sacraments controversy and almost a decade after the expulsion of the Jesuits (an affair in which Manneville was deeply involved), this Jansenist was now wholly engaged in a fiscal battle against the arbitrary authority of royal administration.[80]

The boldest gesture of resistance, which far surpassed that of the courts and the city of Caen, was staged by the Norman nobility.[81] In 1772 an unlikely group of individuals, including former *parlementaires* (Fossé, Janville, Néville, and Montpinçon), nobles of the sword (Manneville and the comte de Trie), and the lawyer Le Maître, joined together to lead the nobility of the province. Fossé and Manneville were Jansenists, as was Le Maître, and they had all worked together years before to expel the Jesuits. According to Trie, they and the others were drawn to this other cause in 1772 by a common desire to halt "the arbitrary increases in the *vingtième* that were imposed on us" and "the unprecedented harassment endured by the nobility of Normandy."[82] The group drafted a petition, which would become known as the *Requête au Roi*, and traveled the Norman countryside from the pays de Bray to the Cotentin peninsula, organizing small gatherings of nobles in châteaux. Although, in the words of one royal official, the nobles were committing an "enormous crime" by participating in such "acts of association" –

---

[79] Hippeau, *Gouvernement de Normandie*, V, p. 127, letter from d'Harcourt to Bertin, 18 November 1772.

[80] M. Joly, *Une Conspiration de la noblesse Normande au dix-huitième siècle* (Caen, 1865), pp. 26–8.

[81] The two main accounts of this noble tax protest are Joly, *Conspiration*, and Doyon, *Agent royaliste*, pp. 1–37.

[82] Hippeau, *Gouvernement de Normandie*, V, p. 120, letter to d'Harcourt, 16 November 1772.

assemblies of this kind were illegal under the Old Regime – they eagerly met with each other to discuss the challenge before them and to sign the petition.[83] Estimates of the number of signatures collected vary but at least 271 men signed one copy of the petition, suggesting that a broad segment of the nobility, extending well beyond the judges of the banished parlement, endorsed the statement.[84] D'Harcourt emphasized that the nobles involved were "good general officers" in the military.[85]

Once the signatures were collected, the petition was printed clandestinely by Le Maître, who was embarking on a great career as an underground printer and pamphleteer, and Néville, who had apparently built a printing press in his château in the pays de Caux.[86] These two men churned out copies of the *Requête* and other pamphlets until they were arrested, at which time a certain Pierre Brunier, a prior from Le Maître's neighborhood in Rouen, continued the project.[87] Hot off Néville's press, copies of the petition were distributed to princes who were asked to present the case of the Norman nobility to the king, nobles of other provinces such as Brittany who might be prompted to enter the fray, and readers throughout Normandy and Paris. It is impossible to determine the number of copies printed, but it was at least in the hundreds. Toward the end of the affair, Fossé's daughter was caught smuggling 169 copies of the petition through the customs gate of Paris, and in all likelihood this was only the last of the *Requête*'s several press runs.

The petition bore the unmistakable imprint of the *parlementaires* who helped draft it. It pleaded for the return of the parlement, whose rights of remonstrance and verification of law ensured "wise and tempered government" and maintained the "liberty" of the "nation." The petition, which at one point called itself "remon-

---

[83] Hippeau, *Gouvernement de Normandie*, V, p. 110, letter from Wargemont to d'Harcourt, 5 November 1772.

[84] The *Requête de la noblesse de Normandie* was signed by 221 nobles and received individual endorsements from 50 additional nobles, according to Carcassonne, *Montesquieu*, p. 416, n. 1.

[85] Hippeau, *Gouvernement de Normandie*, V, p. 101, letter to Bertin, 28 October 1772.

[86] Doyon, *Agent royaliste*, pp. 7 and 23. For Le Maître's involvement in illegal publishing in the 1780s, see Jeremy Popkin, "Pamphlet Journalism at the End of the Old Regime," *Eighteenth-Century Studies* 22 (1989), pp. 351–67.

[87] It is possible that Le Maître and Néville printed three other Norman anti-Maupeou pamphlets that circulated around the same time: *Manifeste aux Normands* (n. p., n. d.); *Titres de la province de Normandie* (n. p., n. d.); and *Essai historique sur les droits de la province de Normandie* (n. p., n. d.).

strances," so resembled parlementary remonstrances that Mont-pinçon remarked that "it was [written in] the same style, [and used] the same phrases as remonstrances."[88]

However, the petition developed one aspect of parlementary remonstrances that had been downplayed after those of 10 May 1760: the need for estates. The *Requête* began by reminding the king that his Norman subjects had lost their liberty:

> Indeed, we had Estates, but we are no longer permitted to assemble them, we had a court that served as a depository of our rights and liberties, but it was taken from us; we had solemn titles which assured the perpetuity of our Estates and the irremovability of our Exchequer; their value is unceasingly recognized by Your Majesty, and their constantly modified execution comes to be indefinitely suspended, so that we, who enjoyed all the rights of a free people, have successively lost them and are reduced to the humiliating condition of a conquered people.[89]

What made the loss of liberty so painfully apparent, moreover, was the subsequent attack on property. Indeed, according to the petition, the main consequence of the suppression of "intermediary bodies" was the "devouring arbitrariness" of royal taxes. Indirect taxes were on the rise,

> But the last straw is the inquisition that is conducted in our houses and châteaux as a natural consequence of the promised cessation of the third *vingtième* ... The second *vingtième* is only a prolongation of the previous one, which must therefore be a prolongation of the same product, and the authority of Your Majesty is abused if one doubles and triples it. It is no longer the second *vingtième* that is imposed, it is a *cinquième* that is collected.

Verifications of the second *vingtième* were nothing but disguised tax hikes, and poorly disguised ones at that, for it was the blatantly unlawful way the tax was levied as much as the increase itself that made the nobles feel vulnerable.

> The form by which these taxes are levied is also as contrary to your wishes as it is to general laws and to our charter. Unauthorized commissioners are sent into the countryside to measure, examine, and estimate our fortunes and our land at their will. Their personal judgment becomes the basis of the tax. By the fundamental law of your crown no tax should be collected until after a deliberation of Estates or a legal verification ... The inquisition

---

[88] Hippeau, *Gouvernement de Normandie*, V, pp. 105–8, deposition of Montpinçon, 1 November 1772.

[89] This and other quotations from the *Requête de la noblesse de Normandie* (n.p., [1772]) are from the reprint in Hippeau, *Gouvernement de Normandie*, V, pp. 94–8, Lettre de la noblesse de Normandie au Roi.

of these itinerant commissioners ... is therefore an attack on our security; their operations are tantamount to the misappropriation of funds; their success will complete in one fell swoop the loss of our liberty, the destruction of our laws, the ruin of our commerce, and the desperate misery of the people.

Apparently one need not have been a *parlementaire* losing an office to feel the "arbitrary" effects of the Maupeou coup. Landowners in Normandy and across the *pays d'élections* experienced the coup directly as they watched royal administrators, unleashed in unprecedented numbers, reassess their property for the first time in decades or, in some cases, for the first time ever. As Malesherbes keenly observed, it was "as if [administrators] had wanted to make the people feel all that they had lost in losing its former Magistrates."[90]

To restore their liberty the nobles asked for "mediatory corps" through which they could communicate regularly with the throne. Although the term "mediatory corps" alluded to both the parlement and the estates, the petition emphasized that estates were the more important institution. The parlement might have "stood in for estates" in the latter's absence, but "the magistrates were no more than a supplement to the assembly of the nation." Having seen Maupeou brush the parlements aside and having experienced the subsequent fiscal inquisition, nobles believed that estates could best prevent the state from veering further out of control. For a nobility that felt vulnerable to the blows of a wayward fiscal administration, estates offered protection and an opportunity to stabilize a listing ship of state. Indeed, the 1772 petition, like the parlement's protests of the previous year, issued the strongest call for estates since 1760, when the solicitation for estates was adorned with flowery allusions to paternal justice. In 1772 the call for estates required no ornament but the self-evident necessity of "mediatory corps."

Used three times in an otherwise concise pamphlet, the term "mediatory corps" was of course borrowed from Montesquieu. Montesquieu had coined the phrase to distinguish tempered monarchies, in which a variety of institutions served to diffuse and soften power, from despotic monarchies whose authority was undiluted. In 1772, however, the words "mediatory corps" commingled with the much starker principle of national sovereignty, that is the idea that the king needed the consent of the nation, represented by estates,

[90] Elisabeth Badinter, ed., *Les "remontrances" de Malesherbes 1771–1775* (Paris, 1985), p. 241.

before levying taxes. Although d'Harcourt defended the noble petitioners by claiming that they asked only for provincial estates and not "the Estates of the kingdom," any but the most narrow reading of the document suggests its reference to estates implied the Estates General as well as the provincial estates of Normandy. Just as the "nation" alluded ambiguously to both Normandy and France, "estates" evoked both the Norman estates and the Estates General.

How subversive was this call for estates? In one sense it was not nearly as radical as the anti-*Unigenitus* remonstrances of 1753, which stated explicitly that the parlements had a right to resist the will of the king. But if the call for estates in 1760 and 1772 sidestepped the question of the right of resistance, it was equally significant in that it shifted the mechanism of consent to royal taxes from courts to political bodies that could more effectively utilize it. Further, in 1772 the idea that estates were the preeminent institutions through which the nation expressed its will and exercised its sovereignty was endorsed by a large fraction of the nobility. Loose associations of privileged taxpayers, consisting of individuals ranging from normally silent rural nobles of the sword to ardent Jansenists familiar with the world of clandestine print, were playing with ideas that, a decade earlier, had been forced into public view by the most radical factions within parlement.

Ministers of state certainly understood the challenge posed by the *Requête*. Threatened as much by the content of the petition as by the autonomous collective action that underlay the signing of it, Bertin instructed the intendants of Caen and Rouen to inspect the printing houses of their generality to ensure that no more copies would be printed, and he ordered officers from Châtelet and the royal mounted police to seize the papers and arrest leaders of the noble cabal. (Bertin had originally instructed d'Harcourt to arrest the rebels but the minister discovered that the governor, who was rumored to have been present at one of the larger noble assemblies, could not be trusted). It did not take long for the royal council to subdue the province. Manneville and Le Maître were thrown in the Bastille. Trie and Janville fled to Holland. Fossé escaped to Utrecht but managed to pass copies of the petition to his daughter, who was then thrown in the Bastille for attempting to smuggle them into Paris. And, under the threat of exile, scores of gentlemen wrote retractions in which nobles of the sword emphasized their devotion to royal military service, and legal scholars such as Toustain de

Richebourg admitted that sovereignty resided entirely in the king. Such punitive actions alarmed the editors of the *Journal Historique*, who closely followed the disturbance in Normandy but who mistakenly predicted that "this violent, military, and despotic expedition" into Normandy would further rouse the nobility.[91] In fact, royal repression ended the affair.

In November 1774 the newly acceded Louis XVI reinstalled the old parlements, intending to usher in an age of cooperation between the magistrature and the monarchy. As magistrates reassembled amidst festivals, banquets, and ceremonies, it looked like a new era of good will had indeed arrived. And to some extent it had. Chastened by the experience of the Maupeou coup, the parlements never again mounted the kind of fierce opposition to royal authority that spanned the 1750s and 1760s.[92] But it would be wrong to characterize the parlements as sheepishly following the royal will. The contentious issue of taxation crossed the divide between Louis XV and Louis XVI, between Machault, Bertin, and Terray, on the one side, and Necker and Calonne on the other, to connect the tumultuous third quarter of the century to the Prerevolution of 1787–8. All the ceremony surrounding the coronation of the new king and the restoration of the courts could not efface the deeper problem posed by the continuation of Terray's fiscal policy. The infamous minister might have fallen from power, but royal administrators continued to impose high *capitation* assessments on officers of justice, and, more significantly, to raise the *vingtième* on landowners after verifying their wealth. Indeed, Necker, minister of finance from 1776 to 1781, intensified the campaign to revise the *vingtième* and publicized a language of fiscal equality that Terray had reserved for private correspondence.

As soon as the celebration of Louis XVI's gracious act of restoring the parlements quieted, the parlement of Rouen, together with the parlements of Grenoble and Bordeaux and the *cour des aides* of Paris, assumed its old confrontational posture. As one witness of the return of the Rouen parlement noted, "the king and the parlement remain each in his own, that is to say, weapons in hand, and ready to fight when the occasion presents itself."[93] That occasion presented itself repeatedly from 1775 to 1778 as the court attempted to block the operations of the directors and controllers of the *vingtième*, taking up

---

[91] Quoted in Joly, *Conspiration*, p. 49.   [92] Doyle, "Parlements of France."
[93] Quoted in Floquet, *Parlement de Normandie*, VII, p. 41.

where the city of Caen, lower officers of justice, and the noble signers of the *Requête* left off in 1772. The court railed against the "illegal" increases in the *vingtième* imposed by the dubious edict of November 1771 and denounced all that those increases represented: arbitrary power, the violation of property rights, the stifling of the will of the nation, the sapping of the citizen-taxpayer, and the debilitating absence of estates. After the Maupeou coup, during the reign of Louis XVI, the pressure of the *vingtième* kept this rhetoric alive, especially the call for estates.

Even before Necker introduced his new policies in 1777, the parlement of Rouen leveled charges against royal fiscal administration, now openly integrating the ideas of Montesquieu and Malesherbes. The ideas of Montesquieu, which had cropped up, uncited, in earlier remonstrances and in the *Requête* of 1772, were used to describe the psychological atmosphere of insecurity created by the activities of controllers. Drawing from book 13 of *De l'esprit des lois*, magistrates highlighted the threat to liberty posed by "this mob of agents" who since 1771 had been tormenting taxpayers with "violent investigations into property." Although the remonstrances of the parlement, unlike those of the *cour des aides* of Paris, shied away from the word "despotism," they emphasized the condition of fear and mistrust that Montesquieu associated with a despotic regime. In an age when *vingtième* controllers were operating outside the law and producing "a continual war between the tax collector and the taxpayer," the property-owner was thrown into a constant state of "anxiety" (*l'inquiétude*). His hold on his property was unnervingly tenuous.[94]

That anxiety was aggravated by the "arbitrary" nature of the appeals process available to taxpayers, against which Malesherbes, as president of the *cour des aides*, had been protesting for two decades. Reacting to the inability of intendants and *vingtième* directors to respond adequately to the wave of petitions that flooded their offices in the 1770s, the parlement of Rouen for the first time went into some detail about the problems taxpayers experienced when petitioning for tax reductions. *Vingtième* petitions were "rejected, forgotten, or lost in the offices of directors," while *capitation* petitions "put your [majesty's] subjects in a position of absolute dependence

---

[94] Both quotations are from BN, NAF, 22104, fos. 156–62, remonstrances of 16 July 1777, but see also BN, NAF, 22104, fos. 184–9, remonstrances of 1 September 1775.

on the Intendants."[95] (The phrase "absolute dependence on the Intendants" was plucked right out of Malesherbes' celebrated 1775 remonstrances). Operating according to no general principles, the entire process of petitioning was but a collection of "little tactics used to gain the consent of taxpayers."[96] And it was now known that any reductions granted in the *capitation* were paid for by its so-called free funds, a pool of tax revenue susceptible to mismanagement by the intendant. The parlement of Grenoble was so outraged by the existence of these funds that it asked in 1778 to have its provincial estates restored in order to manage them.

When in 1777 Necker issued two *arrêts du conseil* designed to intensify verifications of wealth, he met vigorous opposition from courts, which answered his appeal to equality with assertions about the respect owed to law, property, and the right to consent to taxation. Even the parlement of Paris, which had been relatively docile in tax affairs, did not take Necker's challenge lying down. Using evidence collected from an inquiry into the abuses of the *vingtième*, it argued that verifications violated the last vestige of the nation's right to consent to taxes.[97] Typically, the parlement of Paris and the crown went on to resolve their differences through a compromise.

In Rouen, where the parlement proved more intransigent, Louis XVI had to force the registration of Necker's decree. This was the first forced registration to take place at the court since 1771, and the parlement struck back forcefully, embarking on a course of opposition that would end in another collective resignation. After claiming that the court's right to free deliberation was founded "on the wish of the Nation, expressed in the cahiers of the Estates General," the remonstrances of 6 August 1778 answered Necker's plea for fiscal equality with a call for the rule of law and a demand for provincial estates. Necker's proposal was a sham: "this plan for new verifications, announced as a principle of distributive justice, is at bottom only a fiscal project designed to swell the revenues of the fisc without making any reductions for taxpayers who are heavily taxed." It was irrelevant that the incomes of landowners had

---

[95] BN, NAF, 22104, fos. 156–62, remonstrances of 16 July 1777; BN, NAF 22104, fos. 164–83, remonstrances of 6 August 1778.
[96] BN, NAF, 22104, fos. 184–9, remonstrances of 1 September 1775.
[97] See Georges Lardé, *Une Enquête sur les vingtièmes au temps de Necker* (Paris, 1920); and Stone, *Parlement of Paris*, pp. 96–100.

increased since their original assessments; increases in *vingtième* assessments for whatever reason violated the edicts that established the tax. Quoting Montesquieu, the magistrates asserted that taxes should be assessed not according to what the people "are able to give," but according to what it "should give" in relation to the "real needs of state," a principle that forms "the basis of civil society." To rein in the abuses of "arbitrary administration" and to apply sound principles of government, the remonstrances asked for the reestablishment of provincial estates which could eventually negotiate *abonnements* with the king. Meanwhile, the parlement would issue an *arrêt de défense* that threatened to prosecute royal officials for reassessing liability to the *vingtième*.

Growing frustrated with the parlement's recalcitrance, Louis XVI summoned a deputation from Rouen to Versailles to announce that he would never grant the "system of independence" for which the remonstrances called. He ordered the magistrates to return to Rouen to register a new ruling, the *lettres-patentes* of 31 August 1778, prohibiting the parlement from interfering in the crown's self-proclaimed project to establish fiscal equality. Necker used this new decree to reiterate the crown's lofty commitment to justice and equality and to castigate the parlement for its attempts to undermine it: "We cannot tolerate, without harming our authority and the well-being of our subjects, having one of our courts ... issue rulings that prohibit the execution of that which we have judged necessary to ordain ... in order to establish more justice and equality in the distribution of a tax which circumstance makes necessary, and in order to give to the less wealthy and weaker taxpayers the means to make themselves heard." Since parish-wide verifications in which village assemblies participated would lead to a more equal distribution of the tax, the parlement was seeking to prosecute precisely those officials whose "mission" it was "to protect the weakest and poorest" subjects.[98]

To the magistrates the royal *lettres-patentes* were so objectionable that, after d'Harcourt forced them to register them, they decided to repeat the dramatic gesture of 1763 and offer their collective resignation prior to judicial vacation. In an *arrêté* of 4 September 1778 the *parlementaires* explained why they took such a drastic step. The *lettres-patentes*, which were "posted and publicized," "presented the officers

---

[98] Floquet, *Parlement de Normandie*, VII, pp. 75–6.

of the court to the eyes of the people as seeking to oppose the fairest project (that of establishing more justice and more equality in the distribution of the *vingtièmes*, and to protect from oppression the weakest and poorest subjects of the king); whereas the efforts and measures of the court had one single goal, ... to prevent augmentations in the *vingtième* that no law authorizes."[99] The decree had made the court look as if it opposed justice and equality, whereas all it was trying to do, the magistrates insisted, was to uphold the law. Necker's deployment of the language of fiscal equality helped to crystallize the ideological positions of crown and parlement: the monarchy represented itself as the hero of fiscal equality, while the parlement portrayed itself as the protector of law and property and the solicitor of estates.

For all its theatrical value, the parlement's resignation did not lead to an impasse. In stark contrast to their behavior in 1763 the magistrates reassembled at the commencement of the judicial year and continued to serve the king as if they had never resigned. Thanks to both the American war, for which Necker never asked a third *vingtième*, and the memory of Maupeou, which kept the parlement of Rouen from pushing matters to extremes, the next few years were relatively calm in Normandy (though the mantle of opposition passed to such parlements as Bordeaux). In 1782 Louis XVI and the parlements came to an agreement that would keep fiscal dispute at bay for a few more years. Louis insisted that the *vingtième* be tripled temporarily until three years after peace was declared but pledged that *vingtième* assessments themselves would never again be touched. To the magistrates of Rouen who had been fighting increases in assessments since 1772 (or really since 1756) this was a crucial concession on the part of the crown, and they registered the edict of July 1782 with minor resistance. Other parlements objected more strenuously – Besançon called for the Estates General and the return of the provincial estates of Franche-Comté – but the crown prevailed and a third *vingtième* was once again imposed throughout the kingdom. Verifications came to a halt, as promised, but in 1786, with the third *vingtième* due to expire, Calonne tried to institute new direct taxes on the privileged. This time such measures would trigger revolution.

---

[99] Floquet, *Parlement de Normandie*, VII, p. 79, n. 1.

In their reactions to universal taxes, judicial institutions added the themes of liberty, despotism, citizenship, and government by estates to the language of justice that permeated the administrative sphere. Several considerations prevent us from reading too much into this new vocabulary. First, it was used to achieve particularistic, conservative goals. The parlement of Rouen employed the word "liberty" in an effort to preserve Norman liberty, that is the sum of liberties and privileges enumerated in the medieval Norman charter, and to maintain the traditional liberty of the court itself, namely its right to exercise authority in its customary jurisdictions without interference from the royal council and its agents. Personal and familial ambition, corporate interest, and regional loyalty shaped parlementary rhetoric as much as did any guiding abstract ideology. Secondly, the protests of the parlement, no matter how vehement, did not significantly hamper the crown. For all the quarreling and dramatic gestures of defiance, monarchs in the end saw their tax decrees registered by the courts and they received most of the additional tax revenue they had demanded.

To measure tax disputes in livres and sols, however, is to miss their most important dimension. The fact is that a lot was said as magistrates exchanged blows with the monarchy, and the gains kings made in financial capital translated into losses in symbolic capital. To some extent, these symbolic or ideological losses were personal; for example, rumors in the city of Rouen that Louis XV was completely unaware of the true burden of taxation tarnished his image. But I would not go so far as to say that tax disputes "desacralized" Louis XV or Louis XVI, let alone the French monarchy in general. More significant (as Miromesnil would come to learn) was the way in which judicial conflict over universal taxes discredited royal fiscal administration and characterized the apparatus of state as a source of despotism. Increases in universal taxes and the administrative practices associated with them tested Bossuet's distinction between absolute and arbitrary authority. As the crown forced the registration of decrees that increased the *capitation* and the *vingtième*, employed ever more administrators to impose those increases and administer the taxes, and locked the courts out of the appeals process, magistrates began to doubt Bossuet's assertion that the French monarchy, although absolute, respected the property of its subjects. The growth of a fiscal administration that could tax elites effectively without their consent, and which was, by nature, arbitrary and unaccountable to those on whom it preyed, signaled the coming of "despotism."

Parlementary discourse did more than criticize the state. It also evoked a form of government that could keep the fiscal-adminis-trative apparatus of state in check and reestablish the proper ties between ruler and ruled. Barely visible in the distant past, that form of government was founded on the principles of liberty and citizen-ship and on the existence of estates. Liberty in this context meant more than just privilege; the parlement of Rouen never once invoked the term "liberty" to assert that elites enjoyed the privilege of exemption from the *capitation* and the *vingtième*. Instead, liberty alluded to freedom from the encroachments of the state, the feeling of security that came with that freedom, and the right of sovereign courts, as temporary organs of the nation, to deliberate on and consent to royal law. Moreover, the "citizen" now under the attack of fiscal agents had in the past experienced liberty directly when he participated in the administration of taxation and willingly gave tributes to the crown. Only one kind of institution was capable of restoring this citizen of old: estates. Provincial estates and Estates General – the magistrates mentioned both but frequently discussed estates in the abstract – allowed citizens to tax themselves through the persons of their deputies, thereby freeing them from the oppression of royal administration.

These constitutional principles did not develop in a vacuum. They emerged during specific fluctuations in universal taxes and were used to contest particular royal claims. In the last few years of the Seven Years War, facing sharp hikes in the *capitation* and *vingtième*, the more radical factions in the parlement of Rouen drew on, redefined, and added to the rhetoric of judicial Jansenism. One key addition to that rhetoric was the call for estates, which, trumpeted in May 1760 only to be muted for the remainder of the decade, came back resoundingly during the Maupeou coup and continued to be heard in the opening years of Louis XVI's reign. The demand for estates and the words and themes that clustered around it took on a vibrancy in the 1770s not simply because of the sudden judicial intervention of Maupeou but because of the protracted and partially successful project to reassess the *vingtième*. It is worth emphasizing that indirect taxes were less likely to provoke this kind of constitu-tional discourse than were direct ones, as Malesherbes explained: "The collection of taxes on goods is not related to the form of government of the state; but the distribution of direct taxes is fundamentally connected to the constitution of the monarchy."[100] I would add that direct taxes striking the privileged, the most sensitive taxpayers in the kingdom, were particularly likely to lead to reconsiderations of the structure of the state and the political role of taxpaying subjects. It would be difficult to imagine, for example, parlements using the word "citizens" to describe taxpayers in the eighteenth century if direct taxation had continued to fall almost exclusively on commoners. But when confronting rises in taxes on elites, magistrates did not hesitate to employ a vocabulary of resistance that, in theory at least, endowed taxpayers with a degree of sovereignty.

Further, the constant stream of tax legislation after 1760 engendered an endless series of disputes that sustained this kind of rhetoric. Over the last three and a half decades of the Old Regime, *vingtième* decrees prolonging, increasing, or redesigning the tax were presented to the sovereign courts as often as every two years on average. The result of this string of decrees was a dramatic rise in the frequency of protest against taxation and a steady outpouring of parlementary remonstrances and rulings that kept the language of judicial opposition alive. Although the quarrels provoked by legislation did not always reach crisis levels, the perpetual cycle of dispute helped to carry parlementary opposition from war to peace and back, from one administration to another, and from one reign to the next. Severe conflict over taxes spanned from the Seven Years War, when religious conflict reached its climax, into and beyond the Maupeou coup, through the American war, to the Prerevolution of 1787–8.

What effect did this have on public opinion? This is the most difficult question of all. The parlement of Rouen developed the technique of printing its remonstrances for public consumption during the refusal of sacraments affair of 1753 and began to use the strategy in the arena of taxation in 1760. During the remainder of the Seven Years War, the parlement printed remonstrances and judicial rulings against taxation on a regular basis in an effort to win the favor of the public and apply pressure on the royal council. Judging from the accounts of contemporary observers such as

---

[100] Badinter, *Remontrances de Malesherbes*, p. 201.

Miromesnil, Bachaumont, and Barbier, it appears that the dissemination of printed protests against tax legislation did much to shape the political attitudes of privileged and nonprivileged subjects alike. Such anecdotal evidence, of which historians must always be suspicious, is supported by the events of 1772 in which lower-level officers of justice, bourgeois, and nobles in Normandy drew on parlementary rhetoric to protest against increases in the *vingtième*. By 1772 the public idioms of the court had become part of a wider culture of resistance to taxation that stretched beyond the perimeters of institutions to privileged taxpayers at large. While this was most visible in Normandy, where the abolition of the parlement prompted elites to take action, it is likely that the same attitudes existed in other provinces where protest continued to emanate from the parlements. After 1772 the collective action of a broad section of the Norman elite was once again eclipsed by the parlement, but it would resurface with a renewed vigor throughout Normandy and the rest of the kingdom in 1789.

CHAPTER 5

Taxation, Enlightenment, and the printed word: debate in the literary sphere

"When a question of political economy is submitted to the judgment of the Public by way of print, the Minister of State immediately obtains the judgment of educated men; not that all educated men write, but they judge the Writers, and the Writers' principles, and their opinion soon forms public opinion. How can the toil and knowledge of a Minister of State make up for such a powerful kind of assistance?"

– André Morellet[1]

Thus far the language that we have examined came from the world of practice. The crown's "equality," the petitioner's "justice," and the magistrate's "liberty" were words deployed in an active political arena where claims were constantly advanced, contested, negotiated, and re-negotiated. This was less the case with language that came from the literary sphere. There, writers sought to transcend narrow interests, be they those of king, subject, or magistrate, and to observe the tax system from the distant and objective vantage point of the public critic. The purpose of the writer was to analyze and resolve conflict rather than engage in it. This is not to say that writers were, in fact, completely objective or disinterested; they were known to use high-minded philosophy in the service of specific political programs, to write from personal experience, and to exhibit the same kind of zealotry they denounced in others. But, in principle, men of letters eschewed particularism and, with apparent sincerity, fashioned their ideas for the general improvement of society.

This chapter examines how the books of the eighteenth century contributed to the dialogue on taxation. It measures the diffusion of texts on the royal finances over the century, and then focuses on a few of the century's most popular works, assessing their intellectual

[1] Morellet, *Réflexions sur les avantages de la liberté*, p. 22.

and rhetorical content and, where possible, considering how readers responded. During the Enlightenment, as literacy rose and commerce in books expanded, writers suggested a number of highly imaginative ways to approach the problem of taxation and the question of the relationship between state and society that underlay it. Themes such as natural law, social contract, republicanism, public opinion, and patriotism were presented to readers on an unprecedented scale, shaping their conceptions of the French polity. It is time to consider how literature may have affected the political outlook of a reading – and taxpaying – public.

THE CIRCULATION OF TEXTS ON THE ROYAL FINANCES

In the early 1780s Necker took the literary world by storm with the publication of two best-selling books on royal finance: the *Compte rendu au Roi* of 1781, which provided readers with figures on the king's revenues and expenses; and *De l'administration des finances de la France* of 1784, a three-volume work illuminating the entire system of state finance. The reception of these texts was nothing short of astounding. The *Compte* ran through at least seventeen editions and 40,000 copies (or as many as 100,000 according to François Metra), while *De l'administration* appeared in twenty editions totaling 80,000 copies.[2] (By contrast, most moderately fashionable books in this period usually went through three or four editions, each producing anywhere from 500 to 3,000 copies).[3] Driving the sensational success of these works were the droves of literate subjects who were eager to read about the kingdom's finances. Even with a sales rate of 3,000 copies a day upon its release, the *Compte* was unable to satisfy demand, prompting at least one frustrated provincial gentleman, faced with a local shortage of the book, to track down a copy himself and deliver a public reading for those in his locality who had not yet seen it. And how many children were there like Auguste Marmont, the future Napoleonic marshal, who were taught to read from the

---

[2] Robert D. Harris, *Necker: Reform Statesman of the Ancien Régime* (Berkeley, CA, 1979), pp. 217–18; Jean-Claude Perrot, "Nouveautés: l'économie politique et ses livres" in *Histoire de l'édition française*, vol. 2, *Le livre triomphant, 1660–1830*, eds. Henri-Jean Martin and Roger Chartier (Paris, 1984), pp. 254–5; and Kenneth Carpenter, "The Economic Bestsellers before 1850," *Bulletin of the Kress Library* (May, 1975), pp. 22–4.

[3] Carcassonne, *Montesquieu*, p. 660; and Maza, *Private Lives*, pp. 122–3.

Compte, copies of which were composed of the same cheap blue paper on which popular fairy tales had been printed for centuries?[4] Why of all things would a budget and a treatise on financial administration elicit such excitement? Necker is often credited with tearing the veil that shrouded the royal finances in secrecy and providing readers with a tantalizing glance at the inner workings of the monarchy. In an age when a writer such as Rodolphe Effer de Sybourg was thrown in prison under the charge of being a "pamphleteer on the finances," Necker's effort to divulge the financial secrets of the state was bound to arouse readers.[5] But it is perhaps more accurate to view Necker's success as a brilliant crescendo to decades of active printing on financial issues.

Some of that printing was sponsored by the monarchy. The *Compte* was not the first text dealing with the sensitive issue of fiscal administration to be approved by royal censors or printed by the royal press. High royal officials such as Moreau de Beaumont, author of *Mémoires concernant les impositions et droits en Europe* (1768), used the royal press to distribute their work, while writers outside the government used government contacts or protectors at court to obtain formal or tacit permission to publish their manuscripts. As an intendant of finance in the 1750s, Vincent de Gournay used his influence with Malesherbes, then director of the book trade, to help several writers interested in political economy avoid state censure.[6]

Those unable to obtain permission to publish found other ways to circulate their work. Owing in large part to foreign presses in Switzerland, the Low Countries, and England, a substantial clandestine book trade developed in France that gave readers access to unauthorized texts written anonymously or under pseudonyms. Of course writers who defied the law by having their work printed without royal approval ran the risk of arrest and imprisonment, but even in these cases the crown could show considerable restraint. When the marquis de Mirabeau was arrested following the 1760 publication of his celebrated *Théorie de l'impôt*, the great care with which royal officials handled him led Madame d'Epinay to comment, "A man had never been arrested like that." Mirabeau was

---

[4] Perrot, "Nouveautés," p. 254; Simon Schama, *Citizens: A Chronicle of the French Revolution* (New York, 1989), p. 92; Harris, *Necker*, p. 218.
[5] Farge, *Subversive Words*, p. 185.
[6] Antoine Murphy, "Le développement des idées économiques en France, 1750–1756," *Revue d'histoire moderne et contemporaine* 33 (1986), pp. 521–41.

politely escorted from his home ("I could come back tomorrow if you haven't the time today," said the arresting officer), incarcerated in the prison of Vincennes for no more than eight hours, and then exiled to Bignon for three months.[7]

Necker's books, then, were hardly the first to delve into matters of finance. On the contrary, they were hawked to a readership that had already been primed by a wealth of literature produced in the preceding decades. Between formal approval, tacit approval, and the clandestine trade, all kinds of printed material on taxation and finance found its way into circulation: books, pamphlets, diction-aries, encyclopedias, and journals. Most texts on finance came in the form of books and pamphlets, which were sold in bookstores, made available in reading rooms, and, after mid-century, reviewed in newspapers. Dictionaries such as the *Dictionnaire des finances* (1727), first published as reference books for professional financiers, were soon directed toward a general readership interested in critical essays on finance and society. Diderot's *Encyclopédie* con-tained many articles of this kind (*"impôt"* by Jaucourt, *"vingtième"* by Damilaville, *"privilège"* by Boucher d'Argis, and *"économie"* by Rousseau), and, in the final years of the Old Regime, another successful encyclopedia, the *Encyclopédie méthodique: finances* (1784–7), devoted three entire volumes to articles relating to finance. Mean-while, periodical journals also appeared, notably the *Ephémérides du citoyen* (1765–72), which reappeared under Turgot's ministry and in 1788 as the *Nouvelles éphémérides économiques*, and the *Journal d'agricul-ture, du commerce, et des finances* (1765–83), offering subscribers the latest opinions and arguments on economics and government finance, two subjects often treated as one by eighteenth-century writers.[8]

Who read texts on finance? To a large extent, the people who read them – urban nobles, men of letters, magistrates, royal officials, and a variety of professionals – came from the same milieu as those who wrote them. Most texts circulated first in manuscript form among the author's friends within the small world of elite associa-

---

[7] Georges Weulersse, *Le mouvement physiocratique en France de 1756 à 1770*, 2 vols. (Paris, 1910), I, pp. 75–6. In its duration Mirabeau's exile seems to be typical for economists: Boisguilbert was exiled for two months in 1707 and Baudeau for two and a half months in the late 1770s. By contrast, the average writer thrown into the Bastille after 1750 stayed there over six months. Chartier, *Cultural Origins*, p. 63.

[8] For dictionaries and periodicals on political economy, see Perrot, "Nouveautés," pp. 246–7.

tional life. Members of salons, provincial academies, and agricultural societies discussed literature on finance and economics and promoted the works they found most interesting; the salon of Madame de Pompadour, for example, was well known for its encouragement of physiocratic works. Thus the reading public for this literary genre was often quite small, as Dupont de Nemours suggested, in a tone of frustration, when he described his audience as "three or four hundred more or less studious people and some seigneurs who remember that they have land." "Nevertheless," he hastened to add, "all these people spread rumors, and their droning converges to form what is called 'public opinion.' "[9]

Occasionally, works on finance penetrated much larger audiences. As literacy rose over the century (to 47 percent for men and 27 percent for women by the 1780s), and as more and more people came to own ever larger libraries, texts on the arts and sciences – and on politics in particular – flourished in both the licit and illicit book trade.[10] The diffusion of books on state finance was part of this wider fashion for political writings: timely pamphlets such as Roussel de la Tour's *Richesse de l'état* (1763) created great sensations; old classics such as Boisguilbert's *Détail de la France* (1695) and Vauban's *Projet d'une Dîme royale* (1707) were read and re-read decade after decade; books with alluring rhetoric such as Mirabeau's *Théorie de l'impôt* (1760) and Necker's *De l'administration* (1784) were veritable best-sellers; and handy, exhaustive works such as the *Encyclopédie méthodique: finances* (1784–7) reached readers by the tens of thousands.[11]

We shall have occasion to explore the intellectual content of these texts. For the moment it is important to consider how the publication of texts on finance evolved over the eighteenth century. Figure 5.1 shows the number of printed texts in five-year intervals from 1695 to 1789.[12] (Note that the final period from 1785 to 1789 is broken down into two parts, 1785 to 1788 and the year 1789).

---

[9] Quoted in Perrot, "Nouveautés," p. 249.
[10] Chartier, *Cultural Origins*, pp. 69–71; François Furet, "La 'librairie' du royaume de France au 18e siècle," in *Livre et société dans la France du xviiie siècle* (Paris, 1965), pp. 19–23; Darnton, *Forbidden Best-Sellers*, pp. 69 and 75.
[11] Darnton states that the *Encyclopédie méthodique* began with a press run of approximately 5,000 copies (*The Business of Enlightenment*, Cambridge, MA, 1979, p. 36), each of which probably reached several readers.
[12] René Stourm, *Bibliographie historique des finances de la France au dix-huitième siècle* (1895; reprint, New York, 1968). Although incomplete, this source provides by far the most comprehensive bibliography of eighteenth-century works on finance. In compiling figure 5.1, I counted works published in more than one year (journals, reprints, multi-volumed texts) for the first

It takes only a moment's glance at this chart to see the mid-century jump in the rate of production of texts on finance. Before 1750 usually no more than a handful of texts were printed every year. During the reign of Louis XIV, very few books and pamphlets were produced, though the ones that did circulate could be quite scathing.[13] Following the death of the Sun King, there was a temporary increase in book production, from 1715 to 1724, owing in part to the relaxation of censorship but also to two extraordinary events: the *chambre de justice* of 1716 in which the crown prosecuted and seized the fortune of royal financiers; and the rise and fall of John Law, the Scot who attempted to merge royal finances with a trading company. Fueled by financial speculation, Law's "system" collapsed in 1720, triggering a bankruptcy of immense proportions that would provide years of grist for the literary mill. Fifteen years after the Law fiasco the incremental rise in texts from 1735 to 1739 was largely due to the writings of Jean-François Melon and Charles Henri Dutot, who were still debating the lessons of Law's experiment.

From 1750 to the Revolution the French book trade experienced a surge in texts on taxation and political economy in general. The causes of this "happy revolution," as one contemporary called it, were manifold.[14] Dupont de Nemours speculated that the "widespread excitement that encouraged minds to study political economy goes back to M. de Montesquieu," whose *De l'esprit des lois* was published in 1748, just before the outpouring of literature illustrated in figure 5.1.[15] Certainly, the publication of Montesquieu's treatise marked a decisive moment in the history of French political thought, but it was not single-handedly responsible for the mid-century upswing in writings on finance.

More important was the emergence of new schools of economic thought, the spectacle of institutional conflict, and the rise and fall of several reform-minded royal ministers. Of the three main schools of

---

year of publication only. All manuscripts and texts without dates (or without firm evidence of possible dates) were excluded. I likewise excluded newspapers and judicial remonstrances on the grounds that the former were too general and the latter were dealt with in the previous chapter as part of the institutional sphere.

[13] The anonymous *Lettres d'un gentilhomme françois sur l'établissement d'une capitation générale en France* (Liege, 1695), for example, accused the king of financing an unjust war with a ruinous and illegitimate new tax.

[14] Quoted in Murphy, "Idées économiques," p. 530.

[15] Quoted in Stourm, *Bibliographie*, p. 94.

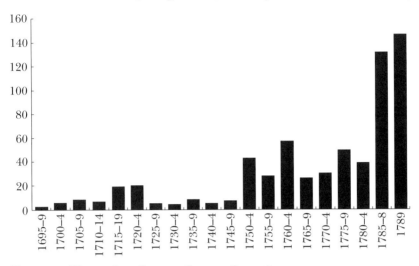

Figure 5.1   The number of texts on finance, 1695–1789.

economic thought – mercantilism, liberalism, and physiocracy – it was the latter that made the largest contribution to the world of print. From the late 1750s Quesnay, Mirabeau, Baudeau, Mercier de la Rivière, Dupont de Nemours, Le Trosne, and many others published profusely on questions of agriculture, the economy, and royal finance, presenting their ideas to readers in books and in journals such as the *Ephémérides*, which produced no fewer than sixty-nine volumes (at 400–500 copies a volume) from 1765 to 1772 and nineteen volumes between 1775 and 1776.[16] Although their immense popularity declined in the 1770s, especially following Turgot's fall in 1776, the physiocrats continued to publish. Mirabeau and Baudeau published as late as 1785 and 1787, respectively, and in 1788 the *Nouvelles éphémérides économiques* made its way into print yet again. The physiocratic school also had its share of detractors who, in turn, made their own literary contributions. Mably, Graslin, Forbonnais, Voltaire, Necker, and Linguet, to mention only the most famous, published all sorts of treatises that attacked physiocracy, from long analytical works such as Graslin's *Essai analytique sur la richesse et sur l'impôt* (1767) and Mably's *Doutes proposés aux Philosophes économistes sur*

---

[16] Perrot, "Nouveautés," p. 254.

l'ordre naturel et essentiel des sociétés (1768) to short biting satires such as Voltaire's *L'homme aux quarante écus* (1767).

Literary debate over finance was not fueled by theoretical rivalry alone, however. Writers in the second half of the century were also drawn to the subject of finance by the dramatic institutional conflicts over royal tax policy that swirled around them. In the early 1750s, for example, a pamphlet war erupted over Machault's attempt to tax the clergy. Immediately after the edict of May 1749 declared that the crown would levy the *vingtième* on ecclesiastical property, a multitude of pamphlets, some commissioned by the crown, appeared in favor of the edict, including Voltaire's famous *La voix du sage et du peuple* (1750) which lambasted the church for its tax privileges. The supporters of ecclesiastical privilege were quick to respond. Joining the church's own formal remonstrances against the edict, numerous tracts, such as Duranthon's *Réponse aux lettres contre l'immunité des biens ecclésiastique* and Gaultier's *Réfutation d'un libelle intitulé la Voix du sage et du peuple*, contested the crown's claims and attempted to refute Voltaire. The number of such protests was probably much larger than figure 5.1 suggests, given that the *arrêt du conseil* of 21 May 1751 banned as many as thirty-seven pamphlets opposing the crown's measures.[17]

Similarly, the peak in new works appearing from 1760 to 1764 reflected the desire of writers to comment on, and of readers to read about, the bitter disputes between the crown and the parlements. During the Seven Years War, controversy over the crown's attempt to increase taxation quickly spilled from the judicial to the literary arena. One pamphlet born of this contentious epoch became tremendously popular: *La richesse de l'état* (1763), written anonymously by Roussel de la Tour, a councilor in the parlement of Paris. Sympathetic to the parlements' complaints and yet quite open-minded about reform, *La richesse* affirmed the opinion of the parlements that the tax system was excessively complicated and subject to the abuse of financiers, and went on to propose the replacement of most existing taxes with a new tax to be levied on all subjects according to their ability to pay. Simple, concise, and initially circulated free of charge, the pamphlet became a sensation in the spring and summer of 1763 as newspapers and critics hailed its patriotism and clarity. "All the public has it in hand," wrote Barbier,

---

[17] The banned pamphlets are listed in Marion, *Machault*, p. 262, n. 4.

"consequently even the people discuss it and wish its implementation." Bachaumont, too, thought its proposals represented "the wish of the nation." The pamphlet provoked more than forty other writers to publish their own opinions on taxation, unleashing an "immense flood" of pamphlet literature that, according to Bachaumont, could fill an entire library. Some of the pamphlets opposing *La richesse*, such as Moreau's *Doutes modestes sur la Richesse de l'état*, were sponsored by the government in an effort to discredit Roussel de la Tour's work and cool the fever for reform among the public, whose interest in finance lent support to the parlements. Miromesnil was probably not the only first president of a parlement to solicit Moreau's *Doutes* from the finance minister and secretly orchestrate its distribution in his locality.[18]

Finally, the post-1750 surge in literature resulted from the controversial tenures of several reformist ministers of state and one extraordinarily liberal director of the book trade, all of whom were interested in influencing public opinion. As director of the book trade, the highest position in the royal literary police, from 1751 to 1763, Malesherbes generously allocated tacit permissions for publication, allowing a freer circulation of texts touching on the sensitive issue of political economy. In the early 1750s, after lifting the prohibition against *De l'esprit des lois*, he actively promoted the work of Jacques-Claude Vincent de Gournay and his cohort of economists (Cantillon, Véron de Forbonnais, Morellet, Dangeul, etc.) who were exploring ideas about the role of the state in the economy.[19] In addition to Malesherbes, a string of finance ministers (Machault, L'Averdy, Terray, Turgot, and Necker) encouraged like-minded authors to voice their views on the kingdom's finances. Baudeau supported L'Averdy's effort to extend the second *vingtième* in the summer of 1767 by publishing *Lettres d'un citoyen à un Magistrat sur les vingtièmes et les autres impôts*, while Turgot helped Richard des Glannières publish his *Plan d'imposition économique et d'administration des finances, présenté à monseigneur Turgot* (1774). No finance minister used and elicited the printed word quite like Necker, however. Besides the minister's own publications, pamphlets for and against his administration rolled off the presses in such prodigious quantities that they

---

[18] Barbier, *Chronique*, VIII, p. 77; Bachaumont, *Mémoires secrets*, I, pp. 254 and 268; Riley, *Seven Years War*, pp. 197–207.
[19] Murphy, "Idées économiques," pp. 521–41.

filled no fewer than three volumes of the *Collection complète de tous les ouvrages pour et contre M. Necker*, edited and re-edited in the early 1780s.

In the last five years of the Old Regime, texts on taxation and finance inundated the kingdom on a wholly new scale. One main current in this flood was stirred by the quarrel between Necker and one of his successors, Calonne, who challenged the validity of the *Compte* and made his own printed appeals to the public. The publicity of this dispute between ministers provoked scores of pamphlets and the publication of at least six state budgets or collections of budgets, all of which were published with the intention of providing the public with a definitive account of the royal finances. One anonymous pamphleteer was so annoyed with the "unparalleled agitation" caused by Necker and Calonne that he failed to see the irony in printing his own condemnation of both ministers for having "spoken too much in public, written too much, and agitated too much the minds of the multitude."[20] Meanwhile, as Calonne and Necker dueled and royal budgets were exposed to the light of day, prerevolutionary political bodies, such as the Assembly of Notables and provincial assemblies, further engaged the reading public by publishing their proceedings. Between 1787 and 1788 the minutes of the provincial assemblies appeared in over twenty publications, including a two-volume summary, which, in turn, encouraged still more essays on financial reform, many of which, like Le Vassor's *Mémoire sur la méthode la plus simple de répartir avec justesse l'impôt de la taille et les autres impositions* (Paris, 1788), were dedicated to "the messieurs composing the provincial assemblies." By 1789 the kingdom was awash in print. Constituents published *cahiers de doléances*; deputies published speeches; the National Assembly published decrees; men of letters continued to publish books; and pamphlet literature soared. In the coming years, the mania for publication would remain intense as revolutionaries looked for ways to put the state on new foundations.

THE IDEAS AND RHETORIC OF LITERATURE ON TAXATION

Having sketched the chronological patterns in which texts on taxation and finance circulated, it is important to push on to an

---

[20] *Lettre de l'auteur de mode françois, ou est agitée la question des assemblées provinciales* (Paris, 1787), pp. 27–8.

examination of the ideas and rhetoric that such texts publicized. How did the language of literature help to shape the issue of taxation? It would not be possible in the space of a single chapter to trace all the ideas about taxation and society from 1695 to the Revolution. Nor would it be desirable, since our aim here is not to construct an exhaustive intellectual history of taxation but to consider ideas that resonated broadly and helped forge new political mentalities. To this end, this study will limit itself to a handful of the century's most popular works, exploring how their authors characterized the problem of taxation and – a more difficult exercise – how such characterizations might have been understood by readers. Leaping from Boisguilbert and Vauban, who at the turn of the century wrote the first modern works of French political economy, to Mirabeau, who captured the public's imagination during the constitutional crises of mid-century, to Necker, who in the 1780s lifted the veil of secrecy from the state in the name of public opinion, it is possible to see how writers over the course of three reigns conceived of and presented the relationship between monarchy, taxation, and society.

Pierre Le Pesant de Boisguilbert, a *lieutenant général* at the *présidial* court of Rouen, and Sébastien Le Prestre de Vauban, a marshal and renowned military engineer, wrote the most popular works of political economy of Louis XIV's reign. Boisguilbert's *Détail de la France*, printed without royal permission in 1695 and censured in 1707, appeared in no fewer than twenty-seven editions in twenty years, while Vauban's *Dîme royale* (1707), which was banned as soon as it appeared, ran through fifteen editions and more than 10,000 copies in the two years following its release.[21] These works figured among a cluster of treatises and memoirs that, calling for a new system of taxation, set the intellectual framework for the creation of the *capitation* and the *dixième*, but the books by Boisguilbert and Vauban stand out for their popularity among the literary elite and for the way they nourished political and economic thought throughout the eighteenth century.[22]

---

[21] Simone Meyssonnier, *La balance et l'horloge: la genèse de la pensée libérale en France au XVIIIe siècle* (Paris, 1989), p. 36; Carpenter, "Economic Bestsellers," pp. 11–13; and Anne Sauvy, "Livres contrefaits et livres interdits," in *Histoire de l'édition française*, p. 108.

[22] It is difficult to pinpoint the exact influence of Boisguilbert and Vauban on the creation of these two taxes. The first writer to discuss a tax that would strike the privileged as well as the nonprivileged was Paul Hay du Châtelet in *Traité de la politique de la France* (1669). By the second half of Louis XIV's reign, several royal officials were boldly considering the

To understand the success of the *Détail* and the *Dîme royale*, it is necessary to put the books in the context of the economic and financial crises that plagued France in the second half of Louis XIV's reign. This was a period of continuous economic and demographic decline or at least stagnation, punctuated by severe famines in 1693–4 and 1708–9, the first of which was very present in the minds of both writers as they set pen to paper. (Boisguilbert wrote the *Détail* in the midst of the first famine and Vauban completed his first financial and demographic works and began writing the *Dîme royale* in its immediate aftermath). The second half of Louis' reign was also a period of heavy fiscal exaction, as the aging king borrowed and taxed his way through the extremely expensive wars of the League of Augsburg (1689–97) and the Spanish Succession (1701–14). It was against this bleak backdrop that the two writers developed new strains of criticism that would blossom during the Enlightenment.

Both Boisguilbert and Vauban began their work from the same starting point: the poverty of the people. Boisguilbert described in detail the disastrous state of affairs into which the kingdom had plunged since 1660, the year in which, he claimed, the economic product of the kingdom began shrinking by 500 million livres annually. By the time he wrote the *Détail* in 1695, the magistrate from Rouen believed that the economic "gangrene" overtaking France had cost the kingdom as much as half its resources. Vauban, less prone to metaphor but no less struck by the kingdom's poverty, conveyed the dismal state of affairs with demographic statistics. He estimated that 10 percent of the population was reduced to begging; 50 percent was extremely poor; 30 percent was burdened with debt and lived in very difficult circumstances; and only the remaining 10 percent, a group that included affluent nobles, clergymen, office-holders, and merchants, enjoyed wealth of any significance.[23]

It was on behalf of the poor that both authors claimed the right to speak to king and public. Boisguilbert, who later wrote his *Factum de la France* "in the name of the people," explained in the *Détail* that the country was losing its economic power because the "self-interest" of

establishment of new universal forms of taxation. See Guéry, "La capitation," pp. 1043–6; Bonney, "Le secret," pp. 385–91; McCollim, "Fiscal Policy," pp. 279–311; and Jean Meuvret, "Comment les Français du xviie siècle voyaient l'impôt," *Études d'histoire économique* (Paris, 1971), pp. 300–1.

23 Pierre Le Pesant de Boisguilbert, *Détail de la France* (1695), in *Economistes-financiers du XVIIIe siècle*, ed. Eugène Daire (1843; reprint, Osnabrück, 1966), p. 250; and Sébastien Le Prestre de Vauban, *Projet d'une dîme royale* (1707), in ibid., pp. 34–5.

the few influenced policy more than the "general interest" of the people, "who have no one to make themselves heard." He asserted that his plan would help 15 million persons, while hurting only those "who grow rich from the ruin of king and people." Vauban, too, announced that his plan was written "in favor of the poor" who have "no way to represent their misfortune to His Majesty." "I feel obliged by my honor and my conscience," he wrote, "to represent to His Majesty that ... in France not enough attention has been paid to the common people." If taxation were distributed more fairly, "we would not see as many great fortunes, but we would see fewer poor people."[24]

That these authors tended to divide the kingdom into economic categories of rich and poor rather than social or legal groups is highly significant. Classifying members of society by their wealth avoided the use of language that might legitimize inequalities. To compare the lot of a rich man with that of a poor man is not like comparing a noble with a peasant, for the latter terms resist comparison. This is not to say that the classifications of Boisguilbert and Vauban were new and that others before them had not made appeals on behalf of the poor. But, unlike the earlier pleas of, say, Fénelon, those of Boisguilbert and Vauban were not founded solely on notions of Christian mercy and justice. They were based instead on political and economic axioms. The two authors were not asking the king to show pity for poor people by lowering taxes; they were presenting laws of political economy whose logic demanded a more equitable system of taxation.

Boisguilbert and Vauban did not, however, allude to the same laws or offer identical proposals. Boisguilbert's analysis concentrated on natural law and economic development, blaming the impoverishment of France on Louis XIV's unnatural fiscal policies, which disrupted a "natural state" of economic growth. It was as unnatural for a society to overburden the poor and relieve the rich as it was for the body to expose its delicate parts and protect its strong ones:

The poor, in the body of the State, are the eyes and skull, and are, therefore, the most weak and delicate parts; the rich are the arms and the

---

[24] Boisguilbert, *Détail*, pp. 218 and 250; Vauban, *Dîme royale*, pp. 44 and 138. Although many writers expected tax reform to diminish the distance between rich and poor, few advocated using progressive taxation toward this end. Jean-Pierre Gross, "Progressive Taxation and Social Justice in Eighteenth-Century France," *Past and Present* 140 (August, 1993), pp. 79–126.

rest of the body. The blows that strike the body for the needs of the state are nearly imperceptible when they fall on the strong and robust parts, but fatal when they reach the weak areas, which represent the impoverished.[25]

More than just a rhetorical convenience, Boisguilbert's metaphor of the body politic was loaded with meaning. By associating the poor with the eyes and skull and the rich with the arms, the metaphor inverted traditional understandings of the social body in which the poor were the arms and hands (the instruments of labor) and the king was the head, the part of the body that orchestrated the movement of all the other parts.[26] The metaphor also rooted Boisguilbert's argument in the idea of nature as a progressive historical agent. Protecting the poor was a natural act that would allow the political body to be healthy and grow. France did not need a "miracle" to experience prosperity; "it is necessary only to let nature act by stopping the perpetual violence done to her." "Let nature act" (*laissez agir la nature*) and "let nature do" (*laissez faire la nature*): these were key phrases for Boisguilbert, as they would be for Gournay, to whom the term "laissez-faire" is usually attributed. The laws of nature, if only allowed to work, would restore France to health.[27]

Boisguilbert asserted that France was decaying because royal tax policy was not aligned with the laws of nature. Natural law demonstrated that "consumption" drove the economy, yet since 1660 taxes had crippled the general population's capacity to consume. The problem was not that taxes were too high – the author insisted that aggregate taxes had not increased in the past thirty years – but that they were raised in a way that fostered economic decline. The *taille*, "the sworn enemy of consumption," was levied so as to ruin the poorest third of the population, preventing this segment of society from purchasing the most basic goods.[28] How could an economy expand when so many consumers had so little money to spend? To make matters worse, taxes on goods raised prices, putting articles of consumption still further beyond the reach of the poor. Both the *taille* and indirect taxes reduced consumption, slowed the economy, and, consequently, made it harder for the king to raise revenue.

[25] Boisguilbert, *Factum de la France* (1705), in *Economistes-financiers du XVIIIe siècle*, ed. Eugène Daire (1843; reprint, Osnabrück, 1966), p. 336.

[26] William Sewell, "Etat, Corps, and Ordre: Some Notes on the Social Vocabulary of the French Old Regime," in *Sozialgeschichte Heute, Festschrift für Hans Rosenberg zum 70 Geburtstag*, ed. Hans-Ulrich Wehler (Göttingen, 1974), pp. 49–68.

[27] Boisguilbert, *Détail*, p. 239; and *Factum*, p. 280.   [28] Boisguilbert, *Factum*, p. 320.

Boisguilbert's remedy was to realign royal fiscal policy with the natural order of the economy. This would produce so much economic growth that the crown would be able to double its revenue while actually lowering taxes. Economic growth was the grand solution to all of the kingdom's problems: what else could simultaneously improve the financial lot of both taxpayers and the king? Boisguilbert proposed to rebuild the economy by first redistributing the burden of taxation, beginning with the *taille*, which had to be distributed "with justice, that is to say, that the rich pay as rich people, and the poor as poor people."[29] Requiring rich and poor commoners to pay in proportion to their income would leave poor commoners more money after the payment of taxes to invest in the cultivation of their land and to purchase goods. Money spent by the poor, because it contributed to the exchanges that made the economy grow, was far more productive than the idle money hoarded by the wealthy, who spent a much smaller proportion of their income on articles of consumption. Thus, the heightened level of demand that resulted from a shift in the tax burden from poor commoners to wealthier ones would substantially boost the economy. (Boisguilbert did not go so far as to suggest that the privileged should pay the *taille*, but he did propose that clergymen, nobles, office-holders, and residents of privileged cities pay a tax on chimneys, which would be levied roughly in proportion to wealth). Secondly, Boisguilbert insisted that customs barriers inside France be removed and that taxes on goods be reduced in order to lower prices and spur the consumption of commodities. Unburdening trade while making the tax system more equal would allow the economy to expand for the benefit of the king and his people: poor taxpayers would spend on goods what they used to pay in taxes, generating more demand; and the king would receive more revenue from a growing economy without damaging popular consumption.

Although Boisguilbert aimed to strengthen the state, his ideas constituted a serious threat to the traditional authority of the monarchy, as Louis XIV's censors understood when they prohibited the publication of his work. By positing the existence of an alternative order of authority, that of nature, and requiring Louis XIV to design state policy according to it, Boisguilbert was in effect limiting the will of the king. Royal authority, he insisted, must bend to the

---

[29] Boisguilbert, *Détail*, p. 222.

natural laws of economics, which, if unhindered, would harmonize the dissonant, self-interested wills of royal subjects and bring prosperity to the kingdom. By supposing the existence of an economy that was virtually self-generating, the economics of natural law put great trust in the wills of individual consumers, a trust that in absolutist political theory was reserved exclusively for the volition of a monarch who, in principle, orchestrated all movement (economic and otherwise) in the kingdom. "The hearts of the people," Boisguilbert stated, are "always disposed to do good, from the moment their good will is given free reign."[30] It was up to the king to recognize this principle and withdraw his heavy hand from the economy.

Boisguilbert extended the trust he placed in consumers to his own readers. The economist was aware of the revolutionary nature of his conclusions, likening himself to Columbus and Copernicus, whose ideas appeared ridiculous at first, but he was confident in the ability of his readers to apply the powers of reason and follow his argument. No one could claim to be unaware of the economic tragedy unfolding in France: "Everyone, provided that he has common sense, is a competent judge; no one can truly abstain from making pronouncements under the pretext of ignorance." Nor could anyone deny that reform was necessary. To say that the kingdom's finances did not need to be changed was to reveal that one was either an enemy of France or "deprived of sense and reason." The great success of the *Détail* suggests that readers were indeed prepared to entertain the economic liberalism of its author.[31]

Vauban's argument for tax reform was based on the same premise as Boisguilbert's, that unfair taxation overburdened those who were "the most ruined and destitute of the kingdom." In a passage that could easily be mistaken for the revolutionary writing of the abbé Sieyès, the marshal wrote:

It is they [the common people], however, who are the most considerable in terms of their number and the real services that they render to the kingdom. It is they who bear all the taxes, and they who have always suffered the most and who still suffer the most ... It is the common people who, by their work and trade, and by that which they pay the king, enrich him and all the nation.[32]

But, unlike Boisguilbert, Vauban was no great economist and did

[30] Boisguilbert, *Factum*, p. 351.   [31] Boisguilbert, *Factum*, pp. 268, 271, and 319.
[32] Vauban, *Dîme royale*, pp. 44–6.

not explain in any sophisticated way how taxation harmed economic growth. Instead, he offered his readers three "fundamental maxims" of government: "that every subject of a State needs protection"; "that the prince ... can give this protection only if his subjects provide him with the means"; and that, "consequently, every subject is obliged to contribute." These maxims, in turn, had three consequences: that "subjects of all social ranks have a natural obligation to contribute in proportion to their revenue"; "that simply being a subject of this State required one to obey this law"; and "that all types of privileges which lead to exemptions from this contribution are unjust and abusive, and should not prevail." Because the state provided military protection for all its subjects, all its subjects were obliged to contribute to it in proportion to their incomes.[33]

This "natural" law formed the basis of Vauban's work. He believed his maxims to be self-evident and felt little need to demonstrate their validity. Readers who did not agree with his conclusions were instructed simply to go back and reread the maxims, as if their simple logic were irrefutable. Most of the *Dîme royale*, therefore, was devoted to describing what kind of tax best conformed to the above postulates and what kind of bureaucracy could best implement it. Vauban proposed that the existing structure of royal taxation be razed and replaced by one tax and one tax alone, the *dîme royale*, which every subject would pay according to his income from land, pensions, *gages*, wages, bonds, and commerce.[34] Sliding from a rate of 3 to 10 percent, depending on the state's needs, this tax would amply provide the crown with the revenue it required and, to prove this, Vauban included pages and pages of demographic, financial, and economic statistics that few readers were in a position to dispute.

To implement such an immense project, Vauban imagined a rigid bureaucracy based on a military model. The king would commission special intendants to be placed in the provinces for the purpose of collecting information on the property of the entire population. To assist the intendants, Vauban proposed the creation of thousands of "captains" and "lieutenants," drawn from the ranks of parish seigneurs and local gentlemen, who would be paid and called "monsieur" just like military officers. Each officer would compose a

---

[33] Vauban, *Dîme royale*, pp. 47–8.
[34] All other taxes were to be abolished except for a light salt tax and customs taxes collected at French borders.

census of his community and mark down the extent of property belonging to every individual. No detail was to be overlooked: even the number and type of livestock belonging to each subject were to be accounted for. These censuses would then be used to make a master survey of the kingdom's population and wealth, which the crown could use to redistribute the tax burden. By sheer bureaucratic force – through an army of administrators gathering detailed information and overseeing the apportionment of the tax – the crown could enforce the maxim that all subjects must pay taxes in proportion to their wealth.

In its outright condemnation of privilege, the marshal's proposal to establish a new "system" of government finance appeared far more radical than that of Boisguilbert. Indeed, Vauban rebuked the author of the *Détail* for merely tinkering with existing fiscal privileges rather than excising them from the kingdom altogether. Although some readers, including highly placed royal officials whose memoranda were heavily influenced by Vauban, believed the political maxim that everyone had to contribute to the state in equal proportion to their income was quite valid, others thought Vauban's rigorous attachment to equality in taxation radical and dangerous.[35] In 1716 Jean le Pottier asked of the *Dîme royale*, "Does this not intend to destroy the Monarchical State in France in order to introduce a Republican State?"[36] For le Pottier the relationship between fiscal privilege and monarchy was so intimate that to abolish one was to destroy the other.

Both Boisguilbert and Vauban expressed ideas that were to become common in eighteenth-century literature. Boisguilbert's emphasis on natural law and the economy marked the beginning of French economic liberalism and anticipated the theories of the most celebrated political economists of the century, from those who praised commerce in all its forms, such as Gournay and Turgot, to land-obsessed physiocrats such as Quesnay and Dupont de Nemours. Although important differences existed between these types of political economists, they all followed Boisguilbert's example insofar as they envisioned a largely self-regulating and self-improving economy that followed the laws of nature.[37] The political impli-

---

[35] Bonney, "Le secret," pp. 390–1.   [36] Quoted in Meyssonnier, *Balance*, p. 31.
[37] For Boisguilbert's influence on individual thinkers, see Gilbert Faccarello, *Aux origines de l'économie politique libérale: Pierre de Boisguilbert* (Paris, 1986), pp. 27–35; and *Pierre de Boisguilbert ou la naissance de l'économie politique*, 2 vols. (Paris, 1966), I, pp. 507–79. For the development of

cations of this line of thought were profound. By telling their readers that the economy functioned and grew according to an independent, coherent, and discernible set of natural laws, economists implicitly characterized the king as a grand policy-maker who could be judged on his ability to direct the economy in accordance with, or in violation of, the laws of nature. The growth of economic liberalism meant that certain taxes could be criticized not only as unfair or arbitrary but as transgressions against nature herself.

Vauban's "fundamental maxim" that state military protection implied a universal and fair distribution of taxation ("fair" meaning an apportionment based on ability to pay) also became a commonplace. Although more than a few eighteenth-century writers shared the marshal's enthusiasm for statistical evidence and for the creation of a tax in kind, the deeper influence of Vauban manifested itself in the way he emboldened other men of letters to assert that some sort of social contract between ruler and subject rendered tax privileges illegitimate. From the late seventeenth century forward, the idea that military and spiritual service, office-holding, and residency in certain cities and provinces entitled one to tax privileges appeared increasingly retrograde as libraries stocked more and more books elaborating on Vauban's original theme. Although fiscal privilege remained in place until the end of the Old Regime, the concept of it was being discredited by many (but by no means all) citizens of the republic of letters.

If Vauban and Boisguilbert stand out so prominently under the reign of Louis XIV, this is in part due to the relative scarcity of printed material in that period. The reign of Louis XV, by contrast, witnessed a burgeoning of texts on the problem of taxation and political economy, especially in the 1750s and 1760s when France experienced severe constitutional crises. Scanning this abundant literature, one can still identify an author whose works enjoyed a singular success. Victor Riquetti, marquis de Mirabeau, father of the famous revolutionary orator, published two of the century's most popular books, the multi-volumed *L'ami des hommes* (1756–60) and the *Théorie de l'impôt* (1760), the former running through forty editions and the latter through eighteen. The remarkable success of these works led Joseph Schumpeter to rank Mirabeau's contemporary

economic liberalism and natural law after Boisguilbert, see Meyssonnier, *Balance*; Murphy, "Idées économiques," pp. 521–41; and Catherine Larrère, *L'invention de l'économie au XVIIIe siècle* (Paris, 1992).

fame as "much greater than that of any other economist before and after, not excluding A. Smith or K. Marx."[38]

In an age when readers were offered a variety of books on questions of political economy, why was Mirabeau so popular? Having searched the work of the marquis in vain for some brilliant path-breaking economic principle and having found instead a text "completely spoiled by lack of judgment," Schumpeter was baffled by the success of such a mediocre economist. But a broader reading of Mirabeau's work suggests that his success did not lie in his economic theory. Rather, it lay in a rhetoric that fired the political imagination of his readers. During a period when the issue of taxation provoked bitter disputes between the crown and superior courts of law and provincial estates, Mirabeau promised the return of harmony to a troubled kingdom and, more important, added a strikingly moral tone to the otherwise dry logic of political economy. Although Mirabeau is usually remembered for his contribution to physiocracy, a school of economic thought to which he was converted by Quesnay in 1757, his most successful work was a pungent blend of that physiocracy with classical republicanism.[39]

It was politics, not economics, that first drew the marquis to the printing press. His earliest works defended various provincial estates that were at the time engaged in struggles with Louis XV over the introduction of the *vingtième*. Both his 1750 pamphlet, *Mémoire concernant l'utilité des états provinciaux*, and his book of 1751, *Mémoire sur les états provinciaux*, argued for the right of estates to consent to royal taxation. His ardent defense of representative bodies led at least one reader, d'Argenson, to take his anonymous work for that of Montesquieu, but in many ways it bore a greater resemblance to Rousseau.[40] More than a decade before the appearance of the *Social Contract*, the marquis wrote, "Man is made to think himself free and to be enchained – but enchained voluntarily and by bonds of which he senses the necessity rather than the constraint."[41] Perhaps Rousseau was thinking of Mirabeau, whom he admired and later befriended, when he penned his famous lines: "Man is born free,

[38] Quoted in Carpenter, "Economic Bestsellers," p. 18.
[39] For Mirabeau's conversion and contribution to physiocracy, see Elizabeth Fox-Genovese, *The Origins of Physiocracy: Economic Revolution and Social Order in Eighteenth-Century France* (Ithaca, NY, 1976), chs. 4–6.
[40] Carcassonne, *Montesquieu*, p. 233.
[41] [Victor Riquetti, marquis de Mirabeau], *Mémoire sur les états provinciaux* (n. p., [1751]), p. 24.

and he is everywhere in chains"; and liberty is "obedience to a law one prescribes to oneself."[42]

Intellectual genealogy aside, Mirabeau's earliest works suggested that representative institutions made men feel free and, as a result, made them better citizens. The *pays d'états* served as a perfect example. There, political participation produced undeniable benefits: taxes were seen as gifts not spoils; taxpayers did not hide the true value of their property; and people's confidence in government generated an abundance of financial credit. Alternatively, in the *pays d'élections*, where taxation was arbitrarily imposed, royal administrators such as intendants "muted" the voices and "numbed the hearts of those who lived there." "Can the security of this administration [of estates] be compared to that of a young man [an intendant] who comes to a province ignorant of its customs, wealth, commerce, etc.?" To demonstrate just how terrible intendants could be, the marquis recounted an incident in which he overheard an intendant bragging to a crowd of people that he had once raised a man's *capitation* from 30 to 300 livres simply because the man happened to cross his path. The appalling arbitrariness of such an act made any form of representative government look reasonable.[43]

In his next major works, *L'ami des hommes* and *Théorie de l'impôt*, Mirabeau softened his position on the right of corporate bodies to consent to royal law while, at the same time, elaborating a dramatic political rhetoric that we might loosely call republican. Republicanism in prerevolutionary France is a confusing subject because it can be defined in very different ways. On the one hand, the meaning of republicanism stems from the term "republic," which is commonly defined in Montesquieuian terms: as a particular form of government in which "the people composed in corps, or a part of the people, has sovereign power."[44] This is the definition that the revolutionaries would adopt when they set out to destroy the monarchy and establish a "republic" in 1792, and, as a result,

[42] Jean-Jacques Rousseau, *The Social Contract*, trans. Maurice Cranston (New York, 1968), pp. 49 and 65. Despite Mirabeau's early loyalty to the nobility and his later attachment to physiocracy, the similarities between Mirabeau and Rousseau are striking. The two thinkers engaged in a lively correspondence in 1767 in which they candidly discussed their political ideas.

[43] [Victor Riquetti, marquis de Mirabeau], *Mémoire concernant l'utilité des états provinciaux, relativement à l'autorité royale, aux finances, au bonheur, et à l'avantage des peuples* (Rome, 1750), pp. 22 and 38–9.

[44] Quoted in Ran Halévi, "La république monarchique," in *Le siècle de l'avènement républicain*, ed. François Furet and Mona Ozouf (Paris, 1993), p. 166.

French historians tend to use republicanism to refer to the political ideology associated with democratic, as opposed to monarchical, forms of government.[45]

But there is another definition of republicanism, which approaches it not as a theory of, or belief in, a type of non-monarchical government but as an ethos and rhetoric. Anyone familiar with the studies of Pocock, Baker, or Venturi would recognize the features of this second sort of classical republicanism: a vigilant mistrust of state finance and administration; a contempt for luxury and courtly extravagance; a longing for the simple rustic life of the countryside; and an overriding fear that civic virtue, the quality by which men act on behalf of the common good, was inevitably corrupted by greed and hunger for power.[46] Baker further defines republicanism as essentially "will-centered," meaning that its language was organized around the notion of political will as opposed to justice or reason. If we accept this definition of republicanism as a language or set of attitudes, we can consider Mirabeau (and so many others) republicans, even though they never challenged the institution of monarchy itself. Even a rigorous republican like Rousseau said it was possible, though unlikely, for a republic to coexist with a monarchy.[47] Mirabeau, in the *Théorie de l'impôt*, set out to teach his readers precisely how this coexistence could be sustained.

By far the most popular work devoted to taxation since the *Dîme royale*, the *Théorie de l'impôt* recounts the advice given by a "man of genius" to an aging king who has been kept unaware of the corruption that threatened his realm. Raised on splendor and flattery, the king is ultimately unable to understand this genius's "language of truth," but the monarch does listen patiently for three hours as this brilliant councilor warns him of the danger into which the kingdom has fallen.

Through the councilor's voice, Mirabeau succinctly revealed the underlying causes of the kingdom's financial crisis:

Seigneur, you have twenty million subjects more or less. These men all have money; they are all pretty much capable of providing the kind of

---

[45] Jean-Marie Goulemot, for example, recently employed this definition and found republicanism to be "absent" from mainstream eighteenth-century thought. "Du républicanisme et de l'idée républicaine au XVIIIe siècle," in *Le siècle de l'avènement républicain*, p. 52.

[46] J. G. A. Pocock, *The Machiavellian Moment: Florentine Political Thought and the Atlantic Republican Tradition* (Princeton, NJ, 1975); Franco Venturi, *Utopia and Reform in the Enlightenment* (Cambridge, 1971); Baker, *Inventing*.

[47] Rousseau, *Social Contract*, p. 82.

service you are asking for. And yet you are able to obtain neither services without money, nor money to pay for services. In plain language, this means that your people are withdrawing themselves from you without their knowing it. Their wills are still rallied around your person, even though they think that you are isolated from the agents under your authority. Though no one dares say it – since we are living in an indolent and fearful century – your power rests on nothing but the unification of your will with the wills of a strong and active multitude. It follows, then, that the disjuncture of wills is what is cutting the nerve of your power. That is the evil, and this is where it comes from.[48]

These opening lines, the very lines that the lieutenant of police and Louis XV found so disrespectful, express the main thrust of the book. Mirabeau's political universe was composed of two distinct worlds, the "physical" world, of which finance was a part, and an inner "moral" world of individual wills and dispositions on which the physical world rested. The king's power, his material success in the physical world, depended on his ability to order the moral world so that the wills of his subjects were aligned with his own.

Everything depended upon the harmony of wills:

The interest of the poor, the interest of the rich, the interest of the great, the interest of the monarch ..., all this will be but one, when it is not introduced under the insidious pretext of the particular interest of the leader or of heterogeneous and corrupted groups. This collective interest will be indivisible; it will have only one form, one life, one common organization, which will distribute with regularity and proportion the nourishment that revitalizes the leader and all members of society.[49]

In a society where the interests and wills of king and subjects were one, the king could draw power from his subjects' sense of honor, "the most precious treasure of your coffers," and honor's "touch-stone" duty, which should guide the actions of all. If the wills of ruler and subject were aligned, the act of paying taxes would be the primary physical expression of the citizen's duty to the king. "Is the citizen's contribution to the public treasury a tribute or a spoil?" asked the councilor rhetorically. In a perfect world "the question alone would be a crime," he answered: "it is a trusted and precious tribute, and the execution of the first of the physical duties of this world."[50]

But Mirabeau's imaginary kingdom had fallen into a grave moral

---

[48] Victor Riquetti, marquis de Mirabeau, *Théorie de l'impôt* (n. p., 1760), pp. 1–2.
[49] Mirabeau, *Théorie*, pp. 34–5.   [50] Mirabeau, *Théorie*, p. 124.

crisis. Instead of seeking public esteem through service, men and women looked only to the physical world for satisfaction. "Money, this idol of corrupted Nations," was all anyone could think about, as taxpayers clutched their purses and those who served the crown sought personal profit. In times like this when the physical world took precedence over the moral world, the king's finances became strained and bankruptcy was imminent. "If ever a Nation was so weakened and burdened with debt that she was obliged to declare what is called 'bankruptcy,' surely every moral principle of this society would be at that moment completely altered."[51] Financial crisis and moral corruption were but grim reflections of each other.

To Mirabeau the origins of moral and financial crisis were obvious. Instead of sharing a "reciprocal affection" for each other, government and people were constantly at loggerheads. And this was the fault of the state, not the people. Because the king relied on the "arbitrary authority" of administrative agents to force his will on royal subjects, he was gradually leading his subjects into "slavery." Here, Mirabeau returns to the theme of his earlier work that arbitrary administrative power hurt, rather than helped, the state. For a century and a half, he said, monarchs had depended on high and arbitrary levies "as if there were no means of sustaining their Power other than monetary taxes." Although exorbitant taxation boosted the crown's spending in the short term, it produced lawlessness, insecurity, a bloated court, and a nobility reduced to "purely mercenary service."[52]

To "regenerate" the kingdom, the king's adviser suggested two solutions, the first of which entailed establishing a system of finance in which "nothing should nor could be submitted to arbitrariness."[53] Here, Mirabeau put his physiocratic knowledge to work, placing economic principles on an essentially republican foundation. Assuming, as all good physiocrats did, that wealth sprang from the land alone, he proposed that the king replace all taxes with a single tax paid by landowners on the net product of their land. Always touching profit and never capital, this tax would allow for greater investment in agriculture, which, when combined with free trade in grain, would generate economic growth. Economic growth, in turn, would increase revenue for the state as well as for the people.

[51] Mirabeau, *Théorie*, pp. 63 and 233.   [52] Mirabeau, *Théorie*, pp. 170–2.
[53] Mirabeau, *Théorie*, p. 178.

Mirabeau, like Boisguilbert whom he cited, believed firmly that economic growth was the key to relieving the kingdom of its financial problems.

But for Mirabeau free trade and a land tax proportional to income were not enough. The marquis also stressed the citizen's right to consent to taxes, although his discussion of this right was weaker than that found in his early works on provincial estates. At times the *Théorie de l'impôt* sounded decisive on the doctrine of consent: "it is ... the natural and imprescriptible right of people to consent to the demands of the Prince in matters of taxation: it is this consent alone that can produce Law; and all levies not founded on Law were only robbery." But, owing to his conversion to physiocracy, which espoused reform from above, Mirabeau was no longer prepared to follow through on such bold assertions. He ultimately backed down on the necessity of political participation, confessing that the king did not need "the formal consent of the people, as expressed by representative assemblies" as long as the government was "founded on Laws and led by practices which did not contradict the constituent Laws of Humanity and the State." Circumventing the issue of estates, he gently proposed that the king use municipal and provincial assemblies instead of royal administrators to distribute and collect taxes and to raise money for royal loans. Establishing such assemblies would show that the king respected the liberty and property of his subjects, making them all the more willing to contribute to the state, but it would not limit the royal power necessary to impose reforms.[54]

Thus, like Boisguilbert and Vauban, Mirabeau characterized the problem of taxation as a crisis. But whereas his predecessors described the crisis in economic and demographic terms, Mirabeau treated it, as did Rousseau, as a moral problem. Fiscal crises were only physical representations of a fundamental "disjuncture" between the will of the king and those of his subjects. In other words, the ties between subject and monarch were withering, and that decay was reflected materially in the monarch's inability to obtain services, or money for services, from his subjects. Posed in this way, the issue could not be resolved by changes in royal fiscal policy alone, as Boisguilbert and Vauban had suggested. The very relationship between crown and citizen needed to be restructured; arbitrary

[54] Mirabeau, *Théorie*, pp. 165–6 and 173.

authority, which manifested itself in the capricious actions of state administrators, had to be destroyed and replaced by the rule of law and, ideally, representative institutions. A state bound by law and strengthened by the participation of its citizens would promote liberty, security, the sanctity of property, and, most importantly, a sense of duty to the king. That sense of duty, in turn, would unite king and subject, providing the former with a plenitude of money and services.

It is a measure of Mirabeau's often-forgotten literary success that Louis-Sébastien Mercier, in one of the most popular books of prerevolutionary France, *L'An deux mille quatre cent quarante*, included him among the century's most famous authors. Historians today would probably not rank Mirabeau with Montesquieu, Rousseau, and Voltaire, as Mercier did, but the marquis seems to have made as great an impression on the popular writer as he did on so many readers of the day.[55] Barbier noted that the *Théorie de l'impôt* made "a lot of noise" at court but he thought the book "too hard in its expressions addressed to the king." Quesnay learned from the same treatise that "sovereignty and kings are not the same thing . . . This is why most nations cede neither the administration of finances nor the right of taxation to their king."[56] Whether or not Mirabeau would have been pleased with Quesnay's stark conclusion is difficult to say, for the republican physiocrat intended not to challenge the sovereignty of the monarchy but simply to acknowledge the spirited will of the citizenry and imagine a kingdom in which it was united with the will of the king. More to the marquis' liking would have been the "rustic poem" penned by an anonymous reader who named the author of the *Théorie* a great "protector" of the citizen.[57]

The extraordinary popularity of Mirabeau's work was not matched until Necker, minister of finance from 1776 to 1781, published the *Compte* in 1781 and *De l'administration* in 1784, both of which ran through numerous editions and tens of thousands of copies. No two works on finance written by the same author had ever been disseminated so extensively in the history of France. What did the minister tell the thousands of avid readers who rushed to buy his books? Some of what Necker wrote would certainly have seemed familiar to readers of other works on political economy. Like

---

[55] Darnton, *Best-Sellers*, pp. 315 and 327.
[56] Barbier, *Chronique*, VII, pp. 323–34; Quesnay is quoted in Hincker, *L'impôt*, p. 90.
[57] *Annonces*, 28 October 1763.

Boisguilbert and Vauban, Necker railed against privilege, expressed concern for the poor, and suggested that tax reform would "diminish a bit of the immense distance that exists between the conditions of different classes in society." And, like Mirabeau, he thought that finance concerned not only the circulation of money but human political psychology or what Necker liked to call "imagination." "There is a great flaw in the abstract thought of political economy, which is that the effects of opinion and imagination are never taken into consideration." This was regrettable, seeing that financial administration "can have the greatest influence on social virtues and public mores." Bad administration, that which was arbitrary and coercive, damaged the imagination, "because everything that is obscure, uncertain, and indefinite leads to mistrust and fear." The belief that the crown could simply command obedience without openly cultivating it was "the source of great administrative errors in a monarchical State."[58]

Necker reasoned that a change in state administration would produce a change in the spirit of the people. Whereas bad fiscal administration encouraged self-interest and heightened perceptions of social injustice, good administration was capable of "strengthening moral ideas, exciting the imagination, and bundling together various opinions and sentiments with the tie of confidence."[59] But what exactly was a good administration? What kind of government could excite the imagination and build confidence? In answering these questions Necker added something important to the existing stock of ideas on state finance and administration: good administration was "public" administration, which made itself visible to the people and nurtured public opinion. The notion that the monarchy should consult public opinion in matters of finance was certainly not new; the abbé de Saint-Pierre and John Law had entertained similar ideas early in the century.[60] But Necker did more than any other single finance minister or writer to popularize the concept of public opinion, by turning the idea of publicity itself into something of a spectacle. As he rightfully (if immodestly) claimed, his grandiose

---

[58] Necker, *De l'administration*, III, pp. 106–7; I, p. 178; I, p. xiii; I, p. 331; and II, pp. 290–1.
[59] Necker, *De l'administration*, I, p. xii.
[60] Thomas Kaiser, "The Abbé de Saint-Pierre, Public Opinion, and the Reconstitution of the French Monarchy," *JMH* 55 (1983), pp. 618–43; Thomas Kaiser, "Money, Despotism, and Public Opinion in Eighteenth-Century France: John Law and the Debate on Royal Credit," *JMH* 63 (1981), pp. 1–28.

attempt to make the state a public entity introduced "a new *era* in state finance."[61]

It should be stated at the outset that Necker's commitment to the publicity of the state was closely tied to his own. For many of Necker's readers, the minister's public figure and the idea of state publicity were often indistinguishable, an effect sustained by Necker's literary voice, which conflated his public persona with his political ideas. Consider the structure of the *Compte*, a text meant to silence his critics by demonstrating that the monarchy enjoyed a surplus of ordinary revenues. More than just a budget, the *Compte* played with literary genres, appearing simultaneously as private memoir and public royal address, which, sanctioned by the king, served to amplify Necker's own voice. The opening lines of the document convey these ambiguities: "Sire, Having devoted all my time and energy to the service of Your Majesty since [he] called me to the position that I occupy, it is without a doubt invaluable for me to render a public account of the success of my work and of the present state of the finances." The *Compte* was addressed to the king as if it were a private letter. But, in publishing it, Necker was not simply making a supposedly private letter public, a common literary device designed to let the reader imagine that he or she had stumbled onto a private exchange, for he was rendering a "public account."

And yet this was no ordinary public statement. The French government had always addressed the public in the name of the king, but Necker invested the *Compte* with his own voice, making it neither a purely public statement, in which the king's voice would have dominated, nor a purely personal letter, which would not have allowed Necker to claim that he was reaching out to the public. By mixing literary forms he was able to speak directly to the public and excite readers by offering both a sincere private memoir to the king and an address to the public by a government insider.

Necker's subsequent success, *De l'administration*, employed a similar strategy. Although he had fallen from power, the Genevan believed that he "still might be of some service to *la chose publique*" and decided to reenter public life through literature. Ostensibly written as a guidebook for present and future statesmen, the work was clearly designed to engage a wide readership and influence public

---

[61] Necker, *De l'administration*, I, p. cviii; the emphasis is Necker's.

opinion. The introduction declared, "Yes, generous nation, I consecrate this work to you, not with a vain and sumptuous dedication, but with a customary, everyday homage." And the conclusion added: "If it is important to provide instruction for those who one day will participate in Government, it is no less essential to enlighten the tribunal before which they will be called to appear, and this tribunal is that of public opinion."[62]

Although Necker constructed both works to promote his own reputation, they were also designed to show how state publicity and the cultivation of public opinion would strengthen France. First, publicity and its counterpart, public opinion, acted as a check on government. "In France it is the ascendancy of public opinion which, more than anything else, often impedes the abuse of authority." Once the "veil" of state secrecy had been torn away, public opinion would hold state officials accountable for their actions: "darkness and obscurity favor nonchalance: publicity, by contrast, can become an honor and a reward only when one senses the importance of one's duties and has tried to fulfill them." Secondly, public opinion could one day function as a positive force. It could "teach kings their duties," determine which state officials were "the most enlightened, impartial, and upright," instill "patriotism" in a kingdom of deadened sensibilities, and help reason to triumph over "the errors of the imagination," all of which would improve royal finances. As it matured, public opinion would strengthen state credit and prepare the French for tax reform.[63]

If Necker saw public opinion as something of a panacea, it was not a panacea that grew organically from French soil. It had to be cultivated, stimulated, and mobilized, and one way to do this was to establish provincial assemblies throughout France. In 1778 and 1779 Necker succeeded in creating two assemblies, in Berry and Haute-Guienne, both of which assumed a central role in the fiscal administration of their province. The next chapter will examine the political significance of such assemblies; our present purpose is to understand how Necker characterized them to his readers. Both the *Compte* and *De l'administration* claimed that assemblies would "excite the public spirit [and] tie the people to the government with sentiments of goodwill and confidence." When the king imposed

[62] Necker, *De l'administration*, I, pp. i and iv; III, p. 455.
[63] Necker, *De l'administration*, I, pp. lxiv and 61; II, p. 279; and Jacques Necker, *Compte rendu au roi* (Paris, 1781), pp. 1–2.

reform from above without the assistance of assemblies, Necker explained, he was doomed to encounter fatal resistance, since ministers could not effectively defend "an abstract idea" against an always prevailing sense of mistrust. Speaking to the public via preambles to decrees may have helped to influence opinion, but "these words, too often the same to be always true, ultimately had to lose their authority." If reform were introduced by the assemblies themselves, however, it would already have the support of public opinion and therefore be able to take root. "It is very important that the most useful changes be supported by public opinion, and that is precisely the effect of the deliberations of a provincial assembly; its propositions reach the Minister of finances already reinforced by a suffrage."[64]

But would members of the assemblies initiate or even accept reform and, if so, why? This was a question that Necker went to great lengths to answer, first by demonstrating that the assemblies of Berry and Haute-Guienne had already introduced key reforms, from establishing more "proportional equality" in the tax levy to abolishing the royal *corvée* to publishing the minutes of their deliberations for the purpose of enlivening public opinion. But beyond such material evidence, Necker emphasized an implicit connection between representative government, enlightenment, and reform. Broader political participation would free men from mistrust and prepare them for enlightened reform: "Participation in forming the general interest eventually increases the total amount of enlightenment; the publicity of deliberations forces honesty, and the public good emerges slowly, but at least it emerges, and once it is obtained in this way, it supports itself and protects itself from caprice."[65] The very experience of political participation would snuff out self-interest, enhance enlightenment, and "engender a true patriotism." "In the assembly," Necker wrote, "one learns to know and love the public good . . . and to form new ties with the *patrie*." In forming such ties, citizens could not help but recognize "the misery of the most numerous class of taxpayers" and strive to reform the fiscal system.[66]

[64] Necker, *De l'administration*, I, pp. xxi and 61; Necker, *Compte*, pp. 3, 75, and 76.
[65] Necker, *Compte*, p. 74. Elsewhere (*De l'administration*, II, pp. 260–1) he wrote, "It would make a truly interesting spectacle, if these administrations multiplied, to see them enlighten each other and form a general association of enlightenment which would prevail over prejudices and over cruel and unjust customs."
[66] Necker, *Compte*, p. 79; Necker, *De l'administration*, II, pp. 271–2, 278–9, and 283.

What is interesting about his comments on provincial assemblies is that Necker scarcely mentions the king. Whereas Mirabeau's remedies for the kingdom's financial difficulties, which also involved the creation of assemblies, were designed to rekindle citizens' feelings of duty towards the monarch, Necker's remedies sought to instill patriotism, or duty towards the "*patrie.*" In this latter vision the king, no longer the chief solicitor of service, is placed somewhere off-stage to be replaced by the fatherland. To be sure, the monarchy would benefit from the spread of patriotism – the minister's purpose after all was to strengthen the royal finances – but the nation, not the king, was to be the object of patriotic duty. Necker sensed that patriotism would arouse the "imagination" of French citizens in ways that monarchy alone could or did not.

Readers responded with great enthusiasm to Necker's patriotic rhetoric. Although the works of Boisguilbert, Vauban, and Mirabeau prompted responses from several authors, they did not come close to provoking the wave of print that swept France during and after Necker's literary interventions. Considered "spicy" by underground booksellers, works on Necker sold very well, so well that the *Collection complète de tous les ouvrages pour et contre M. Necker* became one of the best-sellers of the 1780s.[67] Of course, a good portion of what was said about Necker was negative. Emanating from circles of highly-placed royal officials, hostile nobles, and physiocrats, the literature against Necker attacked him in both personal and political terms, which is hardly surprising given how he had fused his public persona with his policies. Detractors criticized him as an egotist, a foreigner who did not understand French institutions, and a charlatan out to misinform the public.[68] Even Bachaumont, whose account of the controversy is remarkably even-handed, could not help but fault the minister for both his political positions, in particular his "unconstitutional" assertion that the king could increase taxes at will, and his personal flaws such as his "overweening pride" and preachy prose.[69]

Despite these judgments, it appears that the Genevan banker had more friends than enemies as homage to Necker flourished in a

---

[67] Robert Darnton, *The Literary Underground of the Old Regime* (Cambridge, MA, 1982), p. 127; Robert Darnton, *The Corpus of Clandestine Literature in France, 1769–1789* (New York, 1995), p. 35.

[68] The literature against Necker is discussed in Jean Egret, *Necker, ministre de Louis XVI, 1776–1790* (Paris, 1975), pp. 172–8; Popkin, "Pamphlet Journalism," pp. 357–60; and Georges Weulersse, *La physiocratie à l'aube de la Révolution, 1781–1792* (Paris, 1985), pp. 15–22.

[69] Bachaumont, *Mémoires secrets*, XVII, p. 79; XVIII, pp. 47, 216–17, and 221–4.

variety of forms, from book reviews to engravings to the publication of treatises and budgets. Newspapers enthusiastically welcomed Necker's literary efforts. The editors of *Annonces, affiches, et avis divers de la haute et basse Normandie* underscored the "spirit of patriotism" that his provincial assemblies were bringing to France and honored the selflessness of the author of the *Compte* by excerpting, for their readers' pleasure, the minister's own testimony: "I have renounced, with the mildest personal gratification, serving my friends or looking for the recognition of those who surround me. If someone owes a pension or position to my favor, let him name it. I see only my duty ..." The newspaper also cited Necker's confidence in public opinion: "I have proudly depended on public opinion, which the wicked seek in vain to stop or destroy, but which, despite their efforts, leads to justice and truth."[70]

Artists also praised Necker by producing watercolors and engravings in his honor. One of the most famous engravings was "Virtue rewarded" (illustration 5.1), which, based on a sketch by Antoine Borel, was exhibited at the *Salon de la Correspondance* where Bachaumont and others viewed it.[71] In it the figure of France, standing against a classical backdrop, holds a copy of the *Compte* while pointing to a bust of Necker engraved in a pyramid. At the base of the pyramid are seated Equity, Charity, and Abundance, while to the left we find Economy instructing the muse of history "to erase the word *Impôt* from our annals." Above them "Renown publicizes the happy results of a wise administration of finances."

This engraving illustrates several important points about reader response to Necker. The first is that Borel, at least, championed the minister in classical republican terms, as the emphasis on civic virtue and the classical structure behind the pyramid indicate. Borel seems to have been responding to republican themes present in Necker's own work, such as the selfless devotion to the public good that the minister both effected and tried to elicit from French citizens. This artist certainly found the minister's dramatic declarations of integrity and duty sincere. Secondly, there is the issue of fame and publicity. The bust of Necker and the *Compte* itself appear illuminated at the center of the image, and all figures are turned toward them as "Renown" trumpets the success of good financial administration. By

---

[70] *Annonces*, 10 December 1779, and 9 and 19 March 1781.
[71] BN, Collection de Vinck, P 19560.

5.1 *Virtue rewarded*

depicting an allegory of Necker receiving the reward of fame for his virtue, Borel answered the minister's call for state publicity with a personal publicity campaign on behalf of the minister. By glorifying Necker and his political agenda, this engraving reflected the highly personal and deliberately public literary voice of the *Compte*. Finally, and most importantly for our purposes, while the results of reform are represented by the figures of Charity, Equity, and Abundance, the one specific reform that the engraver highlights is the effacement of taxation from French history. Although the author of the *Compte* never promised the abolition of taxes, his public commitment to fiscal equality and to easing levies on the poor evidently made a great impression. As the next chapter will show, this vision of Necker as a reformer became critical in 1788 and 1789, when the banker and the third estate entered into a revolutionary alliance.

Necker's impact on his readers is further evidenced by the publication of the *Encyclopédie méthodique: finances* (1784–7), a royally approved encyclopedia devoted exclusively to providing the public with "the most complete work yet to be published on finance."[72] The publisher of the encyclopedia was the prominent and successful Charles Joseph Pancoucke who, sensing the demand for literature on finances, commissioned Rousselot de Surgy, a former *premier commis des finances* and practicing royal censor, to be the volume's editor. That a royal censor should take on a project described as "revealing the secret of the state" demonstrates the power of the example set by Necker.[73] There is little doubt that Surgy was consciously following in what he believed were Necker's courageous footsteps. In the preface to the volume Surgy tells his readers about the resistance he encountered when asking "men of state" for information on royal finance. Many refused because they believed that, as "confidants of the state, ... mystery and darkness must never cease to cloak their actions and their speech." The editor was surprised that such backward attitudes were still so widespread "at a moment not long after the general portrait of the finances was placed before the eyes of the public." After the *Compte*, how could "citizens full of love for

---

[72] Jacques-Philibert Rousselot de Surgy, ed., *Encyclopédie méthodique: finances* (Paris, 1784), I, p. 4.
[73] Surgy was one among many administrators inspired to write by Necker. A *vingtième* controller named Rouyer, who published an *Essai sur la répartition de la taille et des vingtièmes* (London, 1788), quoted Necker for its epigraph: "The leveling of Fortunes is not within the power of a Government; but by redistributing Taxes ..., it has the means to ease the condition of the people."

their *patrie*" be stopped from "proposing their ideas, denouncing abuses, and demonstrating the necessity and possibility of reform?" Having sung the praises of publicity, Surgy's preliminary discourse went on to echo Necker's cries against privilege, luxury, self-interest, and the tyrannical practices of fiscal administration. To destroy these vices, the editor urged "a new system of finances" that was to be based on "equality of treatment" and the establishment of provincial assemblies.[74]

Necker's work also inspired the dissemination of state budgets. In 1788, a year after Mathon de la Cour, a writer from a family of Jansenist magistrates, wrote a prize-winning treatise on "the best ways to produce and encourage patriotism in a monarchy," he published the *Collection de comptes rendus*, an assemblage of budgets from the 1750s to the 1780s designed to shape public opinion by letting the public see the interior mechanisms of the state. In the preface the editor described himself as "a citizen strongly attached to his *patrie*" who aimed to ground public opinion in financial fact: "be it in Paris or in the provinces, conversations so often center on taxes and on public revenues and expenses that [the citizen] cannot help but desire some solid foundations and certain facts about these matters." Making facts available to the public, Mathon de la Cour said, would guard public opinion against falsehood: "The examination of revenues and expenses will bear an infinite number of reflections which may avoid or prevent a lot of false speculation, ridiculous projects, unfair reproaches, and poorly founded grumbling." Seizing on the example of expenditure on the royal court, which the budgets showed was not nearly as high as the public imagined it to be, Mathon de la Cour asserted that the job of patriotic royal officials was to expose the state to public view and correct popular misunderstanding. "For a long time administrators have worked to conceal from the public the knowledge of everything that has to do with finances ..., [but] the veil is finally torn; the time has come when the nation, called to meet in provincial assemblies to assist in the projects of administration, must know the bases of administration."[75]

Mathon de la Cour was not the only patriot who helped Necker "tear the veil" of state secrecy. Newly-created provincial assemblies

---

[74] Rousselot de Surgy, *Encyclopédie méthodique: finances*, I, lix, 2, and 7–9.
[75] Mathon de la Cour, *Comptes rendus*, avertissement.

and old provincial estates also began to publish budgets. The commission of the estates of Languedoc, for example, explained why in 1789 it decided to publish its own provincial *Compte rendu*:

Monsieurs the Commissaires thought that by rendering this budget public by way of print, each citizen would be enlightened on the extent and use of taxes and on the expenses of the Province; and that the reflections that this publicity will elicit will indicate to the estates ... which taxes and expenses should be abolished, changed, or reduced.[76]

By divulging the budget, the commission believed it would elicit public opinion on questions of reform. There were also political reasons why the commission wanted to make such an appeal. Its members explained that they had decided to announce a "patriotic" proposal to redistribute the tax burden "more equally" among taxpayers, but the first two orders, the clergy and nobility, prohibited the assembly from discussing the matter. With its plan for reform blocked, the commission published the budget so that details of the province's finances "would be disseminated and known in all the dioceses and in the majority of communities." This would stimulate discussion outside the assembly and force the first two orders to capitulate. Thus, for the commission of the estates, as for Necker and Mathon de la Cour, revealing the budget was more than an act of patriotism; it was a way of galvanizing a movement for reform.

To conclude this exploration into the literary sphere of the Old Regime, it is worth considering Tocqueville's thesis that the rise of the centralized state produced a peculiar type of "literary politics" in which men of letters with little experience in government informed popular political opinion. Tocqueville argued that eighteenth-century writers, because they had little contact with free institutions or everyday political affairs, expounded highly abstract theories of government and society that encouraged their readers to imagine an ideal society.

Beyond real society, the constitution of which was still traditional, confused and irregular, where the laws remained varied and contradictory, the social order divided and fixed, and the burdens unequal, an imaginary society was gradually constructed in which everything appeared simple and

---

[76] AN, H-1 748 (284), *Compte rendu des impositions et des dépenses générales de la province de Languedoc* (Montpellier, 1789). For an example of a budget published by a provincial assembly, see the AN, AD IX 390a, *Compte rendu*, which stated that the commission owed it to its "fellow citizens ... to publish every detail of its operations."

coordinated, uniform, equitable, and rational. Little by little, the imagination of the masses deserted the former society to retire to the latter. Losing interest in what was in order to dream of what could be, people eventually came to live spiritually in this ideal world constructed by writers.[77]

How do our findings compare with those of Tocqueville? The writers examined in this chapter were not unfamiliar with politics: Boisguilbert was a magistrate; Vauban was an army officer; Mirabeau held no office but witnessed real episodes of political conflict which inspired him to write; and Necker was a finance minister. Perhaps they did not interact with what Tocqueville called "free" institutions (for such institutions had all but disappeared according to Tocqueville), but to say that they had no understanding of everyday politics is simply untrue. Indeed, to a large extent it was everyday politics that generated such an abundant literature on state finance, especially in the second half of the eighteenth century when writers, many of whom were well connected with high government officials (if they were not officials themselves), engaged in debate over specific royal policies.

Did these writers help create an "imaginary society ... in which everything appeared simple and coordinated, uniform, equitable, and rational"? This is undeniable. All shared a predilection for abstraction, symmetry, and the formulation of general principles by which the state ought to operate. But to say, as Tocqueville did, that all eighteenth-century political philosophy "consists in this single notion" that writers aimed to "substitute simple and elementary rules, drawn from reason and natural law, for the complicated, traditional customs that governed the society of their day" is to ignore the rich variety of ideas and language that writers offered their readers. Tocqueville avoided the question of differences among writers and instead focused on the physiocrats as the paradigmatic figures of Enlightenment political thought because they best fit his argument that the French embraced state centralization and equality at the expense of political liberty.[78] By reducing all thought to physiocracy, however, Tocqueville marginalized other intellectual traditions that were far more hostile to state power and far more receptive to ideas of liberty, citizenship, and political accountability. In fact, this brief study of the century's most popular works on taxation and finance suggests that, while writers emphasized abstract

---

[77] Alexis de Tocqueville, *L'Ancien Régime et la Révolution* (Paris, 1951), p. 214; my translation.
[78] Baker and Furet make the same point in, respectively, *Inventing*, p. 22, and *Interpreting*, p. 152.

reason over custom, they employed rhetoric that severely criticized efforts to centralize and bureaucratize the state.

At the turn of the eighteenth century Boisguilbert and Vauban proposed that the crown make fundamental changes in state fiscality in order both to improve royal finances and to relieve the poor. Their concern for the down-trodden was remarkable, but what was truly original in both works was the principles on which their arguments were based. Boisguilbert justified his call for tax reform on strictly economic grounds, rather than Christian morality. Insisting that the monarchy do only what the "natural order" of the economy dictated, he argued that a shift in the burden of taxation from poor to rich would generate greater overall consumption, which, when combined with free trade in grain, would bring about economic growth. Growth, in turn, would further relieve the poor and strengthen royal finances. This argument heralded the dawn of economic liberalism in France and, although one of its aims was to revitalize state finance, it prescribed strict limits on the actions of monarchs such as Louis XIV who disregarded the natural laws of economics. Kings had to bow to nature if they wanted to reap her abundance.

Vauban's line of argument, on the other hand, was less censorious of royal power yet more critical of the abuse of social privilege. The *Dîme royale* was based on the notion that there existed a social contract between rulers and ruled, whereby the ruled, in order to obtain military protection, had to contribute equal portions of their income to the state. No one was exempt from the obligations of this contract whatever his socio-legal status. To enforce the contract, the marshal designed an immense military-style bureaucracy capable of determining the wealth of every head of household in the kingdom and extracting a uniformly fixed percentage of income. In Vauban we find the source of Tocqueville's anxiety about the tendency of writers to support state centralization without proper concern for political liberty, but Vauban stands out as an exceptional figure in his devotion to large-scale royal administration.

At mid-century, fighting against the seeds of just the sort of bureaucracy that Vauban had imagined, Mirabeau added a moral, republican tone to the discussion of taxation and finance. A hybrid of republicanism and physiocracy, the *Théorie de l'impôt* did more than seek to rationalize the tax system. It characterized fiscal crisis as a mere physical reflection of a much deeper political crisis in the relationship between the monarchy and its subjects. Arbitrary rule, which Mirabeau equated with a bloated fiscal-administrative state, only antagonized the wills of subjects, making them less inclined to fulfill their duty to the king. Instead of using bureaucratic might to extract money from royal subjects, the crown should cultivate a sense of duty in its citizens so that they would willfully serve the crown or at least make the necessary financial contributions. To instill citizenship in a monarchy: this was Mirabeau's answer to the fiscal and constitutional crises of his day. His language of citizenship and political will reveals that in the latter half of the eighteenth century the rhetoric of republicanism could be employed by the most devout monarchist. Mirabeau dreamed of a throne resting on the solid foundations of a dutiful citizenry – a seemingly benign image – but his repugnance for the corruption that seethed in fiscal administration and his attention to the "wills of a strong and active multitude," while endearing to citizen-readers, were threatening enough to royal authorities to land him in prison.

Necker was no stranger to the notion of citizenship either, but he framed his conception of it around the idea of the citizen's love of his *patrie* rather than his duty to the king. For Necker, the king's fiscal problems stemmed from the fact that the state not only hid itself from the public but failed to allow subjects to participate in it. By publicizing the workings of the state, and by creating representative institutions in the provinces, both patriotism and public opinion would emerge to guide the nation to reform, stability, and fiscal strength. Although Necker was hardly the first to discuss public opinion or to use a language of national patriotism, he certainly did much to popularize both subjects in the field of finance. In the last decade of the Old Regime readers gobbled up his best-sellers and mimicked them by adorning their own artistic and literary contributions with allusions to patriotism, tax reform, and publicity.

The voices that we have heard from the literary sphere during the century of Enlightenment added several important themes to the debate on taxation: natural law, social contract, citizenship, publicity, public opinion, and patriotism. Ideas of natural law and social contract emerged at the turn of the century never to depart. Republican rhetoric joined the discussion at mid-century to become another essential, if sometimes overlooked, discourse of opposition to the administrative state. And the notion of public opinion received its fullest treatment at the end of the century in the work of Necker, who also played with the idea of patriotism in an effort to build stronger and, for the state, more lucrative ties between the citizen and the nation. The century's most popular books all aimed to unify and strengthen the kingdom, suggesting that the king either follow the laws of nature, build a stronger administration, reorder the realm's moral structure, or lay the institutional groundwork for patriotism. Yet as they engaged an ever-growing readership, the same books that sought to revive the kingdom by highlighting the will of the poor consumer, the rational administrator, the duty-bound citizen, or the enlightened patriot may have helped to subvert the authority of the monarchy. Certainly they were not intended to destabilize the regime – their authors would have been offended at the very charge – but their rhetoric, which not only criticized privilege and the fiscal-administrative composition of the state but constructed imaginary alternatives to them, ultimately served to undermine the traditional ordering of society and the claims of absolute monarchy. The next chapter will examine in greater detail how rhetoric from the literary sphere, together with the language of dispute from the administrative and institutional spheres, converged to form a revolutionary discourse at the end of the Old Regime.

PART THREE

From resistance to revolution

Turning taxpayers into citizens: reform, revolution, and the birth of modern political representation

"We only made the Revolution to become the masters of taxation."

– Marc-Antoine Lavie[1]

"It seems that by the force of events Calonne, like Necker, had been led to think that a great revolution in the system of finances was, from that point on, the only remedy that could be applied to the disorders of the day ... Neither Necker, nor Calonne, nor perhaps anyone in France at that moment had foreseen that a great revolution in finances would lead inevitably to a great revolution in the social order."

– François-Nicolas Mollien[2]

In the summer of 1789 France experienced the onset of two revolutions. The first was a revolution against absolutism in which representatives from throughout the kingdom seized the state apparatus and bound the will of the crown to that of a national legislative body. The second was a revolution against privilege. In that revolution deputies from the third estate, with assistance from commoners in Paris and the provinces and from liberal allies in the clergy and nobility, declared themselves representatives of the nation, seized legislative power, and set out to create a new society based on equality before the law. It was the convergence of these two revolutions into a single political moment that gave the French Revolution its extraordinary force. In a matter of months the monarchy surrendered much of its power to the nation, and the National Assembly swept away a regime of privilege that had for centuries defined the political and social life of France. This chapter

---

[1] Quoted in Bossenga, "Taxes," p. 589.
[2] François-Nicolas Mollien, *Mémoires d'un ministre du trésor public, 1780–1815*, 2 vols. (Paris, 1898), I, pp. 123–4.

examines this double revolution by considering how the issue of taxation, already politicized under the Old Regime, became invested with revolutionary meanings. The chapter seeks not only to shed light on the constitutional revolution carried out in the name of liberty but also to explain the mysterious metamorphosis by which the general demand for political liberty translated into more specific claims for political equality. What were the connections between the constitutional and egalitarian revolutions?

Conflict over taxation during the Old Regime was not necessarily revolutionary in itself – one can imagine ways in which the regime could have survived the turbulence of tax disputes and avoided revolution – but the politics of taxation changed dramatically and decisively in the 1780s as it broke from patterns of dispute that had developed in previous decades. This change manifested itself in three overlapping phases: the creation of provincial assemblies in 1778, 1779, and 1787 when the crown attempted to forge a new link between the taxpayer and the state; the constitutional revolution of 1787–9 in which a variety of social groups sought liberty in the reestablishment of older, more powerful estates; and, finally, the meeting of the Estates General in the summer of 1789 when the third estate asserted its own claims to power by stretching the political logic of constitutional revolution. During each phase the conceptual link between taxation and political participation was reformulated and used for different purposes. It is the aim of this chapter to recover and compare those formulations and to consider how they ultimately resulted in the construction of a new polity grounded in the "active citizen."

PROVINCIAL ASSEMBLIES AND THE DAWN OF A "NEW REGIME"

From 1778 to 1787 Louis XVI established nineteen provincial assemblies, scores of district assemblies, and thousands of municipal assemblies, experimenting with what writers and members of the assemblies themselves were beginning to call a "new regime."[3] This new regime of assemblies was designed to assist in the reform of direct taxation by superseding older corporate bodies, such as estates

---

[3] The earliest reference I found to the "new regime" of assemblies is [Jacques-Mathieu Augéard], *Lettre d'un bon François* (n. p., 1781), p. 6.

and parlements, which were known to resist increases in, and the redistribution of, the direct tax burden. Although the assemblies achieved mixed results and did not meet the high expectations of many taxpayers, the literature on their design and the ultimate form they took provide important lessons on the relationship between taxation and representation at the end of the Old Regime.

The idea that new kinds of assemblies could help the crown reform the tax system came originally from the literary sphere, where writers had been making such proposals for decades. During the last thirty years of the Old Regime men such as Mirabeau, Dupont de Nemours, and Le Trosne – all physiocrats – urged a new system of representation that differed markedly from that of estates. Most estates, general or provincial, were divided on the basis of status into three orders, each of which deliberated separately and could cast one vote on matters at issue. The physiocratic assemblies, by contrast, were not to be founded on distinctions of status but were to be single-chamber bodies in which members voted as individuals rather than as members of a particular corporate order. The inspiration behind these assemblies stemmed partly from the notion, common to much Enlightenment thought, that a new institutional space that allowed citizens to reconstitute their ties to each other without respect to corporate status would rid France of the particularism and prejudice, the *"esprit de corps"* in Le Trosne's words, that prevented the kingdom from evolving into a harmonious and rational society in which individuals could discern and pursue the public interest.[4] In this respect, the provincial assemblies would resemble other sites of Enlightenment sociability such as provincial academies, masonic lodges, and salons, whose members attempted to exercise reason in the service of public good.

In conceiving provincial assemblies, the physiocrats also drew from their distinctive understanding of political economy. The physiocratic theory of representation was based on a single fundamental axiom: that all wealth, even that ostensibly produced by commerce and industry, was generated by the so-called "net product" of the land, that is the gross revenue from land minus the costs of production. It followed from this that the most efficient form of taxation was a single land tax that struck landowners in propor-

---

[4] Guillaume François Le Trosne, *De l'administration provinciale et de la réforme de l'impôt* (Basel, 1779), p. 126.

tion to their net product. Physiocrats were certain that this cardinal principle of taxation (in conjunction with a free grain trade) was the key to a prosperous kingdom, but they realized that putting it into practice would be an extremely difficult enterprise. For all their talk of "legal despotism," they understood that the monarchy could not simply impose tax reform by fiat or bureaucratic force, for that only alienated subjects from the government and made tax collection all the more difficult. The taxpaying families of the kingdom, Dupont de Nemours observed in his *Mémoire sur les municipalités*, written at Turgot's request in 1775,

view the authoritative commands for the levy of taxes needed for the maintenance of public order as the law of the strongest, to which there is no other reason to yield than their powerlessness to resist. Consequently, everyone tries to cheat [royal] authority and pass his social burden on to his neighbors. Incomes are hidden, and can only be discovered very imperfectly by a kind of inquisition which would lead one to say that Your Majesty is at war with his people.[5]

It was to end this fiscal war that Dupont de Nemours proposed the establishment of assemblies of male landowners at the village, district, provincial, and national levels that would deliberate on such matters as taxes, public works, and poor relief. The main criterion for entry into village assemblies was the ownership of land. As Dupont de Nemours explained, landowners tended to be well-educated, permanent residents of their village who had a direct interest in local administration, whereas the landless were known to be migratory, poor, and susceptible to corruption. Such qualities made the ownership of land the perfect marker by which subjects worthy of participation in the state could be identified.

But there was another, equally compelling reason to give land-owners a place in the assemblies. Landowners possessed the net product of the land, which, believed to constitute the true tax base of the kingdom, entitled them to political or, more precisely, administrative participation. More than simply stationary and better educated, landowners produced the resources on which the state depended for its revenue and, therefore, deserved a place in government. It is for this reason that Dupont de Nemours proposed a system of voting in the municipal assemblies that was scaled not to the size of one's estate but rather to the amount of net product one

[5] Schelle, *Turgot*, IV, p. 577.

produced. Voting, he suggested, should be pegged directly to net product, so that a middle-level landowner with 600 livres of net product, considered enough to sustain a family, got one vote, a small landowner with 300 livres, what he called a "half-citizen," got half a vote, and a large landowner enjoying 1,200 livres of income got two votes. For if, as Mirabeau suggested, "the sovereign and the owners of the disposable *produit net* . . . comprise the State," then it made sense to allot a greater voice to those with more net product.[6] The landowner deserved a degree of citizenship commensurate to his capacity to pay taxes.

There was also a brilliantly practical purpose in "classifying citizens according to the real usefulness they have to the State."[7] Those who wished to exercise the full measure of their vote in the village assembly would have to declare the entire net product of their land, information which could then be used for the purposes of tax assessment. "The same convention by which votes are distributed will provide the best possible rule for the distribution of the tax burden, and the one least subject to quarrels."[8] The knowledge of landed revenue that would be gleaned at the lowest tier of assemblies would ascend, with a representative, to the district-level assembly, which would distribute the tax burden accordingly on the villages and towns of its jurisdiction. The same upward flow of knowledge and representation (and downward flow of tax allocation) would occur at the levels of the provincial and national assemblies, so that in the end the distribution of taxation across the kingdom would match the net product of individual landowners. Le Trosne followed roughly the same scheme in his own book, aptly titled *De l'administration provinciale et de la réforme de l'impôt*, published four years later in 1779.

The significance of the provincial assemblies, as conceived by Mirabeau, Dupont de Nemours and Turgot, Le Trosne, and later Condorcet, rests in part in their rejection of older forms of representation that were rooted in the traditional socio-legal corporate order of the kingdom. These imagined assemblies would not be divided by order or derive their legitimacy from ancient charters or customary right, like provincial estates; they would be composed of individual land-owning taxpayers who voted by head in common session. But

[6] Quoted in Baker, *Inventing*, p. 239.
[7] Schelle, *Turgot*, IV, p. 619.
[8] Schelle, *Turgot*, IV, pp. 588–9.

perhaps more important than their implicit criticism of existing representative bodies was the way the physiocrats sought to establish a new basis for determining the rights of political participation. The amount of one's taxable profit from land was directly proportional to the degree of voting power one held in the local (and district) assembly.

The provincial assemblies of which the physiocrats dreamed were never actually created of course. Because Turgot never presented Dupont de Nemours' plan to Louis XVI, it was left to Necker to create the first two assemblies in 1778 and 1779, neither of which conformed to the specifications of the physiocrats. Eight years later it looked as if true physiocratic assemblies would be created when, in 1787, Calonne again commissioned Dupont de Nemours to design a new set of assemblies, but Calonne fell from power and was replaced by Brienne, who installed assemblies that mixed Calonne's proposed physiocratic forms with Necker's alternate model. Necker's influence over the structure of the assemblies that were put in place was thus considerable. It is to his ideas that we must turn in order to understand the full significance of this experiment in representation.

Necker's interest in provincial assemblies was not all that different from that of the physiocrats. He too believed that assemblies would spread enlightenment and generate a healthy movement for reform as members participated in public administration; one did not have to be a physiocrat to believe that subjects could learn to love and act on behalf of the public good. Indeed, in terms far more explicit than the physiocrats', Necker sought to demonstrate that the assemblies could provide a way out of the chronic, debilitating patterns of contestation that had come to dominate Old Regime fiscal politics. In 1778 he elaborated his ideas in a memoir to Louis XVI that was so critical of existing institutions that it was later used against the minister as part of a successful effort to bring him down.[9]

On the one hand, the memoir drew from the 1775 remonstrances of the *cour des aides*, written by Malesherbes, to condemn royal bureaucracy in terms unusually harsh for a minister of state. Necker criticized the abuses committed by royal administrators, especially overworked intendants who delegated much of their power to subdelegates and other unaccountable subordinates who were hopelessly "timid before the powerful and arrogant toward the weak."

[9] AN, K 885, no. 5, Mémoire donné au Roy par M. Necker en 1778.

Even more frightening than the bureaucracy itself was the complete lack of recourse against it. Borrowing an example directly from Malesherbes, the finance minister described the injustices committed against subjects who vainly contested their taxes. When a taxpayer protested to a finance minister against an assessment made by a particular intendant, the minister, under the pretense of conducting an impartial examination of the case, merely consulted with the very same intendant. The intendant then either "rejected the appeal, contested the facts, or justified them, always in a way that proved that everything done under his orders has been done legitimately." Invariably persuaded by the justifications of the intendant, the minister wrote back to the disputant and, claiming falsely that he had obtained "an exact knowledge of his affair," handed down a decision that was in truth only "the simple response of the intendant" but which was made to look like "a well-considered judgment of the royal council." The royal council, in other words, was but a fiction covering up the abuses of royal ministers and administrators. It is no wonder, Necker concluded, that taxpayers grew frustrated with royal administration and that intendants were "so strongly feared in the provinces by those who have no connection to the royal court or the capital."[10]

Although Necker reiterated the pronouncements of many sovereign courts in his denunciation of the arbitrary nature of royal administration, he did not shrink from pointing an accusatory finger at the parlements as well. Indeed, the memoir claimed that the crown's abusive bureaucratic and fiscal practices only allowed disingenuous magistrates to intervene on behalf of the people, drawing popular loyalty from the monarchy to themselves:

When the grumbling [of taxpayers] degenerates into general complaint, the Parlement moves to place itself between the King and his people; ... this habituates Your Majesty's subjects to sharing their trust, and to knowing a locus of protection other than that of the love and justice of their sovereign. ... Like every corps that wants to acquire power, the parlements intervene in administrative affairs by speaking in the name of the people and calling themselves the defenders of the rights of the nation. ... It is necessary to remove the support [of public opinion for the parlements] or prepare ourselves for repeated Battles which will disturb the tranquility of

---

[10] The charge of Necker (and Malesherbes) that the royal council was no longer a true council of advisers to the king has been demonstrated by Antoine, *Conseil du roi*.

the reign of Your Majesty and lead either to a degradation of authority or to extreme options whose consequences cannot be adequately assessed.

A more succinct analysis of the relationship between public opinion and the conflicts between the crown and the parlements is difficult to find. Translated into the terms of this study, Necker was saying that tensions in the administrative sphere, brought on by fiscal-administrative pressure, provided the foundation for disputes in the institutional sphere, which allowed the parlements to steal the support of public opinion and to weaken the authority of the king.

There was, however, a way out of this infernal cycle. The king could confide the task of distributing taxes to provincial assemblies. "If I may say," Necker asked, "how can people love the glory of the King, how can they partake of his happiness when he is everywhere the commander and guarantor of the hardest and most rigorous details?" "How can people look well upon the king's orders to send soldiers to the house of a taxpayer, and to sell his furniture and his bed?"

If the best constitution can never guarantee taxpayers from abuses of authority, and if it is the nature of men to consider the severe execution of law as an injustice, is it not fortunate that these complaints and grievances be addressed to the representatives of a province and that the name of your majesty, always dear, be pronounced only for consolation and hope?[11]

Once representative institutions replaced bureaucratic ones, the crown would cease to be a lightning rod for public discontent over taxation; and the parlements could no longer tarnish the king's image before the public.

Did Necker worry that, once established, provincial assemblies would assume the role of parlements or provincial estates by resisting the crown in the name of liberty and the people? Not at all: following the physiocrats, he specified that, unlike these other institutions, provincial assemblies would have no authority to challenge the crown. Whereas the power of the parlements and provincial estates was rooted firmly in centuries-old rights and privileges, the provincial assemblies would inherit no "old conventions" and would not even possess the right to "discuss the amount of taxes that [royal] law has determined." Given only the task of distributing taxes, the members of the assembly would be no different than commissioned

---

[11] Necker, *Compte*, p. 75.

administrators. They certainly would not be true representatives of the people.[12]

If Necker's provincial assemblies resembled physiocratic ones in that they were meant to lead the monarchy out of the morass of contestation, generate public spirit for reform, and provide taxpayers with a means to participate in state administration without granting them sovereignty, there were also important differences between the two. Necker did not believe in the magical properties of the net product of land and did not incorporate the innovative system of voting associated with it. Nor did the provincial assemblies of Berry and Haute-Guienne, the two bodies created with much fanfare by the minister, sit atop a hierarchy of assemblies founded on the village assembly where votes were calibrated according to taxable income. Rather, the two assemblies were staffed by the king, who severed their roots from the local power base by appointing one-third of the deputies and instructing them to co-opt the remaining two-thirds. Moreover, Necker's assemblies maintained certain distinctions among the same three orders (clergy, nobility, and third estate) that had since time immemorial composed estates, a dramatic departure from the plans of physiocrats, which allowed for no social distinction among deputies other than that dictated by differences in taxable wealth.

This does not mean that Necker's assemblies were devoid of originality. On the contrary, in the tradition of the marquis d'Argenson, whose argument for monarchical "democracy" laid out in *Considérations sur le gouvernement ancien et présent de la France* called for the creation of representative institutions that would seal an alliance between crown and people, Necker endowed the assemblies of Berry and Haute-Guienne with two startling novelties: a doubling of deputies from the third estate that made it equal in number to the first two estates combined; and a system of suffrage in which votes were counted by head in common session rather than by order. These two measures denied the privileged orders the authority they traditionally exercised in most estates, and invested third estate deputies with an unprecedented degree of power. Although Necker had created relatively weak representative bodies, he deliberately constructed them to produce "a reasonable Equilibrium among the orders" which prevented the nobility from exercising "too great an

---

[12] Necker, *Compte*, pp. 77–8; and Necker, *De l'administration*, II, pp. 289 and 294.

influence" and provided the third estate with a dominant or at least equal voice. According to the minister's formula, a strong third estate embedded in a compliant institution would produce "a proportional equality in taxation" that would allow the crown "to augment the general tax burden." He never averted his eye from the fiscal improvements that a new balance of representation would yield.[13]

Owing to the resistance of the parlement of Paris and his enemies at court, Necker fell from power in 1781 and was unable to realize his intention to create assemblies in other provinces. The idea of establishing more assemblies, however, did not fall with him. To be sure, his conservative successor, Joly de Fleury, saw only danger in provincial assemblies, but the examples of Berry and Haute-Guienne, extolled by provincial newspapers and academies, had whet the appetites of less fortunate provinces in the *pays d'élections* that had neither estates nor provincial assemblies. When Joly de Fleury considered permitting local nobles to assist subdelegates in drawing the rolls of the *capitation*, the intendant of Caen, Esmangard, balked, explaining that the slightest change in tax administration would ignite hazardous demands for assemblies:

You know the provinces. You know better than anyone the agitation that is produced when new systems are proposed to replace the good, old principles on which the tranquillity of the Government rests. In Normandy ... the frenzy of the provincial assemblies has excited people's minds, which may have dangerous consequences. If you think that the agitation has been extinguished, you are fooling yourself. It is like a fire covered with light cinders; if one does not touch it, it will die down and with time burn itself out. But the least fuel that is added will re-ignite it with a stronger explosion. Although this observation might appear to concern Normandy in particular, I think it applies to most of the provinces, and I do not doubt that my colleagues will tell you the same thing, perhaps more vigorously.[14]

The intendant counseled against any reform that might allow taxpayers the opportunity to form representative bodies:

If you should give the nobility any influence on the distribution of the *capitation* in those generalities where the nobility has presently no influence at all, it would give rise to great hopes. The Gentlemen named by the king would soon be erected as representatives of a corps which would form itself without the permission of the sovereign, and before long one would see the

---

[13] AN, K 885, no. 5, Mémoire donné au Roy par M. Necker en 1778.
[14] BN, JdF 1444, fos. 87–8, letter from Esmangard to Joly de Fleury, 31 October 1781.

nobility claim the right to have a say in the distribution of other taxes, and maybe in all matters of provincial administration.[15]

Following the advice of Esmangard, Joly de Fleury abandoned the idea of introducing any fiscal or administrative reforms that could be misconstrued as a step toward representative government.

Calonne would be less cautious. As servicing the massive debt incurred from the American war became increasingly difficult and as the third *vingtième* neared its expiration in December of 1786, Calonne put together a broad reform package centered around the establishment of a new land tax and the creation of more provincial assemblies. These proposed assemblies, designed by Dupont de Nemours, scarcely differed from the ones the physiocrat had discussed with Turgot twelve years earlier and, like the earlier ones, these never got past the planning stage. The Assembly of Notables convoked by Calonne to approve his reforms ended up disgracing him and having him replaced by a notable, Brienne, who, a more successful negotiator, managed to obtain the Assembly's consent to a modified version of Calonne's reforms. By the end of 1787 provincial assemblies were mushrooming across the *pays d'élections*.

Brienne's assemblies reflected a compromise between the ideas of Calonne and Necker. To satisfy the notables, Brienne retained Necker's model of distinguishing the three orders while doubling the third estate and having deputies vote by head. Deputies at the provincial and district levels were also to be appointed by the king or co-opted by royal appointees. At the same time, the assemblies created in 1787 shared certain features with the physiocratic model. Each province had multiple levels of assemblies, the lowest of which, the municipal assemblies, were composed of deputies elected by all adult males, regardless of socio-legal status, who paid 10 livres a year or more of direct taxes. Here, the physiocratic sliding link between one's degree of political participation and the amount of one's taxable wealth was reduced to a franchise based simply on a minimum direct tax requirement. In this latter version there was no scale of citizenship, only a cut-off between taxpayers who paid substantial to moderate taxes and those who paid very little.

Both physiocratic writers and ministers of state, then, played with new modes of representation as they contemplated the creation of provincial assemblies. All imagined assemblies that would be rela-

---

[15] BN, JdF 1444, fos. 88–9, letter from Esmangard to Joly de Fleury, 31 October 1781.

tively weak, possessing little or no sovereignty with which to challenge the demands of the crown. And all related the assemblies to the payment of direct taxes, either by basing systems of representation on taxable landed wealth (the physiocrats) or minimum tax requirements (Brienne on the lower assemblies), or by designing the assemblies in such a way as to elevate the power of the third estate in order to assure a more equal and potentially greater distribution of taxes (Necker and Brienne on the upper assemblies). As we shall see, all of these ideas entered into the revolutionary dynamic of 1789.

Once constituted, how effective was this "new regime" of assemblies? Did it, as intended, extricate the crown from dispute, provide taxpayers with a sense that they were participating in state administration, and levy taxes more equally? These are important questions, for, if assemblies had achieved what their architects expected of them, they would have resolved the tensions between taxpayers and crown, and between society and state more generally, that created crises like the one that precipitated revolution in 1789. Why did the experiment fail?

In 1787 and 1788 it certainly looked as if the assemblies were going to succeed in restructuring the fiscal and administrative order of the kingdom. Judging from the hostile reactions of intendants and local officers of justice, the new bodies threatened to usurp customary jurisdictions – the territorial boundaries of assemblies traced the outlines of the generalities administered by intendants – and assume institutional authority over the provinces. About half of the intendants were hostile to the assemblies, including Launay, intendant of Caen, who on 6 November 1787 delivered the speech that opened the provincial assembly of Lower Normandy.[16] Launay praised the assembly's project to bring "this equality [of taxation] for which the good citizen has so long yearned but which the powerful ... have always eluded," but insisted that he direct it, relegating the deputies to the role of "witnesses to, and collaborators in, his work."[17] In the coming year, as the assembly carved out an administrative space for itself, the intendant did his best to maintain his grip on public affairs, especially taxation. The struggle that ensued confirms that a new regime was indeed being introduced.

One quarrel with the *commission intermédiaire* of Lower Normandy,

[16] The reactions of intendants are discussed in Peter Jones, *Reform and Revolution in France: The Politics of Transition, 1774–1791* (Cambridge, 1995), pp. 142–3.

[17] AD Calvados, C 7617, Discours prononcé par M. de Launay, 6 November 1787.

the body that exercised the assembly's authority after its plenary session, is particularly revealing. The commission claimed the right to manage tax revenue that was not earmarked for the royal treasury, since the money belonged to the generality and therefore should be managed by the assembly. Launay, who had always handled these funds and was not prepared to relinquish control, responded by telling the commission that the revenues "belong to the King and not to the generality, which is merely charged with paying them." The intendant brought the dispute to the attention of the finance minister, warning that a transfer of jurisdiction in this affair would invest the commission with "incalculable" power, enough "to influence even the constitution of the State." These funds included the free funds of the *capitation*, which Launay distributed at will to pay administrative costs and salaries as well as to provide relief to "unfortunate" families who had been forgotten by "absentee seigneurs." Such "government relief," the intendant emphasized, "must always emanate directly from [the royal] council; ... otherwise, the softest ties that bind the subject to the sovereign would cease to exist, and one of the king's most beautiful prerogatives would be given over to the provincial assembly." Launay argued his case in vain. Lambert, the minister of finance, decided the conflict in the commission's favor, a humiliation that only strengthened the intendant's resolve to make the transfer of power to the provincial assembly as difficult as possible. Conflicts continued to flare over the communication of information on tax reductions granted to payers of the *capitation*, control over revenue from the tax that replaced the *corvée*, and the formation of district assemblies. In all these affairs Launay referred to the moneys collected from taxes as "*deniers royaux*," while the commission called them "*deniers publics*."[18]

Officers of justice were equally threatened by the assemblies. Except for those of Besançon and Bordeaux, all parlements registered the edict of June 1787 creating the provincial assemblies, but most, like Rouen, qualified their registrations with provisions demanding to see decrees that spelled out how the assemblies would

---

[18] AD Calvados, C 8091 and 4397, correspondence between intendant and commission; C 4703 bis, no. 15, letter from Launay to Lambert, 27 February 1788; C 4703 bis, no. 13, letter from commission to Lambert, 20 February 1788; Félix Mourlot, *La fin d'ancien régime et les débuts de la Révolution dans la généralité de Caen, 1787–1790* (Paris, 1913), pp. 56–7, 127, and 133–7; Félix Mourlot, *Rapports d'une assemblée provinciale et de sa commission intermédiaire avec l'intendant, 1787–1790* (Paris, 1902), pp. 1–18.

operate and stipulating that the assemblies could not contract new taxes without parlementary consent. In Normandy the parlement was not the only court to resist the transfer of administrative authority. The lower *élection* courts refused to hand over the rolls of the *taille* to district assemblies, which were now charged with its apportionment among villages, and threatened to prosecute tax collectors who cooperated with the new deputies. When the royal council received word of this, it sent a decree to Normandy's highest tax court, the *cour des aides* of Rouen, supporting the assemblies' administrative claims, but the court refused to register the law, helping to keep the assemblies at bay until 1790 when the Constituent Assembly all but dismantled the administrative power of sovereign courts and firmly delegated the management of the *taille* to the assemblies.[19]

Despite opposition from the intendant and the courts, the provincial assemblies did manage to acquire jurisdiction over several key areas of administration. Not least of these was the levy of the *capitation* and the *vingtième*, over which the provincial and district commissions took complete command. Did the assemblies manage to equalize taxation or blunt the bureaucratic edge of royal administration? They certainly intended to. In a report to the assembly of Lower Normandy, its president, the duc de Coigny, announced that "the aim" of this "new regime" was "the happiness of the people," and that their first duty was "to distribute taxes equitably." The entire system of direct taxation needed attention but especially the *capitation*:

The distribution of this tax has always been known for its arbitrariness, and arbitrariness is a most terrible scourge in matters of taxation ... Your purpose, Messieurs, will be to look for the most appropriate means to make the distribution of this tax more equal, ... [so that] the burden on the rich man would be proportioned to his fortune, and the artisan, who often has no wealth but his work, would receive ... the relief that he expects from the enlightened wisdom of your views.[20]

Coigny's initial confidence in the assembly's ability to transform the fiscal system was shared by other deputies and pro-assembly writers and pamphleteers.

When it came time to make actual changes, however, members of

---

[19] AN, AD IX 390a, *Compte rendu*, part I, ch. I; Mourlot, *Fin d'ancien régime*, p. 133; and Mourlot, *Rapports*, p. 14.

[20] *Procès-verbal des séances de l'assemblée provinciale de basse-Normandie* (Caen, 1788), pp. 110–11.

the assemblies found they could do only so much, as the case of the *capitation* makes clear. Because the provincial assembly had no right to contest the overall weight of the tax, it was forced to distribute the same global sum as in previous years, leaving little room for reform. The correspondence between the provincial commission of Lower Normandy (which took over the intendant's duties) and the district commissions (which replaced the subdelegates) suggests that the new regime quickly slipped into the ruts of the old. The *capitation* rolls hardly changed, and when petitions from taxpayers streamed in, the commissions blindly doled out the same old reductions. District commissions, for example, acquiesced when subdelegates petitioned for the same "light favor" they had been accustomed to receive, and discharged the burden of one of the intendant's lawyers who had asked for the "same privilege" his predecessors enjoyed.[21] Likewise, the rest of the privileged – nobles, officers of justice, bourgeois, *privilégiés*, and state employees – continued to negotiate lower assessments for themselves as if the intendant and subdelegates had never been replaced.

Why did assemblies revert to what they themselves described as outdated, abusive practices? Looking back on its record, the provincial commission blamed its failure to redistribute the *capitation* on "lack of time" and "lack of knowledge."[22] Because they had no more knowledge of the wealth of taxpayers than had the intendant, and because the bureaux were not allowed to lower the overall burden, they were in no position to make any drastic changes. It did not help that the public was watching them closely, comparing their administration with the old one. The members of the district commission of Vire explained that they were afraid of being "recognized as men of the fisc who were even more cruel than their predecessors," a sentiment expressed by their counterparts in Mortain who stated that "if we want to attach the people more and more to the new regime, we must grant unfortunate taxpayers the same kindness they received from the old administration."[23] This was not the time to restrict administrative justice.

---

[21] AD Calvados, C 8110, petitions from subdelegate of Mortain, 26 June 1789, and Frederic Desbordeaux, lawyer for the intendancy, 26 October 1789.
[22] AN, AD IX 390a, *Compte rendu*, part I, ch. I.
[23] AD Calvados, C 8102, letter from the commission of Vire to the provincial commission, 23 January 1789; AD Calvados, C 8116, letter from the commission of Mortain to the provincial commission, 15 July 1788. The bureau of Mortain accused the intendant's agents

Petitions against the *capitation* suggest that royal subjects were deeply disappointed in the so-called "new regime." This was particularly true for officers of justice who since 1769, we recall, were forced to petition annually against high *capitation* assessments. Louis Harvel, a lawyer from Caen, complained that his exorbitant tax assessment was a "revolting" example of "arbitrary" taxation. He believed that his recent marriage had something to do with the increase, but why should a "citizen" be more heavily burdened because "he has fulfilled one of the most noble duties of society?" The increase, he concluded, "was no doubt the work of some poorly informed subordinate." To this lawyer, the new regime was as dependent on the work of incompetent, low-level agents as the old one. Another petitioner, Desmaretz de Monchalon, made an appeal on behalf of the officers of the *bailliage* court of Cotentin, who "have been imposed every year at a fixed but exorbitant sum, which every year forces them to present petitions for reductions to the intendant." "Although this reduction was accorded to them," the petition stated politely, "you can easily see, Messieurs, how such a subjugation has been onerous to each individual member of the court." This plea to cease forcing officers of justice to petition for reductions in inflated assessments was rejected, dimming whatever hopes these officers had in the new representative system. At the very least, they probably came to realize that this new regime, as it stood, was insufficient.[24]

The way in which assemblies handled the *vingtième* tells the same story. Although the two provincial assemblies created by Necker were encouraged to pay the *vingtièmes* by way of *abonnements* and to distribute the tax on the basis of new, fairer tax rolls, the process of redrawing the rolls proved more difficult than expected. After three years the province of Berry had revised the rolls of a third of the parishes in the province, and in the Haute-Guienne roughly the same proportion of nobles had after five years furnished new declarations of wealth as instructed. Even if we do not follow the majority of historians who have seen the glass of reform as two-thirds empty rather than one-third full, it is important to recognize that provincial deputies and taxpayers who expected to benefit from

of spreading the rumor that the funds allotted for tax reductions were now being spent on administrative costs.
[24] AD Calvados, C 8110 and 8115, petitions from Louis Harvel, 31 October 1789, and Desmaretz de Monchalon, 1788.

reapportionment perceived the rate of reform as terribly slow. "Such is our final conclusion," reported Berry's commission on taxation in 1786, "that there reigns in the rolls as much or more confusion than before the *abonnement* and that, having become responsible for a debt that weighs equally on all property, we have not taken a single step to distribute it with justice."[25]

Members of the assemblies of Lower Normandy soon shared the pessimism of their more experienced colleagues in Berry. Brienne also allowed the assemblies he created to pay *abonnements* for the *vingtième*, a concession for which the deputies were grateful since they wanted desperately to distribute and collect their own taxes, as provincial estates did, without the "arbitrary" interference of administrators who operated "in the shadow of mystery."[26] But the differences between assemblies and estates became clear when it came time to negotiate the size of the *abonnement*. Because they had no long-standing customs, rights, or privileges, and because they owed their existence to the good will of the royal minister with whom they were bargaining, assemblies could not exert the same kind of pressure on the crown as estates. Whereas estates could persuade the crown to accept *abonnements* that were well below what royal agents could have collected, assemblies ended up paying the same or even more than they had paid in the past. In 1788, after much negotiation, Lower Normandy ultimately settled for an *abonnement* of 2,112,000 livres, which was 304,000 livres more than the generality of Caen had paid without an *abonnement* in 1787.[27]

The acceptance of such a large *abonnement* exposed the assembly to public criticism and weakened its legitimacy. Pamphlets charged that the deputies were not real representatives at all, for true representatives would not have allowed the *vingtième* to increase beyond levels set by despotic administrators.[28] Well aware of the dangers of this kind of attack, one deputy from the provincial commission of Lower Normandy worried that the increase in the *vingtième*

will have the worst possible effect on everyone's attitudes, and will end up strengthening the existing prejudice in this generality against the operations of the Provincial assembly. The hope of a good future will not obliterate the

---

[25] The figures and quotation are from Rioche, *Vingtièmes*, pp. 121–4.
[26] AD Calvados, C 8169, letter from Montfarville to the district commission of Saint-Lo.
[27] AD Calvados, C 8159, records of the *abonnement* negotiation.
[28] See, for example, *Essai sur les assemblées provinciales, ou réflexions d'un patriote sur les effets qui en sont résultés* (London, 1789).

present evil from the mind of the people, and it is essential to prevent an absolute loss of confidence.[29]

To prevent an "absolute loss of confidence," the commission decided against conducting any investigations into the wealth of taxpayers. Such investigations would be "an object of anxiety, mistrust, and fear, and the unfavorable opinion that the people would have of the assembly's efforts would necessarily result in the spread of grievances."[30] Hence the commission decided to distribute the *abonnement* according to old tax rolls drawn by royal administrators. Contrary to expectations that taxpayers were now finally going to oversee the assessment of their taxes, hundreds of parish assemblies, which were supposed to redistribute the *vingtième*, were given no authority to revise the rolls. Resorting to the old rolls had serious consequences for the commission, as a deputy from the district of Saint-Lo understood when he commented with regret that the whole operation "will always appear in the eyes of the people as fixed by the arbitrariness of a small number of men whose interests and competence are under suspicion. Public hatred will therefore focus on them alone."[31]

Although provincial assemblies did introduce reforms here and there, they failed in general to realize the new regime that many taxpayers, writers, and deputies had rather optimistically imagined. For every enthusiastic pamphleteer who claimed that merely reading the published minutes of provincial assemblies gave one the thrilling impression that one was participating in government, there were hundreds of subjects who, watching their taxes remain the same or even rise, found little solace in the *procès verbaux*.[32] Both for the majority of taxpayers, who desired institutions powerful enough to shield them from the arbitrary exactions of the monarchy, and for nonprivileged taxpayers and liberal elites, who wanted an immediate and thorough redistribution of the tax burden, the experience of the provincial assemblies was disappointing. Although the assemblies suggested possibilities for radically new forms of representation – a fact of fundamental importance – they did not meet the high

---

[29] AD Calvados, C 8159, anonymous "observations."
[30] AD Calvados, C 8159, letter from the provincial commission to the controller-general, 3 May 1788.
[31] AD Calvados, C 8169, letter from Montfarville to the district commission of Saint-Lo.
[32] *De l'influence des administrations provinciales sur les moeurs et l'opinion* (Paris, 1788), p. 30.

expectations they had first aroused, leaving taxpayers on the lookout for other solutions.

Whatever their strengths and weaknesses, successes and failures, the provincial assemblies did not, as their founders hoped, neutralize the resistance of the sovereign courts and put a stop to the deleterious cycle of fiscal contestation. In 1787 and 1788 Louis XVI resumed the monarchy's long-term campaign to increase taxes on "the wealthiest class of his subjects," to use Lamoignon's words, by attempting to establish a new land tax that would reach property still untouched by the *vingtième* and, when that failed, resorting to the contentious policy of increasing the *vingtième* through reevaluations.[33] This was to be the last fiscal push of the Old Regime and it set off a storm of dispute as severe as that of 1763 or 1771–2. To fend off the crown, the Assembly of Notables, parlements, writers, local officials, and ordinary taxpayers reissued the call for estates, which, first sounded in the early 1760s, had grown louder the following decade during and after the Maupeou coup. Once again the attempt to increase universal taxes provoked demands for the return of estates, the only institutions, it was understood, that could protect the liberty of taxpayers and put an end to "despotism." This time, however, the monarchy would yield.

The first call for the Estates General came oddly enough from the Assembly of Notables in 1787. When Calonne convoked this body of royal nominees, he believed, as did most everyone who followed government affairs, that it would submissively approve new taxes. The sentiment of the Austrian ambassador to Versailles, that the convocation of notables was "no more than a petty trick to raise more money," was seconded by the arbiters of Paris fashion, who welcomed a new style of vest on which was embroidered an image of Louis XVI sitting among the notables, with his left hand holding a caption that read "the golden age," while his right hand picked the vest's pocket.[34] What a shock it must have been, then, to see hand-picked notables react so defiantly when confronted with proposals for new taxes.

---

[33] Jules Flammermont, ed., *Les remontrances du parlement de Paris au XVIIIe siècle*, 3 vols. (Paris, 1888–98), III, p. 678.
[34] Quoted in Munro Price, *Preserving the Monarchy: The Comte de Vergennes, 1774–1787* (Cambridge, 1995), p. 225; Bachaumont, *Mémoires secrets*, XXXIV, p. 327.

Faced with the prospect of a land tax that would renew investigations into landed revenue and a stamp tax that would strike royal creditors, office-holders, and merchants, the notables dug in their heels and raised the constitutional issue of consent to taxation. Rather than respond to the pressure of universal tax increases with defensive pronouncements about the inviolability of fiscal privileges, many notables countered royal claims with their own demand for a system of representation based on the consent of parlements, provincial assemblies, and, above all, provincial and national estates. Whether this counter-demand represented a full "mutation" in elite political culture, as Vivian Gruder contends, is open to debate – since the 1760s courts of law had preferred invoking principles of consent to arguing on the basis of fiscal privilege alone – but it is clear that the Assembly's stress on the periodicity of estates and its willingness to discuss the possibility of establishing fiscal equality in exchange for a number of constitutional safeguards against fiscal and administrative abuses inaugurated the so-called Prerevolution.[35]

The resistance of the Assembly of Notables strengthened the resolve of the parlement of Paris, which had long left serious protest against taxation to its provincial counterparts. This court now followed the lead of the Notables and issued its first call of the century for the Estates General. When presented with the stamp tax edict in July 1787, the parlement stated its wish "to see the Nation assembled before the introduction of any new tax," since "it alone can eradicate great abuses and offer great resources."[36] The parlement was more explicit in its rejection of the edict announcing the land tax: "the Nation, represented by the Estates General, is alone in possessing the right to grant the King the necessary taxes."[37] Abdicating its authority to represent the nation in matters of taxation, the parlement threw its weight behind the Estates General, apparently believing that the benefits of a stronger institutional check on the crown's fiscal appetite outweighed the risk of jurisdic-

---

[35] Vivian Gruder, "A Mutation in Elite Political Culture: The French Notables and the Defense of Property and Participation, 1787," *JMH* 56 (December 1984), pp. 598–634. Although claims for representation stemmed from a long history of tax conflicts within France, American constitutional ideas were also influential. See Franco Venturi, *The End of the Old Regime in Europe, 1776–1789*, trans. R. Burr Litchfield (Princeton, NJ, 1991), I, pp. 3–143; Dale Van Kley, ed., *The French Idea of Freedom: The Old Regime and the Declaration of Rights of 1789* (Stanford, CA, 1994), pp. 75–6, 158–60; and Daniel Mornet, *Les origines intellectuelles de la Révolution française, 1715–1787* (reprint, Lyons, 1989), pp. 439–50.

[36] Flammermont, *Remontrances*, III, p. 674, remontrances of 26 July 1787.

[37] Flammermont, *Remontrances*, III, p. 676, *arrêté* of 30 July 1787.

tional rivalry. The stakes of this gamble were far higher than the magistrates of Paris could have imagined.

Not yet willing to bow to the parlement's demands, Louis XVI forced the registration of both tax edicts and exiled the court to Troyes after it objected that the forced registration of the land tax was "a veritable attack on property."[38] Because the exile had the effect of making the stamp and land taxes appear all the more illegitimate – even the town criers of Paris refused to announce their establishment[39] – the newly appointed minister Brienne offered a compromise: he would withdraw the stamp and land tax edicts and instead reimpose and reform the two *vingtièmes*. The first *vingtième* would be levied indefinitely, the second through 1792; the rolls of both would be subject to revision. Brienne also declared that the Estates General would meet by 1792, a remarkable concession that bought a financially strapped monarchy some time. The parlement accepted.

The sublime image on the horizon of the Estates General, however, could not blot out the more immediate specter of investigations into property. The wording of the *vingtième* edict of October 1788 clearly signaled the coming of another round of verifications in which directors and controllers would resume their work throughout the *pays d'élections*, disturbing the tranquility that had reigned there since 1782. It was this renewal of verifications to which the young Parisian councilor Goislard de Montsabert objected when he delivered the famous speech that led to his arrest and to a royal coup against the judiciary not unlike the one inflicted by Maupeou. How familiar this speech must have seemed, as Goislard de Montsabert brought before the attention of the parlement "an abuse contrary to the laws and to the tranquility of citizens" committed by "individuals known by the name of controllers of the *vingtième*, armed with ministerial orders, [who] pour into the countryside."[40] To no avail the councilor invoked the parlement's proviso of 1763 that prohibited augmentations in the tax, and reminded his colleagues of the statement their court had made in 1778, that the voluntary declarations of property submitted by payers of the *vingtième* represented a vestige of the nation's right to consent to the tax. The issue of

---

[38] Flammermont, *Remontrances*, III, pp. 689–90, *arrêté* of 13 August 1787.
[39] Louis Meyniel, *Un facteur de la Révolution française: la querelle des impôts au parlement de Paris en 1787 et 1788* (Paris, 1907), p. 89.
[40] Quoted in Rioche, *Vingtièmes*, pp. 130–1.

reassessing the *vingtième* reappeared in terms strikingly similar to those of the previous decade.

Nowhere was this more true than in the provinces, where the edict of October 1788 provoked an outcry from several parlements. The parlement of Normandy, reacting with characteristic defiance, took up precisely where it left off in opposing the augmentations of the 1770s. Adopting and hastily printing an *arrêté* in December, the court charged the crown with imposing a higher *vingtième* under "the specious pretext of trying to establish equality in the distribution of the tax," which leaves "every property-owner uncertain and fearful of soon seeing, at the whim of fiscal greed, a renewal of inquisitions on their land." To ward off imminent "tyrannical verifications," the parlement drew on what was now a thirty-year-old dictum, a "public and recognized principle," a "national truth": that only the "three Orders of the State can consent to a new tax." Had not the king admitted as much when he agreed to call the Estates General? The court added that, with the Estates General, the estates of Normandy should also be reestablished so that the province would possess a body through which it could levy its own taxes.[41]

Weeks after the publication of the *arrêté*, during which time the Norman parlement conducted extensive research into the history of the *vingtième*, the court issued its last great tax remonstrances of the century, summing up three decades of protest.[42] Predictably, the magistrates reiterated the old theme of the "terror" instilled by *vingtième* administrators whose "inquisitorial regime" was outdone only by inquisitions into religious belief and political opinion. Royal agents, the remonstrances said,

are going to search through public records to find property titles of all kinds, leases, contracts of sale, declarations of the centième denier, etc. In the absence of titles, they inform themselves of everything regarding the value of property; relations based on friendship, hate, jealousy are all accepted indiscriminately: if they sometimes ask property-owners to present their leases, they do so with little faith in their validity.

The most extraordinary feature of the remonstrances of 5 February was their keen sense of history from which they drew the conclusion that the parlement was absolutely incompetent to restrain royal power. This too was an old theme going back to 1760 but it was expressed here in remarkably desperate terms. The magistrates

[41] AD Calvados, C 6518, *arrêté* of 20 December 1787.
[42] *Remontrances du parlement de Normandie au roi . . . , 5 février 1788* (n. p., [1788]).

recounted the history of the *vingtième*, laying emphasis on the steady stream of decrees extending, doubling, and tripling the tax, and on the violations of the proviso inscribed in the court's register since 1756 that forbade the revision of rolls. The crown had run roughshod over that proviso from 1772 to 1782 (as evidence magistrates must have obtained from the *chambre des comptes* of Rouen showed) and it appeared as if the new edict before them was about to "plunge Normandy back into all the calamities from which the vigilance of the Parlement sought to protect it." Such a history led the magistrates to the dramatic if inevitable conclusion that the court could no longer exercise its two basic functions: those of granting the Prince "the consent and obedience of the Peoples" and guaranteeing the people that "the duration and weight of taxation will not exceed the limits prescribed by the law establishing it." The parlement was in no position to fulfill either obligation: "Your Parlement, Sire, now finds itself reduced to a level of powerlessness that makes it impossible to fulfill this double duty, to administer this double guarantee effectively." History did not lie. "For thirty years the nation has been the victim and plaything of the financial administration." For thirty years, since the moment the crown began to force the registration of universal tax increases, the parlement had proved incapable of protecting French taxpayers. "After so many false promises, after the non-fulfillment of so many laws," how could the court give any assurances to the people? If the registration of tax decrees had become an "insufficient sign of the consent of the Peoples, it was even a weaker guarantee of the period and amount of taxation."

But now the Nation finally understood this. "The abusive excess made for some years of the faculty of borrowing and taxing awoke the Nation from its slumber, enlightened it on its true rights. It reproached us for having jeopardized [these rights] with registrations made too often and too easily; it refuses to recognize us as its representatives." It was time for the court and the fisc, both of which had betrayed the nation, to step aside and let taxation be sanctioned by estates, a right no less "imprescriptible" for having been suspended. The meeting of the Estates General was of course crucial in this respect, but the "most dear hope" of the magistrates of Rouen was the return of the provincial estates of Normandy.[43]

---

[43] For the court's longing for provincial estates, see also the *Lettre du parlement de Normandie au roi, pour demander les anciens états de la province* (n. p., [1788]), which argued that the coming of

That hope was given new life in August 1788 when, in order to stave off bankruptcy, Louis XVI moved the date of the Estates General up to 1 May 1789 and announced his intention to establish provincial estates in provinces where they had been suppressed. The royal lip-service paid to the reinstallation of estates spurred an outpouring of books, pamphlets, and petitions in the fall of 1788 acclaiming the coming of a constitutional revolution in which fiscal and administrative authority would devolve upon estates all across the kingdom. The highly visible struggle for provincial estates in Dauphiné only fueled the desire for similar institutions elsewhere, from the periphery of France (Provence, Hainault, and Franche-Comté), where the appeal for estates might be expected, to the very heart of the kingdom, the Île de France.[44]

Writers in Normandy, including the editors of the Norman newspaper, dug deep into the history of the province, approaching the reinstatement of the estates of Normandy as a return to a pre-absolutist past. To revive this past age, they gave accounts of the history of the estates, analyzed old *cahiers* written by Norman ancestors, and published the Norman charter of 1134. Taking this historical line of inquiry to an extreme, J. L. LeNoir began work on a catalogue of all the acts and titles relating to the province of Normandy, its gentleman and seigneurs, and its principal cities. For LeNoir the creation of estates signaled the possibility of a return to an age in which charters, ancient privileges, and personal titles acted as "the surest safeguard and the most solid foundation of our rights, properties, status, and condition."[45]

A corollary to the thesis that estates could best combat the claims of the monarchy was that the newly created provincial assemblies were but "a new form of executive power" imposed on the people by "a unilateral contract."[46] The leading publicist for the estates of Normandy was a certain de la Foy, a nobleman and lawyer at the parlement of Rouen whose enthusiasm for estates was exceeded only by his disdain for assemblies. Author of two influential pamphlets

---

the Estates General and the existence of provincial assemblies in no way made the need for provincial estates less urgent.

[44] The pamphlet *A Messieurs les propriétaires et habitans de Paris et de l'Isle de France* (n. p., n. d.) went back to 1561 to find a precedent for the convocation of provincial estates in the Île de France.

[45] J. L. LeNoir, *Collection chronologique des actes et des titres de Normandie* (n. p., 1788), pp. 7–8.

[46] [J.-R. Loyseau], *Les états provinciaux comparés avec les administrations provinciales* (Paris, 1789), p. 246. Criticism of this kind began soon after the first assemblies were created by Necker. See [Augéard], *Lettre d'un bon François*.

and a book, he argued that the rights of Normandy as stipulated by the Norman charter had, on the whole, been respected until the seventeenth century. In that century, however, "all was lost" when "Richelieu suddenly commissioned thirty-five intendants of justice to the provinces, and administration completely changed." As "the power of the intendants did not stop growing," the estates disappeared and the burden of taxation soared. According to de la Foy, the provincial assemblies were simply a new phase in this long-term evolution of state centralization. Instead of giving "representatives to the people," the assemblies only provided more "administrators, tax assessors, and tax collectors to the fisc." Short vitriolic descriptions of provincial assemblies and the deputies who staffed them punctuated de la Foy's work: "agents of the fisc," "an establishment of spies," "the little fiscal committees," "a multitude of arrogant little administrators," "the new fiscal assemblies," "agitators of the ministerial will," "these sad daughters of ministerial despotism." With the memory of "arbitrary" increases in the *vingtième* in the 1770s fresh in his mind, the author warned that the assemblies would reintroduce "inquisitions" and attack the "liberty" of Norman taxpayers. The only political body capable of blocking the crown's demands was the provincial estates, an institution rooted in the medieval past, confirmed by the Norman charter, and composed of "real representatives," "freely chosen" by those whom they represented. "It is up to our estates," he wrote, "to suggest the best way to reconcile the existence of privileges and sacred rights of property with . . . the taxes for which the State has demonstrated its need."[47]

As writers and *parlementaires* campaigned for the provincial estates of Normandy, officials all over the province rushed petitions to Versailles. The governor of Normandy, the duc d'Harcourt, solicited the royal council and commissioned several researchers, including LeNoir, to examine the archives of the *chambres des comptes* of Paris and Rouen for records of the estates of Normandy.[48] The municipal officers of Caen also expressed their desire to see the estates of the province assemble before those of the nation "to grant and consent

---

[47] G. de la Foy, *Parallèle des assemblées provinciales établies en Normandie, avec l'assemblée des états de ce duché* (n. p., 1788), pp. 17–18, 22, and 25–26; G. de la Foy, *Addition au parallèle* (n. p., 1788), pp. 32 and 34; [G. de la Foy], *De la constitution du duché ou état souverain de Normandie* (n. p., 1789), p. 275.

[48] Hippeau, *Gouvernement de Normandie*, V, p. 467; and VI, pp. 93–4 and 96, letters from LeNoir to d'Harcourt, 30 October 1788, d'Harcourt to Villedeuil, 21 January 1989, and Necker to d'Harcourt, 25 January 1789.

to taxes that the king solicited."[49] Even members of the district assemblies, the supposed allies of ministerial despotism, petitioned for provincial estates. Unlike the recently created network of assemblies to which they belonged, the estates could "freely and legally offer ... the aid needed to maintain the dignity of the crown and to satisfy the true needs of state."[50] The strength of the movement for provincial estates reminds us that in 1788 and 1789 not everyone focused exclusively on the advent of a national assembly. For many Normans, the coming of the Estates General was viewed, above all, as an opportunity to retrieve their provincial estates and win back the right to tax themselves.

The demand for government by national and provincial estates reached its climax in the winter and spring of 1789 as the three orders gathered to elect deputies to the upcoming Estates General. During the elections, constituents from each order drafted *cahiers de doléances*, lists of grievances that deputies to the Estates General were to take with them to Versailles. Although the *cahiers* did not anticipate all that would come in the Revolution, they did sketch the blueprint for a constitutional monarchy in which the crown would be held in check by permanent representative bodies designed to provide greater participation in the formation of law. Strikingly, all three orders converged on this idea. The large sample of noble *cahiers* studied by Chaussinand-Nogaret shows that, while half called for a written constitution, all (100 percent) solicited a permanent or periodic Estates General, 81 percent asked for the return of provincial estates everywhere, and 41 percent stated specifically that provincial estates should be empowered to levy taxes.[51] Such demands – the word grievances hardly does them justice – were also put forward by the third estate and to a lesser extent by the clergy. In the principal *bailliages* of Caen and Coutances, constituents from all three orders instructed their deputies to fight for a written constitution and periodic meetings of both the Estates General and the provincial estates of Normandy.[52]

[49] Hippeau, *Gouvernement de Normandie*, V, pp. 446–50, letter from the city of Caen to the king, 22 October 1788.

[50] Hippeau, *Gouvernement de Normandie*, V, pp. 462–6, letter from the assembly of Caen to the king, 25 October 1788.

[51] Chaussinand-Nogaret, *French Nobility*, pp. 150–6.

[52] *AP*, II, pp. 486–97, *cahiers* from Caen; and III, pp. 48–57, *cahiers* from Coutances. Local third estate *cahiers* also suggested periodic meetings of the Estates General; see, for example, Hippeau, *Gouvernement de Normandie*, VIII, pp. 87–9, *cahier* of the parish of Saint-Jean.

The emphasis on the periodicity of both provincial estates and the Estates General suggests the extent to which constituents were imagining a new (or, in the minds of some, newly restored) political order. At the heart of this constitutional order stood the principle that the monarchy needed the consent of estates to impose taxes, a demand made in 90 percent of noble *cahiers* and probably an equally high proportion of *cahiers* from the third estate. Such stipulations in favor of constitutional monarchy were almost always associated with the idea that the nation, as a collectivity of taxpayers, had the right to make law. The *cahier* of the nobility of the *bailliage* of Caen, for example, informed its deputies "that in a monarchical state, the nation consents to or refuses taxes; that [the nation] participates with the prince in the formation of laws, ... and that the monarchy, which is obliged to observe them, is alone charged with executive power."[53] For all three orders the right of the nation to "consent to or refuse taxes" was the essence of a constitutional government in which legislative power was to be divided from executive power.

Found in many philosophical and judicial tracts of the century, these ideas were easier to state than to implement, but the electorate of 1789 moved France a step closer to constitutional revolution by developing a way to ensure that its demands would be met. Constituents declared in their *cahiers* that future tax revenues would be withheld until their wishes for a written constitution and periodic estates were fulfilled. Asserting control over the flow of tax revenue was the easiest and most effective way of transferring legislative authority to estates, since tax money was the one thing that royal subjects had to negotiate with. How else could constituents and their deputies apply pressure to a monarchy that they believed had a long history of ignoring the will of the nation? As the third estate of Coutances told its deputies, "the first purpose of the deliberations of the Estates General is to secure firmly the constitution of the State by fundamental laws ..., and no taxes are to be voted before this constitution is settled and secured." Once the constitution was sanctioned, deputies could then go on to vote for taxes – but only taxes that would expire before the next meeting of the Estates General. "No taxes will be granted," the nobles of Coutances stated in accordance with the majority of noble *cahiers*, "but for the interval

[53] *AP*, II, p. 488.

between one session of the Estates General and the next, and all taxation will cease by right at that fixed time." Such an arrangement, their noble brothers in Caen added, would guard against "abuses of arbitrary power."[54]

The desire for estates to be called periodically was not new – deputies to the Estates General of 1614 and earlier had asked for the same thing – but in 1789 taxpayers, noble and commoner alike, backed their claims with a threat to cut off the flow of revenue on which the monarchy so heavily depended. With this threat constituents passed from soliciting fundamental political change to demanding it by asserting their authority as taxpayers.

And in this they were largely successful. Although most provinces never retrieved their own estates, the impulse to wrest the authority to tax from the crown, to create a strong representative national body, to separate legislative and executive power, and to rid France of the "arbitrary" practices of royal fiscal administration shaped many of the stirring events of the early revolution. On 17 June 1789, the very day the National Assembly was born, its members unanimously declared that royal taxes, "not having been consented by the nation, are all illegal and are consequently null in their creation and extension," though the Assembly would allow them to be collected temporarily.[55] In this single act the National Assembly assumed the power to destroy as well as create taxes, making itself a formidable rival of the crown. Two months later the Declaration of the Rights of Man declared that citizens have a right to consent to taxation (article 14), that state officials are accountable to society (article 15), and that "those who solicit, expedite, execute, or order the execution of arbitrary orders should be punished" (article 7). The constitution of 1791 further elaborated these principles by marking in greater detail the boundaries between executive and legislative power. Here was a liberal revolution sustained by a critical mass of more or less reform-minded clergymen, nobles, officeholders, bourgeois, and common people, all of whom had reasons

---

[54] *AP*, III, p. 488; and III, pp. 52 and 54. According to Chaussinand-Nogaret (*French Nobility*, p. 154), 68 percent of noble *cahiers* instructed deputies to grant taxes only until the next session of the Estates General. This method of assuring the periodicity of the estates appeared in local third estate *cahiers* as well. See *AP*, II, pp. 497–8, *cahier* of the merchants' guild of the city of Caen; and AD Calvados, 16B, nos. 8 bis and 267, *cahiers* of the parishes of Saint-Benin and Clinchamps.

[55] Bloch, *Contributions directes*, decree of 17 June 1789.

for wanting to control or at least restrain the fiscal-administrative machinery of the monarchy.

THE EMPOWERMENT OF THE THIRD ESTATE AND SOCIAL REVOLUTION

It is not all that difficult to imagine the French Revolution stopping there, as many conservative deputies wanted it to. Following the British model, French representative institutions would have gradually come to represent broader sections of society as the social movements of the nineteenth century applied pressure on the state. But the French Revolution was, in reality, much more than a constitutional or liberal revolution. It was also a social revolution that suppressed legal and fiscal privilege, abolished the nobility, established equality before the law, and instituted the widest suffrage Europe had ever witnessed. Given what we know about the politics of taxation under the Old Regime, it is much easier to explain the coming of a liberal revolution against "ministerial despotism" than an egalitarian revolution against the upper orders; debate over taxation was cast more often in terms of political liberty than political equality (even if fiscal equality was widely discussed). But the two revolutions, liberal and social, may have been more closely linked than we think, insofar as they both hinged on the relationship between taxation and representation.

This link is discernible if we examine the moment the social dimension of the Revolution first appeared, when the critical question arose of how the Estates General would vote. Would the body vote according to "the forms of 1614," that is by order as it had the last time it met, so allowing the first and second estates to dominate the proceedings, or would deputies vote by head, giving the third estate an equal voice? (The number of third estate deputies had been doubled by the royal decree of 27 December 1788 so that it equaled that of the clergy and nobility; vote by head, then, would invest the third estate with exactly equal representative power). This burning question, too hot for Louis XVI and his ministers to handle, shifted the public's attention from questions concerning the relationship between king and nation to those regarding the distribution of power within the nation itself. "The public debate has changed," observed the journalist Mallet du Pan in January 1789. "Now the king, despotism, the constitution are merely secondary: it is a war between the Third Estate and the two other orders," a war that the third estate and its allies would win.[56]

To win that war, to assert itself in the struggle over the Estates General, the third estate appropriated the fiscal logic of constitutional revolution and extended it to make claims for political equality. If the payment of taxes invested subjects with the status of citizenship and entitled them to some form of political participation, whether in estates or assemblies, then did not the third estate, which carried most of the kingdom's tax burden, deserve at least equal representation in the Estates General? In 1789, the third estate waved its impeccable record of taxpaying as if it were a first-class ticket to national politics.

To make the most of their bid for power, leaders of the third estate sharply differentiated their estate from the other two, characterizing it as the only estate untainted by privilege. Their most vocal spokesperson, the abbé Sieyès, was particularly adept at drawing Manichean distinctions between estates, although he saved his most severe criticism for the privileges attached to nobility rather than those enjoyed by his own order, the clergy. "It is not the difference of profession, wealth, or enlightenment which divides men," he wrote; "it is the difference of interest. And presently, there are only two interests, that of the privileged and that of the nonprivileged." The interest of the privileged was by definition corporate: "the moment ministers of state stamp the quality of privilege on a citizen, they open his soul to particular interests ... and he believes himself to be obliged first and foremost to the interests of his caste." Because the privileged individual could think only of advancing his cast's interest, Sieyès continued, the status of citizenship was "destroyed" in him; "he is incapable of public-mindedness and an enemy of common law." To give the two privileged orders the upper hand in the Estates General, therefore, was to turn the nation over to those who were least capable of acting on its behalf. Would it not be wiser to give a stronger voice to the third estate, which, composed of nonprivileged subjects, could recognize and act in the interest of common good?[57]

When Sieyès spoke of privilege he meant all forms of it: fiscal, legal, professional, seigneurial, and honorary. But many writers and caricaturists in 1789 focused on fiscal privilege, reinforcing the

[56] Quoted in Doyle, *Origins*, p. 147.
[57] Emmanuel-Joseph Sieyès, *Qu'est-ce que le Tiers Etat?* (1789; reprint, Paris, 1988), pp. 67, n. 1, and 177; Emmanuel-Joseph Sieyès, *Essai sur les privilèges* (n. p., 1788), pp. 2 and 16–17.

notion that the three estates were divided between two corrupt privileged orders and one worthy nonprivileged one. The Norman lawyer Thouret, undoubtedly an avid reader of Sieyès, suggested that the privileged were incapable of seeing past their personal financial interests: "the two privileged Orders have an interest apart from the general interest of the Nation; it is that of the extension or at least preservation of their pecuniary privileges."[58]

The fiscal privileges associated with the first two estates were described with great resentment. Listen to the hostility vented in this anonymous pamphlet:

> The clergy is too rich . . .: its exemptions are the cause of the surcharge on the people . . . The nobles that we call seigneurs have great possessions and great exemptions. These privileges make my blood boil! . . . Are not all citizens equally the subjects of the king? Do they not all equally have rights to his kindness? . . . All children should be treated by their father the same way.[59]

The same emotion was expressed in many images produced at the time of the meeting of the Estates General. In illustrations 6.1 and 6.2 the third estate, represented by a peasant, is bearing the (tax) burden of the clergy and the nobility. In the first image, "Let's hope that I will soon be done with this," a peasant carries a prelate and a noble on his back, and a scrap of paper in his pocket lists several taxes (*sel, tabac, taille, corvée, dîme*, and *milice*) that weighed heavily on the peasantry. And just in case the viewer fails to associate the figurative weight of taxation with the literal weight of the noble and prelate, the caption spells out the theme of the image by stating that it is an "allusion to taxes, the weight of which falls entirely on the people: not only do clergymen and nobles pay nothing, but they obtain the gifts and pensions that exhaust the State, and the unfortunate cultivator can hardly furnish his own subsistence." The image of weight was also evoked in "The past age," in which a peasant is crushed by a rock bearing the weight of the noble and clergyman standing on it. Inscribed in the rock are the words, *Taille, Impôts, et Corvées*, implying that the fiscal oppression of the third estate was the direct result of the tax privileges of the first two orders. No surprise that the two taxes named explicitly in this

---

[58] [J.-P. Thouret], *Mémoire présenté au roi par les avocats au parlement de Normandie, sur les Etats-généraux* (n. p., [1789]).

[59] Hippeau, *Gouvernement de Normandie*, VI, pp. 371–82, Réflexions toutes simples et toutes naturelles d'un Normand.

A FAUT ESPERER Q'EU JEU LA FINIRA BEN TOT.

l'auteur en Campagne Ap. 1789.

6.1   *Let's hope that I will soon be done with this*

Le temps passé les plus utiles étoient foulés aux pieds.

6.2   *The past age*

illustration were those from which the clergy and nobility were notoriously exempt.[60]

Other prints imagined the third estate winning the fight against privilege. The engraving "I knew our turn would come" (illustration 6.3) reverses the image in "Let's hope" as the peasant now rides on the back of the noble, who leans on a clergyman with a slip of paper in his pocket which reads "Land Tax," a tax that was expected to strike the church directly and make nobles pay more. The cleric also holds the scales of justice, which evenly weigh "Relief of the People" and "Equality and Liberty," all of which would come to France if the third estate were to triumph over privilege. The same theme of tax redistribution manifests itself in "The present time demands that each support the great Burden" (illustration 6.4), in which taxation is again depicted in the form of a heavy rock, but now the rock, bearing the inscription "Land Tax," is shouldered by members of all

---

[60] BN, Collection de Vinck, P 21193 and 21184. The latter print was engraved by Villeneuve and published in *Révolutions de Paris*.

6.3   *I knew our turn would come*

Le temps present veut que chacun suporte le grand Fardeau &c.

6.4   *The present time demands that each support the great Burden*

three orders, not the lone peasant. It is the clergymen in the middle who, with the assistance of the noble and peasant, bears the burden of the national debt.[61]

The most elaborate if least famous depiction of a successful fight against fiscal privilege is found in "He would like to knock down that which sustains them" (illustration 6.5), an image of conflict over taxation between the privileged orders on the one side, and Necker and the third estate on the other. It is a less harmonious picture than the previous two but it still promises victory. On the left Necker holds a scale weighed down with taxes and says to the king, "Sire, this is not just." In the middle of the print the privileged, represented by a high clergyman, a *parlementaire*, a high noble, and two lower nobles try to pull down a tree filled with members of the third estate and held by Necker, who tells the third estate not to fear. Behind the tree, the swords of two figures clash; one of them, representing the

---

[61]   BN, Collection de Vinck, P 21197 and 21186.

6.5 *He would like to knock down that which sustains them*

third estate (or perhaps Necker), says, "Oh you [tu] will pay," to which the other responds, "I am Noble." To the far right, Necker and Louis XVI help France to her feet.[62]

What is striking in all these images is the precision with which illustrators matched fiscal privilege with the upper two orders and the lack of privilege with the third estate, a representation of privilege that does not entirely conform to what we know was, by 1789, an extremely complicated fiscal system in which certain direct taxes reached upward to the nobility and certain exemptions spread down into the third estate. Certainly the leaders of the third estate – the deputies, writers, illustrators, and engravers who supported its cause – enjoyed direct tax privileges by virtue of offices they held or of residence in a privileged city or province; Sieyès himself benefited from the privileges of the church. However, in caricatures and pamphlets championing the third estate the complex realities of the distribution of privilege across the social hierarchy were simplified to draw a clear line of battle between the nonprivileged and the privileged. Small wonder that it was a peasant, a figure notably unsoiled by privilege, who was chosen to personify the third estate.

The failure to depict accurately the convolution of fiscal privilege in eighteenth-century society has many explanations. William Sewell attributes Sieyès' distortions to a "rhetoric of amnesia" that allowed the abbé to channel a general critique of privilege into an exclusive attack on the nobility. Sieyès unconsciously substituted the privileges of the nobility for all privileges in order to avoid the prickly question of those belonging to the clergy and the upper strata of the third estate. This same sort of amnesia is evident in these caricatures, which, unlike the writings of Sieyès, included the clergy in their attack on fiscal privilege but conveniently forgot about the privileges belonging to the third estate. Sewell ultimately explains such "collective amnesia" by arguing that the utilitarian consciousness of the Enlightenment distanced the French from the corporate society to which they belonged. "The more the language of utility dominated public discourse, the more the realities of a society of privileged estates and bodies disappeared from view."[63]

In the case of fiscal privilege in particular, however, other explanations are possible. First, many members of the third estate, who had only a vague idea of how the fiscal system as a whole actually

---

[62] BN, Collection de Vinck, P 19600. [63] Sewell, *Rhetoric*, p. 143.

functioned, could easily imagine nobles not paying any taxes at all. The *cahier* of the parish of Saint-Pair, for example, complained that military nobles "pay the *capitation* only on their income from their position, protecting their property from any tax."[64] In reality, military nobles did pay the *capitation* on their property as well as on their position – the amount they paid as officers was deducted from their residential assessments – but the Byzantine, secret nature of royal administration made it impossible for anyone to know for sure what nobles or anyone else paid in the end. In an age when rumors about taxation could not be verified by a public record, members of the third estate were apt to minimize the degree to which the *capitation* and the *vingtième* struck the nobility.

Secondly, leaders of the third estate may have deliberately distorted representations of privilege to bolster their political position. Given the extent and visibility of direct tax privileges enjoyed by the upper third estate, I find this explanation more plausible than that of a passive amnesia. Advocates for the third estate understood that any successful bid for power on the basis of tax payments would have to be predicated on a conception of society that smoothed over the rough edges of a complex system of privilege and exaggerated fiscal differences between their estate and the two above them. It was not as if such exaggerations ran directly counter to the actual incidence of taxation; after all, as I demonstrated in chapter 2, even the lion's share of universal taxes (let alone the *taille*) fell on commoners. The undeniable fact that the third estate constituted the bulk of the nation's taxpayers made it easier to depict the politically useful image of an unprivileged third estate carrying the entire burden.

The reaction of the nobility and clergy to this image of privilege is revealing. A minority of nobles and clergymen proudly clung to their tax exemptions. In an attempt to shift criticism back onto the monarchy, the noble author of *Le seul intérêt de tous, par un gentilhomme de Normandie* emphasized that the "abuses" of the current regime and the "hardship" suffered by citizens were caused by an expanding royal administration, not by the privileged orders. The fiscal privileges of the nobility, he insisted, were perfectly defensible since "every gentlemen is a soldier by birth" and, as such, merited

---

[64] Quoted in Armand Brette, "La noblesse et ses privilèges pécuniaires en 1789," *La Révolution Française* 51 (August 1906), p. 118.

exemption from the *taille*. Toustain de Richebourg, a Norman who had participated in the *vingtième* revolt of 1772, claimed in his pamphlet *Aux Français, par un ami des trois ordres* that "ten noble families picked at random provide incomparably more services and military sacrifices than the same number of third estate families." Hence fiscal privilege was entirely legitimate. This notion also showed up in noble electoral assemblies such as that of the *bailliage* of Caen, in which one nobleman told his peers that tax privileges were valid because "the French nobility has always sacrificed its life and its fortune for [the monarchy's] preservation and expansion."[65]

But, on the whole, most nobles and clergymen joined the assault on fiscal privilege by dramatically renouncing their exemptions, a step that implicitly validated the third estate's dictum that "He is not a citizen who does not pay taxes."[66] From the fall of 1788 to the spring of 1789, group by group, the privileged declared publicly that they were abandoning their fiscal privileges. Deputies to the first Assembly of Notables had hinted that they were prepared to renounce their tax privileges in exchange for a greater degree of political participation and constitutional safeguards for their property, but the first formal renunciation came from the dukes and peers of the kingdom in a published letter to the king in December 1788. The same month the magistrates of the parlement of Paris followed suit in a nearly unanimous vote, and soon such acts of renunciation were repeated by nobles and clergy in the provinces as they prepared their *cahiers* for the Estates General. In the *bailliage* of Caen, the nobility informed the third estate that, "[i]n order to cement the union of the three orders, the order of the Nobility of the *bailliage* of Caen has deliberated and decided to bear Taxes in perfect equality, in proportion to the wealth of each, claiming to reserve only the sacred Rights of property and the distinctions necessary in a monarchy."[67] The nobility was offering to pay equal taxes if certain "distinctions" were maintained, one of which, it was understood, was deliberating and voting by order in the Estates General. The clergy of Caen also renounced its privileges: "wishing to maintain and cement the union so desirable among the three orders, the order

[65] Hippeau, *Gouvernement de Normandie*, VI, pp. 402–17, 206–10, and 257–63.
[66] Quotation from the *cahiers* of the third estate of Nemours, as cited in John Markoff, *The Abolition of Feudalism: Peasants, Lords, and Legislators in the French Revolution* (University Park, PA, 1996), p. 142.
[67] AD Calvados, 16 B 5, Voeu émis par la noblesse du bailliage de Caen, 20 mars 1789.

of the Clergy consents henceforth to Taxes, in whatever form, on all property." Dominated by lower members of common birth, the clergy of Caen was sympathetic to the aspirations of the third estate and made no claims regarding vote by order.[68]

As both Gruder and Chaussinand-Nogaret stress, some of these renunciations reflected true patriotic sentiment and liberalism. De Montchalon, president of the second order of the *bailliage* of Coutances, said that, moved by the "example of patriotism" set by the peers of the kingdom and "struck with the great truth that the first title in the State is that of citizen," he and his fellow nobles "have made the honorable agreement to renounce all pecuniary privilege and to consent to an equal distribution of taxes." In Rouen, one of the few *bailliages* in which nobles refused to abandon their privileges, the second order was sharply divided. The comte de Blagny urged his fellow nobles that taxation "should never separate their status as gentlemen from their status as French citizens," but his words failed to convince the majority: 160 voted against renunciation, 106 voted for it. Taking their cause to the *Journal de Normandie*, the "106" publicly implored the majority to change its opinion: "Reunite us then and say: for my *patrie*, for my king, through love, I abandon."[69]

The rhetoric in pamphlets also suggests that some nobles were sincerely thrilled to shed their privileges and assume the status of citizen. One gentleman-pamphleteer, paraphrasing Sieyès, stated that privilege isolated the nobility from the "general interest":

Nobles of Normandy! Let us begin by showing our sentiments in a clear and precise way to all our fellow citizens; ... Let us make it known to them that we are bound to the nation, to the *patrie*, by the same ties and same interests as them. ... This truth will be all the better demonstrated by making them an offer to share the burden of taxes with complete equality.[70]

Not all acts of renunciation were motivated by such liberal or patriotic passions, however. To balance Revisionism's tendency to emphasize the progressiveness of the nobility, it is worth pointing out that some nobles shrewdly calculated that surrendering the battle of

---

[68] AD Calvados, 16 B 2, Voeu émis par le clergé du bailliage de Caen, 20 mars 1789.
[69] Hippeau, *Gouvernement de Normandie*, VI, p. lxiii, Montchalon to the general assembly of Coutances; and VI, p. 86, declaration of the comte de Blagny, 22 April 1789. The quotation of the "106" is from Chaline, *Godart de Belbeuf*, p. 491.
[70] *Mon Opinion Motivée, ou le voeu d'un gentilhomme normand à la noblesse normand* (n. p., n. d.).

privilege could help them win the war over the vote in the Estates General. Believing that the legislative authority derived from voting by order far outweighed the advantages of their pecuniary privileges, and not wanting what remained of these privileges to burden them in the race for representative power, deputies of the first two estates pitched them overboard. As early as 30 October 1788 the comte d'Osseville, a noblemen from Carentan, hatched a plan to dupe the third estate into relinquishing its demands for equal representation in the Estates General. "An idea came to me," he wrote, informing the duc d'Harcourt of his ploy, "to inspire the order of the nobility to offer the third its privileges in matters of taxation at the opening of the Estates General. By this means, we would disarm the third, whom we must pay off a bit, and the clergy, defeated by this act, will become taxpayers like other citizens."[71] By graciously yielding its privileges and disarming the third, the nobility could expect to win the crucial issue of the vote. D'Osseville did not worry about the loss of tax privileges; nobles were paying taxes anyway, he pointed out. What mattered was that the monarchical state be constrained, and that the nobility command a powerful voice in the body that was to constrain it.

No matter their motivations, the clergy and the nobility came to the Estates General in May 1789 with the intention of formally yielding their tax privileges. On 19 May, in a meeting of the first estate, the abbé Coster, archbishop of Verdun, moved that the clergy renounce its fiscal privileges. Overcoming the predictable opposition of many bishops, the motion was pushed through by a large majority of lower clergy: 156 members voted in favor of the motion; 46 voted for the motion provided that the clergy delay informing the third estate of its deliberation; and 26 voted against it outright.[72] This was a major turning point in the history of the French church, which more than any other corporate body in the kingdom had escaped royal taxation.

The nobility followed the clergy's example but agreed to give up its fiscal privileges only on the strict condition that the verification of the credentials of deputies would proceed by order, a provision that, if accepted by the third estate, would lay the groundwork for voting by order. To some noble deputies even this was too large a conces-

[71] Hippeau, *Gouvernement de Normandie*, VI, pp. 5–7, letter of 30 October 1788.
[72] AN, C 26, no. 177, deliberations of the clergy, 19 and 20 May 1789; Thibault and Coster, *Les séances des députés du clergé aux Etats-généraux* (Paris, 1917), pp. 95–6.

sion, but the majority supported it: 143 deputies voted in favor of yielding their fiscal privileges to the third estate; 52 voted for the resolution with various stipulations; 28 abstained; and 12 voted against it.[73] In the end, the nobles renounced their privileges as the vast majority (88.5 percent) of their *cahiers* had instructed.[74]

Despite the drama with which the two first orders shed themselves of their tax privileges, the third estate was singularly unimpressed. Although it welcomed the news of the renunciations, it did not, as conservative nobles hoped, lose sight of the key issue at hand; it refused to budge from the demand that the estates vote by head in common session. After the nobility hardened its own demand for separate orders, the third estate, together with a handful of clergymen who defected from their order, broke the deadlock by declaring itself the National Assembly on 17 June 1789. This single act, sanctioned by the king after much indecision, marked a critical turning point in the Revolution. On the one hand, it reflected a pivotal moment when constitutional and social revolution intersected. The very first act of the National Assembly was to seize legislative control over royal taxation, a move that allowed the third estate both to place constitutional limits on the fiscal authority of the crown and to flex its newly found representative muscle. On the other hand, the events of 17 June 1789 transformed the practice of representation itself. As Ran Halévi has suggested, representation under the Old Regime was predicated on that regime's particularism, according to which representatives were by custom bound strictly to the "imperative mandates" of their constituents. On 17 June, however, third estate deputies broke their mandates by declaring themselves representatives of the entire nation. No longer mere mouthpieces of their particular constituency, the deputies claimed to be the voice of an indivisible national will.[75]

Although historians have been more interested in the consequences of this transformation in political representation, some going so far as to read in it the ultimate collapse of individual rights

[73] AN, C 26, no. 178, deliberation of the nobility, 22 and 23 May 1789; *Procès-verbal des séances de la chambre de l'ordre de la noblesse aux Etats-généraux* (Versailles, 1789), pp. 67–89 and 102–3. Some nobles claimed that their mandates prevented them from deciding tax matters before a constitution was written, while others moved that certain exemptions be kept in place for poor nobles.

[74] Chaussinand-Nogaret, *French Nobility*, p. 153.

[75] Ran Halévi, "La révolution constituante: les ambiguités politiques" in *The Political Culture of the French Revolution*, ed. Colin Lucas (Oxford, 1988), pp. 69–96.

and the coming of the Terror, it is worth pausing to consider the ideological roots of the third estate's seizure of power. Why was the third unwilling to compromise with the nobility? Why did it not settle for fiscal equality, a remarkable concession on the part of the first two orders, and withdraw its bid for equal representative power?

In part because the third estate understood fiscal privilege to be wholly unjustified in the first place. The "gift" of fiscal equality was no gift at all; it was a right and, as such, deserved no reciprocal gesture of goodwill. Anticipating the renunciations of the privileged, Sieyès stated, "Yes, you will pay, not by generosity, but by justice; not because you want to, but because you should."[76] The clergy's justification for tax privileges – that its wealth was not its own but belonged to God and could be used only for the purposes of the spiritual mission of the church – had been under siege for decades, since Machault attempted to impose the *vingtième* on church lands, so it is hardly surprising that, by 1789, the third estate and many nobles expected the crown to tap the rich resource of ecclesiastical property. Voltaire's campaign had borne fruit.

Historians have been less quick to point out that the nobility's justification for privilege – that it was exempt from certain direct taxes because it contributed to the crown in the form of personal military service – was also wearing thin. It is difficult to determine exactly when the perception emerged that noble military service no longer warranted tax privileges. As chapter 5 demonstrated, many of the most popular writings on taxation since Louis XIV denied the legitimacy of the nobility's tax privileges on the abstract grounds of political economy or of a contract between ruler and ruled, but by the 1770s and 1780s philosophes, writers, and statesmen were suggesting explicitly that the justification of military service no longer carried weight. Mercier, Turgot, Malesherbes, and Condorcet all cast doubt on the reasoning behind noble tax privileges and stressed that common soldiers contributed as much service to the crown as did the nobility of the sword.[77]

---

[76] Sieyès, *Tiers Etat*, pp. 97–8. Similarly, when the notables renounced their privileges, Morellet replied: "In asking that taxes be shared with the most complete equality, it is not a favor the Third is soliciting, it is a justice that should be done ... Above all, they should not do this as an act of generosity, since no Order of citizens whatever has the right to be generous towards a people." Quoted in Jean Egret, *The French Prerevolution 1787–1788*, trans. Wesley D. Camp (Chicago, 1977), p. 202.

[77] [Louis-Sébastien Mercier], *The Year 2440* (in Darnton, *Best-Sellers*, p. 334); Louis-Sébastien

One of the most thorough critiques of privilege based on military service was written in 1787 by a tax assessor from Aix named Pascalis. According to Pascalis, warfare and the army had changed completely since the age when tax privileges were granted to the nobility. Gone was the *ban et arrière-ban*, the feudal arrangement by which the king called his faithful lords and their vassals to war. (On the wane under Louis XIII, the *ban et arrière-ban* was officially suppressed by Louis XIV during the War of the League of Augsburg, the same war in which the king began to tax the nobility through the *capitation*). Gone too was the "old chivalry" in which knights adorned themselves with lances, armor, and liveries. The army was now organized on the basis of "modern discipline": "nothing resembles less a present-day army unit," the author observed, "than a Corps of fief-holders armed and equipped for war." In the "modern" army it was obvious that the nobility no longer served the crown personally, and Pascalis insisted that nobles stop saying that they did: "cease, cease, therefore, speaking to us of a service that you no longer render." And cease, Pascalis continued, speaking of the privileges supposedly justified by such a service. If the nobility's claim of personal service was false, so too was its right to tax exemption.[78]

In 1789 leaders of the third estate adopted similar arguments to deflate the magnanimity of the noble's abandonment of their privileges. In his *Requête au Roi* one attorney from Cotentin stated that, before the reign of Charles VII, nobles did indeed perform military services, "that is, they provided soldiers and the costs of war," but after Charles VII "nobles no longer made war at their own expense. They became hired soldiers like the People" and were therefore no longer entitled to tax privileges.[79] A much angrier Norman author wrote:

Mercier, *Le Tableau de Paris* (reprint, Paris, 1982), p. 98; Gerald Cavanaugh, "Turgot: The Rejection of Enlightened Despotism," *FHS* 6 (Spring 1969), p. 58, n. 98; Badinter, *Remontrances de Malesherbes*, p. 235; and Keith Baker, *Condorcet: From Natural Philosophy to Social Mathematics* (Chicago, 1975), p. 255.

[78] Pascalis, *Mémoire sur la contribution des trois ordres aux charges publiques et communes de la province* (Aix, 1787). This pamphlet elicited great interest, to judge from the diary of Parisian bookseller Siméon-Prosper Hardy: "we owe [Pascalis] our gratitude for having so well shown, so solidly established, so energetically defended the rights of the Third Estate, the interests of the poor, which have been sacrificed up until now to the vanity of the Great, the nobles, the clergy; at the same time [the third estate] was made prey to the cupidity, the voracity even, of the vampires of Taxation and Finance." Quoted in Egret, *Prerevolution*, p. 209.

[79] *Requête au Roi, par un avocat de l'ordre du Tiers … de Cotentin* (n. p., 1789).

You [the nobility] risk your fortune and your life for the defense of the *patrie*? Does not the third estate do as much? Count, of three thousand fighters, how many are you? Of 100,000 dead, how many do you lose? To what do you owe your loftiness, your glory, if not to the worth of the soldier? Is this not often the advice given by old veterans? You bring pride and splendor into our camps; your haughty manner discourages soldiers and causes desertions. Was this how the leaders of the Franks conducted themselves? Were not the Franks who marched under them their companions? . . . When it comes time to contribute to public taxes, do not look to pass them on to the third estate.[80]

That it did not accept justifications for privilege only partially explains the third estate's indifference to the acts of renunciation. The third's resolve was also rooted in the belief that it fully deserved the political power it demanded. It mattered little that the nobility was willing to pay its fair share of taxes if the order was intent upon keeping an unfair share of constitutional power. Again, Sieyès' voice is testimony to the determination of the third estate. The abbé understood that renunciations of privilege were designed intention-ally to "distract" the third estate from "the necessity that it be *something* in the Estates General."[81] But why did members of the third estate believe so deeply that they had the right to be "some-thing" in the Estates General in the first place?

To answer this question we must take a closer look at the logic by which the third estate claimed that it, as the estate that paid the nation's taxes, was entitled to equal representation. To some extent, the third estate's line of reasoning – and its confidence in that line of reasoning – was rooted in the debate over taxation that had raged in France for three decades, as magistrates, physiocrats, and ministers of state each formulated a logic of representation that the third estate would extend and modify for its own purposes.

As chapter 4 demonstrated, privileged taxpayers in various parle-ments had struggled since 1760 against increases in universal taxes by advancing the principle that they – as taxpayers – were entitled to representation in provincial estates and Estates General. Parlemen-tary rhetoric had already turned taxpayers into citizens, even if magistrates had no intention of empowering the third estate (as the Paris parlement's ruling of 23 September 1788 in favor of the "forms

[80] Hippeau, *Gouvernement de Normandie*, VI, pp. 297–307, Le Tiers-Etat de Normandie éclairé, ou ses droits justifiés.
[81] Sieyès, *Tiers État*, pp. 93–4.

of 1614" made apparent). Clearly, the magistrates did not grasp the full implications of their language of resistance.

Physiocratic political economists also associated taxation with representation, building a more explicit connection between the two by conceiving of provincial assemblies in which one's political voice was based not on membership in one of the three estates but on one's taxable wealth. The physiocrats were not trying to empower the third estate either, although the notion that the basis of representation should shift from that of corporate identity to social utility became a key idea in 1789.

Finally, the crown helped construct the logic by which the third estate would radicalize the constitutional revolution by creating provincial assemblies in which the number of third estate deputies equaled those of the clergy and nobility and in which votes were to be counted by head. Members of the third estate never forgot that the crown had designed the assemblies to their benefit, as one author emphasized when he spoke of the bodies as "the first aid offered to the third estate in its former state of ruin."[82] Although Necker refrained from explicitly linking the third estate's enhanced presence in the provincial assemblies to its right as an estate of taxpayers to have equal power, he went on to affirm the connection between the distribution of taxation and the proportionality of deputies when he decided to double the third estate at the Estates General. The *Résultat du conseil* of 27 December 1788, admittedly, did not say why the third estate deserved to be doubled, but it did declare that the geographical spread of representatives was to be based on the population and tax contributions of each *bailliage*.[83] If the crown was distributing geographical representation according to taxation, there was no reason to believe it was not doing the same with regard to social representation. Barentin, the keeper of the seals, came close to saying as much when, in the speech that opened the Estates General, he recognized "the nearly universal cry" for the doubling of the third estate "on which the principal burden of taxation weighs."[84] But royal ministers, no less than physiocrats and *parlementaires*, were wary of endowing the third estate with too much power, for although Necker doubled the third estate, neither he nor any other minister was willing to take the next step of imposing the vote by head.

[82] De Servan, *Réflexions sur la réformation des états provinciaux* (n. p., 1789), p. 15.
[83] *AP*, I, p. 498.
[84] *Réimpression de L'Ancien Moniteur* (Paris, 1847), I, séance of 5 May 1789.

This the third estate would have to do itself. To complete the process of transplanting a system of equal representation, residing in weak provincial assemblies, into the Estates General, an institution with real sovereignty, leaders of the third estate developed mathematical formulas that directly related its tax burden to its political rights. The result was a modern arithmetic of representation based on the two variables of taxation and population. (One could add economic productivity as a third variable but it was not as widely used as the other two). Arguing for an equal proportion of third estate to first and second estate deputies at the upcoming Estates General, one third estate deputy to the Assembly of Notables said, "if numbers are considered, . . . the proportion would be more than ten to one; if tax contributions, more than double; if degree of utility, are not commerce, the arts, and agriculture in the hands of this Order?"[85] The ubiquitous Sieyès also played with the "principles according to which one can determine the proportion of representatives." Having implied that the privileged orders did not deserve a place in the Estates General since they were not part of the nation, Sieyès went on to make a separate argument that used population and tax contributions as coefficients of representative power. Estimating that the third estate paid more than half the taxes and constituted nearly the entire population, he asked the reader if this order was demanding too much when it claimed an equal voice in the Estates General.[86]

Experimenting with this arithmetic of political representation, it should be emphasized, was not restricted to philosophers or deputies. In towns and villages across Normandy (and other provinces) members of the third estate put this logic to use as they sought to empower their order in provincial estates and the Estates General. Let us reason along with the mayor of Granville, a small town in the generality of Caen, who suggested that the size and structure of the impending provincial estates of Normandy should correspond to the demographic and fiscal composition of the province:

Considering all the importance that the Third Estate has acquired since its emancipation from feudal tyranny, considering its great population in Normandy, and the enormous sum of taxes that it is charged to acquit based on its industry, it is only fair that the king grant this province a number of freely elected representatives proportionate to its political influence.

---

[85] Quoted in Egret, *Prerevolution*, p. 199.   [86] Sieyès, *Tiers Etat*, pp. 71–5.

To calculate the exact number of representatives to which the estates of Normandy was entitled, the mayor took as his model the newly established estates of Dauphiné, a most "equitable" body because it had a doubled third estate and voted by head. Since Normandy was three times more populous than Dauphiné, and paid five times more taxes, he argued that the estates of Normandy should be four times the size, with 96 members of the clergy, 192 members of the nobility, and 288 members of the third estate. The coefficient four reflected the average of the coefficients for population and tax contribution. For this local mayor, as for Sieyès, representation had become calculable according to a mathematical formula that would yield a strong third estate in both provincial and national estates.[87]

The municipality of Cherbourg employed a similar argument in its petition to the king on the formation of the Estates General. Less mathematically precise, this petition discarded the variable of population to speak only of taxes. "If the Third supports the greatest share of public taxes," it stated, "it is fair, Sire, that in the Assembly where the French people will decide the great sacrifices necessary to pay off the national debt, the two first orders, which have always evaded taxes by virtue of their influence and privileges, be sufficiently counterbalanced by the third."[88]

The principle that representation of the three orders should be scaled to tax contributions was even more rigorously laid out in pamphlets. The author of *Le Tiers-Etat de Normandie, ou ses droits justifiés*, the very same pamphlet that lashed out against the haughtiness of noble army officers, demonstrated exactly why the third estate was entitled to power. The clergy and the nobility, the author admitted, possessed more property than the third estate, but representation should be based not on property, but on tax payments. (Here the pamphleteer parted ways with the more conservative physiocrats who, holding on to their economic theory, refused to separate tax payments from the value of landed property). Using statistics from Necker's books, the pamphlet showed that the clergy, in proportion to its wealth, paid fifteen times less than the third

---

[87] Hippeau, *Gouvernement de Normandie*, V, pp. 438–41, deliberations of the hôtel de ville of Granville, 17 October 1788.

[88] Hippeau, *Gouvernement de Normandie*, VI, pp. 202–6, letter from the municipal officials of Cherbourg to the king, 22 December 1788. The vicomte Le Veneur made the same argument: "this division of the three orders may cause the most frightening injustices since it would make it possible for the first two orders to impose the burden of taxation on the third, keeping that order enslaved." Hippeau, *Gouvernement de Normandie*, VI, p. 125.

estate, and the nobility just as little. The author then asserted his political rights in the following terms:

I contribute in taxes double, triple, quadruple, quintuple what you [the clergy and the nobility] do ...; therefore, my deputies should be in proportion to my contribution ... To sum up, of the 585 million livres of total tax revenue, the clergy supports only 11 million, the nobility almost as much; It is the third estate that pays the rest. And they want to limit the deputies of the third estate to the Estates General![89]

For this and other pamphleteers and for municipal officers throughout and beyond Normandy it was but a short step from recognizing the political rights of taxpayers in general to adding up the rights that belonged to the third estate in particular. Representation had become calculable, and the weight of taxation was a key coefficient in this new political arithmetic.

As deputies from the third estate traveled to Versailles, they carried this logic with them. When the orders met, and the clergy and nobility renounced their privileges, the gesture only reinforced the conviction of the third estate. Did not the renunciations imply that the privileged were interested in becoming full taxpaying citizens and that the third estate, whose credentials in the area of taxation were second to none, were indeed better prepared to represent the nation? Only with great confidence in this fiscal logic of political entitlement could the deputies of the third estate and their allies, on 17 June 1789, seize control of royal taxation, assume responsibility for the debt, and declare themselves the true representatives of the French nation. Though it manifested itself in a political arena, this was the first decisive step toward social revolution.

REVOLUTION AND THE "ACTIVE" CITIZEN

Technically, the story of the origins of the Revolution stops there and that of its course begins. This chapter concludes by considering how the bond between taxation and representation that helped produce the two revolutions of 1789 became enshrined in the civic order of the early Revolution only to be eclipsed in 1792–3 by a more radical philosophy of popular sovereignty.

---

[89] Hippeau, *Gouvernement de Normandie*, VI, pp. 297–307, Le Tiers-Etat de Normandie éclairé, ou ses droits justifiés.

From 1789 to 1792 the theoretical shift in sovereignty from the crown to the nation was put into practice as so-called "active citizens," granted the coveted right to vote in elections, replaced the office-holders and administrators of the Old Regime with a slew of elected officials. Isser Woloch has enumerated the many positions that came to depend on election: "mayors, municipal councils, urban sectionary officials, national guard officers, district administrative councils and syndics, departmental administrative councils and syndics, justices of the peace, civil court judges, departmental criminal court judges, public prosecutors, members of the national *Tribunal de Cassation*, parish priests, bishops, and of course legislative deputies."[90] The length of this list suggests the extent to which the authority of the revolutionary state inhered in its citizenry.

It also suggests the extent to which that authority came to rest on the nation's taxpayers, since at every tier of representative government participation was defined in part by tax contributions. At the base of the electoral pyramid stood a large pool of active citizens who, unlike their "passive" counterparts, were eligible to vote in municipal assemblies in which they elected both local officials (mayors, justices of the peace, national guard officers) and "electors" who would go on to attend district assemblies and vote for higher regional officials and national representatives. According to the decree of 14 December 1789, to become an active citizen one had to be a French male of more than 25 years of age who had lived in the same canton for at least a year, was not a domestic, and paid direct taxes in the amount equivalent to at least three days' wages. Such conditions for active citizenship yielded the widest suffrage in Europe at the time, enfranchising at least 4,300,000 French men, or 61.5 percent of men over 25 years of age. In certain areas such as the district of Versailles, Patrice Gueniffey has found, the suffrage was even broader, extending to over 80 percent of all male direct taxpayers; 5 percent were excluded for being domestics and 15 percent for tax payments that were too low.[91]

Tighter restrictions applied to the two levels of participation above municipal elections. Those elected to office or to the position

---

[90] Isser Woloch, *The New Regime: Transformations of the French Civic Order, 1789–1820s* (New York, 1994), p. 63.
[91] Patrice Gueniffey, *Le nombre et la raison: la Révolution française et les élections* (Paris, 1993), pp. 89–92, 97, and 100.

of elector had to show proof of direct tax payments in the amount of at least ten days' wages, a stipulation that approximately 2,700,000 men, or 38.6 percent of adult males, could meet. And at the crest of the new system of representative government, where the deputy to the National Assembly sat, a special tax qualification called the *marc d'argent* required representatives to pay direct taxes in the amount of at least 53 livres, a feat that scarcely more than 1 percent of the entire population could achieve.

Given the emphasis that the representative system placed on taxation, it is hardly surprising that the electoral lists of the early revolution were often nothing but tax rolls inherited from the Old Regime. When a would-be active citizen presented himself to local election officials, they simply checked his status by consulting various direct tax rolls: rolls for the *taille, capitation, vingtième,* withholding taxes, and other local land taxes – "generally all taxes other than those paid on the consumption of goods."[92] That Old Regime direct tax rolls were used as electoral lists reveals two important aspects of revolutionary active citizenship. First, citizenship had nothing to do with indirect taxes, which, unlike direct taxes, were utterly condemned by the *cahiers* of 1789 and became a common target of tax revolts throughout the Revolution. Discredited by abstract physiocratic theory but also associated in the popular imagination with corruption and profiteering, indirect taxes provided no sound foundation for the construction of citizenship.[93] Direct taxes, alternatively, were considered legitimate, if in desperate need of reform, and were understood to form the backbone of the new constitutional government. As the debate over taxation since mid-century had already made clear, the levy of direct taxes had special political implications.

The second observation about the use of direct tax rolls for the verification of citizenship has to do with the spread of universal taxes in the last century of the Old Regime. To peg citizenship to direct taxation would have been unthinkable without the *capitation* and the *vingtième,* taxes that guaranteed privileged property-owners a place in the new polity before the 1791 tax reforms were introduced. How

[92] Quoted in Gueniffey, *Nombre,* p. 86.
[93] Markoff, *Abolition of Feudalism,* pp. 100–9 and 233–40; and Bryant Ragan, "Rural Political Activism and Fiscal Equality in the Revolutionary Somme," in *Re-creating Authority in Revolutionary France,* ed. Bryant Ragan and Elizabeth Williams (New Brunswick, NJ, 1992), pp. 36–56.

absurd the very idea of the citizen-taxpayer would have seemed to most elites had they not already been paying direct taxes and demanding, as taxpayers, a participatory role in government for some time.

In 1791 the relationship between taxation and representation was further reinforced by the unveiling of both a written constitution and a new system of taxation. The ill-fated constitution of 1791 not only declared that the distribution of seats in the national legislature would be based on territory, population, and taxation, meaning that of the 745 seats available 249 would be apportioned to 83 departments following their direct tax contributions, but it also reaffirmed the distinction between active and passive citizenship, raising the legitimacy of tax qualifications to new constitutional heights. The *marc d'argent*, it is true, was abolished but the qualifications for second-tier electors were tightened considerably to restrict the number of active citizens eligible for office or for voting in the most important elections.

In tandem with the constitution came the final destruction of the Old Regime tax system, still largely intact despite promises made on the night of 4 August 1789, and the creation of three new direct taxes: the *contribution foncière* (a land tax modeled on the *vingtième*), the *contribution mobilière* (a tax on non-landed wealth), and the *patente* (a fee imposed on businesses). These taxes were presented to the public as the heart of a new social contract between taxpayer and state, the essence of which was denoted by a change in the word for tax. Whereas the old words *impôt* and *imposition* were associated with the "barbarous nomenclature" of the Old Regime, the committee of taxation explained, the new word for tax, *contribution*, "better expresses the share that each citizen must provide to help pay for the necessary costs of society." And where the old vocabulary indicated the "arbitrary power" by which taxation was imposed, the new one evoked the principle that taxes were created by the "general will." In a somewhat circular logic that betrays the irreconcilability of Rousseauian popular sovereignty with a tax-based system of representation, the Assembly also declared that, if the general will created the new taxes, the new taxes would also create citizens whose wills would produce the general will in the future. "Your political existence," proclaimed the deputies, "stems from the fact that each citizen, by the share that he gives in proportion to his income, obtains a useful share of all public services – services paid for by the like contributions that all fellow citizens have pooled with his."[94]

From 1789 to 1791 there were several justifications for making the "political existence" of French citizens dependent on taxation. Sieyès, who originated the idea of a distinction between active and passive citizenship, characterized active citizens as "shareholders in the great social enterprise," a metaphor that suggests that those with a financial stake in government were entitled to full political participation. Thus he proposed the creation of a voluntary tribute of 3 livres and 12 livres, respectively, for active citizens and electors, to be paid in addition to regular taxes. It was the voluntary aspect of the tribute, which implied a certain amount of devotion to the public good, that mattered most to Sieyès.[95] But after the popular violence of the summer and fall of 1789, and in particular that of the October Days, deputies in the National Assembly began to contend that taxpayers of some substance, alone, should be allowed to make decisions about the national debt, taxes, and poor relief that supposedly affected only them. Turning Sieyès' argument into an instrument of social exclusion, conservative deputies used fiscal criteria for active citizenship to bar the poorest classes from political participation. If the Revolution had promised to empower the taxpayer, many deputies were quick to define exactly which tax-payers – those with enough property to have a stake in government – would actually exercise the right to vote.[96]

Two additional arguments were advanced in defense of tax qualifications: that the indigent were too dependent on social super-iors and too susceptible to influence and "corruption" to be trusted with the vote; and that a screen was necessary to sift the talented from the untalented and the qualified from the unqualified, a mechanism of particular importance for the selection of second-tier electors, government officials, and national deputies, all of whom needed the skills, integrity, and composure to run the country. In making these arguments, moderate and conservative deputies suc-ceeded in using the connection between taxation and representation

[94] *AP*, XVIII, pp. 158–9, report of the committee of taxation; Bloch, *Contributions directes*, pp. 263–4, Address to the French, 24 June 1791.

[95] William Sewell, "Le citoyen/la citoyenne: Activity, Passivity, and the Revolutionary Concept of Citizenship" in *The Political Culture of the French Revolution*, ed. Colin Lucas (Oxford, 1988), pp. 105–24; and Guineffey, *Nombre*, p. 58.

[96] See, for example, the speeches of Dupont de Nemours and de Cazalès (*AP*, IX, pp. 479 and 598).

not only to shore up constitutional revolution but to place social limits on it as well.[97]

From the very beginning the left contested the logic by which political rights were distributed according to tax contributions, even though that logic had initially helped the third estate assert itself. The most lively debate in the National Assembly occurred over the *marc d'argent*, which its adversaries said set up an "aristocracy of the rich," not of the talented or virtuous, and stifled the will of electors who might want to elect deputies who could not meet the stringent tax criteria. It was in the context of this debate that Roederer made the stunning remark that "Rousseau, if he were still alive, would never be able to seat himself among you."[98] (Apparently, Rousseau paid less than 53 livres a year in direct taxes). But the more interesting discussion unfolded over the issue of the tax qualification for active citizenship. Debated three times – in October of 1789, when the decree establishing the criteria for active citizenship was first adopted, in January and February 1790, when deputies claimed that certain municipalities were deliberately setting the value of a day's work at excessively high levels so as to limit the number of poorer active citizens, and in April and May 1791, after the committee on the constitution proposed to exclude passive citizens from the national guard and deny them the right of petition – the question of a tax qualification for the right to vote elicited from the left a potent rhetoric of popular sovereignty. Drawing from the radical Rousseauian elements of the Declaration of the Rights of Man, deputies on the left claimed that all male citizens without distinction shared in the sovereignty of the nation and possessed the right to vote. Did not the Declaration state that men are born and remain free and equal in rights, and that all citizens have the right to take part in the formation of law? For Grégoire it sufficed that voters in primary assemblies simply be good citizens with sound judgment and a French heart.[99]

Underpinning the argument against legislated tax qualifications for active citizenship was the principle that active citizenship for adult males was an eternal right, founded on nature, reason, and justice, that could not be modified by legislative will. The most articulate advocate of this idea was Robespierre, who led the charge

---

[97] See, for example, the remarks of Démeunier in *AP,* IX, p. 479.
[98] *AP,* X, p. 415.   [99] *AP,* IX, p. 479.

against all attempts to limit the suffrage. "The right of the citizen is a natural right which every member of a political society should enjoy," he argued before the National Assembly; "for this he does not need the intervention of the legislator."[100] Legislating a right that already existed in nature was not only redundant but dangerous, especially if legislators defined that right according to a flimsy and ever-changing tax system. Condorcet noted the ironies of a political order in which rights would rise and fall with taxes like ships on the tide: "Is it not rather amusing," he wrote, "that liberty should diminish with taxes, and that the better we will be governed [and the lower the tax burden], the less we will be free?"[101] Robespierre further illustrated the capriciousness of pegging rights to taxes by citing the example of Artois, where many direct taxes had long been converted into indirect taxes, so reducing the number of active citizens. Did this mean that upon leaving Artois and settling elsewhere a passive citizen could pass into the privileged ranks of active citizens? How arbitrary such a political order seemed:

But how was one able to imagine making the sacred rights of men depend on the mobility of systems of finance, on variations, on the patchwork that makes up different parts of the same State? ... And what does it matter, indeed, that 20 or 30 sols [a day's wage] compose the elements in the calculations that decide my political existence? Do not those who earn only 19 sols have the same rights? And are the eternal principles of justice and reason, on which these rights are founded, able to bend themselves to the regulations of a variable and arbitrary tariff?

"It is not at all taxation which makes us citizens," Robespierre proclaimed.[102]

In the summer of 1792, after a series of defeats on the matter since October 1789, Robespierre's call for universal male suffrage was finally answered. Severing a tie between taxation and representation that had helped make the Revolution possible but that was now being used to restrict its expansion, the Paris section of Théatre-Français, under Danton's leadership, threw its doors open to passive citizens in July. Several other sections, ignoring the legal distinction between active and passive citizenship, followed the example of the radicals in Théatre-Français and created a movement in Paris for universal male suffrage. The constitution of 1793, bowing before the influence of such radicals, was drafted in the same spirit: it made no

---

[100] *AP*, XIX, p. 771.   [101] Quoted in Gueniffey, *Nombre*, p. 86.
[102] *AP*, XI, pp. 318 and 320–5.

mention of active or passive citizenship and extended the right to vote and be elected to all male citizens. And of the distribution of seats in the legislature, the constitution stated emphatically that "population is the only basis for national representation."[103]

It is here that the debate over taxation and the political order that began under the Old Regime truly ends, and the experiment with popular sovereignty begins. The National Convention of 1795 would of course rewrite the constitution yet again, reinserting the direct tax requirement for citizenship, a requirement that would become all the more restrictive during and after the Directory as indirect taxes were reintroduced and direct taxes fell. But the struggle between advocates of liberal and popular forms of suffrage would become one of the Revolution's legacies to the nineteenth century, until universal male suffrage was permanently established under the Third Republic.

[103] Jacques Godechot, *Les Constitutions de la France depuis 1789* (Paris, 1970), p. 84.

Conclusion: liberté, égalité, fiscalité

As debate over the origins of the French Revolution becomes ever more sophisticated, taking up cultural and intellectual questions in addition to social and economic ones, it is sometimes easy to forget that what made the Revolution possible was that royal subjects, including a crucial number of vocal elites, believed that they were being oppressed. Such forgetfulness is not completely accidental. In his path-breaking book, written two decades ago, François Furet redirected revolutionary historiography away from Marxian social and economic interpretations toward intellectual and cultural ones by insisting that "we stop regarding revolutionary consciousness as a more or less 'natural' result of oppression and discontent."[1] Given that Furet goes on in the next sentence to call revolutionary consciousness a "strange offspring of *philosophie*," I take this statement to mean that the development of new philosophical ideas, rather than oppression and discontent, was responsible for the formation of revolutionary consciousness. That Furet attempted to locate the origins of the Revolution in philosophical societies and in the Rousseauian notion of an indivisible general will confirms this interpretation.

But does it make sense to bifurcate the world of ideas and that of experience in such a stark manner? Cannot an attitude like "discontent" or a feeling of "oppression" be both culturally constructed – as part of a story people tell themselves about the world – and rooted in unarticulated social experience? In taking up the problem of taxation and political culture this study presumes that it can. It is entirely legitimate to consider discontent and oppression as origins of the Revolution as long as we are careful not to reduce either to pure social "reality" or cultural "construction."

---

[1] Furet, *Interpreting*, p. 27.

311

This approach is particularly useful in coming to terms with the role played by elites in the transformation of political culture at the end of the Old Regime. Why privileged property-owners, whether noble or bourgeois, capitalist or non-capitalist, adopted anti-absolutist political ideology and joined together to bury "despotism" is a perplexing question, especially since recent work on absolutism emphasizes the ways in which the so-called "absolutist" state went out of its way to cater to elites. Indeed, contrary to older interpretations of absolutism which suggest that Louis XIV tamed the nobility by means of his majestic presence and firm political resolve, historians today stress the degree to which the Sun King secured the stability of the absolutist state by co-opting and collaborating with the privileged. The characteristically insightful words of William Beik on this subject are worth quoting at length:

> Absolutism was the political manifestation of a system of domination protecting the interests of a privileged class of officers and landed lords ... In the seventeenth century, ... the social reputation which assured domination was guaranteed by seigneurial authority, *plus* economic advantage, *plus* privileged status by the crown. It was still possible to maintain social prominence solely through ancestral title or seigneurial possessions, but it was increasingly difficult. Now dominance on the land was also measured by special status with respect to laws, taxes, and enforcement mechanisms and by control of a share of the "official" power of command. In other words, social position was increasingly dependent on privileges created and defended by the state and on offices and titles which were defined in relation to the state.[2]

This was the absolutist system that Louis XIV perfected, a world in which the glue of privilege held together an alliance between the crown and a land- and office-holding elite. If the basic outlines of this regime of privilege persisted through the eighteenth century, as they appear to have done, the question of elite resistance to the state and participation in the Revolution becomes all the more mystifying. Why would elites challenge a monarchy that was reinforcing their social position?

This study suggests one possible answer by focusing on long-term changes in state fiscality. As European states engaged each other in a fiscal race for military power, the eighteenth-century French monarchy introduced new forms of taxation that disregarded long-established customs of privilege and were based, in principle, on

---

[2] Beik, *Absolutism*, pp. 335–6.

fiscal equality. Although universal taxes were not nearly effective enough to break the "symbiotic relationship" between privilege and the state that defined so much of the Old Regime – this was never their intention – they were nonetheless heavy enough to disturb that relationship and alarm those who were benefiting from it.[3] Noble landowners and other privileged groups in the *pays d'élections*, who had always enjoyed and were still enjoying substantial exemptions from the *taille*, now confronted the *capitation* and the *dixième/vingtième*, the latter of which made particularly significant inroads into their income. Provinces that were *pays d'états* were better protected from new modes of taxation, but even there the privileged experienced an increase in their overall direct tax burden as universal taxes rose. Further, the *capitation* and the *dixième* cut into the pensions, *gages*, and salaries that the crown distributed to all kinds of royal subjects from the haughtiest courtier to the most demure provincial postmaster. And although the clergy of France seems to have escaped royal taxation altogether, it was compelled to increase its gifts to the crown in order to dispel threats of a full tax levy. When we take into account the ability to pay, privileged taxpayers were not heavily burdened compared with their nonprivileged counterparts, who had to pay the new taxes in addition to the *taille*, but it remains true that the privileged in the eighteenth century began – for the first time – to pay regular direct taxes against which they possessed no special privileges. From 1695 to 1789, as elites maintained privileges with respect to older direct taxes, universal taxes struck them with greater and greater force, creating an entirely new social being: the privileged taxpayer.

Most disturbing to that oxymoronic creature, the privileged taxpayer, was the way in which universal taxes were levied. The *capitation* and the *vingtième* ushered in a set of administrative procedures that fundamentally changed the way the state intervened in society. Deliberately avoiding the communal and judicial administration associated with the *taille*, the crown entrusted jurisdiction of universal taxes to provincial intendants who, funding ever larger staffs with revenue from the *capitation*, investigated the wealth of taxpayers (with startling thoroughness from 1772 to 1782), drafted the tax rolls, oversaw collection, and, most significantly, handled appeals, an area of administration wholly reserved to the courts with

---

[3] The phrase "symbiotic relationship" is from Bien, "System of State Credit," p. 92.

respect to the *taille*. Barred from contesting their *vingtième* or *capitation* in court, taxpayers were forced instead to submit petitions to royal administrators who, while likely to make concessions to payers of the *capitation*, were rarely moved to negotiate over the *vingtième*. The transfer of authority over tax administration to intendants and their staffs created a field of direct contact between royal agents and individual elites, dramatically heightening the presence of royal administration in the lives of privileged royal subjects.

That presence and the resulting birth of the privileged taxpayer provoked tremendous conflict and debate, the study of which, I hope to have shown, illuminates important changes in French political culture. It is commonly asserted that from the seventeenth to the eighteenth century the dominant types of revolt changed from widespread popular tax uprisings to more restricted subsistence and anti-seigneurial riots.[4] Yet this and other recent studies demonstrate that, at the level of both popular and elite politics, taxation remained a highly contentious issue down to the Revolution. At the popular level, anti-tax and subsistence "incidents" were equally frequent in the eighteenth century, whereas anti-seigneurial violence was far behind, if on the rise.[5] Further, at the level of high politics and literary debate, taxation was a far more provocative problem in the eighteenth century than it had ever been, even in the *grand siècle* when taxation soared. Part of the reason that taxation became so contentious at the higher levels of society was because, although taxation as a whole did not substantially increase in real terms over the eighteenth century, direct taxation was changing form and spreading up the social hierarchy. As new taxes began to reach the privileged, the structure of contestation and the content of debate transformed significantly.

The structure and language of contestation over universal taxes was apparent in three overlapping arenas: administrative, institutional, and literary. In the administrative sphere taxpayers swamped the offices of intendants (and higher authorities) with petitions for reductions in assessments, supporting their claims with a rhetoric of justice. In the case of the *vingtième*, justice was simply a

---

[4] Emmanuel Le Roy Ladurie, "Révoltes et contestations rurales en France de 1675 à 1788," *Annales* 29 (1974), pp. 6–22; Chartier, *Cultural Origins*, pp. 141–5.

[5] Guy Lemarchand, "Troubles populaires au XVIIIe siècle et conscience de classe: une préface à la Révolution française," *Annales historiques de la Révolution française* 279 (1990), pp. 32–48; Markoff, *Abolition of Feudalism*, pp. 264–9.

matter of proving that one's income was not as high as administrators believed, a feat that few taxpayers could accomplish. In the
case of the *capitation*, appeals for justice were much richer. Nobles of
the sword complained ever so politely that it was not fair to demand
an "exorbitant" *capitation* from those who already served the king
personally in his army. Pitting an older and, in their eyes, more
legitimate form of contributing to the state against a new treacherous
one, they asked intendants and finance ministers to do justice by
lifting the burden of taxation in recognition of personal and familial
loyalty and sacrifice. Officers of justice mentioned service too, but
their petitions against the *capitation* reveal a higher degree of resentment of royal administration, especially after 1769 when, their
assessments having jumped, they had to submit to the humiliating
annual routine of supplicating commissioned administrators. Even
petitioners who expressed no explicit hostility to royal administrators
indicted them indirectly by claiming that other taxpayers were being
treated more favorably: princes complained that other princes were
better cared for; brothers looked jealously at one another; officers
compared themselves with their peers. The steady flow of appeals
for distributive justice suggest that many privileged taxpayers
believed that the crown was spreading the *capitation* unfairly.
Although rhetoric from the administrative sphere struck a tone of
ingratiation, the persistent drone for "justice" betrays a distinct
frustration with royal fiscal administration.

The frustration embedded in petitions was aired publicly and
given ideological force by such regional institutions as provincial
estates and parlements. The parlement of Rouen provides a particularly clear example of the way in which sovereign courts
publicized anti-absolutist language in an effort to shield the provinces from universal taxes. Although the parlement cooperated
with royal authority on many fronts, it began, in 1760, when the
capitation and *vingtième* were doubled and tripled, to develop a potent
critique of royal fiscal administration. Converting rhetoric they had
used in earlier disputes over Jansenism, the magistrates of Rouen
claimed that "despotism," once present in the "arbitrary" power of
the episcopate, was now at hand in the "arbitrary" levy of taxes.
The increases in universal taxes from the Seven Years War on, the
forced registrations that made those increases possible, the increasingly thorough practice of verifying personal declarations of wealth
submitted by property-owners liable to the *vingtième*, and the admin-

istrative as opposed to judicial character of the process of lodging appeals against assessments all bore witness to the "despotic" nature of the monarchy's ever more intrusive fiscal-administrative apparatus.

Not limiting itself to a discourse of condemnation, the parlement also elaborated principles of liberty, national sovereignty, and citizenship to suggest the possibility of a return to a legitimate form of rule. If sometimes these principles amounted to little more than an appeal for a tempered monarchy in which the king was to be lightly restrained by courts of law, at other times they were arranged to make a much more subversive call for a system of government by estates that could more effectively bind the will of the monarchy to the nation. Although they had been highly reluctant in the sixteenth and seventeenth centuries to call for estates, since estates were known to rival the jurisdiction of law courts, magistrates responded to increases in universal taxes after 1760 by demanding the installation of these bodies, which they believed would provide greater leverage against the fiscal claims of the crown. More revealing than the invocations of estates themselves was the language in which parlements such as that of Rouen couched their appeals. The semantic range of the word "liberty," which traditionally meant the free exercise of privileges, extended to include the right of the nation to consent to taxation, while that of "citizen" referred not to a mere royal subject, bourgeois, or Catholic entitled to receive the sacraments, but to an individual who taxed himself by way of his deputies' consent. These statements may have been made in the course of narrow jurisdictional disputes with the crown but their words alluded to larger constitutional problems.

And such words, it is worth recalling, were deliberately set down in print before the public, a tactic developed during Jansenist disputes and now applied to fiscal contestation. Although the impact of parlementary anti-tax rhetoric on public opinion is hard to measure, the dissemination of such rhetoric during the Seven Years War certainly weakened France's ability to borrow from a European "public" of creditors, while at home it contributed to the deterioration of Louis XV's image. There was a more enduring legacy, however. The language of remonstrances and other printed material emanating from the court between 1760 and 1788 helped to build a delicate alliance between nobles of the sword and those of the robe and, more generally, between privileged and nonprivileged taxpayers, all of whom came to agree that the fiscal machinery of the royal state was veering out of control and needed to be constrained. By 1772 sections of the vague "public" to which the parlement of Rouen had long appealed rose up in the absence of the court to join in revolt against the *vingtième* and to demand the return of estates. As military nobles, former *parlementaires*, and city officials drafted their own "remonstrances," it became clear that there was indeed a social analog (and a dangerously active one at that) to the "public" to which the court had spoken.

The problem of taxation also drew attention from writers who, increasingly after mid-century, published their own criticisms of the kingdom and imagined the possibility of a different political and social order. An examination of the most popular books on finance and taxation suggests that readers were exposed to entirely new realms of thought. During the second half of the reign of Louis XIV, Boisguilbert evoked the possibility of an economy that could run of its own volition and improve itself, were it not subject to the jolting interventions of the monarchy. If the crown could subordinate its will to natural economic law by providing tax relief for poor consumers and freeing the grain trade, France could become a prosperous kingdom. Less oriented toward the economy but equally compelling was the work of Vauban, who explained to his readers that, because all members of society benefited from royal protection, all should contribute equally (that is, in proportion to their ability to pay) to financing that protection, regardless of claims to fiscal privilege. Neither Bosiguilbert nor Vauban, it should be added, paid much attention to the society of orders. Rather, anticipating much of the political and economic thought of the Enlightenment, they described a society of individual taxpayers, each of whom, whether rich or poor, producer or consumer, officer or civilian, counted as a basic building block of a unified economic and political system.

The most popular book of the century devoted exclusively to taxation appeared in 1760, the *Théorie de l'impôt* by Mirabeau. This best-seller combined physiocratic and republican ideas to argue that France's fiscal troubles were essentially reflections of a deeper "moral" crisis in which the will of the people was alienated from that of the crown. The marquis urged the king not only to follow the physiocratic program of replacing all taxes with a single direct tax on land, but as well to rally his subjects to the throne by appealing to their sense of duty and citizenship rather than bludgeoning them with bureaucratic coercion. In the 1780s, the fabulously popular Necker reexamined this idea of citizenship, but replaced Mirabeau's focus on kingship with an emphasis on national patriotism and the publicity of the state. If state institutions were turned into public bodies, citizens would come to the support of their nation and the problem of taxation would be resolved. Although all of these writers aimed to strengthen the state, their work may well have undermined the foundations of a monarchy that, although changing, could not possibly keep pace with the imagination and reformist impulses of the Enlightenment.

The patterns of conflict and the themes of debate in the administrative, institutional, and literary spheres were not inherently revolutionary, but in the 1780s the issue of taxation took a decisive turn. Recognizing the need for some form of representation, the crown drew from the literature of political economy and created provincial assemblies that were designed to mend the frayed ties between property-owning taxpayers and the state. It soon became obvious, however, that the assemblies had no sovereign power with which to contest the monarchy, so that, after a final attempt to raise taxes on the privileged, calls rang out for a more thoroughgoing reform in which genuine constitutional power – the right to consent to taxation – would be granted to provincial estates and the Estates General. This was a thirty-year-old demand but it was now seconded by the Assembly of Notables and the parlement of Paris after decades of dispute had generated a consensus that liberty, citizenship, and property could be protected only if taxpayers were treated as citizens who possessed a share of sovereignty and taxed themselves. When Louis XVI at last agreed to convoke the Estates General (and to restore provincial estates as well), the constitutional revolution was under way.

The logic that tied taxation to citizenship and representation did more than justify constitutional revolution, however. It also opened the way for social revolution by providing the third estate and its allies with a conceptual tool for the seizure of power. Radicalizing the constitutional revolution already in progress, leaders of the third estate reasoned that if taxpayers were indeed citizens who deserved some form of political representation, as *parlementaires* as well as the political economists and finance ministers who recommended the establishment of provincial assemblies all claimed, then the third estate, which characterized itself as the estate that supported most of the nation's taxes, was entitled to at least equal representation in the Estates General. Inserting its impeccable record of taxpaying into mathematical formulas for political representation, the third estate easily justified the revolutionary assertion that it deserved a strong voice in any national representative body. At the end of the Old Regime and early in the Revolution, liberal political principle, as much as Rousseauian radicalism, cleared a path for social revolution.

TOCQUEVILLE AND HABERMAS RECONSIDERED

The process by which taxation became politicized and invested with revolutionary meaning, involving realignments between monarchy and social hierarchy and shifts in ideology, has important implications for our understanding of Tocqueville and Habermas. And since historians of eighteenth-century France have in the past decade relied heavily on the conceptual frameworks of both thinkers, it is worth elucidating a few of these implications.

The story of universal taxes presented in this book, while in accord with a Tocquevillian state-centered approach, casts doubt on two of Tocqueville's main axioms: that the rise of the monarchy from the fifteenth century down to the Revolution was predicated on the constant proliferation of social privilege; and that equality under the Old Regime rose at the direct expense of liberty. There is obviously a good deal of truth to the first axiom. We know that the monarchy used privilege for fiscal purposes as it distributed tax exemptions, social status, and financial monopolies to corps of venal office-holders, the clergy, provincial estates, municipalities, and guilds, all in return for credit at low rates of interest. But Tocqueville believed that the crown also made use of privilege for non-financial reasons. Privilege, that is social privilege and not the kind of corporate political prerogatives that royal subjects often associated with liberty, was essential to the growth of the state, he argued, because it undermined the power of the nobility by transforming it from a vigorous ruling order into an impotent caste of individuals. Privilege comforted nobles and other potentially powerful subjects in their exile from rule, making them content to stand by and watch royal administration expand into a colossus. Tocqueville's understanding of the political processes surrounding the growth of privilege explains why an historian like himself, who is known for emphasizing the strength of the central state to the point of exaggeration, never so much as entertained the idea that this same state was capable of attacking or even eroding privilege. To attack privilege would have been to lay siege to the very foundations of royal power.

Yet this is exactly what the crown did, albeit in an attenuated fashion, when it established universal taxes in the eighteenth century. By superimposing the *capitation* and *dixième/vingtième* on the *taille*, the monarchy ate away at the fiscal immunities of elites and disturbed the state-sponsored system of privilege that pervaded Old Regime society. Over the course of the eighteenth century, particularly from the 1760s onwards, it became clear that the monarchy was capable of limiting fiscal privilege and taxing elites in ways that were previously unthinkable let alone feasible. Apparently, privilege could undergo contraction as well as expansion.

If Tocqueville's highly deterministic account of absolutism fails to take seriously the possibility of a partial contraction in fiscal privilege at the end of the Old Regime, it is no wonder that he also downplayed resistance to that contraction. In fact, he downplayed all resistance to the state and muted all forms of political contestation in order to stress the silent inevitability with which administrative centralization progressed. Tocqueville's tendency to foreground the rise of the state by marginalizing political conflict makes his designation as figurehead of the new political history of eighteenth-century France, much of which emphasizes contestation, an ironic one, but that tendency stems from an axiom deeply embedded in his work: that liberty and equality were antithetical historical forces. As royal administrators increasingly intervened in society, Tocqueville argued, they severed the natural, communal ties of obligation that had held subjects together and had legitimized the inequalities among them, replacing those ties with much more restrictive bonds between individuals and the state. The consequence was a decline in liberty and a rise in the spirit if not the fact of equality, both of which, so his argument goes, led directly to revolution. While the decline in liberty stifled the will and undermined the institutional wherewithal to check the advancement of state centralization, the desire for equality, fanned by abstract political literature, drove revolutionaries to invest still more power in an already formidable central state so that they could sweep away the debris of privilege that had been accumulating relentlessly for centuries.

But was equality the inverse of liberty in the eighteenth century?

Again, there is some truth to this axiom. It is undeniable that the growth of the administrative state, although not as inevitable or all-encompassing as Tocqueville suggests, and the writings of intellectuals, if not always as abstract and naïve as he would have us believe, did encourage a spirit of egalitarianism. Not only did the crown establish new taxes on the privileged, so inviting the nonprivileged to imagine the possibility of fiscal equality and thus making the privileges that remained all the more unbearable;[6] it also amplified the voice of the third estate when it created provincial assemblies with a doubled third estate and vote by head. Further, writers in the embryonic field of political economy cultivated egalitarian sentiment when many of them denied the legitimacy of tax privileges and treated individuals simply as economic producers and consumers without reference to their status in the socio-legal corporate order.

But the politics of taxation suggests that demands for equality also grew out of intense conflict and a deep concern for political liberty. Contestation in the administrative sphere, admittedly, did not always take the form of forceful opposition – and in this respect my evidence squares with that of Tocqueville, whose research was based on administrative documents – but resistance to the state took a more confrontational tone among the sovereign courts. As the monarchy laid heavier fiscal demands on the privileged, courts of law and privileged taxpayers vociferously defended themselves in the name of "liberty," a word that, hardly on the wane in the eighteenth century, came to evoke such weighty notions as respect for law, the rights of the nation, citizenship, and political participation. Instead of declining, the pursuit of liberty flourished to such an extent that it helped to lay the groundwork for political equality. Consider the claims for political equality advanced by leaders of the third estate in 1789. In asserting that the third estate, as an order of taxpayers, was entitled to equal political power, members of the third estate were drawing not only from the examples of the provincial assemblies or from the encouraging words of a statesman such as Necker but also, in an implicit way, from the language of parlementary opposition, which had ceaselessly invoked a relationship between tax-paying and sovereignty. Those who spoke for the third estate in 1789, in other words, were interested not so much in destroying liberty as in

---

[6] In 1714 the mere existence of the *dixième* emboldened parish assessors in Caen to attempt (unsuccessfully) to levy the *taille* on the privileged as well as on the nonprivileged. AN, G-7 219, nos. 19 and 22.

extending and democratizing it (even if efforts at democratization went on to subvert individual rights later in the Revolution). Thus Tocqueville may have been right to underscore the relationship between French state formation and the rise of democracy, but that relationship was not always as direct as he insisted. Between administrative centralization and democratic equality there was a crucial middle step: resistance to the state. It was reactions to a changing state, as much as the state itself, that helped to produce the language and ultimately the act of revolution.[7]

The importance of resistance to the state did not escape Habermas. The opening chapters of *The Structural Transformation of the Public Sphere* explain clearly how the emergence of a public sphere in Europe resulted from friction between a bureaucratizing mercantilist state and an ascendant capitalist bourgeoisie irritated by that state's intrusions. Yet whereas Habermas applies this hypothesis with only minor adjustments to the "model case" of Britain, he jettisons it altogether when he turns to France. Finding in the French case neither a strong bourgeoisie, nor a free press, nor a connection between the mercantilism of the late seventeenth century and a public sphere that by his reckoning was born a century later, he adopts a strictly Kantian perspective and emphasizes the autonomous development of a republic of letters, which served as a benign, mildly political precursor to the fully politicized public sphere of the Revolution. The precociousness and influence of the French republic of letters are not in question here but Habermas' exclusive emphasis on them is. Taxation is one issue among many that demonstrates that there was more to the making of the public sphere than the spread of printed matter, the development of new kinds of sociability, and changes in reading practices. There was also constitutional conflict. Constitutional strife generated more than its share of

---

[7] Although it contradicted his main thesis, Tocqueville was more willing to entertain this interpretation than was his foremost interpreter, Furet, who went to great lengths to emphasize the Rousseauian as opposed to the liberal dimension of the Revolution. In the eleventh chapter of the second part of *The Old Régime and the French Revolution*, Tocqueville admitted that opposition to the state enjoyed a healthy resonance under the Old Regime (compared with his own day) and that "it would be absurd to suppose that such virile virtues [of the men who made the Revolution] could have sprung from a soil on which all liberty had been extinguished." In the same spirit, he relegated the following assertion to his notes where it would do little harm to his overall argument: the meaning of democracy "is intimately related to the idea of political liberty. To call 'democratic' a government in which political liberty is absent is to utter an obvious absurdity." Quoted in Furet, *Interpreting*, p. 147.

publicity and produced a highly politicized public sphere well before the Revolution. Literary figures both great and small, it is true, sustained the publicity surrounding constitutional conflict as they wrote on behalf of a particular party or in an effort to find a way to minimize conflict altogether, but the principal source of such conflict in the case examined here lay in a Lockeian struggle over property and over competing notions of the proper balance of power between taxpayers and the monarchy.

In other words, we need not follow Habermas' lead in abandoning his own theoretical insight that "official interventions into the privatized household" helped to trigger the coming of a critical public sphere.[8] If we recognize that the "carrier" of the public was not the bourgeoisie alone, and that the state's intervention in the economy was not exclusively mercantilist in nature, we can begin to develop a more accurate interpretation of the role played by state–society interaction in the formation of the public sphere. As the example of taxation reveals, royal administrators did use new bureaucratic procedures to investigate the ownership of property and to tax income that for centuries privileged subjects had regarded as, in the words of Saint-Simon, "the secret of their families."[9] Further, magistrates and other privileged subjects responded to this intrusion by publicizing the notion that despotism was present in the fiscal and administrative apparatus of the monarchy and that taxpayers possessed political rights, thereby initiating a debate that would eventually become revolutionary. In this respect, new forms of direct taxation, rather than the economic regulations and customs duties that Habermas associates with mercantilism, provoked an oppositional public sphere; and, in addition to writers, it was courts of law and a wider circle of privileged and nonprivileged taxpayers, not a capitalist bourgeoisie, that led and composed the public.

As the crown began to appropriate the property of the privileged in a direct and routine fashion, it became the target of new kinds of public criticism that would open the door to revolutionary demands. The eighteenth-century monarchy was, in the end, strong enough to make significant changes in its fiscal and administrative structure and so alter the way elites experienced the state, but it was far too weak to contain the contestation or to direct the debate that such changes set in motion.

[8] Habermas, *Public Sphere*, p. 24. [9] Quoted in Bonney, "Le secret," p. 385.

Select bibliography

Archival sources

ARCHIVES NATIONALES, PARIS

Series AD IX. Collection Rondonneau
Cartons 81–82. Royal decrees on the *capitation*.
Carton 390a. *Compte rendu par le commission intermédiaire provinciale de Basse Normandie.*
Carton 470. Royal decrees on the *taille*.
Cartons 400–401. Royal decrees on the *dixième*.
Cartons 491–492. Royal decrees on the *vingtième*.

Series AP. Archives Privés
Carton 144 AP 101, 114, 132. Memoirs of d'Ormesson, intendant of finance.

Series C. Assemblées Nationales
Carton 26. Minutes of the assemblies of the clergy and nobility, 1789.

Series D VI. Comité des Finances
Cartons 2, 9, 12, 14–19, 24, 38. Correspondence and memoirs of the committee. Petitions against taxes, 1790–1.

Series F-4. Ministère de l'Intérieur: Comptabilité Générale
Cartons 1076–1116, 1940, 1945, 2022. Budgets and records of the Royal Treasury.

Series F-5 I. Ministère de l'Intérieur: Comptabilité Départementale
Cartons 1–3. Provincial and departmental finances, 1788–90.

Series G-7. Contrôle Général des Finances
Cartons 215–219. Correspondence between ministers of finance and intendants of Caen, 1695–1715.

Cartons 1132–1137. Correspondence, memoirs, and accounts on the *capitation*, 1695–1718.

Cartons 1138–1140. Correspondence, memoirs, and accounts on the *dixième*, 1710–17.

Carton 1849. Minutes of the royal council under the Regency.

Cartons 1909–1914. Tax contracts of receivers-general, 1761–3.

Series H-1. Pays d'Etats. Pays d'Elections. Intendances
Carton 29. Estates of Artois.

Carton 141, 173. Estates of Burgundy. Petitions of parlement of Dijon.

Cartons 345–347, 527, 550–551. Estates of Brittany.

Cartons 748 (284), 870–871, 878, 898, 1093. Estates of Languedoc.

Carton 1231. Estates of Provence.

Carton 1463. Correspondence between Terray and intendants, 1771–3. Disputes over the *vingtième* in Caen.

Series K. Monuments Historiques
Cartons 879–887, 900. Ministerial memoirs on finance. Remonstrances of clergy, courts, and estates.

Series KK. Registres
Carton 355. Royal accounts, 1662–99.

Series O-1. Maison du Roi
Cartons 656–657, 724, 729. Taxes on royal pensions. Petitions from pensioners.

Series P. Chambres des Comptes et Comptabilité
Cartons 5074, 5105–5105 bis, 5133, 5169–5170 bis, 5195, 5224, 5239–5262, 5263–5269, 5270–5271, 5295–5298 bis, 5392–5392 bis, 5416–5417 bis, 5442, 5557, 5591, 5688, 5743 bis–5744, 5764–5765, 5838. *Capitation* rolls. *Etat des finances. Etats au vrai* for the *capitation* and *vingtième*, 1760s-80s.

Series R-2. Papiers des Princes
Carton 501. Tax disputes involving the vicomte de Turenne.

Series Z-1P. Chambre Ecclésiastique des Décimes
Carton 10. *Capitation* roll for the diocese of Paris, 1696.

BIBLIOTHÈQUE NATIONALE, PARIS

Cabinet des Estampes
Collection de Vinck. Engravings, watercolors, and prints on Necker and the events of 1789.

Collection Joly de Fleury

1444. Correspondence between royal ministers and intendants. Memoirs on finance and administration.

1448–1449. Correspondence. Memoirs. Figures on the *vingtième* for the kingdom.

Manuscrits Français

6877. Royal response to remonstrances against the *vingtième*.

8852. Letter from Pontchartrain to intendants on the establishment of the *capitation*.

11152. Memoirs on finances.

11162. Accounts of the *vingtième*.

11906. Disputes over the *capitation*.

14080. *Capitation de la Cour*.

14083. Memoirs on taxation.

16524. Papers of Harlay, president of the parlement of Paris.

17430. Letter from Pontchartrain to Harlay on the establishment of the *capitation*.

21812. Memoir on provincial intendancies by d'Aube.

Nouvelles Acquisitions Françaises

22104. Remonstrances and letters of the parlement of Rouen to Louis XVI.

ARCHIVES DÉPARTEMENTALES DU CALVADOS

Series 16 B. Preparations for the Estates General

Cartons EIII, 1475. Letters of convocation.

Cartons 2 and 5. Assemblies of the clergy and nobility of Caen.

Cartons 8 bis, 9, 16, 33, 267, 269, 299, 453. Local *cahiers de doléances*.

Series C. Provincial Administration before 1790

Cartons 4387–4398, 4517–4523, 6516. Correspondence on the *taille* and taxation.

Cartons 4524–4535, 4701–4712 bis. Correspondence, memoirs, and accounts on the *capitation*.

Cartons 4536–4674. *Capitation* rolls for nobles, officers of justice, *privilégiés*, employees, bourgeois, and guilds.

Cartons 4675–4700, 6517. Petitions against the *capitation*. Investigations into delinquent taxpayers.

Carton 4713. Correspondence on the *dixième*.

Cartons 5284–5292. Petitions against the *dixième*.

Cartons 5293–5295, 5940–5954, 6518. Correspondence on the *vingtième*.

Cartons 5342, 5395, 5396, 5594, 5631, 5635, 5722. Rolls of the *vingtième*.

Cartons 5899–5911. Petitions against the *vingtième*.

Cartons 5964–5967. Accounts of the *vingtième*.

Carton 6044. Constraints against recalcitrant taxpayers.
Cartons 7611–7618. Records of the provincial assembly of Lower Normandy.
Cartons 7619–7630. Records of the commission of Lower Normandy.
Cartons 8088–8089. The provincial assembly and taxes for 1788 and 1789.
Cartons 8090–8142. The provincial assembly and the *capitation*.
Cartons 8158–8178. The provincial assembly and the *vingtième*.
Cartons 9388, 9389, 9869. Registers of the *bureaux du contrôle*.

ARCHIVES DÉPARTEMENTALES DE LA SEINE-MARITIME

Series 1B. Records of the Parlement of Rouen
Cartons 230, 253, 261, 268, 276, 278. Secret registers of the parlement.
Cartons 5532. Documents on the censorship of parlementary publications.
Cartons 5445. Assorted parlementary remonstrances.

Series C. Provincial Administration before 1790
Cartons 481–486. Accounts of the *vingtième* for the generality of Rouen.

BIBLIOTHÉQUE MUNICIPALE DE ROUEN

Montbret Collection
P 11904 and 12295. Assorted parlementary remonstrances.

Published primary sources

Annonces, affiches, et avis divers de la Haute et Basse Normandie. Rouen, 1762–85.
Argenson, René-Louis, marquis d'. *Considérations sur le gouvernement ancien et présent de la France*. Amsterdam, 1764.
[Augéard, Jacques-Mathieu]. *Lettre d'un bon François*. N. p., 1781.
Bachaumont, Louis Petit de. *Mémoires secrets pour servir à l'histoire de la république des lettres en France*, 36 vols. London, 1777–89.
Badinter, Elisabeth, ed. *Les "remontrances" de Malesherbes, 1771–1775*. Paris, 1985.
Barbier, Edmond. *Chronique de la régence et du règne de Louis XV, 1718–1763*, 8 vols. Paris, 1857–8.
[Baudeau]. *Lettres d'un citoyen à un magistrat, sur les vingtièmes et les autres impôts*. Amsterdam, 1768.
Baudry, F., ed. *Mémoires de Nicolas-Joseph Foucault*. Paris, 1862.
Bloch, Camille, ed. *Les contributions directes; instructions, receuil de textes et notes*. Paris, 1915.
 ed. *Procès-verbaux du comité des finances de l'Assemblée Constituante*. Rennes, 1922.
Boisguilbert, Pierre Le Pesant de. *Détail de la France*, 1695. In *Economistes-*

financiers du XVIIIe siècle, ed. Eugène Daire, 1843. Reprint, Osnabrück, 1966: 180–266.

Factum de la France, 1705. In *Economistes-financiers du XVIIIe siècle*, ed. Eugène Daire, 1843. Reprint, Osnabrück, 1966: 267–351.

Boislisle, A. M. de, ed. *Correspondance des contrôleurs généraux des finances avec les intendants des provinces, 1683–1715*, 3 vols. Paris, 1874–97.

  ed. *Mémoires de Saint-Simon*, 41 vols. Paris, 1879–1928.

Bossuet, Jacques-Bénigne. *Politique tirée des propres paroles de l'Ecriture sainte*, ed. Jacques Le Brun. Geneva, 1967.

Brette, Armand, ed. *Receuil de documents rélatifs à la convocation des Etats Généraux de 1789*. Paris, 1894.

[Brienne, Étienne Charles Loménie de]. *Compte rendu au roi, au mois de Mars 1788, et publié par ses ordres*. Paris, 1788.

Compte générale des revenus et des dépenses fixés au premier de mai 1789. Paris, 1789.

Compte rendu des impositions et des dépenses générales de la province de Languedoc. Montpellier, 1789.

De Servan. *Réflexions sur la réformation des états provinciaux*. N. p., 1789.

Desmaretz, Nicolas. *Mémoire sur l'administration des finances*. N. p., n. d.

Diderot, Denis and Jean Le Rond d'Alembert, eds. *Encyclopédie, ou Dictionnaire raisonné des sciences, des arts, et des métiers*, 35 vols. Neufchatel, 1751–80.

Essai sur les assemblées provinciales, ou réflexions d'un patriote sur les effets qui en sont résultés. London, 1789.

Flammermont, Jules, ed. *Les remontrances du parlement de Paris au XVIIIe siècle*, 3 vols. Paris, 1888–98.

[Forbonnais, François Véron de]. *Recherches et considerations sur les finances de la France depuis l'année 1595 jusqu'à l'année 1721*, 6 vols. Liège, 1758.

Foy, G. de la. *Addition au parallèle*. N. p., 1788.

  Parallèle des assemblées provinciales établies en Normandie, avec l'assemblée des états de ce duché. N. p., 1788.

[Foy, G. de la.] *De la constitution du duché ou état souverain de Normandie*. N. p., 1789.

Guyot, Joseph N. *Répertoire universel et raisonné de jurisprudence civile, criminelle, canonique, et bénéficiale*, 17 vols. Paris, 1784.

Hippeau, Célestin, ed. *Le gouvernement de Normandie au XVIIe et au XVIIIe siècle d'après la correspondance inédite des marquis de Beuvron et des ducs d'Harcourt, lieutenants-généraux et gouverneurs de la province*, 9 vols. Caen, 1863–70.

De l'influence des administrations provinciales sur les moeurs et l'opinion. Paris, 1788.

Isambert, F.-A., Jourdain, A.-J.-L., and Decrusy, eds. *Recueil général des anciennes lois françaises depuis l'an 420 jusqu'à la Révolution de 1789*, 29 vols. Paris, 1822–33.

LeNoir, J. L. *Collection chronologique des actes et des titres de Normandie*. N. p., 1788.

Le Trosne, Guillaume François. *De l'administration provinciale et de la réforme de l'impôt*. Basle, 1779.

Lettre de l'auteur de mode françois, ou est agitée la question des assemblées provinciales. Paris, 1787.

Lettre de M. Chancelier au parlement de Rouen, ou réponse aux remontrances de ce parlement. N. p., n. d.

Lettre du parlement de Normandie au roi, pour demander les anciens états de la province. N. p., [1788].

Lettres d'un gentilhomme françois sur l'établissement d'une capitation générale en France. Liège, 1695.

Le Verdier, P. *Correspondance politique et administrative de Miromesnil premier président du Parlement de Normandie,* 5 vols. Paris, 1899–1903.

[Loyseau, J.-R.]. *Les états provinciaux comparés avec les administrations provinciales.* Paris, 1789.

Mathon de la Cour, Charles-Joseph, ed. *Collection de comptes rendus, pièces authentiques, états et tableaux concernant les finances de France.* Lausanne, 1788.

Mavidal, M. J. and M. E. Laurent, eds. *Archives parlementaires de 1787 à 1860,* 82 vols. Paris, 1879–1913.

Mémoires pour servir à l'histoire du droit public de la France en matières d'impôts. Brussels, 1779.

Mirabeau, Victor Riquetti, marquis de. *L'ami des Hommes, ou traité de la population,* 2 vols. Avignon, 1758–60.

Mémoire concernant l'utilité des états provinciaux, relativement à l'autorité royale, aux finances, au bonheur, et à l'avantage des peuples. Rome, 1750.

Mémoire sur les états provinciaux. N. p., [1751].

Théorie de l'impôt. N. p., 1760.

Mon Opinion Motivée, ou le voeu d'un gentilhomme normand à la noblesse normand. N. p., n. d.

Montesquieu, Charles-Louis de Secondat, baron de. *De l'esprit des lois,* 2 vols, 1748. Reprint, Paris, 1979.

Moreau de Beaumont, Jean-Louis, ed. *Mémoires concernant les impositions et droits en Europe,* 4 vols. Paris, 1768.

Morellet, abbé André. *Réflexions sur les avantages de la liberté d'écrire et d'imprimer sur les matières de l'administration.* London, 1775.

Necker, Jacques. *Compte rendu au roi.* Paris, 1781.

De l'administration des finances de la France, 3 vols. Paris, 1784.

Nouvelles remontrances du parlement de Normandie au roi. N. p., [1760].

Objets de remontrances, arrêtés par le parlement séant à Rouen . . . le 16 juillet 1763. N. p., [1763].

Pascalis, *Mémoire sur la contribution des trois ordres aux charges publiques et commune de la province.* Aix, 1787.

Précis de ce qui s'est passé au Parlement séant à Rouen, depuis la S. Martin jusques et y compris le 19 Novembre 1763. N. p., n. d.

Procès-verbal des séances de l'assemblée provinciale de basse-Normandie. Caen, 1788.

Procès-verbal des séances de la chambre de l'ordre de la noblesse aux Etats-généraux. Versailles, 1789.

Relation de ce qui s'est passé au Parlement séant à Rouen, au sujet des édits et déclarations du mois d'avril 1763. N. p., [1763].

Remontrances du parlement de Normandie au roi . . . , 5 février 1788. N. p., [1788].

Remontrances du parlement de Rouen au sujet de l'édit du mois du février dernier, & de la déclaration du 3 du même mois. N. p., [1760].

Remontrances du parlement séant à Rouen, au roi, au sujet de l'édit et la déclaration du mois d'Avril dernier. N. p., [1763].

Le Renard pris au trébuchet: dialogue entre la capitation et Gruet. N. p., 1716.

Réponses du roi, lettres de jussion et de cachet, arrêtés et itératives remontrances du parlement à Rouen, au sujet de l'édit du mois de février dernier et de la déclaration du 3 du même mois. N. p., n. d.

Requête au Roi, par un avocat de l'ordre du Tiers . . . de Cotentin. N. p., 1789.

[Roger]. *Dialogue entre un auteur et un receveur de la capitation.* Amsterdam, 1767.

Rousseau, Jean-Jacques. *Discours sur l'économie politique.* Reprint, Paris, 1990.

The Social Contract, trans. Maurice Cranston. New York, 1968.

[Roussel de la Tour]. *La richesse de l'état.* N. p., [1763].

Rousselot de Surgy, Jacques-Philibert, ed. *Encyclopédie méthodique: finances*, 3 vols. Paris, 1784–7.

Rouyer. *Essai sur la répartition de la taille et des vingtièmes.* London, 1788.

Schelle, Gustave, ed. *Oeuvres de Turgot et documents le concernant*, 5 vols. Paris, 1913–23.

Sieyès, Emmanuel-Joseph. *Essai sur les privilèges.* N. p., 1788.

Qu'est-ce que le Tiers Etat?, 1789. Reprint, Paris, 1988.

Tableau des impositions que supporte une propriété de 6,122 livres dans la province de l'Isle de France. N. p., n. d.

Thibault and Coster. *Les séances des députés du clergé aux Etats-généraux.* Paris, 1917.

[Thouret, J.-P.]. *Mémoire présenté au roi par les avocats au parlement de Normandie, sur les Etats-généraux.* N. p., [1789].

Vauban, Sébastian Le Prestre Seigneur de. *Projet d'une dîme royale*, 1707. In *Economiste-financiers du XVIIIe siècle*, ed. Eugène Daire, 1843. Reprint, Osnabrück, 1966: 31–152.

Secondary works

Anderson, Perry. *Lineages of the Absolutist State.* London, 1974.

Antoine, Michel. *Le conseil du roi sous le règne de Louis XV.* Geneva, 1970.

Le dur métier du roi. Paris, 1986.

Louis XV. Paris, 1989.

"La monarchie absolue." In *The Political Culture of the Old Regime*, ed. Keith M. Baker, Oxford, 1987: 3–24.

"Les remontrances des cours supérieures sous le règne de Louis XIV (1673–1715)." *Bibliothèque de l'École des Chartes* 151 (1993): 87–122.

Ardant, Gabriel. *Histoire de l'impôt.* Paris, 1971.

Badinter, Elisabeth, ed. *Les "remontrances" de Malesherbes, 1771–1775.* Paris, 1985.

Baker, Keith Michael. *Condorcet: From Natural Philosophy to Social Mathematics.* Chicago, 1975.

"Defining the Public Sphere in Eighteenth-Century France: Variations on a Theme by Habermas." In *Habermas and the Public Sphere*, ed. Craig Calhoun. Cambridge, MA, 1992: 181–211.

Inventing the French Revolution: Essays on French Political Culture in the Eighteenth Century. Cambridge, 1990.

ed. *The Political Culture of the Old Regime*, vol. 1 of *The French Revolution and the Creation of Modern Political Culture*, 3 vols. Oxford, 1987–9.

Behrens, C. B. A. "Nobles, Privileges, and Taxes in France at the End of the Ancien Régime." *Economic History Review* 2nd ser. 15 (April 1963): 451–75.

"A Revision Defended: Nobles, Privileges, and Taxes in France." *French Historical Studies* 9 (1976): 521–31.

Beik, William. *Absolutism and Society in Seventeenth-Century France: State Power and Provincial Aristocracy in Languedoc.* Cambridge, 1985.

"A Social Interpretation of the Reign of Louis XIV." In *L'état ou le roi: les fondations de la modernité monarchique en France (XIVe-XVIIe siècles)*, ed. Neithard Bulst, Robert Descimon, and Alain Guerreau. Paris, 1996: 145–60.

Urban Protest in Seventeenth-Century France: The Culture of Retribution. Cambridge, 1997.

Bell, David A. *Lawyers and Citizens: The Making of a Political Elite in Old Regime France.* Oxford, 1994.

Bercé, Yves-Marie. *History of Peasant Revolts: The Social Origins of Rebellion in Early Modern France*, trans. Amanda Whitmore. Ithaca, NY, 1990.

Besnier, R. "Les vérifications des vingtièmes en Normandie." *Normannia* (1930): 754–84.

Bickart, Roger. *Les parlements et la notion de souveraineté nationale au XVIIIe siècle.* Paris, 1932.

Bien, David D. "Manufacturing Nobles: The Chancelleries in France to 1789." *Journal of Modern History* 61 (September 1989): 445–86.

"Offices, Corps, and a System of State Credit: The Uses of Privilege under the Ancien Régime." In *The Political Culture of the Old Regime*, ed. Keith M. Baker. Oxford, 1987: 89–114.

"Old Regime Origins of Democratic Liberty." In *The French Idea of Freedom: The Old Regime and the Declaration of Rights of 1789*, ed. Dale Van Kley. Stanford, CA, 1994: 23–71.

Bluche, François. *Les magistrats du parlement de Paris au XVIIIe siècle*, 2nd edn. Paris, 1986.

Bluche, F. and J.-F. Solnon. *La véritable hierarchie sociale de l'ancienne France: le tarif de la première capitation, 1695.* Geneva, 1983.

Bonney, Richard, ed. *Economic Systems and State Finance.* Oxford, 1995.

"France, 1494–1815." In *The Rise of the Fiscal State in Europe, c. 1200–1815*, ed. Richard Bonney. New York, 1999.

Political Change in France under Richelieu and Mazarin, 1624–1661. Oxford, 1978.

"'Le Secret de Leurs Familles': The Fiscal and Social Limits of Louis XIV's *Dixième*." *French History* 7 (1993): 383–416.

Bosher, John. *French Finances, 1770–1795: From Business to Bureaucracy.* Cambridge, 1970.

Bossenga, Gail. *The Politics of Privilege: Old Regime and Revolution in Lille*. Cambridge, 1991.

"Taxes." In *A Critical Dictionary of the French Revolution*, ed. François Furet and Mona Ozouf; trans. Arthur Goldhammer. Cambridge, 1989: 582–9.

Braudel, Fernand and Ernest Labrousse, eds. *Histoire économique et sociale de la France*, vols. I and II. Paris, 1970–77.

Brette, Armand. "La Noblesse et ses privilèges pécuniaires en 1789." *La Révolution Française* 51 (August 1906): 97–124.

Brewer, John. *The Sinews of Power: War, Money, and the English State, 1688–1783*. Cambridge, MA, 1990.

Briggs, Robin. *Communities of Belief: Cultural and Social Tension in Early Modern France*. Oxford, 1989.

Bruguière, Michel. *Gestionnaires et profiteurs de la Révolution: L'administration des finances françaises de Louis XVI à Bonaparte*. Paris, 1986.

Pour une renaissance de l'histoire financière, XVIIIe-XXe siècles. Paris, 1992.

Campbell, Peter R. *Power and Politics in Old Regime France 1720–1745*. London, 1996.

Carcassonne, Elie. *Montesquieu et le problème de la constitution française au XVIIIe siècle*. Reprint, Geneva, 1970.

Carpenter, Kenneth. "The Economic Bestsellers before 1850." *Bulletin of the Kress Library* (May 1975): 1–29.

Cavanaugh, Gerald. "Nobles, Privileges and Taxes in France: A Revision Reviewed." *French Historical Studies* (Fall 1974): 681–92.

Censer, Jack and Jeremy Popkin, eds. *Press and Politics in Pre-Revolutionary France*. Berkeley, CA, 1987.

Chaline, Olivier. *Godard de Belbeuf: le parlement, le roi et les Normands*. Luneray, 1996.

Chartier, Roger. *The Cultural Origins of the French Revolution*, trans. Lydia G. Cochrane. Durham, NC, 1991.

The Cultural Uses of Print in Early Modern Europe, trans. Lydia G. Cochrane. Princeton, NJ, 1987.

Chaussinand-Nogaret, Guy, "Le fisc et les privilégiés sous l'ancien régime." In *La fiscalité et ses implications sociales en Italie et en France aux XVIIe et XVIIIe siècles*. Rome, 1980.

The French Nobility in the Eighteenth Century: From Feudalism to Enlightenment, trans. William Doyle. Cambridge, 1985.

Clamageran, J. J. *Histoire de l'impôt en France*, 3 vols. Paris, 1867–76.

Cobban, Alfred. *A History of Modern France 1715–1789*. London, 1957.

Collins, James B. *Classes, Estates, and Order in Early Modern Brittany.* Cambridge, 1994.

    Fiscal Limits of Absolutism: Direct Taxation in Early Seventeenth-Century France. Berkeley, CA, 1988.

    The State in Early Modern France. Cambridge, 1995.

Crouzet, François. *La grande inflation: la monnaie en France de Louis XVI à Napoléan.* Paris, 1993.

Cubells, Monique. *La Provence des lumières. Les parlementaires d'Aix au XVIIIe siècle.* Paris, 1984.

Darnton, Robert. *The Forbidden Best-Sellers of Pre-Revolutionary France.* New York, 1996.

Davis, Natalie. *Fiction in the Archives: Pardon Tales and their Tellers in Sixteenth-Century France.* Stanford, CA, 1987.

Dessert, Daniel. *Argent, pouvoir, et société au Grand Siècle.* Paris, 1984.

Doyle, William. *Officers, Nobles and Revolutionaries: Essays on Eighteenth-Century France.* London, 1995.

    Origins of the French Revolution. Oxford, 1980.

    The Parlement of Bordeaux and the End of the Old Regime 1771–1790. New York, 1974.

    Venality: The Sale of Offices in Eighteenth-Century France. Oxford, 1996.

Doyon, André. *Un agent royaliste pendant la Révolution: Pierre-Jacques Le Maître (1790–1795).* Paris, 1969.

Duby, Georges. *The Three Orders: Feudal Society Imagined*, trans. Arthur Goldhammer. Chicago, 1978.

Dupâquier, Jacques, ed. *Histoire de la population française*, 4 vols. Paris, 1988.

Durand, Y. *Les fermiers généraux au XVIIIe siècle.* Paris, 1971.

Echeverria, Durand. *The Maupeou Revolution: A Study in the History of Libertarianism, France 1770–1774.* Baton Rouge, LA, 1985.

Egret, Jean. *The French Prerevolution 1787–1788*, trans. Wesley D. Camp. Chicago, 1977.

    Louis XV et l'opposition parlementaire, 1715–1774. Paris, 1970.

    Necker, ministre de Louis XVI, 1776–1790. Paris, 1975.

    Le parlement de Dauphiné et les affaires publiques dans le deuxième moitié du XVIIIe siècle, 2 vols. Paris, 1942.

Eisenstein, Elizabeth. "Who Intervened in 1788? A Commentary on *The Coming of the French Revolution.*" *American Historical Review* 71 (October 1965): 77–103.

El Kordi, Mohamed. *Bayeux aux xviie et xviiie siècles: contribution à l'histoire urbaine de la France.* Paris, 1970.

Esmonin, Edmond. *Etudes sur la France des XVII et XVIII siècles.* Paris, 1964.

    La taille en Normandie au temps de Colbert, 1661–1683, 1913. Reprint, Geneva, 1978.

Faccarello, Gilbert. *Aux origines de l'économie politique libérale: Pierre de Boisguilbert.* Paris, 1986.

Farge, Arlette. *Subversive Words: Public Opinion in Eighteenth-Century France*, trans. Rosemary Morris. University Park, PA, 1995.

Félix, Joël. *Économie et finances sous l'Ancien Régime: guide du chercheur, 1523–1789*. Paris, 1994.

Fitzsimmons, Michael P. "Privilege and the Polity in France, 1786–1791." *American Historical Review* 92 (1987): 269–95.

Floquet, Amable. *Histoire du parlement de Normandie*, 7 vols. Rouen, 1840–3.

Fogel, Michèle. *Les cérémonies de l'information dans la France du XVIe au XVIIIe siècle*. Paris, 1989.

Ford, Franklin L. *Robe and Sword: The Regrouping of the French Aristocracy after Louis XIV.* New York, 1953.

Forster, Robert. *The House of Saulx-Tavanes: Versailles and Burgundy 1700–1830.* Baltimore, MD, 1971.

  Merchants, Landlords, Magistrates: The Depont Family in Eighteenth-Century France. Baltimore, MD, 1980.

  The Nobility of Toulouse in the Eighteenth Century: A Social and Economic Study. Baltimore, MD, 1960.

Fox-Genovese, Elizabeth. *The Origins of Physiocracy: Economic Revolution and Social Order in Eighteenth-Century France.* Ithaca, NY, 1976.

Fréville, Henri. *L'intendance de Bretagne (1689–1790)*, 3 vols. Rennes, 1953.

Furet, François. *Interpreting the French Revolution*, trans. Elborg Forster. Cambridge, 1981.

  "La 'librairie' du royaume de France au 18e siècle." In *Livre et société dans la France du xviiie siècle*. Paris, 1965.

Furet, François and Mona Ozouf. *Le siècle de l'avènement républicain*. Paris, 1993.

Goodman, Dena. "Public Sphere and Private Life: Toward a Synthesis of Current Historiographical Approaches to the Old Regime." *History and Theory* 31 (1992): 1–20.

Goubert, Pierre. *The Ancien Régime: French Society, 1600–1750*, trans. Steve Cox. New York, 1969.

Grosclaude, P. *Malesherbes: témoin et interprète de son temps.* Paris, 1961.

Gross, Jean-Pierre. "Progressive Taxation and Social Justice in Eighteenth-Century France." *Past and Present* 140 (1993): 79–126.

Gruder, Vivian R. "A Mutation in Elite Political Culture: The French Notables and the Defense of Property and Participation, 1787." *Journal of Modern History* 56 (1984): 598–634.

  The Royal Provincial Intendants: A Governing Elite in Eighteenth-Century France. Ithaca, NY, 1968.

Gueniffey, Patrice. *Le nombre et la raison: la Révolution française et les élections.* Paris, 1993.

Guéry, Alain. "Etat, classification sociale et compromis sous Louis XIV: la capitation de 1695." *Annales E.S.C.* 41 (1986): 1041–60.

  "Les finances de la monarchie française sous l'ancien régime." *Annales E.S.C.* 33 (1978): 216–39.

Guihenneuc, L. *Étude sur la capitation proprement dite dans la province de Bretagne de 1695 à 1788*. Rennes, 1905.

Habermas, Jürgen. *The Structural Transformation of the Public Sphere: An Inquiry into a Category of Bourgeois Society*, trans. Thomas Burger. Cambridge, MA, 1989.

Halévi, Ran. "La révolution constituante: les ambiguités politiques." In *The Political Culture of the French Revolution*, ed. Colin Lucas. Oxford, 1988: 69–96.

Hanley, Sarah. *The "Lit de Justice" of the Kings of France: Constitutional Ideology in Legend, Ritual, and Discourse*. Princeton, NJ, 1983.

Harris, Robert D. "French Finances and the American War, 1777–1783." *Journal of Modern History* 42 (June 1976): 233–258.

    Necker, Reform Statesman of the Ancien Régime. Berkeley, CA, 1979.

Hazard, Paul. *The European Mind: The Critical Years, 1680–1715*, trans. J. Lewis May. New York, 1990.

Herlihy, David and Christianne Klapisch-Zuber. *Tuscans and Their Families: A Study of the Florentine Catasto of 1427*. New Haven, CT, 1985.

Hincker, François. *Les français devant l'impôt sous l'ancien régime*. Paris, 1971.

Hirschman, Albert O. *The Passions and the Interests: Political Arguments for Capitalism before Its Triumph*. Princeton, NJ, 1977.

Hoffman, Philip T. "Early Modern France, 1450–1700." In *Fiscal Crises, Liberty, and Representative Government, 1450–1789*, ed. Philip T. Hoffman and Kathryn Norberg. Stanford, CA, 1994: 226–52.

Hudson, David. "The Parlementary Crisis of 1763 in France and Its Consequences." *Canadian Journal of History* 7 (1972): 97–117.

Hufton, Olwen. *Bayeux in the Late Eighteenth Century: A Social Study*. Oxford, 1967.

Joly, M. *Une conspiration de la noblesse Normande au dix-huitième siècle*. Caen, 1865.

Jones, Colin. "Bourgeois Revolution Revivified: 1789 and Social Change." In *Rewriting the French Revolution*, ed. Colin Lucas. Oxford, 1991: 69–118.

Jones, Peter. *Reform and Revolution in France: The Politics of Transition, 1774–1791*. Cambridge, 1995.

    "Reforming Absolutism and the Ending of the Old Regime in France." *Australian Journal of French Studies* 29 (1992): 220–8.

Jouhaud, Christian. "Révoltes et contestations d'Ancien Régime." In *Histoire de la France*, ed. André Burguière and Jacques Revel. Paris, 1990, vol. 3: 18–99.

Kaiser, Thomas E. "The Abbé de Saint-Pierre, Public Opinion, and the Reconstitution of the French Monarchy." *Journal of Modern History* 55 (1983): 618–43.

    "Money, Despotism, and Public Opinion in Eighteenth-Century France: John Law and the Debate on Royal Credit." *Journal of Modern History* 63 (1981): 1–28.

Kaplan, Steven L. *Bread, Politics, and Political Economy in the Reign of Louis XV,* 2 vols. The Hague, 1976.

    The Famine Plot Persuasion in Eighteenth-Century France. Philadelphia, PA, 1982.

Keohane, Nannerl O. *Philosophy and the State in France: The Renaissance to the Enlightenment.* Princeton, NJ, 1980.

Kwass, Michael. "A Kingdom of Taxpayers: State Formation, Privilege, and Political Culture in Eighteenth-Century France." *Journal of Modern History* 70 (1998): 295–339.

    "*Liberté, Egalité, Fiscalité*: Taxation, Privilege, and Political Culture in Eighteenth-Century France." PhD thesis, University of Michigan, 1994.

Labrousse, Ernest. *Esquisse du mouvement des prix et des revenues en France au XVIIIe siècle.* Paris, 1933.

Lardé, Georges. *La capitation dans les pays de taille personelle.* Paris, 1906.

    Une enquête sur les vingtièmes au temps de Necker. Paris, 1920.

Larrère, Catherine. *L'invention de l'économie au XVIIIe siècle: du droit naturel à la physiocratie.* Paris, 1992.

Le Goff, T. J. A. *Vannes and Its Region: A Study of Town and Country in Eighteenth-Century France.* Oxford, 1981.

Le Roy Ladurie, Emmanuel. "Révoltes et contestations rurales en France de 1675 à 1788." *Annales E.S.C.* 29 (1974): 6–22.

Lemarchand, Guy. *La fin de féodalisme dans le pays de Caux.* Paris, 1989.

    "Troubles populaires au XVIIIe siècle et conscience de classe: une préface à la Révolution française." *Annales historiques de la Révolution française* 279 (1990): 32–48.

Levinger, Mathew. "La rhétorique protestaire du parlement de Rouen." *Annales E.S.C.* (May–June 1990): 589–613.

Lizerand, Georges. "Observations sur l'impôt foncier sous l'ancien régime." *RHES* 36 (1958): 18–44.

Lucas, Colin. "Nobles, Bourgeois, and the Origins of the French Revolution." *Past and Present* 60 (August 1973): 84–126.

Luethy, Herbert. *La banque protestante en France de la révocation de l'Edit de Nantes à la Révolution,* 2 vols. Paris, 1959–61.

Lynn, John. "Recalculating French Army Growth during the *Grand Siècle,* 1610–1715." *French Historical Studies* 18 (Fall 1994): 881–906.

McCollim, Gary. "The Formation of Fiscal Policy in the Reign of Louis XIV: The Example of Nicolas Desmaretz, Controller-General of Finances (1708–1715)." PhD thesis, Ohio State University, 1979.

Major, J. Russell. *Renaissance Monarchy to Absolute Monarchy: French Kings, Nobles, and Estates.* Baltimore, MD, 1994.

Marion, Marcel. *Dictionnaire des institutions de la France aux XVIIe et XVIIIe siècle.* Paris, 1923. Reprint, Paris, 1989.

    Histoire financière de la France depuis 1715, 5 vols. Paris, 1919–28.

    L'impôt sur le revenu sous l'ancien régime. Paris, 1901.

Les impôts directs sous l'ancien régime, principalement au XVIIIe siècle. Paris, 1910.

Machault d'Arnouville, étude sur l'histoire du contrôle général des finances de 1749 à 1754. Paris, 1892.

Markoff, John. *The Abolition of Feudalism: Peasants, Lords, and Legislators in the French Revolution.* University Park, PA, 1996.

Martin, Henri-Jean and Roger Chartier, eds. *Le livre triomphant. 1660–1830,* vol. 2 of *Histoire de l'édition française,* 1984. Reprint, Paris, 1990.

Mathews, George T. *The Royal General Farms in Eighteenth-Century France.* New York, 1958.

Mathias, Peter and Patrick O'Brien. "Taxation in Britain and France, 1715–1810." *Journal of European Economic History* 5 (1976): 601–50.

Maza, Sarah. *Private Lives and Public Affairs: The Causes Célèbres of Prerevolutionary France.* Berkeley, CA, 1993.

Meek, Ronald L. *The Economics of Physiocracy: Essays and Translations.* Cambridge, MA, 1963.

Merrick, Jeffrey W. "Conscience and Citizenship in Eighteenth-Century France." *Eighteenth-Century Studies* 21 (Fall 1987): 48–70.

The Desacralization of the French Monarchy in the Eighteenth Century. Baton Rouge, LA, 1990.

Mettam, Roger. *Power and Faction in Louis XIV's France.* London, 1988.

Meuvret, Jean. "Comment les Français du xviie siècle voyaient l'impôt." *Études d'histoire économique.* Paris, 1971: 295–308.

Meyer, Jean. *La noblesse bretonne au XVIIIe siècle,* 2 vols, 1966. Reprint, Paris, 1985.

"Un problème mal posé: la noblesse pauvre – l'exemple breton au xviiie siècle." *Revue d'histoire moderne et contemporaine* 18 (April–June 1971): 161–88.

Meyniel, Louis. *Un facteur de la Révolution française: la querelle des impôts au parlement de Paris en 1787–1788.* Paris, 1907.

Meyssonnier, Simone. *La balance et l'horloge: la genèse de la pensée libérale en France au XVIIIe siècle.* Paris, 1989.

Michaud, Claude. *L'eglise et l'argent sous l'ancien régime.* Paris, 1991.

"La participation du clergé de France aux dépenses de la monarchie à la fin de l'ancien régime." In *Etat, finances, et economie pendant la Révolution française.* Paris, 1991: 3–10.

Mitard, Stanislas. *La crise financière en France à la fin du XVIIe siècle: la première capitation (1695–1698).* Rennes, 1934.

Morineau, Michel. "Budgets de l'Etat et gestion des finances royales en France au dix-huitième siècle." *Revue Historique* 264 (1980): 289–336.

"Budgets populaires en France au xviiie siècle." *Revue d'histoire économique et sociale* 50 (1972): 203–37 and 449–81.

Mornet, Daniel. *Les origines intellectuelles de la Révolution française, 1715–1787.* Reprint, Lyons, 1989.

Mosser, Françoise. *Les intendants des finances au XVIIIe siècle: les Lefevre d'Ormesson et le "département des impositions" (1715–1777).* Geneva, 1978.

Mourlot, Félix. *La fin d'ancien régime et les débuts de la Révolution dans la généralité de Caen, 1787–1790*. Paris, 1913.

——— *Rapports d'une assemblée provinciale et de sa commission intermédiaire avec l'intendant, 1787–1790*. Paris, 1902.

Mousnier, Roland. *The Institutions of France under the Absolute Monarchy, 1598–1789*, 2 vols, trans. Brian Pearce. Chicago, 1979–84.

Murphy, Antoine. "Le développement des idées économiques en France, 1750–1756." *Revue d'histoire moderne et contemporaine* 33 (1986): 521–41.

Musset, Jacqueline. *L'intendance de Caen: structure, fonctionnement et administration sous l'intendant Esmangart, 1775–1783*. Condé-sur-Noireau, 1985.

Norberg, Kathryn. "The French Fiscal Crisis of 1788 and the Financial Origins of the Revolution of 1789." In *Fiscal Crises, Liberty, and Representative Government, 1450–1789*, ed. Philip T. Hoffman and Kathryn Norberg. Stanford, CA, 1994: 253–98.

Ozouf, Mona. "L'opinion publique." In *The Political Culture of the Old Regime*, ed. Keith M. Baker. Oxford, 1987: 419–34.

Palmer, R. R. *The Age of the Democratic Revolution*, 2 vols. Princeton, NJ, 1959.

Parker, Geoffrey. *The Military Revolution: Military Innovation and the Rise of the West, 1500–1800*. Cambridge, 1988.

Perrot, Jean-Claude. *Genèse d'une ville moderne: Caen aux XVIIIe siècle*, 2 vols. Paris, 1975.

——— *Une histoire intellectuelle de l'économie politique (XVII-XVIIIe siècle)*. Paris, 1992.

——— "Introduction à l'emploi des registres fiscaux en histoire sociale: l'exemple de Caen au XVIIIe siècle." *Annales de Normandie* (1966): 33–63.

——— "Nouveautés: l'économie politique et ses livres." In *Histoire de l'édition française*, vol. 2, *Le livre triomphant, 1660–1830*, ed. Henri-Jean Martin and Roger Chartier. Paris, 1984: 240–57.

——— *Pierre de Boisguilbert ou la naissance de l'économie politique*, 2 vols. Paris, 1966.

Pocock, J. G. A. *The Machiavellian Moment: Florentine Political Thought and the Atlantic Republican Tradition*. Princeton, NJ, 1975.

——— *Virtue, Commerce, and History: Essays on Political Thought and History Chiefly in the Eighteenth Century*. Cambridge, 1985.

Poggi, Gianfranco. *The State: Its Nature, Development, and Prospects*. Stanford, CA, 1990.

Popkin, Jeremy. "Pamphlet Journalism at the End of the Old Regime." *Eighteenth-Century Studies* 22 (1989): 351–67.

Préel, Yves. *L'impôt direct au XVIIIe siècle: les vingtièmes dans la généralité de Caen*. Caen, 1939.

Price, Munro. *Preserving the Monarchy: The Comte de Vergennes, 1774–1787*. Cambridge, 1995.

Ragan, Bryant. "Rural Political Activism and Fiscal Equality in the Revolutionary Somme." In *Re-creating Authority in Revolutionary France*, ed. Bryant Ragan and Elizabeth Williams. New Brunswick, NJ, 1992.

Ravitch, Norman. *Sword and Mitre: Government and Episcopate in France and England in the Age of Aristocracy*. The Hague, 1966.

Renouvin, Pierre. *Les assemblées provinciales de 1787. Origines, développements, résultats.* Paris, 1921.

Riccomard, Julien. "Les subdélégués des intendants aux XVIIe et XVIIIe siècles." *L'information historique* 24 (1962): 139–48, 190–5, and (1963): 1–7.

Richet, Denis. "Autour des origines idéologiques lointaines de la Révolution française: élites et despotisme." *Annales, E.S.C.* 24 (1969): 1–23.

La France moderne: l'esprit des institutions. Paris, 1973.

"La monarchie au travail sur elle-même?" In *The Political Culture of the Old Regime,* ed. Keith M. Baker. Oxford, 1987: 25–40.

Riley, James C. "French Finances, 1727–1768." *Journal of Modern History* 59 (1987): 209–43.

The Seven Years War and the Old Regime in France: The Economic and Financial Toll. Princeton, NJ, 1986.

Rioche, Augustin. *De l'administration des vingtièmes sous l'ancien regime.* Paris, 1904.

Robin, Régine. *La société française en 1789: Semur-en-Auxois.* Paris, 1970.

Robinne, Paul. "Les magistrats du parlement de Normandie à la fin du XVIIIe siècle (1774–1790)," 2 vols. Thèse de l'École des Chartes, 1967.

Roche, Daniel. *France in the Enlightenment,* trans. Arthur Goldhammer. Cambridge, MA, 1998.

Rogister, John. *Louis XV and the Parlement of Paris, 1737–1755.* Cambridge, 1995.

Root, Hilton. *The Fountain of Privilege: Political Foundations of Markets in Old Regime France and England.* Berkeley, CA, 1994.

Peasants and King in Burgundy: Agrarian Foundations of French Absolutism. Berkeley, CA, 1987.

Rothkrug, Lionel. *Opposition to Louis XIV: The Political and Social Origins of the French Enlightenment.* Princeton, NJ, 1965.

Schnerb, R. *Les contributions directes à l'époque de la Révolution.* Paris, 1933.

"La répartition des impôts directs à la fin de l'Ancien Régime." *Revue d'histoire économique et sociale* 38 (1960): 129–45.

Scott, James C. *Domination and the Arts of Resistance: Hidden Transcripts.* New Haven, CT, 1990.

Sewell, William H., Jr. "Le citoyen/la citoyenne: Activity, Passivity, and the Revolutionary Concept of Citizenship." In *The Political Culture of the French Revolution,* ed. Colin Lucas. Oxford, 1988: 105–24.

"Ideologies and Social Revolutions: Reflections on the French Case." *Journal of Modern History* 57 (March 1985): 57–85.

A Rhetoric of Bourgeois Revolution: The Abbé Sieyes and "What Is the Third Estate?" Durham, NC, 1994.

Skocpol, Theda. *States and Revolutions: A Comparative Analysis of France, Russia, and China.* Cambridge, 1979.

Smith, Jay M. *The Culture of Merit: Nobility, Royal Service, and the Making of Absolute Monarchy in France, 1600–1789.* Ann Arbor, MI, 1996.

Solomon, Robert C. *A Passion for Justice: Emotions and the Origins of the Social Contract.* Reading, MA, 1990.

Sonenscher, Michael. *Work and Wages: Natural Law, Politics, and Eighteenth-Century French Trades.* Cambridge, 1989.

Stone, Bailey. *The French Parlements and the Crisis of the Old Regime.* Chapel Hill, NC, 1986.

The Genesis of the French Revolution: A Global-Historical Interpretation. Cambridge, 1994.

The Parlement of Paris, 1774–1789. Chapel Hill, NC, 1981.

Stourm, René. *Bibliographie historique des finances de la France au dix-huitième siècle,* 1895. Reprint, New York, 1968.

Swann, Julian. *Politics and the Parlement of Paris under Louis XV, 1754–1774.* Cambridge, 1995.

Tackett, Timothy. *Becoming a Revolutionary: The Deputies of the French National Assembly and the Emergence of a Revolutionary Culture (1789–1790).* Princeton, NJ, 1996.

Taylor, George. "Noncapitalist Wealth and the Origins of the French Revolution." *American Historical Review* 72 (1967): 469–96.

"Revolutionary and Non-revolutionary Content in the *Cahiers* of 1789: An Interim Report." *French Historical Studies* (1972): 479–502.

Tilly, Charles. *Coercion, Capital, and European States, AD 990–1992.* Cambridge, MA, 1992.

ed. *The Formation of National States in Western Europe.* Princeton, NJ, 1975.

Tocqueville, Alexis de. *The Old Régime and the French Revolution,* trans. Stuart Gilbert. Garden City, NY, 1955.

Touzery, Mireille. *L'invention de l'impôt sur le revenu: la taille tarifée, 1715–1789.* Paris, 1994.

Van Kley, Dale. *The Damiens Affair and the Unraveling of the Ancien Régime, 1750–1770.* Princeton, NJ, 1984.

The Jansenists and the Expulsion of the Jesuits from France, 1757–1765. New Haven, CT, 1975.

The Religious Origins of the French Revolution: From Calvin to the Civil Constitution, 1560–1791. New Haven, CT, 1996.

ed. *The French Idea of Freedom: The Old Regime and the Declaration of Rights of 1789.* Stanford, CA, 1994.

Venturi, Franco. *Utopia and Reform in the Enlightenment.* Cambridge, 1971.

Vignes, J.-B. Maurice. *Histoire des doctrines sur l'impôt en France.* Paris, 1909.

Villain, Jean. *Les contestations fiscales sous l'ancien régime dans les pays d'élections de taille personelle.* Paris, 1943.

Le recouvrement des impôts directs sous l'ancien régime. Paris, 1952.

Walzer, Michael. *Spheres of Justice.* New York, 1983.

Weir, David R. "Les crises économiques et les origines de la révolution française." *Annales E.S.C.* 46 (July–August 1991): 917–47.

"Tontines, public finance and revolution in France and England, 1688–1789." *Journal of Economic History* 49 (1989): 95–124.

Wells, Charlotte C. *Law and Citizenship in Early Modern France.* Baltimore, MD, 1995.

Weulersse, George. *Le mouvement physiocratique en France de 1756 à 1770*, 2 vols. Paris, 1910.

White, Eugene Nelson. "Was There a Solution to the Ancien Régime's Financial Dilemma?" *Journal of Economic History* 49 (1989): 545–68.

Woloch, Isser. *The New Regime: Transformations of the French Civic Order, 1789–1820s.* New York, 1994.

Index

abonnements, 207
  and the clergy, 109, 159
  in the *pays d'états*, 95–100
  and provincial assemblies, 270–2
  and royal princes, 104–5
absolutism, 49
  and alliance between state and elites,
    23–4, 312
  historiography of, 4, 5, 6, 7, 9–10, 11, 14,
    312, 320
  limits and challenges to, 19, 38, 60, 157,
    163, 166, 168–9, 209–10, 228, 237–8,
    251, 252, 255, 278, 315–16
  new stage of, 60–1, 114–15
affaires extraordinaires, 34, 45–6
Alençon, 73, 134–5, 156
Anderson, Perry, 14
Annales school, 10, 63, 65
*Annonces, affiches, et avis divers de la haute et basse
  Normandie*, 172, 184, 244
Argenson, René Louis de Voyer de Paulmy,
  marquis d', 106, 161, 232, 263
arrêt de défense, 87, 186–7, 189, 193, 207
Artois, 35, 99n75, 309
Assembly of Notables, 222, 265, 273–4, 293,
  301, 318
Assembly of the Clergy, 27, 30, 119, 155, 156
  see also clergy of France
Aube, François Richer d', 148
Aux Français, par un ami des trois ordres, 293

Bachaumont, Louis Petit de, 181, 191n65, 212,
  221, 243, 244
Baker, Keith M., 4, 8n12, 10n16, 16, 234,
  249n78
ban et arrière-ban, 298
bankruptcy, 3, 13, 63, 114, 218, 278
  and justification for universal taxes, 46–7,
    190
  magistrates' indifference to, 182
  Mirabeau on, 236

  personal, 130–1
Barbier, Edmond, 97, 167, 172, 177, 185, 212,
  220–1, 238
Barentin, Charles de Paule de, 300
Baudeau, Nicolas, 219, 221, 216n7
Bâville, Nicolas de Lamoignon de, 56
Bayeux, 81n37, 128, 131, 134, 135, 148
  capitation in, 76n23, 77n26
  capitation dispute between bailiff and
    subdelegate of, 121–3
  land tax on clergy in, 112
  vingtième in, 90, 93–4
Behrens, C. B. A., 14–15, 63–4, 66
Beik, William, 23–4, 312
Bertin, Henri Léonard Jean-Baptiste, 175,
  178, 188, 198, 204
  and "Anglican principles," 185
  crackdown on *Requête au Roi*, 203
  on credit and tax disputes, 173–4
  and military justification for tax increases,
    37
  opposition to provincial estates, 176, 179
Bien, David D., 12, 31, 106n91, 313n3
Blagny, comte de, 294
Bluche, François, 64, 65, 69
Boisguilbert, Pierre Le Pesant de, 237, 239,
  249
  and consumption, 226–7, 250
  literary success of, 217, 223, 243
  and natural economic law, 225–8, 250,
    317
  political implications of, 230–1
  on poverty, 224–5
  Vauban's opinion of, 230
Bonney, Richard, 35, 64–65
Borel, Antoine, 244–6
Bosher, J. F., 64, 65
Bossenga, Gail, 12
Bossuet, Jacques-Bénigne, 168–9, 209–10
Boucher d'Argis, Antoine-Gaspard, 216
Bourges, 72n16, 73, 76, 85n48, 90–1, 94

Brienne, Étienne Charles Loménie de, 47, 112, 260, 265, 266, 271, 275
Brittany, 103, 159, 194, 200
  methods of tax payment in, 95–6, 99–100
  royal taxation on, 97–9
  social incidence of *capitation* in, 100–1
  social incidence of *dixième/vingtième* in, 101
Bureaux du contrôle, 57, 87, 149, 276
Bureaux des finances, 48–9, 105, 134–5
Burgundy, 95, 102, 73n18, 99n75

Caen
  bailliage of, 280–2, 293–4
  capitation in generality of, 71–84, 105
  city of, 91, 279–80
  dixième/vingtième in generality of, 84–94, 105, 271
  generality of, 50, 156, 301, 321n6
  intendancy of, 54–6, 58, 59, 120
  land tax on clergy in, 112, 114
  revolt against *vingtième* in, 196–204
  taille in generality of, 83–4, 105
  tax petitions from residents of, 120–54
  University of, 165
  see also Normandy
cahiers de doléances, 222, 278
  and calls for constitutional change, 280–2
  and indirect taxes, 305
  and parlementary right to deliberate, 206
  and renunciations of fiscal privilege, 293–4, 296
Calonne, Charles Alexandre de, 204, 208, 255
  and convocation of Assembly of Notables, 273
  and creation of provincial assemblies, 260, 265
  and quarrel with Necker, 222
Camus de Pontcarré, Geoffroy-Macé, 147–8
Camus de Pontcarré de Viarme, 189–90
Cantillon, Richard, 221
capitation, 292, 298
  1709 sale of exemptions from, 110–11
  and active citizenship, 305–6
  administration of, 51–60, 264–5, 313–14
  on the bourgeoisie, 81–2, 113
  on the clergy, 108–111, 114, 313
  on commoners, 72–4, 75, 83, 102, 103, 114, 313
  free funds of, 55, 59, 206, 267
  global weight of, 67–8
  Mirabeau's criticism of, 233
  on the nobility, 74–7, 100–3, 113, 313

  on officers of justice, 77–80, 105–7, 113, 114, 314
  origins of, 17, 33–8, 223
  on Paris, 107–8, 114
  parlementary discourse on, 156–7, 159, 161–5, 170, 176, 178–9, 192, 196, 204, 205–6, 209–10, 315–17
  in the *pays d'états*, 95–103, 113, 313
  petitions for reductions in, 120–37, 139, 314, 315
  on the privileged, 72–4, 75, 91, 94–5, 113, 313, 320
  on the *privilégiés*, 80–1, 113, 314
  and provincial assembly of Lower Normandy, 267, 268–70
  reductions granted by administrators, 74–6, 77–9, 84, 140–1, 142–54, 314
  on the royal court, 103–5, 114, 314
  royal rhetoric on, 41–6, 62
  tariff of, 64, 65, 68–70
Cavanaugh, Gerald C., 14, 64, 66
Chaline, Olivier, 168
Chambre des comptes (Brittany), 100
Chambre des comptes (Paris), 279
Chambre des comptes (Rouen), 179, 277, 279
Chambres de justice, 69, 218
Chambres des comptes, 55, 62, 71, 155
Charles VII, 25, 298
Chartier, Roger, 4, 5
Chaussinand-Nogaret, Guy, 146–7, 280, 294
Cherbourg, 81n37, 135–6, 138, 151, 302
citizenship, 5, 12, 17, 19, 156, 249, 282, 321
  active citizenship, 1, 2, 256, 303–10
  and Mirabeau, 233, 235, 237–8, 251, 317–18
  and Necker, 242–3, 251–2, 318
  in parlementary discourse, 18, 19, 162, 163, 164–5, 166, 169–70, 173, 176, 179, 184, 205, 210–11, 275, 299, 316–17
  and political claims of third estate, 284, 285, 293, 299
  and provincial assemblies, 257, 259, 265, 266
  and reader response to Necker, 244, 246–7, 248
  and renunciations of fiscal privilege, 294, 295, 303
  and revolt against *vingtième*, 196, 198
  in tax petitions, 136, 138, 270
  see also Estates General; liberty; provincial estates
classical republicanism, 214, 234
  and Mirabeau, 232–8, 250–1, 317
  and reader response to Necker, 244–6

clergy, 3, 41, 66, 71, 103, 114, 155–6, 192, 248,
255, 282, 283–4, 296, 300, 304
attestations of poverty by, 129, 149
cahiers de doléances of, 280
and the *capitation*, 44, 68, 80, 109–11
and the *dixième/vingtième*, 110–11, 159, 220,
297
fiscal privileges of, 24–8, 30–1, 227, 297,
319
of the frontier, 109
and land tax in Caen, 112–13
and political claims of third estate, 302–3
and provincial assemblies, 263
and renunciation of fiscal privilege, 293–4,
295
and representations of fiscal privilege,
284–92
taxes internal to, 112
voluntary gifts of, 110–12, 313
wealth of, 108, 111, 224
see also Assembly of the Clergy; Jansenism
Coigny, Marie-François-Henri de
Franquetot, duc de, 268
Collins, James B., 23–4, 95n69
Compte rendu au roi, 214–15, 222, 238, 240, 241,
244–7
Condorcet, Marie-Jean-Antoine-Nicolas,
marquis de, 259, 297, 309
conseil supérieur (Bayeux), 196–7
conseils supérieures, 86, 194, 195
Constituent Assembly, 1, 268
constitution of 1791, 282, 306
constitution of 1793, 309–10
contribuable, 52
contribution foncière, 306
contribution mobilière, 306
contrôleur général
office of, 53, 53n76, 176
see also Bertin; Brienne; Calonne;
Desmaretz; Joly de Fleury; Lambert;
L'Averdy; Law; Machault;
Pontchartrain; Silhouette; Terray;
Turgot
Coster, Sigisbert-Etienne, abbé, 295
Cotentin, 199, 270, 298
cour des aides (Paris), 41, 79, 204, 205, 260–1
and jurisdiction over the *capitation* and
vingtième, 53–4, 160–1, 165
and call for Estates General, 171n21, 194
see also Malesherbes
cour des aides (Rouen), 27, 179, 268
cours des aides, 50, 62
Coutances, 84, 149
bailliage of, 280, 281–2, 294
city of, 81n37

credit, 12, 195, 274, 319
and fiscal inequality, 23–4, 114
international market for, 173–4, 179–80,
316
and Necker's idea of public opinion, 241
and provincial estates, 99–100, 233
sustained by universal taxes, 35, 36, 46–7
and venality, 30–1
see also bankruptcy; debt (personal); debt
(royal); venality of office

Damilaville, Etienne No(l, 216
Dangeul, Louis-Joseph Plumard de, 221
debt (communal)
and liability to *taille*, 49–53, 58
debt (national), 47, 289, 302, 303, 307
debt (personal), 224
as metaphor in Jansenist controversy, 166
and payment of *vingtième*, 89n60, 137–9
and petitions against *capitation*, 126, 128–9,
131
debt (royal), 12, 65, 114, 167, 236
attitude of magistrates toward, 182
and clerical debt, 30–1
and provincial debt, 99–100
and universal taxes, 35, 36, 37, 43, 45–7,
61, 265, 271
see also, bankruptcy; credit; venality of
office
De l'administration des finances, 214, 217, 238–9,
240–2
Declaration of the Rights of Man and
Citizen, 282, 308
desacralization of the monarchy, 158, 209
see also Louis XV (popular perceptions of)
Desmaretz, Nicolas, 35–6, 121, 122–3, 126
despotism, 1, 5, 18, 121, 156, 158, 273, 283,
312, 323
and judicial Jansenism, 11, 166, 168–9, 173,
189, 315
and judicial tax protest, 159, 162, 164, 165,
168–9, 173, 189, 193, 205, 209–10, 315,
323
and physiocracy, 258
and provincial assemblies, 279–80
Dessert, Daniel, 23, 32–3
Détail de la France, 217, 223–8, 230
Diderot, Denis, 130, 216
direct taxes, 13, 14–15, 17, 23, 26, 46, 61, 62,
64, 66, 71, 82, 84, 92, 95, 107–8, 113,
114, 127, 208, 291, 292, 313, 314, 317, 323
and active citizenship, 304–6, 308, 309, 310
and constitutional thought, 211
and provincial assemblies, 256–7, 265,
266, 268

relative weight of, 67–8
see also capitation; dixième; taille; vingtième
dixième
    administration of, 52, 56, 58, 64–5, 70–1,
        87, 90
    on the clergy, 110–2
    as example of fiscal equality, 321n6
    and feudal dues, 137–8
    global weight of, 67–8
    incidence in Brittany, 96–9
    incidence in generality of Caen, 84–5
    incidence in Languedoc, 96–9
    origins of, 17, 33, 35–6, 37, 179, 223,
        223n22
    parlementary opposition to, 159–60
    petitions against, 121, 122, 123, 125, 126n22,
        141n68
    royal rhetoric on, 42–3, 45, 46–7, 62
    as withholding tax, 104–7, 113, 313
    see also vingtième
Domat, Jean, 124
Doyle, William, 64, 80, 113n111, 195n71
Dupont de Nemours, Pierre-Samuel, 217,
    218, 219, 230, 257–60, 265
Duranthon, Antoine, 220
Dutot, Charles Henri, 218

élections, 31
    and administration of *taille*, 48–51,
        57–8
    and jurisdiction over *capitation* and
        vingtième, 54
    of Bayeux, 90, 93, 134
    of Caen, 79, 90
    of Mortain, 197
    and provincial assemblies, 268
    see also pays d'élections
Encyclopédie méthodique: finances, 216, 217, 246
*Encyclopédie, ou Dictionnaire raisonné des sciences,
    des arts, et des métiers*, 127, 129, 216
England, 14, 215, 283, 322
    fiscal-military rivalry with, 34–6
    and French constitutional rhetoric, 181,
        185, 185n54, 190
    and international credit, 173–4, 179–80
Epinay, Louise-Florence-Pétronville de Lavive
    d', 215–16
equality, 2, 9, 17, 19
    and Tocqueville, 6, 10, 249, 319–22
    *see also fiscal equality, political equality,
        third estate*
Esmangard, Charles François Hyacinthe, 78,
    139, 141, 150, 264–5
Estates General, 25, 206, 256, 257, 263, 278,
    280, 285, 318

call for by Norman nobility, 202–3, 317
calls for by parlements, 162–3, 165, 170–1,
    171n21, 173, 179, 194, 194n70, 196, 205,
    208, 209, 210, 316
calls for during Prerevolution, 273–7
debate over vote at, 283–4, 296–303,
    318–19
demands for periodicity of, 280–2
see also provincial estates
états des finances, 105
états au vrai, 66, 71

Febvre, Lucien, 63
Fénélon, François de Salignac de la Motte,
    225
fiscal equality, 31–2, 33, 114, 153, 274, 287,
    297, 313, 320–1
    Boisguilbert and, 227, 231
    Mirabeau and, 236–7
    Necker and, 242, 246–7, 264
    nobility's espousal of, 293–4
    and provincial assemblies, 264, 266
    royal rhetoric of, 17, 37–8, 41–3, 42n37,
        48, 61, 81n39, 86–7, 197, 204, 206, 207,
        208, 213, 276
    Vauban and, 229–31
Fogel, Michèle, 39
Fontette, Jean François Orceau de, 88,
    92n66, 139, 140n66, 141, 142, 196–7,
    198
Forbonnais, François Véron de, 219, 221
Forster, Robert, 101–2
Fossé, Antoine-Augustin Thomas du, 166,
    168, 176, 181, 186, 189, 199–200, 203
Foy, G. de la, 278–9
Furet, François, 4, 5, 9–10, 311

gages, 30, 56n87, 79–80, 83n41, 90, 104,
    105–6, 106n91, 128, 134–5, 229, 313
Gaultier, Jean-Baptiste, 220
General Farms, 29, 80–1, 106
    see also indirect taxes
Glannières, Richard des, 221
Goislard de Montsabert, Anne Louis de, 275
Granville, 81n37, 301
Graslin, Jean-Joseph, 219
Gruder, Vivian, R., 274, 294
Gueniffey, Patrice, 304
Guéry, Alain, 64–5, 69
guilds, 15, 28, 30, 48, 130, 319
    capitation and *vingtième* on, 70, 81n39, 89,
        107–8, 136–7
Guynet d'Arthel, François, 122–3

Habermas, J(rgen, 5, 6–9, 10, 40, 319, 322–3

Halévi, Ran, 296
Harcourt, Anne Pierre, duc d', 92n66, 133,
    180, 185–7, 200, 203, 207, 279, 295
*He would like to knock down that which sustains
    them*, 289–91

I knew our turn would come, 287–9
indirect taxes, 34, 64, 80, 106, 108, 113, 201,
    226, 309, 310
    constitutional insignificance of, 210, 305
    relative weight of, 66
intendants of finance, 37, 52–3, 53n76, 55,
    86, 122n11, 142, 215
    see also Ormesson
intendants (provincial), 34, 35, 40, 59, 106,
    198, 203
    and administration of universal taxes,
        51–9, 77, 78–9, 80, 81, 85, 87–9, 96,
        110, 112, 195, 196–7, 313–14
    growth of intendancies, 54–7
    and jurisdiction over *taille*, 49–51
    Mirabeau's criticism of, 233
    Necker's criticism of, 260–1
    opposition of courts to, 160–1, 164, 165,
        169, 179, 205–6
    opposition of privileged to, 199, 279
    and provincial assemblies, 264, 266–7,
        268, 269, 270, 279
    and responses to tax petitions, 71, 74, 84,
        139–54
    tax petitions to, 120–39, 153–4, 315
    and Vauban's *dîme royale*, 229
    see also Aube; Caen (intendancy of);
        capitation (free funds of); Esmangard;
        Fontette; Guynet; La Briffe de Ferrières;
        Launay; Vastan

Jansenism, 8, 11–12, 13, 198–9, 247
    and parlement of Rouen, 166, 168–71, 189,
        203, 210, 315
    and parlement of Paris, 160
    and printing of remonstrances, 172–3,
        316
    and provincial parlements, 167
    see also Fossé; Le Maître; Manneville
Janville, Louis François Pierre Louvel de,
    199, 203
Jaucourt, Louis, chevalier de, 216
Joly de Fleury, Jean François, 264–5
Jouhaud, Christian, 120–1
Journal de Normandie, 294
justice, 18, 19, 42, 156, 179, 209, 225, 227, 234,
    244, 287, 297
    administrative justice, 53–4, 140–53, 154,
        261, 269, 271

distributive justice, 129–39, 206, 315
    in frame of petitions, 120, 124, 213, 314
    personal justice, 127–9
    in petitions against *capitation*, 125–37, 139,
        153–4, 315
    in petitions against *dixième/vingtième*, 125,
        137–9, 153, 314–15
    and royal authority, 124, 164, 202, 153–4
    royal rhetoric of, 197, 206, 207–8

Kaplan, Steven L., 13

La Briffe de Ferrières, Louis Arnauld de,
    147–8
Labrousse, Ernest, 2
Lambert, Claude Guillaume, 267
Languedoc, 56, 95, 159
    Compte rendu of, 248
    methods of tax payment in, 95–7, 99–100
    and origins of *capitation*, 45
    royal taxation on, 97–100
    social incidence of *capitation* and *vingtième*
        in, 101–3
La richesse de l'état, 217, 220–1
La Rochefoucauld, François, duc de, 1
Launay, François de, 121–3
Launay, Louis Guillaume René Cordier de,
    266–7
L'Averdy, Clément Charles François de, 37,
    100, 188, 189–90, 191, 192
Law, John, 218
lawyers, 3, 5, 12, 50, 194n70, 199, 278, 285
    intendants' consultation with, 54, 269
    and petitioners, 124n19
    as petitioners, 121, 150, 270
    and publicity of remonstrances, 172–3
    see also Barbier; Le Maître; Le Paige
Le Couteulx, Barthélemy-Thomas, 189–90
Le Goff, T. J. A., 101
Le Maître, Pierre-Jacques, 173, 199–200, 203
LeNoir, J. L., 278, 279
Le Paige, Louis Adrien, 168, 171, 171n21, 176
*Le seul intérêt de tous, par un gentilhomme de
    Normandie*, 292–3
Le Tiers-État de Normandie, ou ses droits justifiés,
    298–9, 302–3
Le Trosne, Guillaume François, 219, 257, 259
Le Vassor, 222
Let's hope that I will soon be done with this, 285–7
liberty, 5, 18, 19, 156, 158, 173, 193, 209, 213
    and active citizenship, 309
    and Mirabeau, 232–3, 237–8
    and political equality, 256, 283, 287, 319,
        321
    and privilege, 170, 209, 210, 316

and property, 184–5, 194, 201–2, 205, 318
and provincial assemblies, 262, 279
in rhetoric of judicial Jansenism, 166, 168, 170
and right of parlementary deliberation, 170, 176, 177, 179, 185, 188, 200, 210
and self-taxation through estates, 162–3, 164–5, 170, 176, 196, 201, 202, 210, 256, 273, 316, 318
and Tocqueville, 6, 10, 249, 250, 319–21, 322n7
Limoges, 73, 76, 79, 90–1, 94
Linguet, Simon-Nicolas-Henri, 219
Lizerand, Georges, 64n4
Locke, John, 184, 323
Loisel, Antoine, 124
Louis XIV, 38, 47, 69, 103, 109, 124, 160, 168, 172, 298
and absolutism, 60
books on finances under, 218, 223–5, 227, 231, 250, 297, 317
and creation of universal taxes, 33, 34–6, 64, 110, 179–80
finances of, 29, 34
and regime of fiscal privilege, 23–4, 312
rhetoric of tax decrees under, 41–6
and suppression of *ban et arrière-ban*, 298
and tax jurisdiction of intendants, 51–2
Louis XV, 29, 30, 31, 37, 54, 99–100, 138, 182, 194, 204
books on finances under, 231, 232, 235
and increases in *capitation* and *vingtième*, 36–7
and parlement of Rouen, 175–7, 180–1, 183, 187, 188, 190–1
popular perceptions of, 174, 183–4, 209, 316
rhetoric of tax decrees under, 42, 45, 46–7
Louis XVI, 25, 88, 104, 111, 289–91
and creation of provincial assemblies, 256, 260
and parlement of Rouen, 204–8, 209, 210
and Prerevolution, 273, 275, 278, 283, 318
rhetoric of tax decrees under, 42–3, 45, 47
Luxembourg, Charles-François de Montmorency, maréchal de, 177

Mably, Gabriel Bonnot de, 172, 219
Machault d'Arnouville, Jean Baptiste de, 204, 221
and levy of *vingtième* on clergy, 111, 159, 220, 297
and verifications of *vingtième*, 85, 87, 160
and *vingtième* in *pays d'états*, 96–7, 159

Malesherbes, Chrétien-Guillaume de Lamoignon de, 41, 297
on direct versus indirect taxes, 210–11
as director of book trade, 215, 221
influence on Necker, 260–1
influence on parlement of Rouen, 165, 205–6
on *vingtième* verifications, 202
see also cour des aides (Paris)
Manneville, Jean-Robert Gosselin de, 90, 198–9, 203
marc d'argent, 305, 306, 308
Marion, Marcel, 13, 62–3, 64, 96, 146, 157
Mathias, Peter, 64–5
Mathon de la Cour, Charles-Joseph, 247, 248
Maupeou, René Nicolas Charles Augustin de, 159, 204, 208, 275
judicial reform and *vingtième*, 57, 85–6, 194–6
opposition to, 195–204, 205, 210, 211, 273
Melon, Jean-François, 218
Mémoire concernant l'utilité des états provinciaux, 232–3
Mémoire sur les états provinciaux, 232–3
Mémoire sur les municipalités, 258–9
Mercier, Louis-Sébastien, 40, 238, 297
Mercier de la Rivière, Pierre-Paul, 219
Meyer, Jean, 76n25, 101
Michelet, Jules, 2, 3
Mirabeau, Victor Riquetti, marquis de, 215, 217, 219, 223, 239, 249
and provincial estates, 232–3
literary success of, 231–2, 238
and provincial assemblies, 243, 257, 259
and Rousseau, 232–3, 233n42
Théorie de l'impôt, 233–8, 250–1, 317–18
see also classical republicanism; physiocracy
Miromesnil, 37, 182, 209, 212, 221
on factions in parlement of Rouen, 174, 178, 181–2, 183–4, 186, 189–90, 192
on kingship, 38, 175, 176–7, 179, 180, 189, 190–1
on public opinion, 39, 173, 174–5, 178, 179, 183, 188, 191, 192–3
against forced registration, 177, 185
Montchalon, 294
Montesquieu, Charles Louis de Secondat, baron de, 218, 232, 233, 238
influence on parlement of Rouen, 164, 165, 205, 207
influence on *Requête au Roi*, 202
Montpinçon, Louis-Raoul Bombel de, 199, 201
Moreau, Jacob-Nicolas, 221
Moreau de Beaumont, Jean Louis, 37, 215

Morineau, Michel, 64, 65
Morellet, André, 191, 213, 221, 297n76
Marmont, Auguste, 214–15

National Assembly, 222, 255, 280, 305
  birth of, 282, 296
  debate over citizenship in, 307–9
national sovereignty, 1, 8, 12, 19, 158, 238,
    255, 296, 303, 321
  and active citizenship, 304, 308
  and *cahiers de doléances*, 281–3
  and parlement of Rouen, 163, 170–1, 173,
    176, 185–6, 205, 206, 210, 277, 316
  and Prerevolution, 274, 275, 277
  and *Requête au Roi*, 202–3
natural law, 18, 42, 214, 249, 251
  and Boisguilbert, 225–8, 230–1, 250
  and Vauban, 229
Necker, Jacques, 28, 82, 112, 139, 150, 155,
    204, 205, 219, 223, 249, 255, 302
  and fiscal equality, 37, 42, 205–8
  as friend of third estate, 289–91, 300, 321
  literary success of, 214–6, 217, 221–2, 238
  and patriotism, 243, 251, 318
  and provincial assemblies, 241–3, 251,
    260–6, 270–1, 300
  and public opinion, 39, 239–42, 251, 318
  reader response to, 243–8, 251
  and verifications of *vingtième*, 89, 93–4,
    205–8
Néville, François-Claude Le Camus de, 199,
    200
newspapers, 7, 216, 220
  discussion of assemblies and estates in,
    264, 278
  and publicity of parlementary
    remonstrances, 172, 173, 179–80, 184,
    196
  and publicity of royal law, 40–1
  reviews of financial literature in, 216, 220,
    244
  *see also Annonces, affiches, et avis divers de la
    haute et basse Normandie*; *Journal de
    Normandie*
nobility, 3, 19, 32, 56, 66, 216, 243, 248, 255,
    278, 282, 283
  and Boisguilbert, 225, 227
  cahiers de doléances of, 280–2
  capitation on, 68–9, 74–7, 80, 81, 82, 84,
    100–3, 103–5, 105–6, 113–14, 121–2,
    313
  dixième/vingtième on, 90–4, 100–3, 103–5,
    105–6, 113–14, 313
  and fiscal coercion, 58–60
  fiscal privileges of, 24–8, 48, 284–92, 312

and historiography of fiscal privilege,
    13–15, 23–4, 63–6
  in language of royal decrees, 41–2, 44, 62
  and military justification for fiscal
    privilege, 297–9, 126–7, 153, 160, 162,
    297–9
  and military service, 26, 27–8, 44, 47,
    126–7, 153, 160, 162, 203
  and parlement of Rouen, 160, 162, 170,
    192–3, 316
  and participation in levy of *capitation*, 164,
    264–5
  and provincial assemblies, 263–4, 269,
    270, 300
  renunciation of tax privileges, 292–7
  and representation at Estates General,
    294–5, 301–3, 315
  and revolt against *vingtième*, 196, 198–204,
    205, 212, 317
  tax petitions of, 123, 126–8, 131, 140, 142,
    143, 145–6, 146–8, 149, 153, 154, 315
  and Tocqueville, 6, 319
  and Vauban, 224, 225
Normandy, 26, 31, 93, 156, 157, 170–1
  charter of, 176, 201, 209, 278–9
  and literature of Prerevolution, 285, 292,
    293, 294, 298–9
  opposition to *vingtième* in, 196–204, 212
  political claims of third estate in, 301–3
  taxes in, 89, 194
  *see also Annonces, affiches, et avis divers de la
    haute et basse Normandie*; Caen; *Journal de
    Normandie*; parlement of Rouen;
    provincial assemblies (Lower
    Normandy); provincial estates
    (Normandy)

O'Brien, Patrick, 64, 65
Ormesson, Marie-François Lefevre d', 52,
    86, 119, 129, 135, 138n59, 142, 152
  see also intendants of finance
Osseville, comte d', 295

Paris, 8, 12, 40, 41, 54, 62, 109, 165, 255
  public opinion in, 8, 12, 40–1, 54, 62, 167,
    247, 273
  remonstrances of parlement of Rouen in,
    173, 181, 184
  and *Requête au Roi*, 200, 203
  revolutionary sections of, 309–10
  royal taxation in, 71, 103, 107–8
  Treaty of, 181
  see also cour des aides (Paris), parlement of
    Paris
parlement of Aix, 159–60, 161, 167, 171n21

parlement of Besançon, 135, 160, 167, 171n21, 182, 182n49, 208, 267
parlement of Bordeaux, 59, 106, 159–60, 161, 182, 182n49, 194n70, 196, 204, 208, 267
parlement of Dijon, 134, 135, 152, 159–60, 182, 194n70
parlement of Grenoble, 161, 167, 171n21, 181, 182, 204, 206
parlement of Paris, 25, 38, 106, 158, 185n54, 188, 220, 264
  Jansenism and, 160, 166, 167, 168, 172
  and Prerevolution, 274–5, 293, 299, 318
  and proviso against *vingtième*, 87–8, 191
  relative docility of, 159–60, 161, 167, 171, 171n21, 194n70, 206
parlement of Rennes, 106, 159–60, 182, 196, 171n21, 194n70
parlement of Rouen, 156–7, 199, 209, 278, 315–16
  arrêt de défense of, 186–8
  and British constitutional thought, 184–5
  and delegations to Versailles, 175–7, 190–1, 207
  early opposition to universal taxes, 158–60
  factions within, 174–5, 178, 181, 183, 189–90, 192–3
  and forced registrations, 177–8, 179, 180, 185–6, 193, 206, 315
  and indifference to bankruptcy, 182
  and Jansenism, 166–73, 181–2, 210, 315
  Maupeou's abolition of, 194–6, 200, 204
  opposition to *vingtième* verifications, 161, 196, 204–7, 275–7, 315–16
  and petitions, 205–6
  and provincial assemblies, 267–8
  and proviso against *vingtième*, 87, 161, 195, 196, 208
  and public opinion, 173–5, 179–80, 183–4, 192–3, 194, 212, 316–17
  and publicity of disputes, 183–184, 186–8, 191–3, 196, 207–8, 211
  and publicity of remonstrances, 171–4, 179–80, 184, 185, 211, 316–17
  remonstrances of, 159, 160, 161–6, 175–6, 178–9, 184–5, 200–1, 205–7, 211, 276–7
  resignation of, 183, 188, 207–8
  taxes on magistrates of, 89, 93, 105–6
  and theory of classes, 170–1
  see also citizenship; despotism; Estates General; liberty; Miromesnil; national sovereignty; provincial estates (Normandy)
parlement of Toulouse, 159–60, 161, 170n20, 181, 182, 182n49, 186, 194n70
parlements, 11–12, 119, 121, 155–6, 159, 161,
  172, 176, 193, 204, 208, 211–12, 220–1, 315
  historiography of, 157–8
  and Maupeou coup, 86, 194–6, 202
  Necker's criticism of, 261–2
  and Prerevolution, 273, 299
  and provincial assemblies, 256–7, 267–8
  taxes on, 105–6, 152
The past age, 285–7
patente, 306
patriotism, 214, 220, 243, 244, 247, 248
  and Necker, 241, 242, 251, 252, 318
  and renunciations of fiscal privilege, 294
pays d'élections, 55, 70
  capitation in, 71–84, 113, 313
  compared with *pays d'états*, 95, 96, 97, 99, 100, 103
  dixième / vingtième in, 84–95, 113, 194, 195, 202, 275, 313
  levy of *taille* in, 48–51
  Mirabeau on, 233
  and provincial assemblies, 264, 265
pays d'états, 70, 104, 155
  Mirabeau on, 233
  royal taxation in, 95–103, 113, 313
Perrot, Jean Claude, 73, 91–2
petitions, 16, 18, 119–20, 213
  and appeals against *taille*, 50–1
  from bourgeois against *capitation*, 135–7, 154
  and distributive justice, 124, 129–39, 150–2, 153–4, 315
  and family relations, 130–3, 154
  intendants' responses to, 139–41, 146–53
  from nobles against *capitation*, 84, 125–7, 133–4, 153, 154, 315
  from office-holders against *capitation*, 134–5, 154, 270, 315
  and parlementary remonstrances, 160, 162, 205–6, 315
  and personal justice, 124, 127–9, 148–50, 153
  process of petitioning against universal taxes, 52–3, 120–4, 139–41, 144–5
  and provincial assembly, 269–70
  reductions granted to bourgeois petitioners, 82, 146
  reductions granted to noble petitioners, 74–6, 143, 145–6, 146–8
  reductions granted to officers of justice, 77–9, 143, 146
  reductions granted to *vingtième* petitioners, 84, 141–2, 145
  and revolt against *vingtième*, 198–9
  and verifications of *vingtième*, 57, 87, 88

petitions (*cont.*)
  against *vingtième*, 125, 137–9, 153, 154, 314–15
physiocracy, 217, 219, 305
  and Boisguilbert, 230–1
  Mirabeau's adherence to, 232, 236–8, 250, 317
  and opposition to Necker, 243
  and representation in provincial assemblies, 257–60, 262, 263, 265–6, 299, 300, 302
  and Tocqueville, 249
Pocock, J. G. A., 234
political equality, 255–6, 283, 284, 320–2
  and Estates General, 283–303
  and active citizenship, 308–10
  in provincial assemblies, 263–4
  see also third estate
political representation, *see* Estates General, provincial estates, provincial assemblies, third estate
Pompadour, Jeanne Antoinette Poisson, marquise de, Mme de, 217
Pontcarré, Louis-François de, 106
Pontchartrain, Louis Phélipeaux, comte de, 34, 38, 121
The present time demands that each support the great Burden, 287–9
privilege (fiscal), 1, 17, 19, 23–4, 32–3, 60–1, 71, 113–15, 252, 255, 274, 283, 312, 313
  and bourgeoisie, 28, 107, 150
  and clergy, 25–8, 30, 108, 110–13, 220, 292
  and liberty, 170, 209, 210, 316
  Marion on, 13, 62–3, 157
  Michelet on, 2
  and Necker, 239, 247
  and nobility, 25–8, 103, 127, 292, 297–9
  in *pays d'états*, 29, 95–7, 271, 279
  recent historiography of, 12, 13–15, 63–5
  renunciations of, 293–6
  representations of, 284–92, 297, 202–3
  in taxpayers' petitions, 121, 122, 269
  Tocqueville on, 6, 319–21
  Vauban's rejection of, 229–30, 231, 250, 317
  and venality of office, 29–32
  see also clergy; fiscal equality; nobility; provincial estates; *taille*
Projet d'une Dîme royale, 217, 223–5, 228–30, 234, 250
property, 17, 19
  and call for provincial estates, 279
  of clergy, 27, 111–12, 220, 297
  and active citizenship, 307
  and Habermas, 323

and Mirabeau, 233, 237–8
and parlementary discourse, 164, 166, 168–9, 184, 194, 201–2, 205–6, 208, 209, 275–6, 318
of parlementary magistrates, 182
and petitions, 125, 130–3, 135, 148, 152
and power struggle at Estates General, 302
and provincial assemblies, 258–9, 271, 302
and renunciation of fiscal privilege, 293–4
in Revisionism, 3
seizures of, 58–9, 198
and tax assessment, 42, 56–7, 70, 89–95, 145, 273, 292
and Vauban's *dîme royale*, 229–30
and venality, 31, 194
and *vingtième* verifications, 87–9, 92–4, 194–6
Provence, 29
  provincial estates of, 95, 278
provincial assemblies, 222, 256–7, 260, 265–6, 274, 300, 301, 318, 321
  Brienne's creation of, 265, 266
  demand for, 264–5
  fiscal operations of, 268–73
  Mirabeau's proposal for, 237
  Necker's creation of, 241–3, 244, 247, 260–4, 266, 300
  opposition of intendants to, 266–7
  opposition of judicial officers to, 267–8
  physiocratic conception of, 257–60, 265, 266, 300
  and provincial estates, 278–9
provincial assembly of Berry, 241, 242, 263, 264, 270–1
provincial assembly of Haute-Guienne, 241, 242, 263, 264, 270
provincial assembly of Lower Normandy, 121
  dispute with intendant, 266–7
  dispute with judicial officers, 267–8
  and levy of *capitation*, 268–70
  and levy of *vingtième*, 270–2
provincial estates, 30, 119, 120, 155, 156, 206, 208, 209, 273, 274, 280, 315, 319
  compared with provincial assemblies, 256–7, 259, 262, 263, 271, 278–9
  Mirabeau on, 232–3, 237
  universal taxation and, 95–103, 112, 159
  see also pays d'états; provincial estates (Brittany); provincial estates (Languedoc); provincial estates (Normandy); provincial estates (Provence)
provincial estates (Brittany), 95–103, 159
provincial estates (Languedoc), 45, 95–103, 159, 248

provincial estates (Normandy)
  calls for during Prerevolution, 278, 279, 280, 318
  comparisons with provincial assembly of Lower Normandy, 271, 278–9
  demand for periodicity of, 280–2
  Norman nobility's call for, 196, 201–3, 205, 316
  parlement of Rouen's call for, 162–5, 170–1, 173, 176, 179, 184, 196, 205, 207, 208, 210, 276–7, 299, 316
  representation of third estate at impending, 301–2
provincial estates (Provence), 29, 95, 278
public opinion, 5, 8, 12, 16, 17, 38
  and Habermas, 6–7, 8, 9, 322–3
  and international credit, 173–4, 179–80
  Necker's conception of, 89, 239–43, 244–6, 251, 261–2
  and opposition to *vingtième*, 196–204
  and the parlement of Rouen, 156, 157, 158, 168, 173–5, 178, 179–80, 183–4, 185, 188, 192–4, 211–12, 276, 316–17
  and provincial assemblies, 271–3
  as reflected in *cahiers de doléances*, 280–2
  and representations of privilege, 284–92
  and writers, 213, 214, 246–8
  see also publicity
publicity
  of books on finance, 214–22, 246–8, 317–18
  of parlementary rulings and remonstrances, 159, 160, 161, 171–3, 178, 179–80, 184, 185, 186–7, 191–2, 211
  of royal decrees, 38–47, 89, 186–8, 191, 207–8

Quesnay, François, 219, 230, 232, 238

Requête au Roi, 199–204, 205
Résultat du conseil, 300
Revisionism, 3–5, 8, 11, 14, 63–4, 294–5
Richelieu, Armand, cardinal duc de, 26, 279
Riley, James C., 64–5, 73
Robespierre, Maximilien, 308–9
Roederer, Pierre-Louis, 308
Rouen, 223
  intendant of, 203
  nobles from *bailliage* of, 294
  rumors in city of, 178, 183, 209
  vingtième in generality of, 89
  see also cour des aides (Rouen); *chambre des comptes* (Rouen); parlement of Rouen
Rousseau, Jean-Jacques, 8, 40n50, 216, 319, 322n7

and active citizenship, 306, 308
and general will, 9, 10, 306, 311
and Mirabeau, 232–3, 234, 237, 238
Roussel de la Tour, Pierre Philippe, 217, 220–1
Rousselot de Surgy, Jacques-Philibert, 246–7
royal council, 71, 78, 103, 111, 122, 166, 169, 187
  and administrative centralization, 48–9, 51–4, 145, 165
  and appeals against universal taxes, 52–3
  fiction of, 261, 261n10
  see also contrôleur général; intendants (provincial); intendants of finance
royal court, 155, 198, 247
  and tax petitons, 120, 133–4, 261
  and universal taxes, 70, 103–5, 114
  see also, parlement of Rouen (delegations to Versailles)

Saint-Simon, Louis de Rouvroy, duc de, 56, 323
Schnerb, Robert, 64n4
Scott, James C., 123
seigneurial dues, 2, 70, 94, 137–9
Seven Years War
  pamphlet literature during, 220–1
  parlementary opposition during, 86, 167, 173–4, 179–81, 189, 193, 210, 211, 315, 316
  tax increases of, 36–7, 45, 72, 73, 76, 77, 81, 97, 113, 194
Sewell, William H., Jr., 291
Sieyès, Emmanuel Joseph, abbé, 228
  and active citizenship, 307
  and political claims of third estate, 297, 299, 301, 302
  and representations of privilege, 284, 285, 291, 294
Silhouette, Étienne de, 36–7
social contract, 1, 18, 214, 231, 232, 250, 251, 306–7
Solnon, J.-F., 64–5, 69
subdelegates, 54, 55, 260
  and *capitation* petitions, 141, 148, 151
  and tax administration, 56, 58, 81, 121–3, 264–5, 269
  taxes on, 80, 122
  see also capitation (administration of); intendants (provincial)

Taille, 43, 66, 71, 87, 93, 105, 134, 181, 222, 305, 320
  administration of, 48–52, 54, 55, 56, 57–8, 120, 140, 268, 313–14

Taille (cont.)
  Boisguilbert's criticism of, 226–7
  and creation of universal taxes, 33–5
  declining relative weight of, 67–8, 113
  exemptions from, 24–33, 44, 80, 81, 107,
    109, 114, 153, 159, 285, 292–3
  incidence of, 82–4, 95, 101–2, 292
  reform of, 32, 32n25
tax revolts, 3, 18, 119, 120–1, 149, 305, 314
  against the *vingtième*, 196–204, 211, 293,
    317
taxes
  see *capitation*; *contribution foncière*; *contribution
    mobilière*; *direct taxes*; *dixième*; indirect
    taxes; *patente*; privilege (fiscal); *taille*; tax
    revolts; *vingtième*
Taylor, George, 3–4
Terray, Joseph Marie, 119, 152, 221
  and *capitation* tariff on officers of justice,
    78–9, 113
  and *dixième* on pensions, 104, 113
  and fiscal equality, 42n57, 204
  and verifications of *vingtième*, 86–9, 93,
    97–9, 113, 194–5, 196–8
Théorie de l'impôt, 215, 217, 231–2, 233–8,
    250–1, 317–18
third estate
  cahiers de doléances of, 280–1
  privileges within, 14, 28, 64
  and representation at Estates General, 19,
    255–6, 283–4, 293, 294, 295, 296–303,
    308, 318–19, 321–2
  and representations of privilege, 284–92
  and representation in provincial
    assemblies, 263–6
  taxation of, 25–6, 95, 101
Thouret, Jacques-Guillaume, 285
Tocqueville, Alexis de, 71
  and historiography, 5–10, 12, 14, 64
  and administrative justice, 53
  and literary politics, 248–50
  reconsideration of, 319–22, 322n7
Toustain de Richebourg, Charles Gaspard,
    203–4, 293
Touzery, Mireille, 32n25
Trie, Michel-Nicolas, comte de, 199, 203
Turgot, Anne Robert Jacques, 40n50, 73, 230,
    297
  and provincial assemblies, 258–60, 265
  publishing on finance under, 216, 219,
    221
  and verifications of *vingtième*, 88–9, 93

Valognes, 50–1, 81n37, 135–6, 151
Van Kley, Dale K., 13, 166–8

Vannes, 101
Vastan, Félix Aubéry de, 120, 125
Vauban, Sébastien Le Prestre de, maréchal
    de, 217, 249
  and poverty, 224–5, 250
  and *Projet d'une dîme royale*, 223, 228–31,
    237, 239, 243, 250, 317
venality of office, 23, 34, 45–6, 49, 304, 312
  and assets of magistrates, 182
  and exemption from *taille*, 28, 28–32, 231
  and Maupeou coup, 194
  and representations of privilege, 291
  and tariff of *capitation*, 68–70
  and universal taxation, 56, 57, 77–81,
    89–90, 104–6, 114, 127, 128
  see also *affaires extraordinaires*; *gages*
Venturi, Franco, 234
Vignon, Elizabeth, 50–1
Vincent de Gournay, Jacques Claude, 215,
    221, 226, 230
vingtième, 292, 293, 306
  and active citizenship, 305–6
  administration of, 51–60, 70–1, 313–14
  in Brittany, 95–103, 313
  on clergy, 108–11, 297
  on commoners, 95, 101, 102, 103
  global weight of, 67–8
  incidence in generality of Caen, 84–5
  on industry, 89–90
  in Languedoc, 95–103, 313
  literary debate on, 216, 220–1, 232, 279,
    297
  on lower-level office-holders, 90
  on nobility and privileged, 90–5, 101–3,
    104–5, 113–14, 313, 320
  origins of, 33, 36–8
  on Paris, 107–8
  parliamentary discourse on, 156–7, 159–65,
    170, 174, 179, 181–2, 192–3, 204–12, 273,
    275–7, 315–17
  petitions for reductions in, 120–1, 125,
    137–9, 153
  and provincial assemblies, 265, 268,
    270–3
  reductions granted by administrators,
    140–2, 152, 154, 314
  revolt against, 194–204, 317
  royal rhetoric on, 41–3, 45–7
  and seigneurial dues, 137–9
  verification and reassessment of, 55–7,
    85–9, 92–5, 141, 160–1, 191, 195–6,
    201–2, 206–8, 270–2, 275–7, 315–16
  see also *dixième*
Vire, 77, 81n37, 121, 130, 140, 269
Virtue rewarded, 244–6

Voltaire, François Marie Arouet, 219–20,
238, 297
Vovelle, Michel, 13–14

War
   and creation of universal taxes, 33–8
   as justification for universal taxes,
   43–5

War of American Independence, 37, 45, 47,
89, 97, 208, 211, 265
War of Austrian Succession, 36, 45, 46–7
War of the League of Augsburg, 34, 43–4,
224, 298
War of the Spanish Succession, 29, 34, 35–6,
46, 224
Woloch, Isser, 304